stop

blu manga are published in the original japanese format

go to the other side and begin reading

High school is difficult enough, especially when you live in the shadow of your stunningly attractive older brother...

Kotori is often teased for being superficial, and with a gorgeous brother like Kujaku, you can't really blame him for thinking that looks are everything. However, once Akaiwa steps into the picture, Kotori's life is heading for a lesson in deep trust, self-confidence, and abiding love.

Price: $9.99
Available Now!

© 2003 SUZUKI TANAKA

OT
OLDER TEEN

Here's a dog that will make you beg.

When Ukyo rescues a stray dog and names it Kuro, he soon learns that he may have found a rare breed—his new dog can talk and magically transform into a hunky human! With his dog now taking the form of a hot man and licking him in various places, what is Ukyo to do?!

From the creator of BLU's Wild Rock.

FOR MATURE AUDIENCES ONLY

Price: $9.99
Available Now!

This "Pure Romance" is anything but...

Passing his college entrance exams isn't the only thing Misaki has to worry about! Being romanced by a suave and older tutor is the concern especially when the tutor in question is his brother's best friend and a famous porn novelist! Suddenly Misaki's "normal" life transforms into an educational journey filled with unfamiliar feelings and nonstop insanity.

A YOUNG PRINCE TRAINS FOR BATTLE BUT INSTEAD LEARNS TO LOVE!

WHEN CHRIS AND ZEKE MEET IN MILITARY SCHOOL, THEY EMBARK ON A LIFE-LONG RELATIONSHIP FRAUGHT WITH DANGER, TREACHERY, AND ABOVE ALL, LOVE.

BLACK KNIGHT IS A SWEEPING ROMANTIC FANTASY EPIC ABOUT THE RELATIONSHIP BETWEEN A DASHING PRINCE AND HIS GUARDSMAN, WITH PLENTY OF SWORD ACTION TO KEEP BOYS' LOVE FANS ENTICED AND ENTHRALLED!

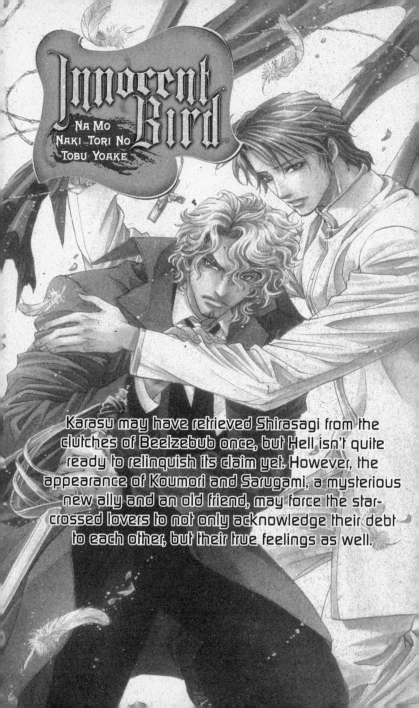

Innocent Bird

Na Mo Naki Tori No Tobu Yoake

Karasu may have retrieved Shirasagi from the clutches of Beelzebub once, but Hell isn't quite ready to relinquish its claim yet. However, the appearance of Koumori and Sarugami, a mysterious new ally and an old friend, may force the star-crossed lovers to not only acknowledge their debt to each other, but their true feelings as well.

INNOCENT BIRD VOLUME 1
Created by Hirotaka Kisaragi

NAMO NAKI TORI NO TOBU YOAKE Volume 1 © HIROTAKA KISARAGI 2002
First published in Japan in 2002 by KADOKAWA SHOTEN PUBLISHING CO., LTD.,
Tokyo. English translation rights arranged with KADOKAWA SHOTEN PUBLISHING
CO., LTD., Tokyo through TUTTLE-MORI AGENCY, INC., Tokyo.

English text copyright © 2007 BLU

ISBN: 978-1-59816-831-0

First Printing: March 2007
10 9 8 7 6 5 4 3 2 1
Printed in the USA

Hi, everybody! Nice to meet you...or long time no see.

Since I decided to "draw a piece about an angel and a devil who don't resemble what they really are," I have somehow managed to make it through this first volume--thanks to cooperation of my editors. In the second volume, the story's background will be explained in a bit more detail. I hope you look forward to finding out if Karasu's and Shirasagi's feelings get closer little by little... or not.

With sincere appreciation for my editors (for whom I'm causing troubles before every deadline), I say--see you in the second volume.

—Hirotaka Kisaragi

The Dawn of the Nameless Bird

~INNOCENT BIRD~
Vol. I

Hirotaka Kisaragi

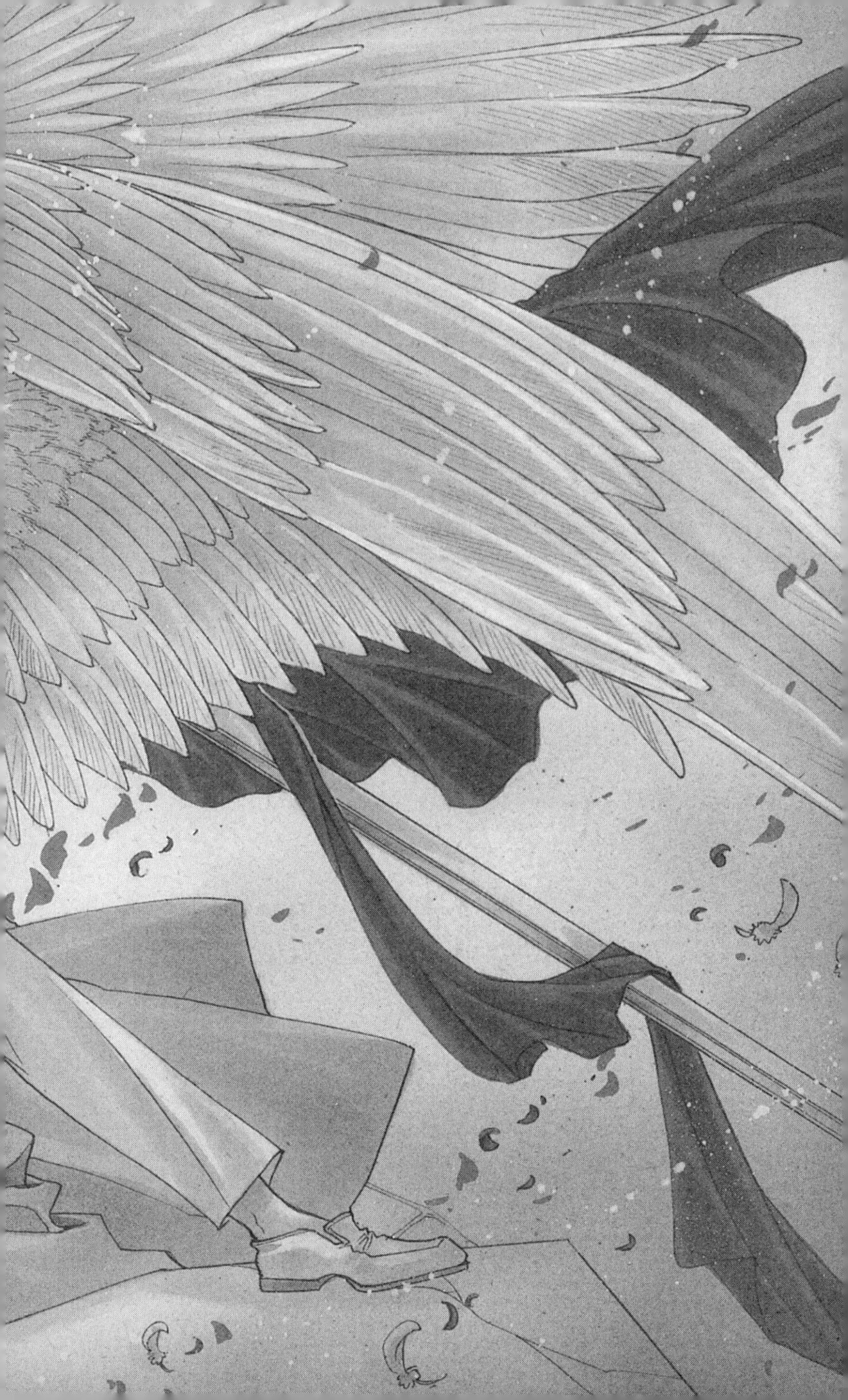

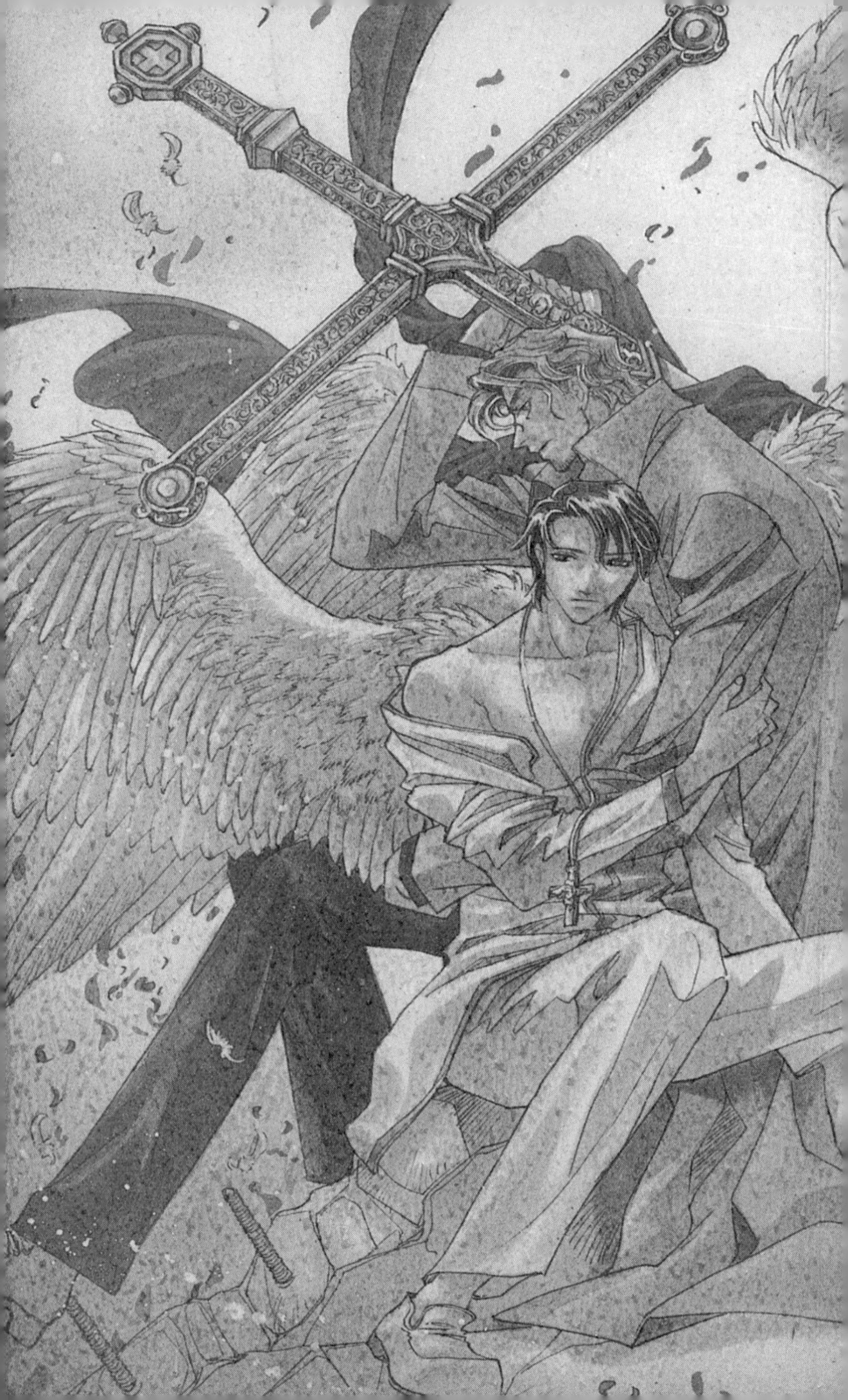

The Dawn of the Nameless Bird
~INNOCENT BIRD~ Vol.1

CONTENTS

Episode 1.................................. 5

Episode 2.................................. 37

Episode 3.................................. 73

Episode 4.................................. 105

***

My Sweet Darling.................... 139

Postscript................................ 191

0

Episode 1

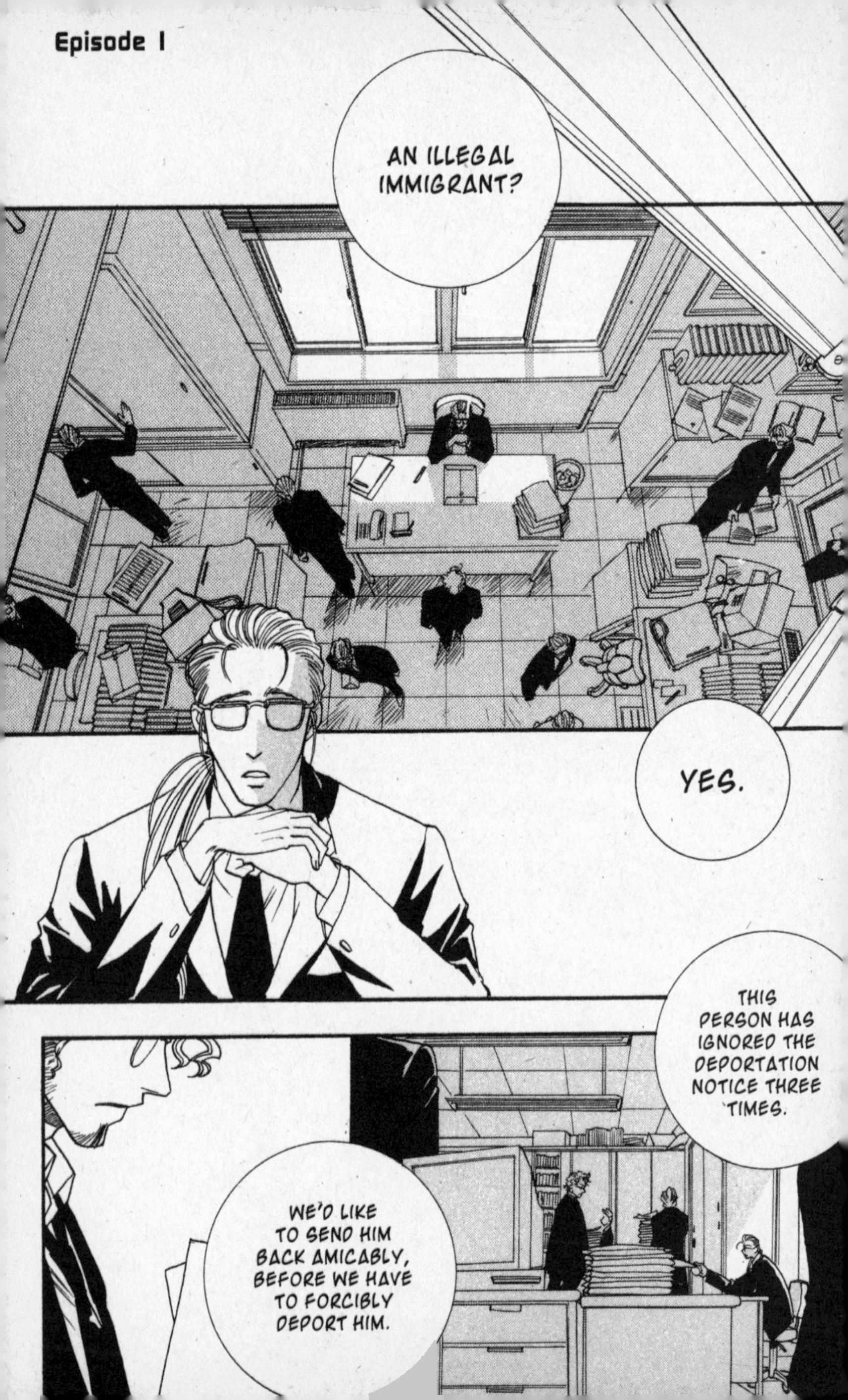

AN ILLEGAL IMMIGRANT?
YES.
THIS PERSON HAS IGNORED THE DEPORTATION NOTICE THREE TIMES.
WE'D LIKE TO SEND HIM BACK AMICABLY, BEFORE WE HAVE TO FORCIBLY DEPORT HIM.

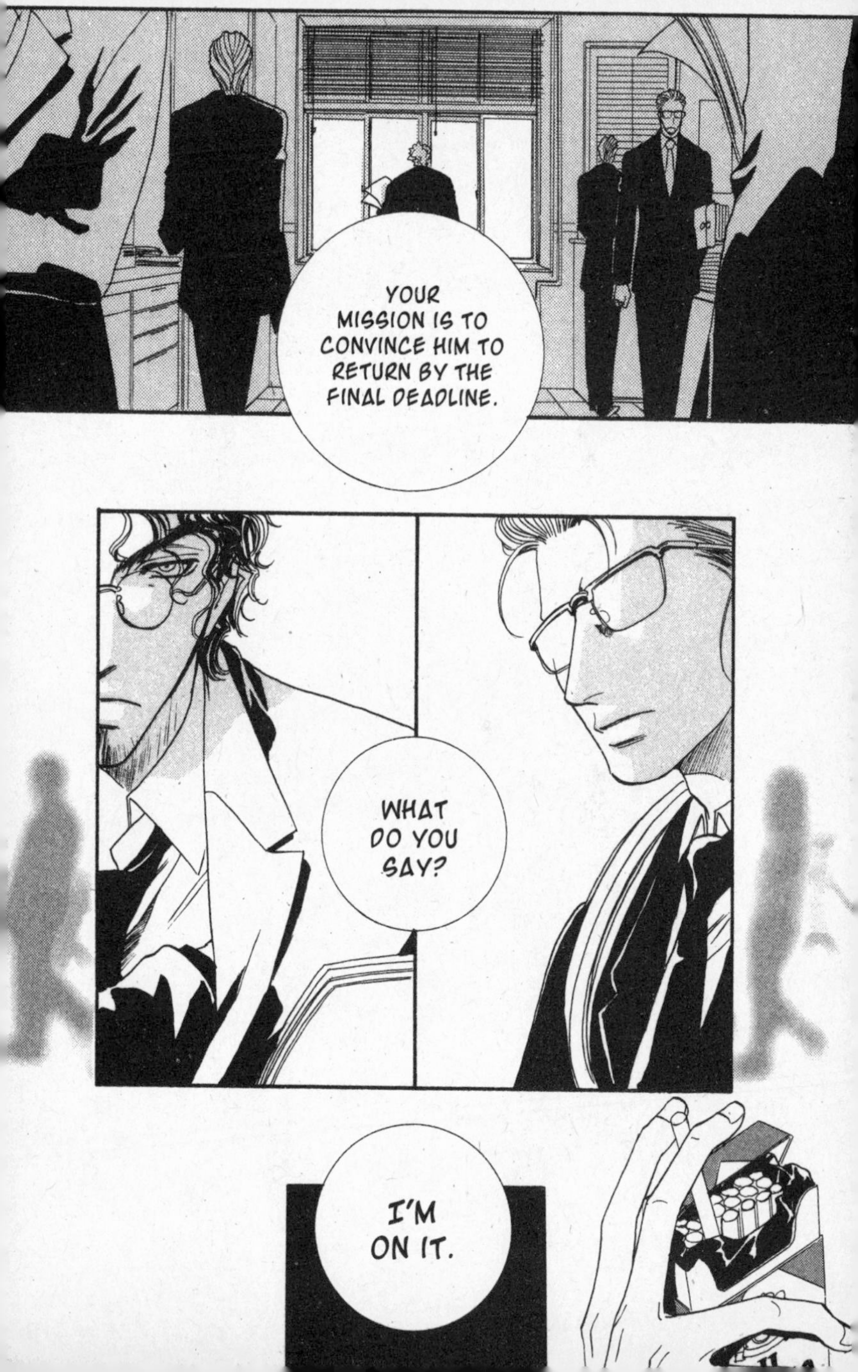
YOUR MISSION IS TO CONVINCE HIM TO RETURN BY THE FINAL DEADLINE.
WHAT DO YOU SAY?
I'M ON IT.

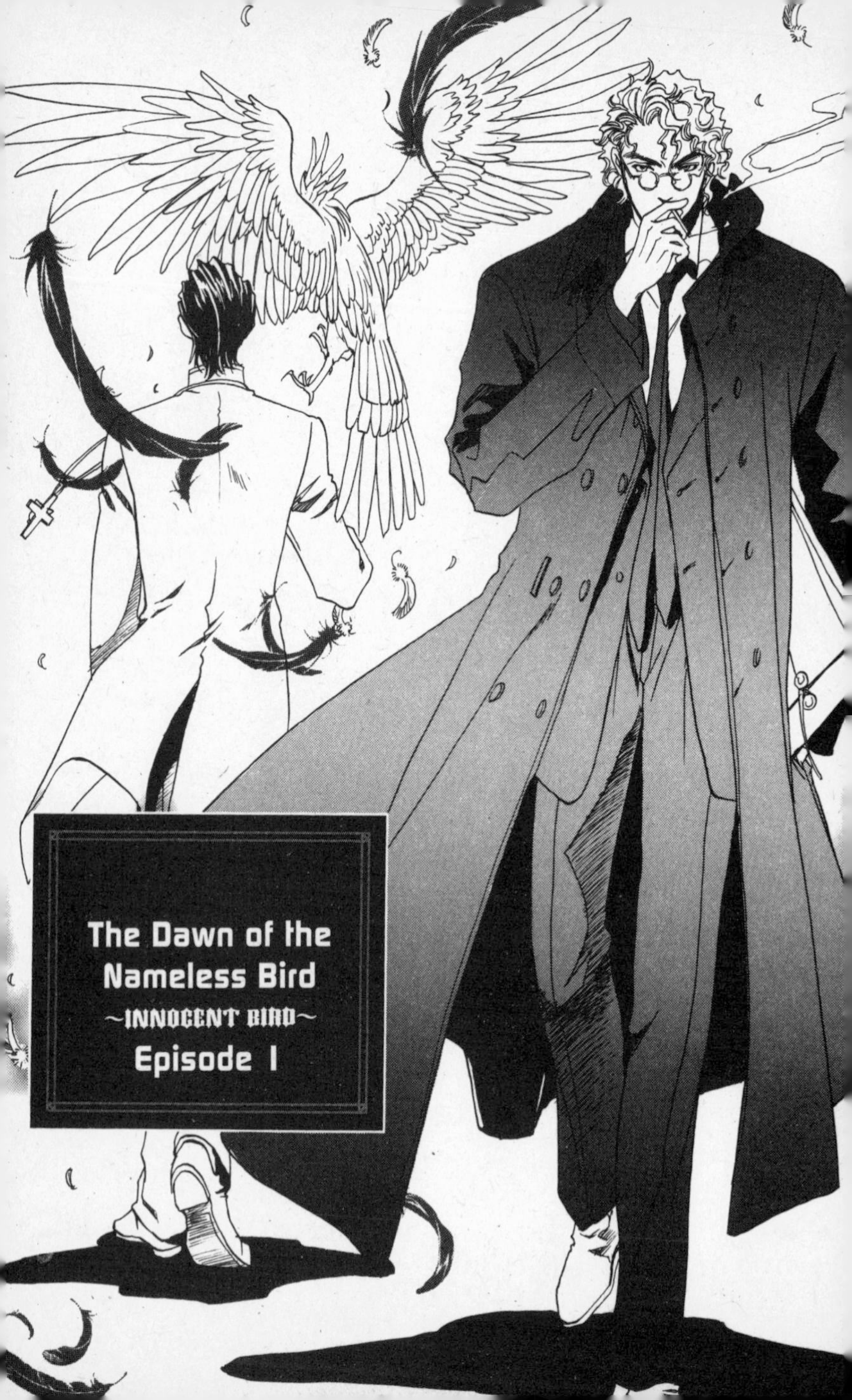
The Dawn of the Nameless Bird
~INNOCENT BIRD~
Episode 1

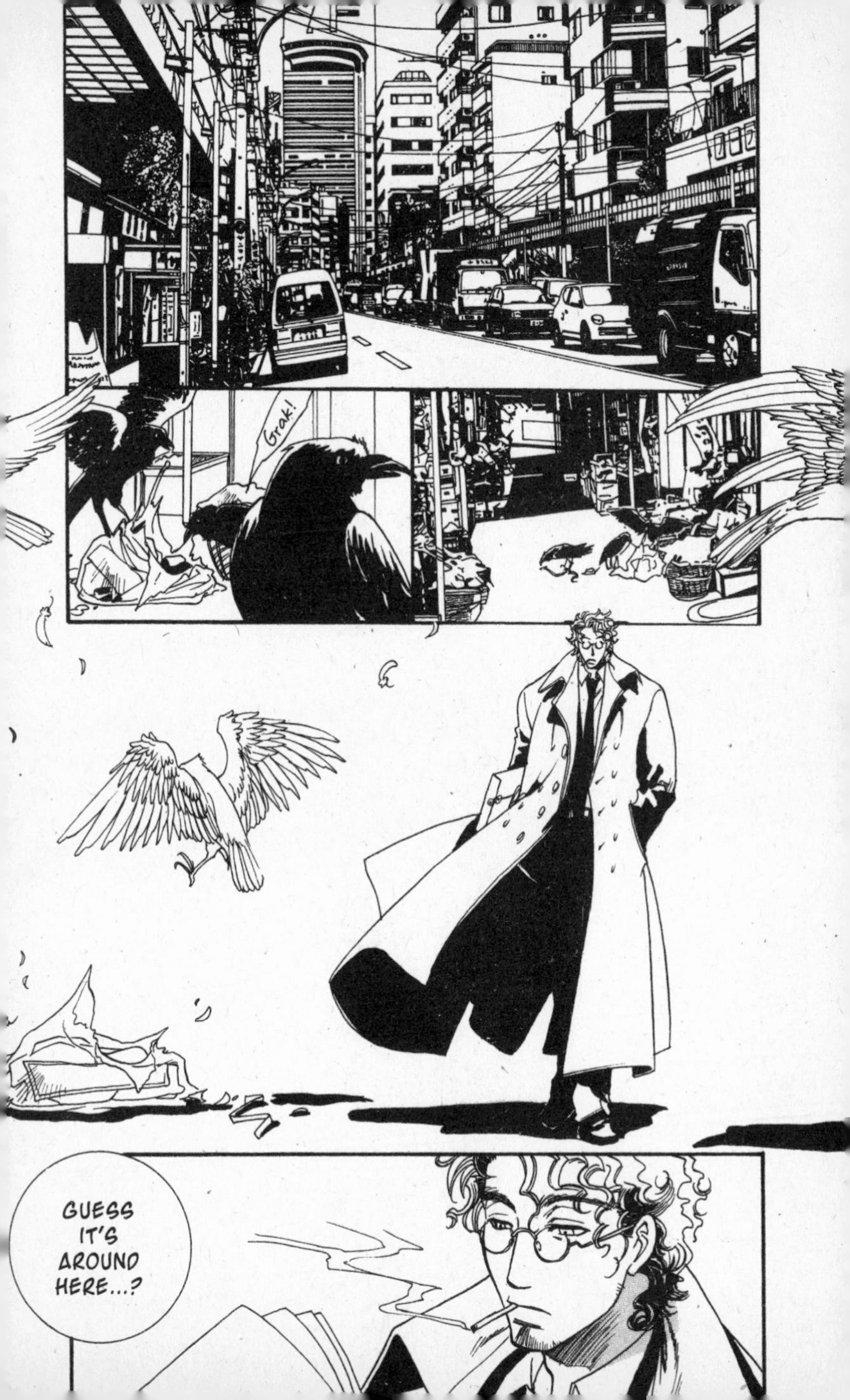
Grak!
GUESS IT'S AROUND HERE...?

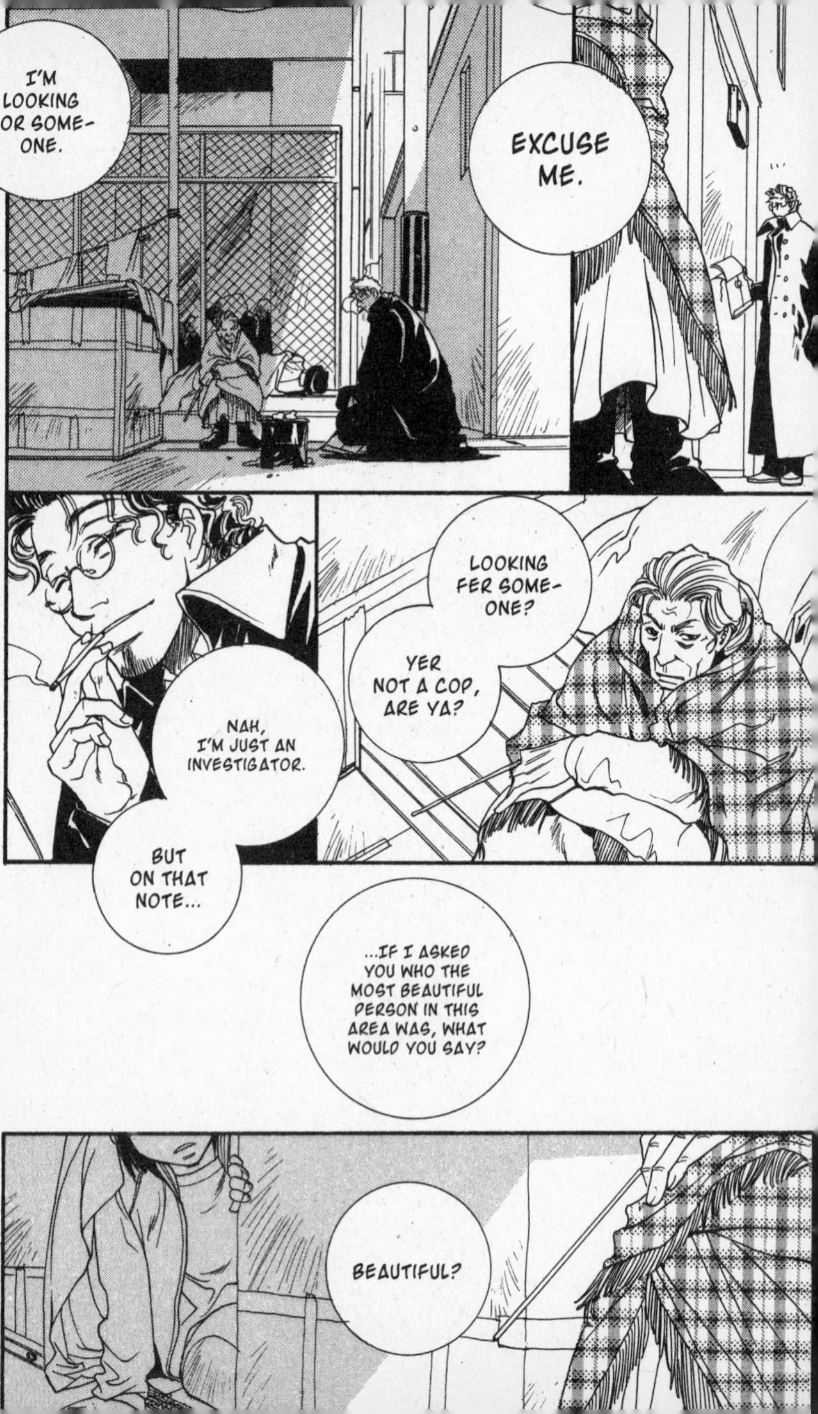
EXCUSE ME.
I'M LOOKING FOR SOME-ONE.
LOOKING FER SOME-ONE?
YER NOT A COP, ARE YA?
NAH, I'M JUST AN INVESTIGATOR.
BUT ON THAT NOTE...
...IF I ASKED YOU WHO THE MOST BEAUTIFUL PERSON IN THIS AREA WAS, WHAT WOULD YOU SAY?
BEAUTIFUL?

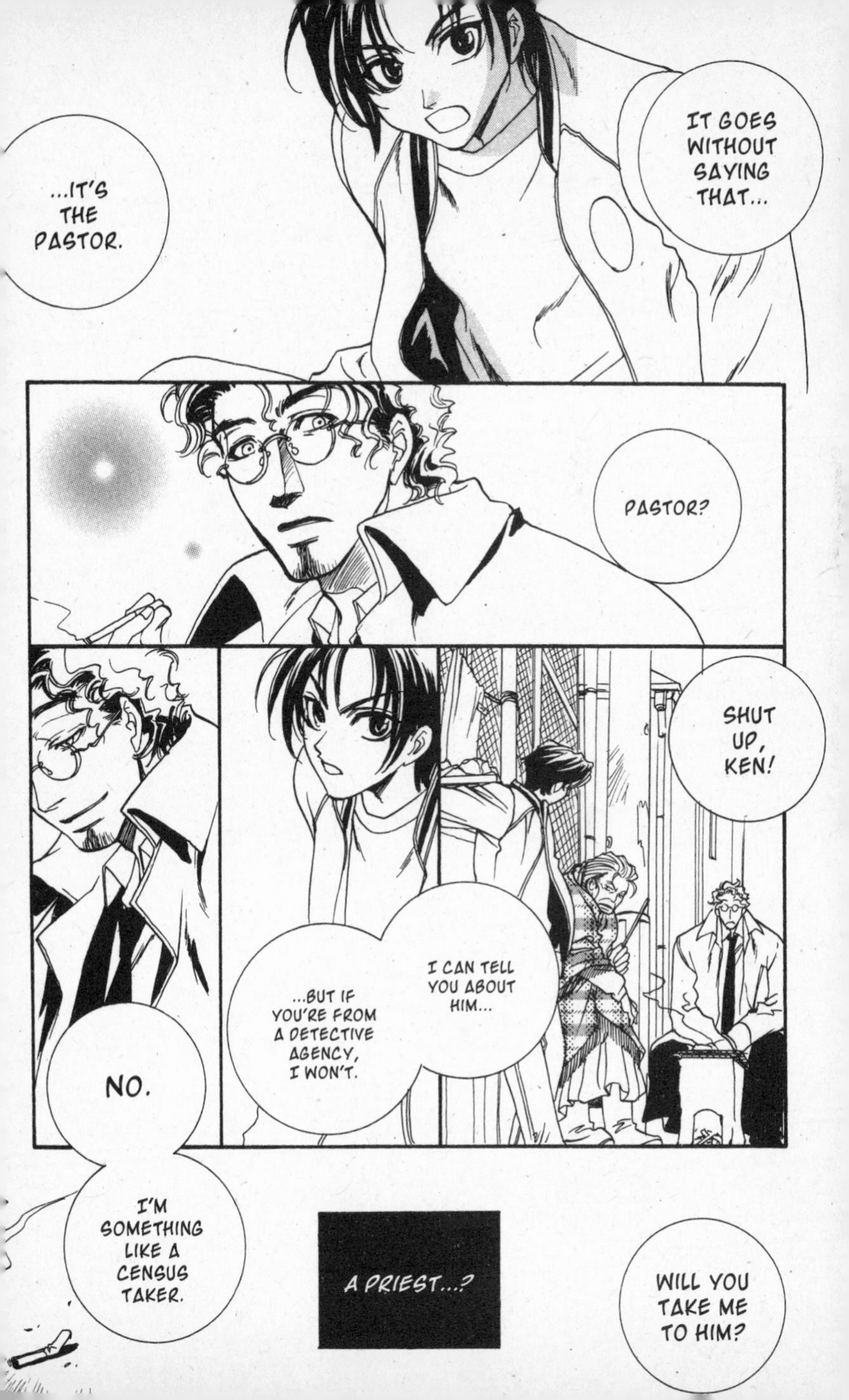
IT GOES WITHOUT SAYING THAT...
...IT'S THE PASTOR.
PASTOR?
SHUT UP, KEN!
I CAN TELL YOU ABOUT HIM...
...BUT IF YOU'RE FROM A DETECTIVE AGENCY, I WON'T.
NO.
I'M SOMETHING LIKE A CENSUS TAKER.
WILL YOU TAKE ME TO HIM?
A PRIEST...?

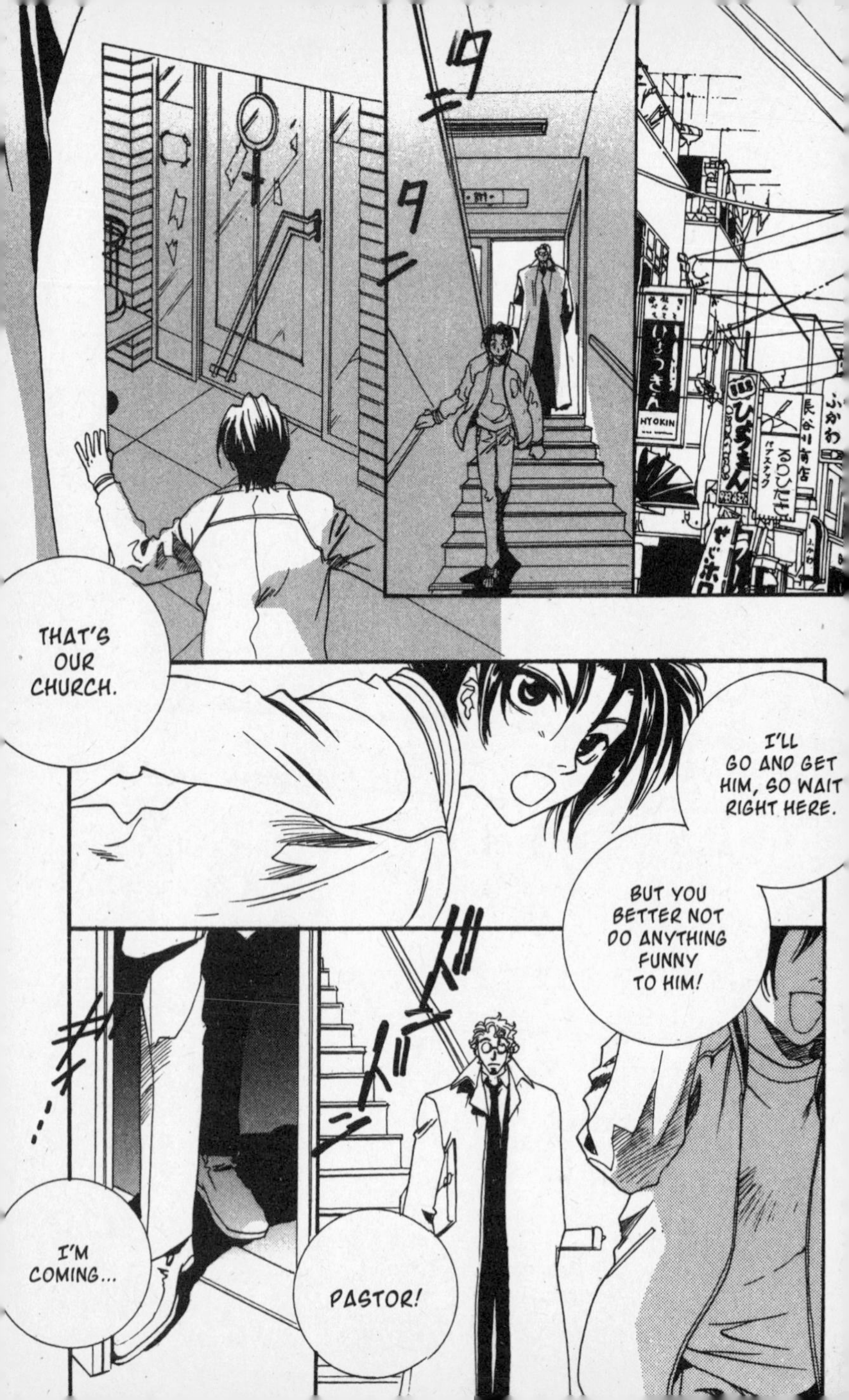
HYOKIN
THAT'S OUR CHURCH.
I'LL GO AND GET HIM, SO WAIT RIGHT HERE.
BUT YOU BETTER NOT DO ANYTHING FUNNY TO HIM!
PASTOR!
I'M COMING...

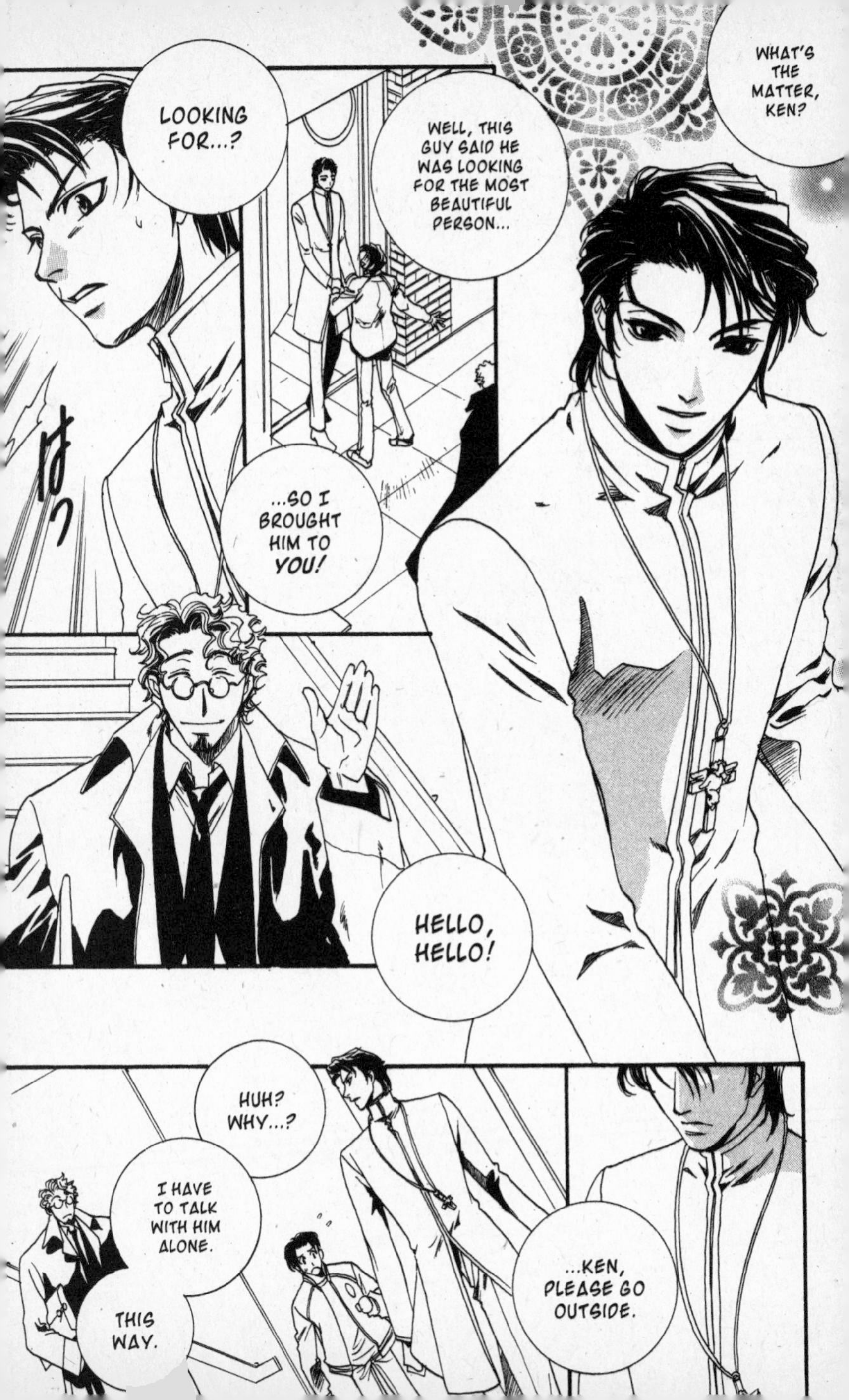

WHAT'S THE MATTER, KEN?
WELL, THIS GUY SAID HE WAS LOOKING FOR THE MOST BEAUTIFUL PERSON...
...SO I BROUGHT HIM TO *YOU!*
LOOKING FOR...?
はっ
HELLO, HELLO!
...KEN, PLEASE GO OUTSIDE.
HUH? WHY...?
I HAVE TO TALK WITH HIM ALONE.
THIS WAY.

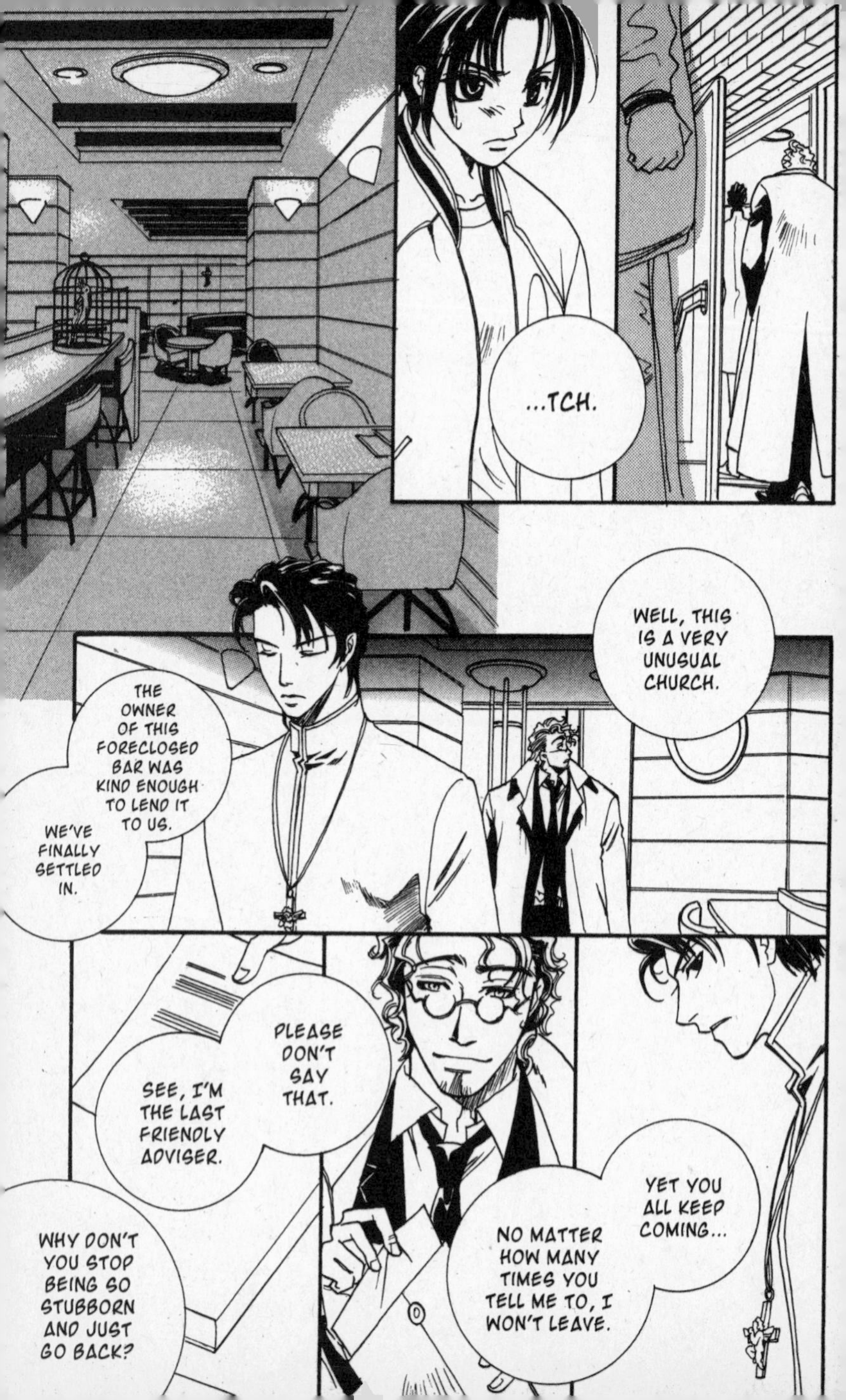
...TCH.
WELL, THIS IS A VERY UNUSUAL CHURCH.
THE OWNER OF THIS FORECLOSED BAR WAS KIND ENOUGH TO LEND IT TO US.
WE'VE FINALLY SETTLED IN.
YET YOU ALL KEEP COMING...
NO MATTER HOW MANY TIMES YOU TELL ME TO, I WON'T LEAVE.
PLEASE DON'T SAY THAT.
SEE, I'M THE LAST FRIENDLY ADVISER.
WHY DON'T YOU STOP BEING SO STUBBORN AND JUST GO BACK?

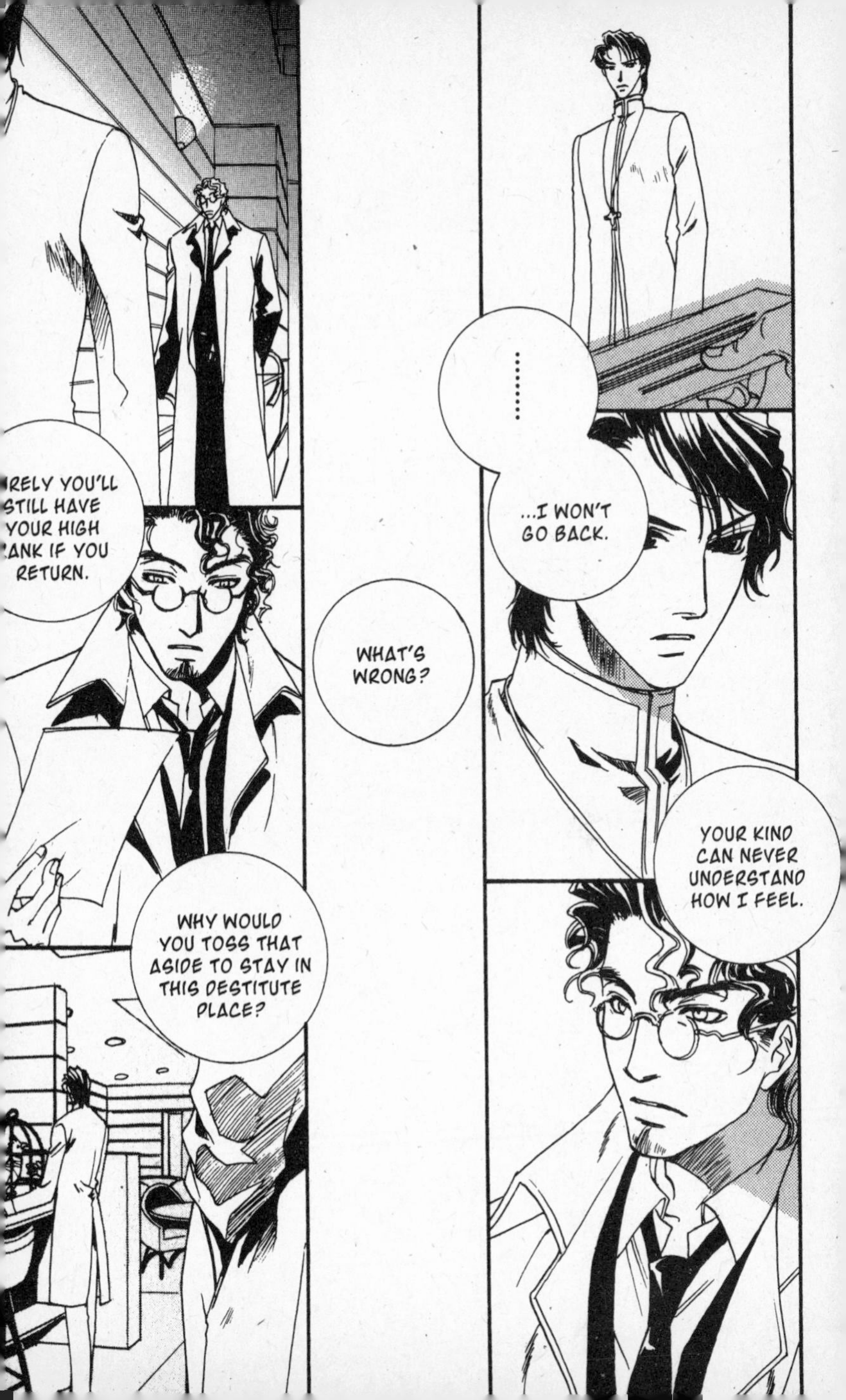
……
...I WON'T GO BACK.
YOUR KIND CAN NEVER UNDERSTAND HOW I FEEL.
WHAT'S WRONG?
RELY YOU'LL STILL HAVE YOUR HIGH ANK IF YOU RETURN.
WHY WOULD YOU TOSS THAT ASIDE TO STAY IN THIS DESTITUTE PLACE?

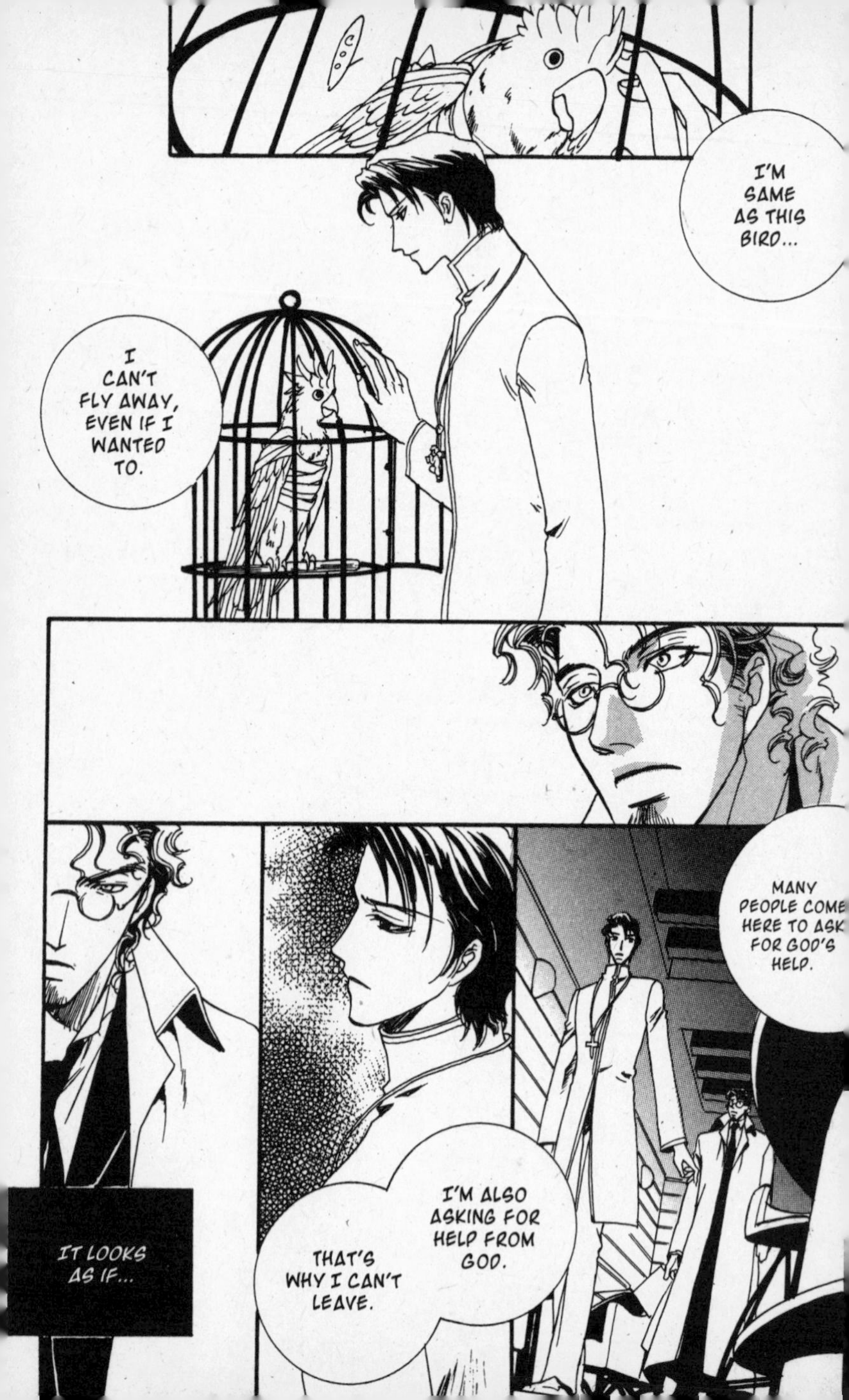
I'M SAME AS THIS BIRD...
I CAN'T FLY AWAY, EVEN IF I WANTED TO.
MANY PEOPLE COME HERE TO ASK FOR GOD'S HELP.
I'M ALSO ASKING FOR HELP FROM GOD.
THAT'S WHY I CAN'T LEAVE.
IT LOOKS AS IF...

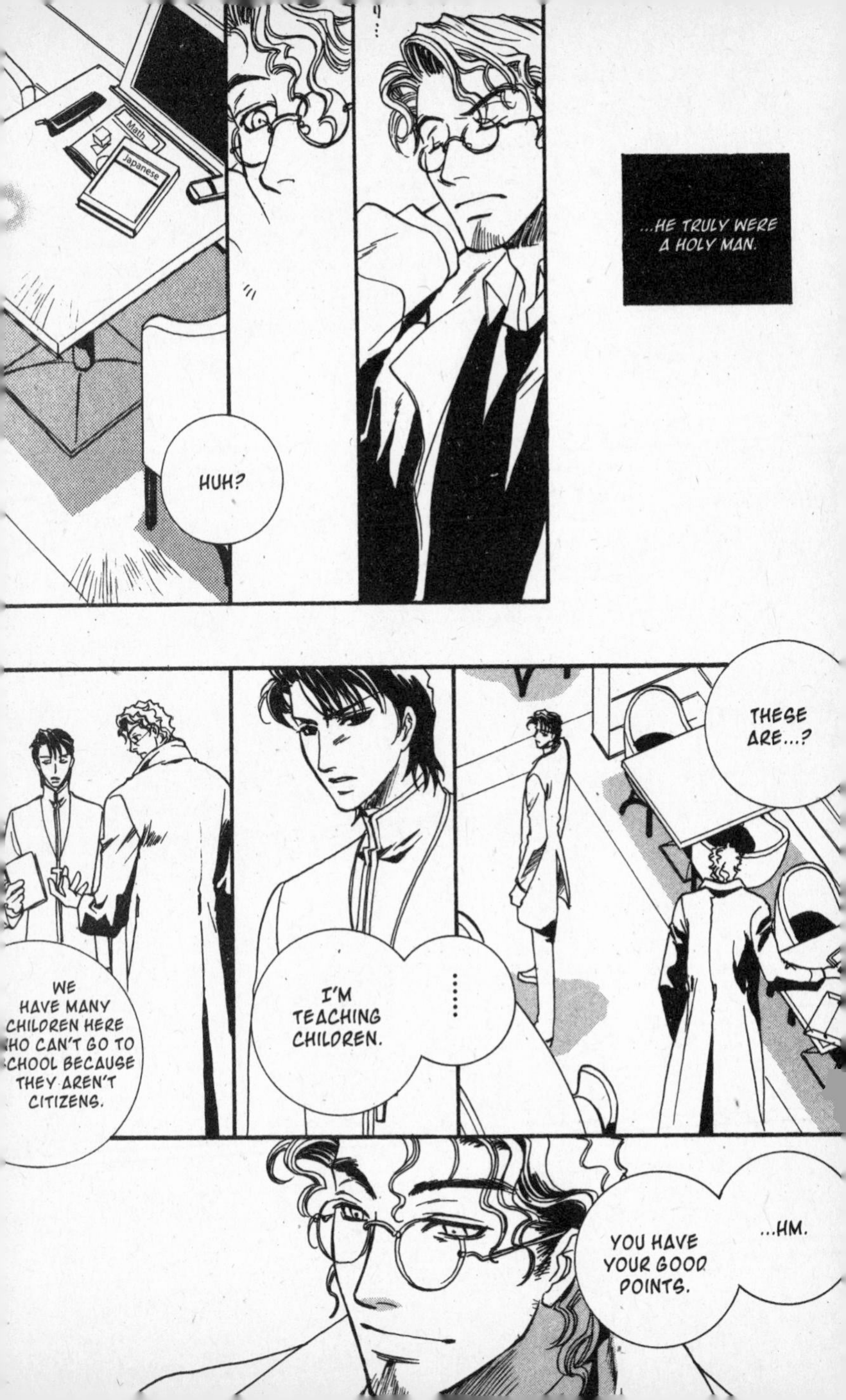
...HE TRULY WERE A HOLY MAN.
HUH?
Math
Japanese
THESE ARE...?
......
I'M TEACHING CHILDREN.
WE HAVE MANY CHILDREN HERE HO CAN'T GO TO CHOOL BECAUSE THEY AREN'T CITIZENS.
...HM.
YOU HAVE YOUR GOOD POINTS.

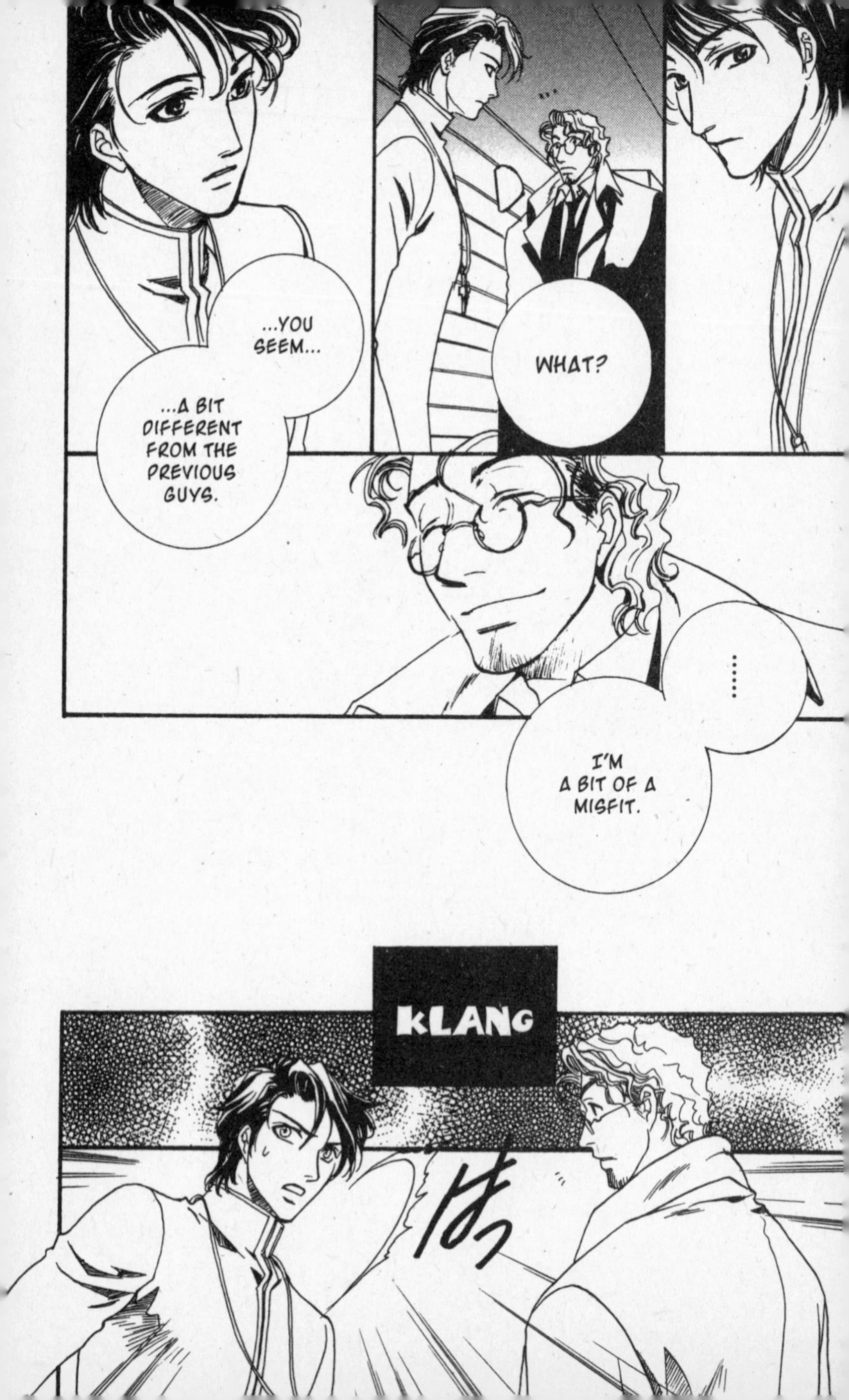
WHAT?
...YOU SEEM...
...A BIT DIFFERENT FROM THE PREVIOUS GUYS.
......
I'M A BIT OF A MISFIT.
KLANG
はっ

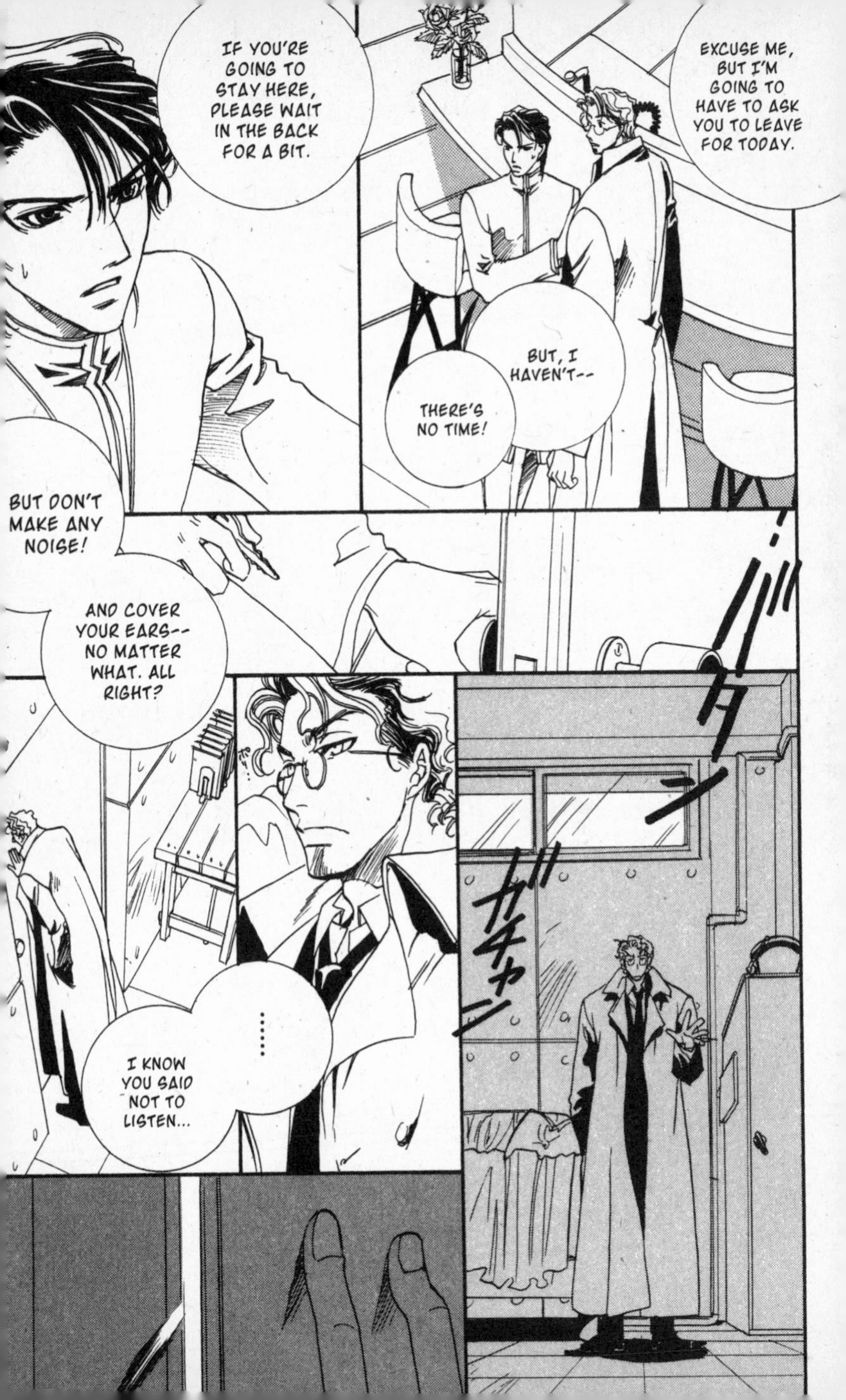
EXCUSE ME, BUT I'M GOING TO HAVE TO ASK YOU TO LEAVE FOR TODAY.
BUT, I HAVEN'T--
THERE'S NO TIME!
IF YOU'RE GOING TO STAY HERE, PLEASE WAIT IN THE BACK FOR A BIT.
BUT DON'T MAKE ANY NOISE!
AND COVER YOUR EARS--NO MATTER WHAT. ALL RIGHT?
バタン
ガチャン
......
I KNOW YOU SAID NOT TO LISTEN...

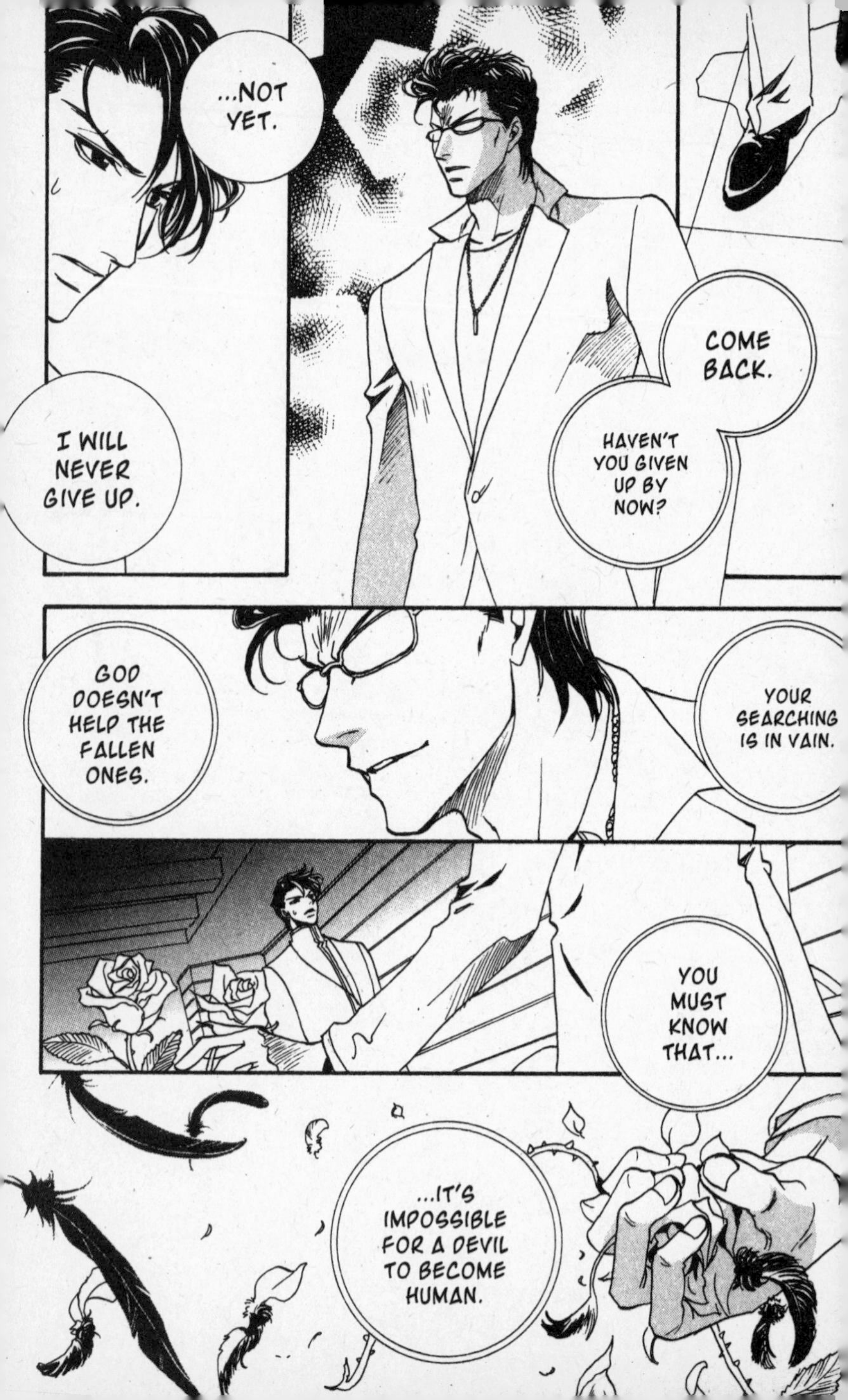
COME BACK.
HAVEN'T YOU GIVEN UP BY NOW?
...NOT YET.
I WILL NEVER GIVE UP.
YOUR SEARCHING IS IN VAIN.
GOD DOESN'T HELP THE FALLEN ONES.
YOU MUST KNOW THAT...
...IT'S IMPOSSIBLE FOR A DEVIL TO BECOME HUMAN.

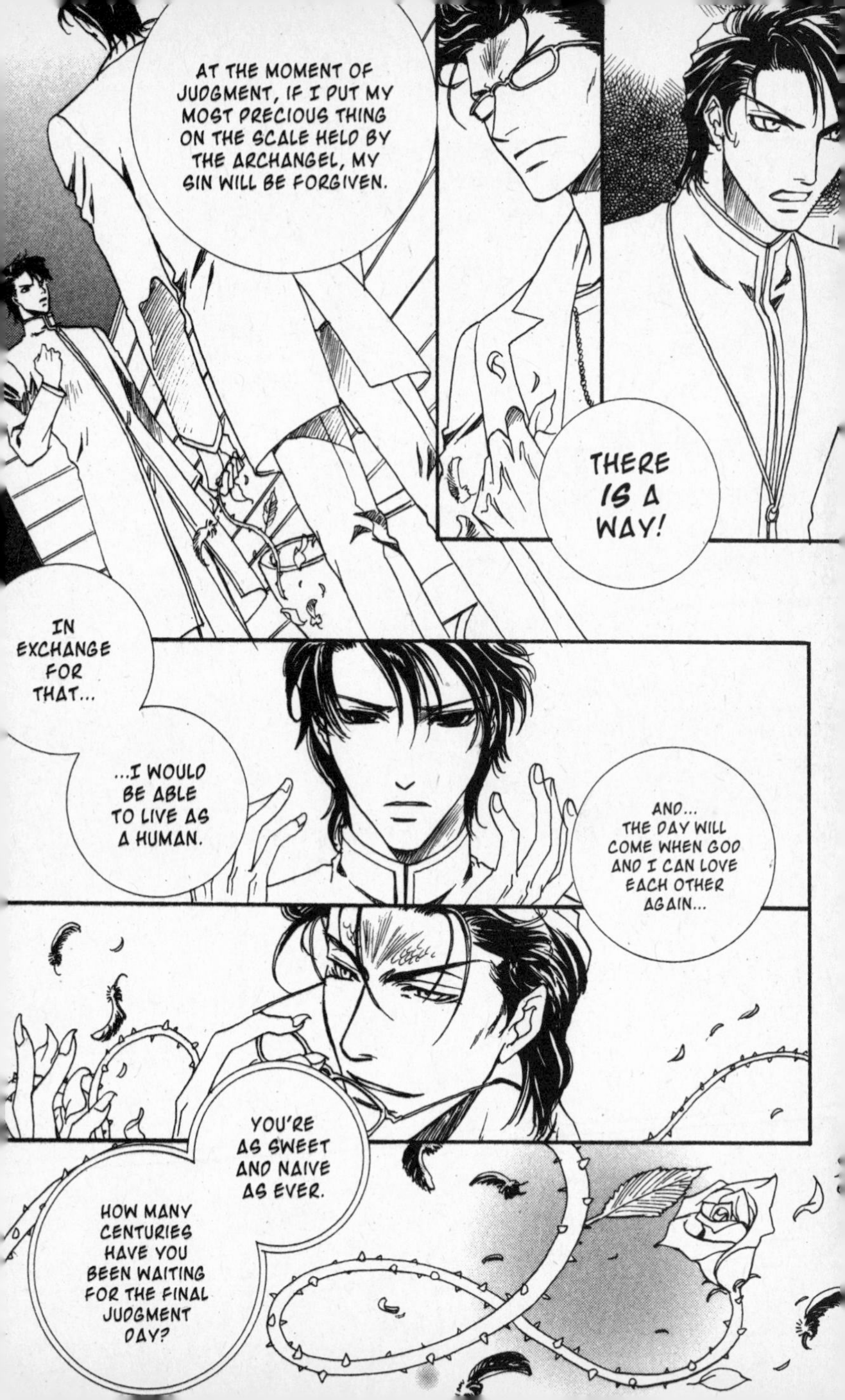
THERE IS A WAY!
AT THE MOMENT OF JUDGMENT, IF I PUT MY MOST PRECIOUS THING ON THE SCALE HELD BY THE ARCHANGEL, MY SIN WILL BE FORGIVEN.
IN EXCHANGE FOR THAT...
...I WOULD BE ABLE TO LIVE AS A HUMAN.
AND... THE DAY WILL COME WHEN GOD AND I CAN LOVE EACH OTHER AGAIN...
YOU'RE AS SWEET AND NAIVE AS EVER.
HOW MANY CENTURIES HAVE YOU BEEN WAITING FOR THE FINAL JUDGMENT DAY?

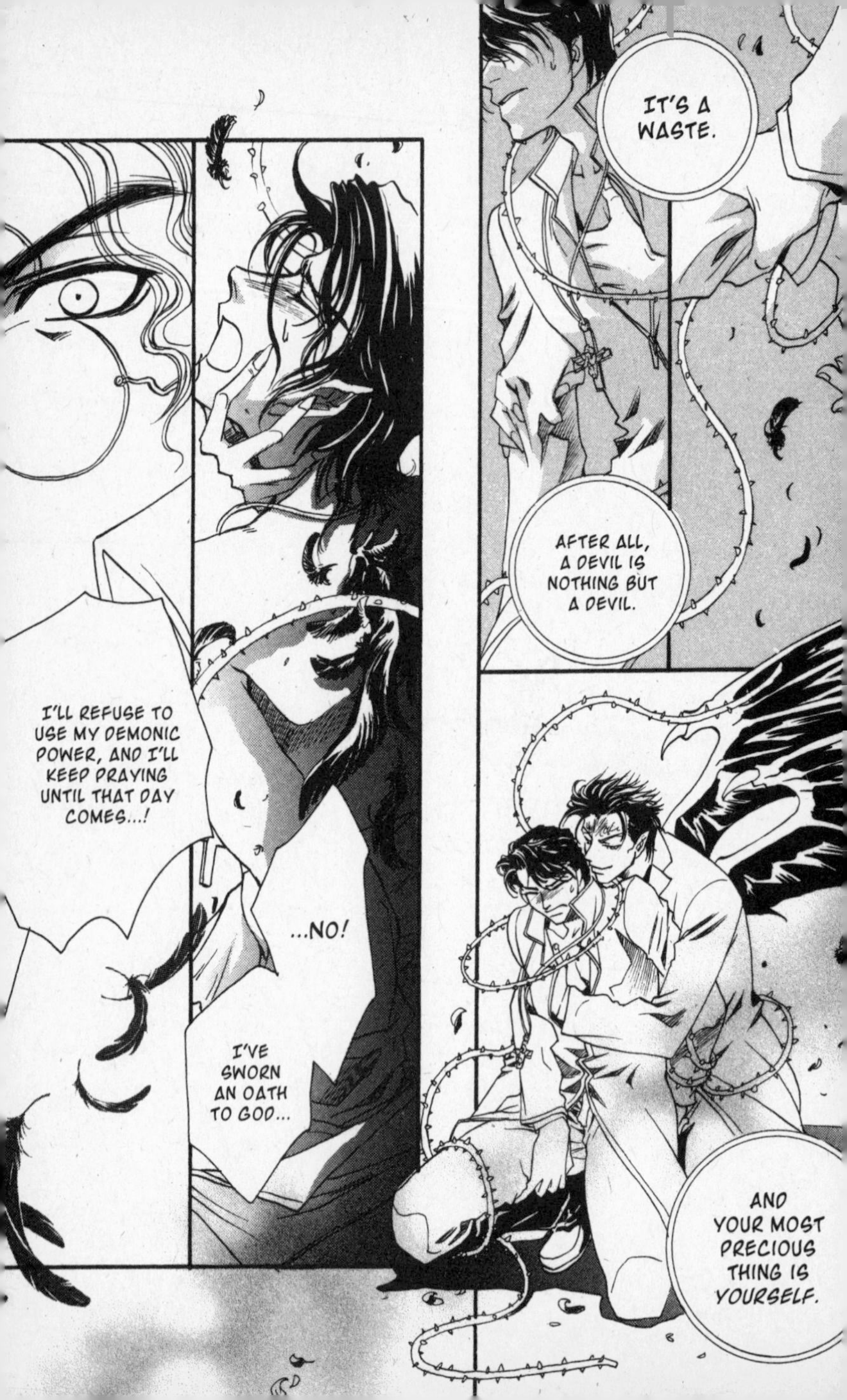
IT'S A WASTE.
AFTER ALL, A DEVIL IS NOTHING BUT A DEVIL.
AND YOUR MOST PRECIOUS THING IS YOURSELF.
...NO!
I'VE SWORN AN OATH TO GOD...
I'LL REFUSE TO USE MY DEMONIC POWER, AND I'LL KEEP PRAYING UNTIL THAT DAY COMES...!

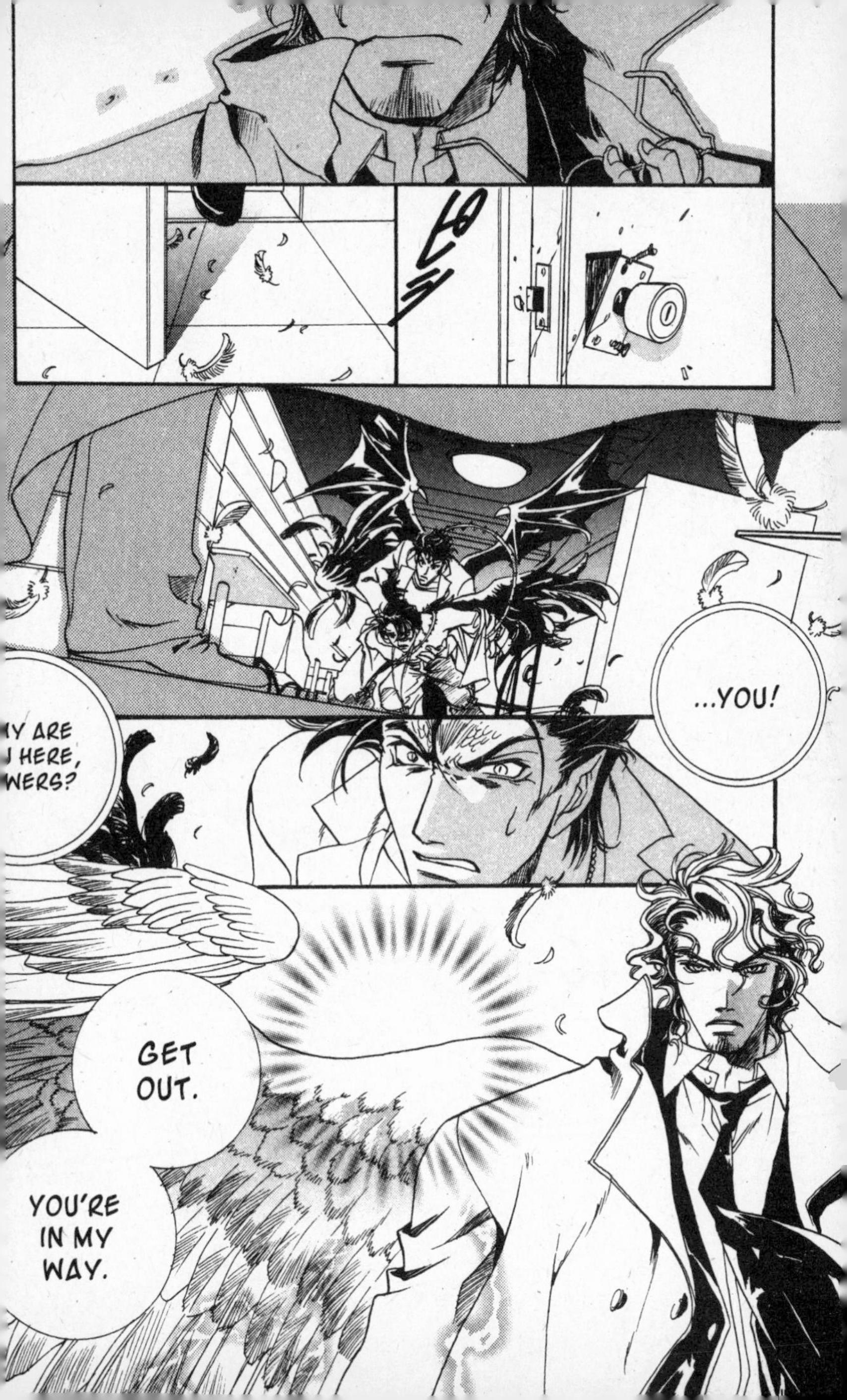
...YOU!
Y ARE U HERE, WERS?
GET OUT.
YOU'RE IN MY WAY.

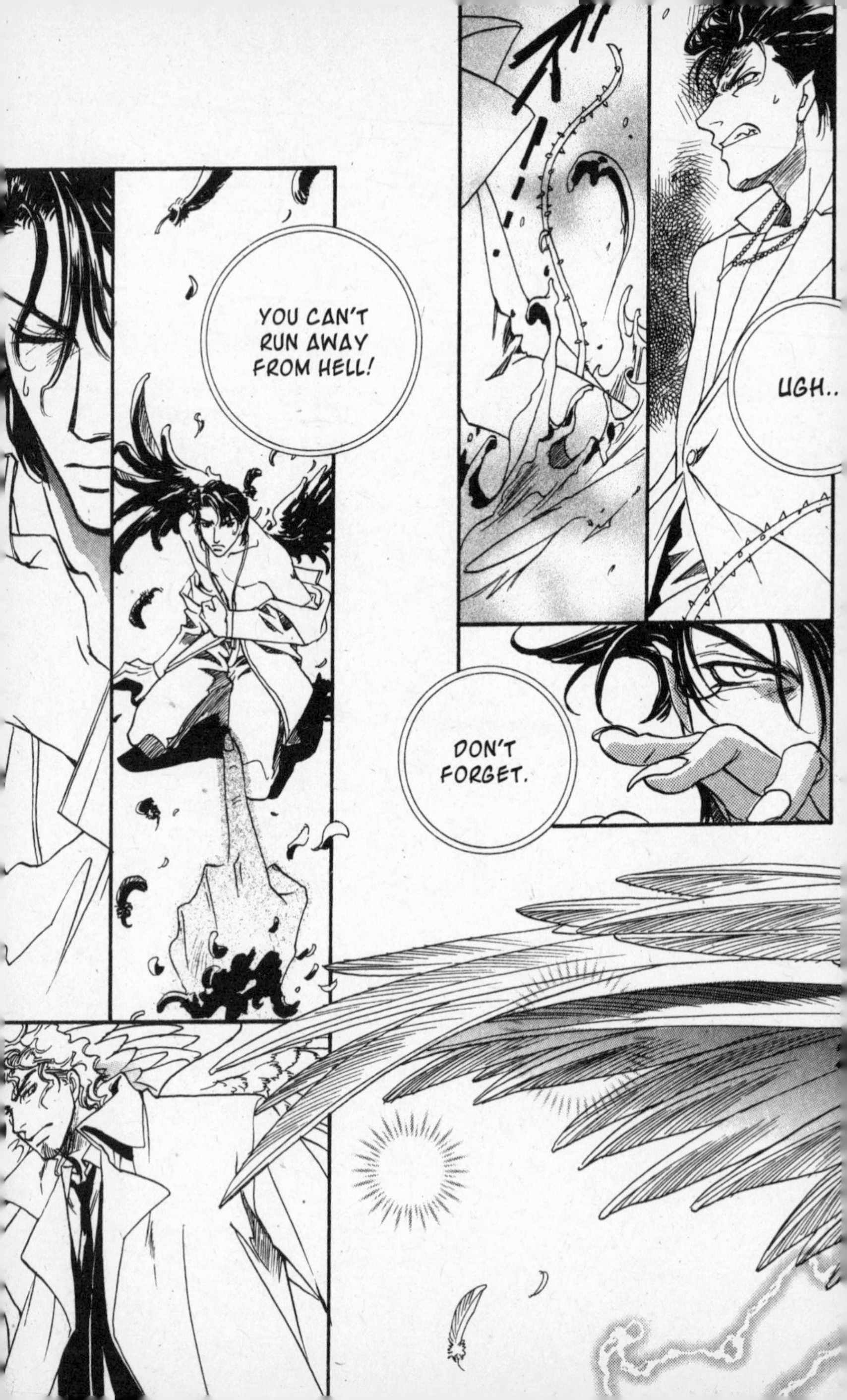
UGH..
DON'T FORGET.
YOU CAN'T RUN AWAY FROM HELL!

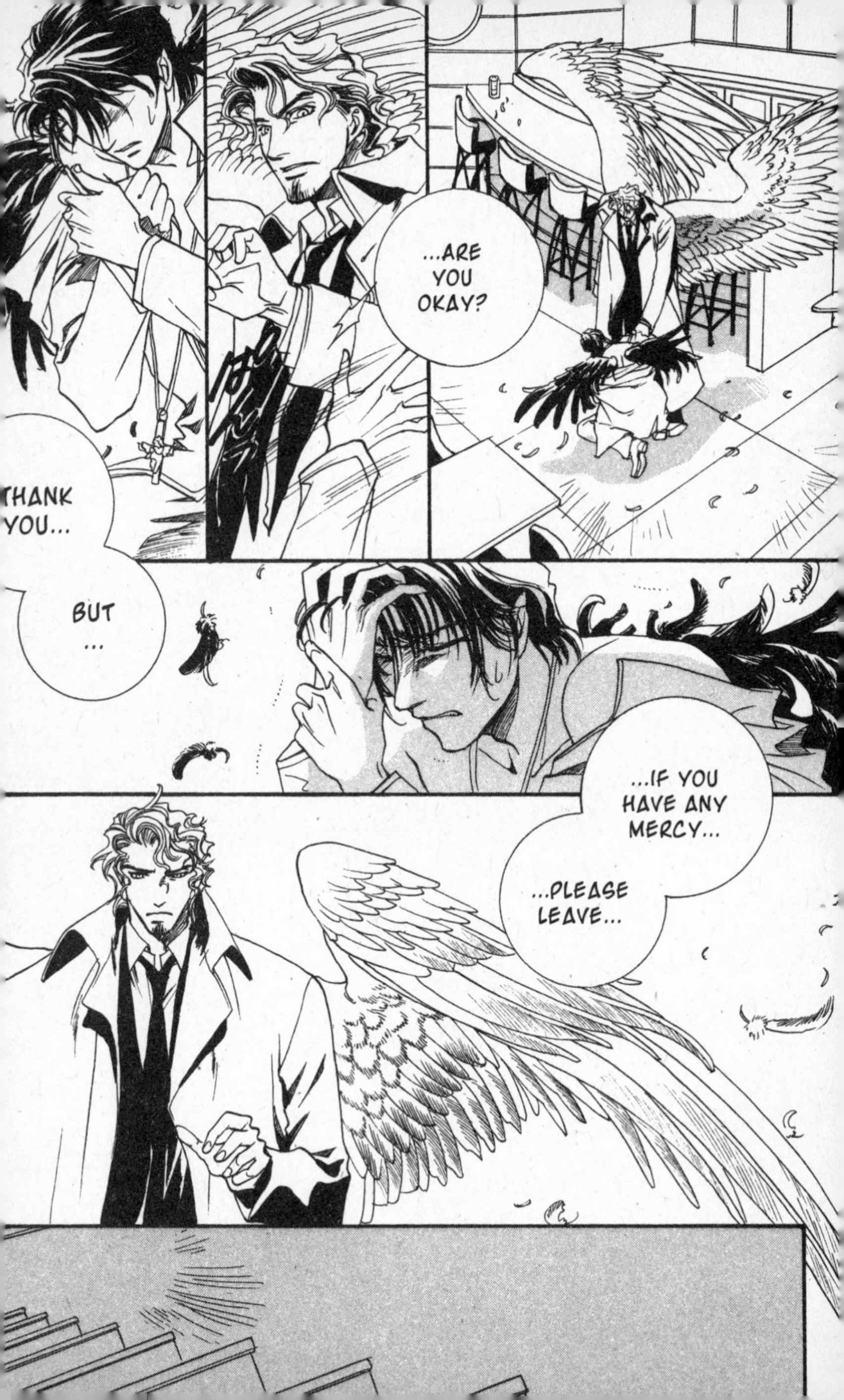
...ARE YOU OKAY?
THANK YOU... BUT ...
...IF YOU HAVE ANY MERCY...
...PLEASE LEAVE...

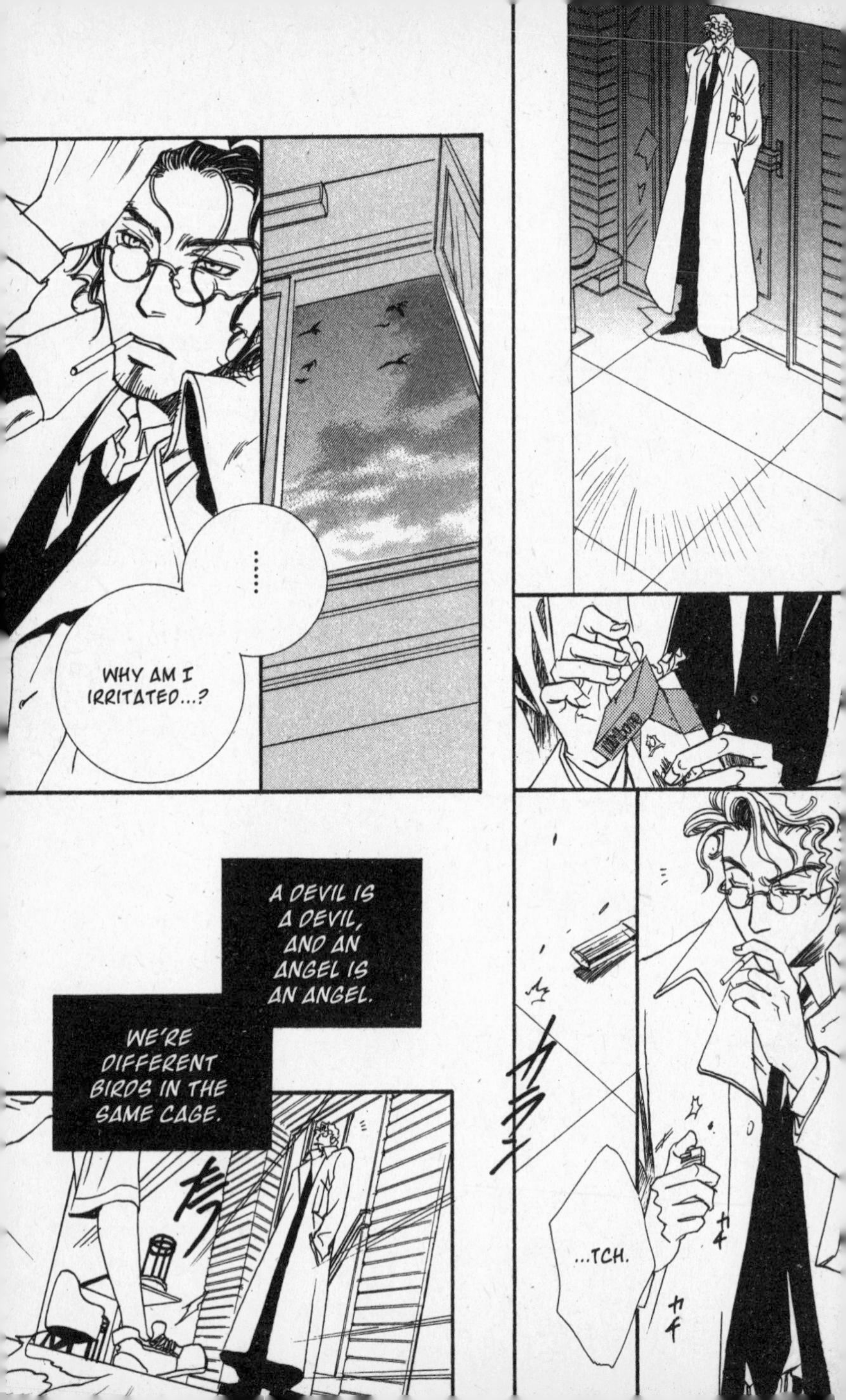

...TCH.
......
WHY AM I IRRITATED...?
A DEVIL IS A DEVIL, AND AN ANGEL IS AN ANGEL.
WE'RE DIFFERENT BIRDS IN THE SAME CAGE.

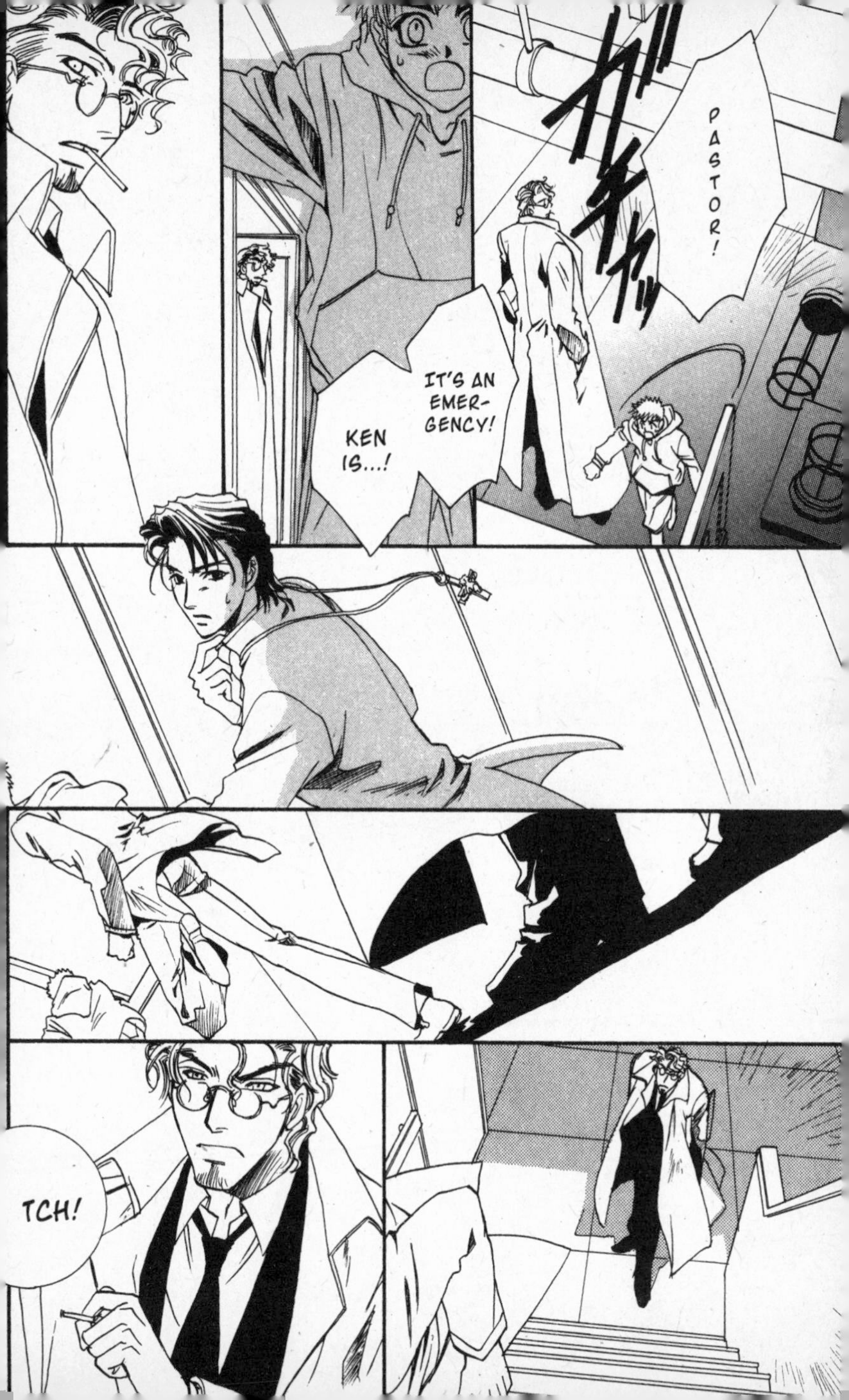
PASTOR!
ガチャッ
IT'S AN EMER-GENCY! KEN IS...!
TCH!

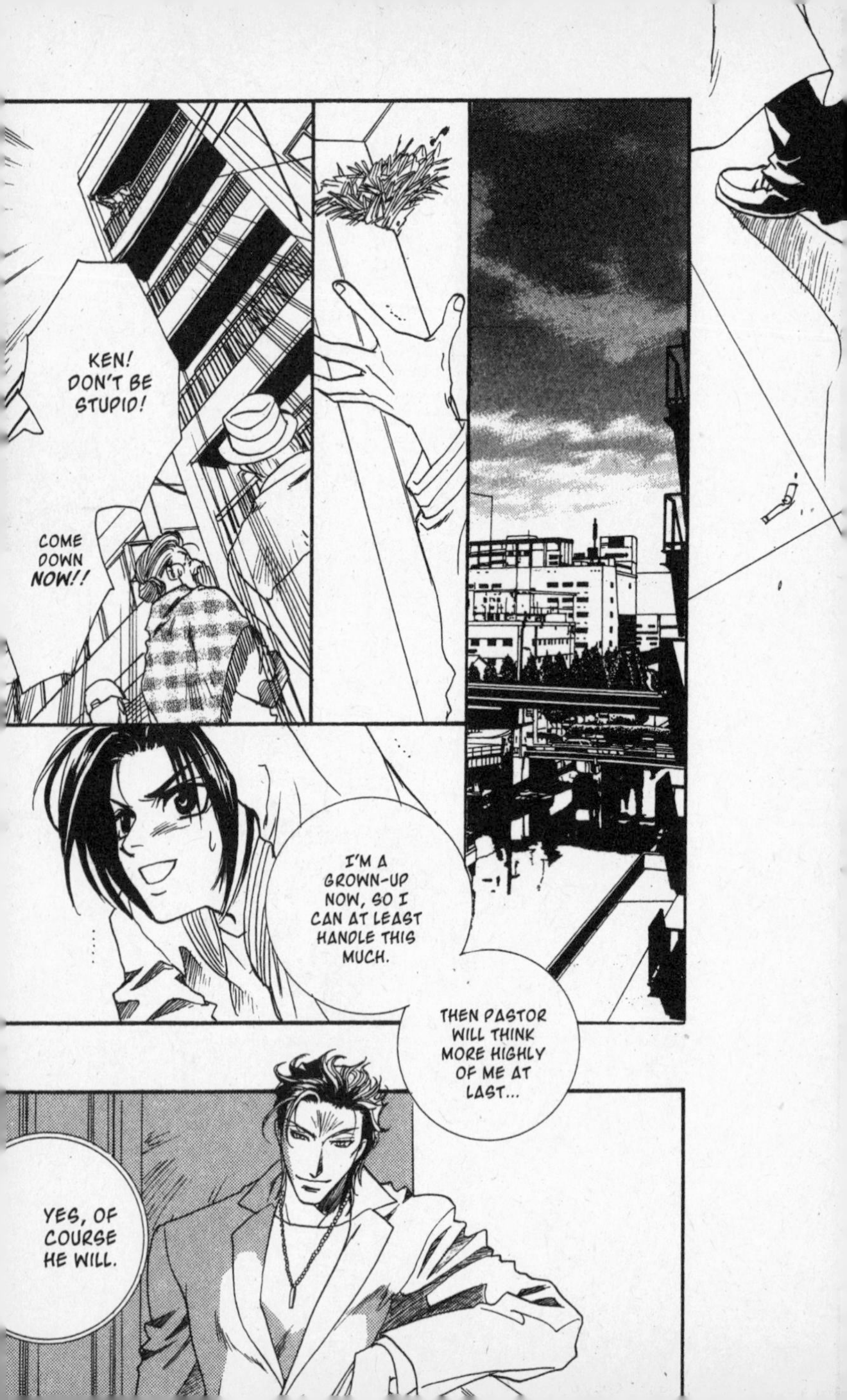
KEN! DON'T BE STUPID!
COME DOWN NOW!!
I'M A GROWN-UP NOW, SO I CAN AT LEAST HANDLE THIS MUCH.
THEN PASTOR WILL THINK MORE HIGHLY OF ME AT LAST...
YES, OF COURSE HE WILL.

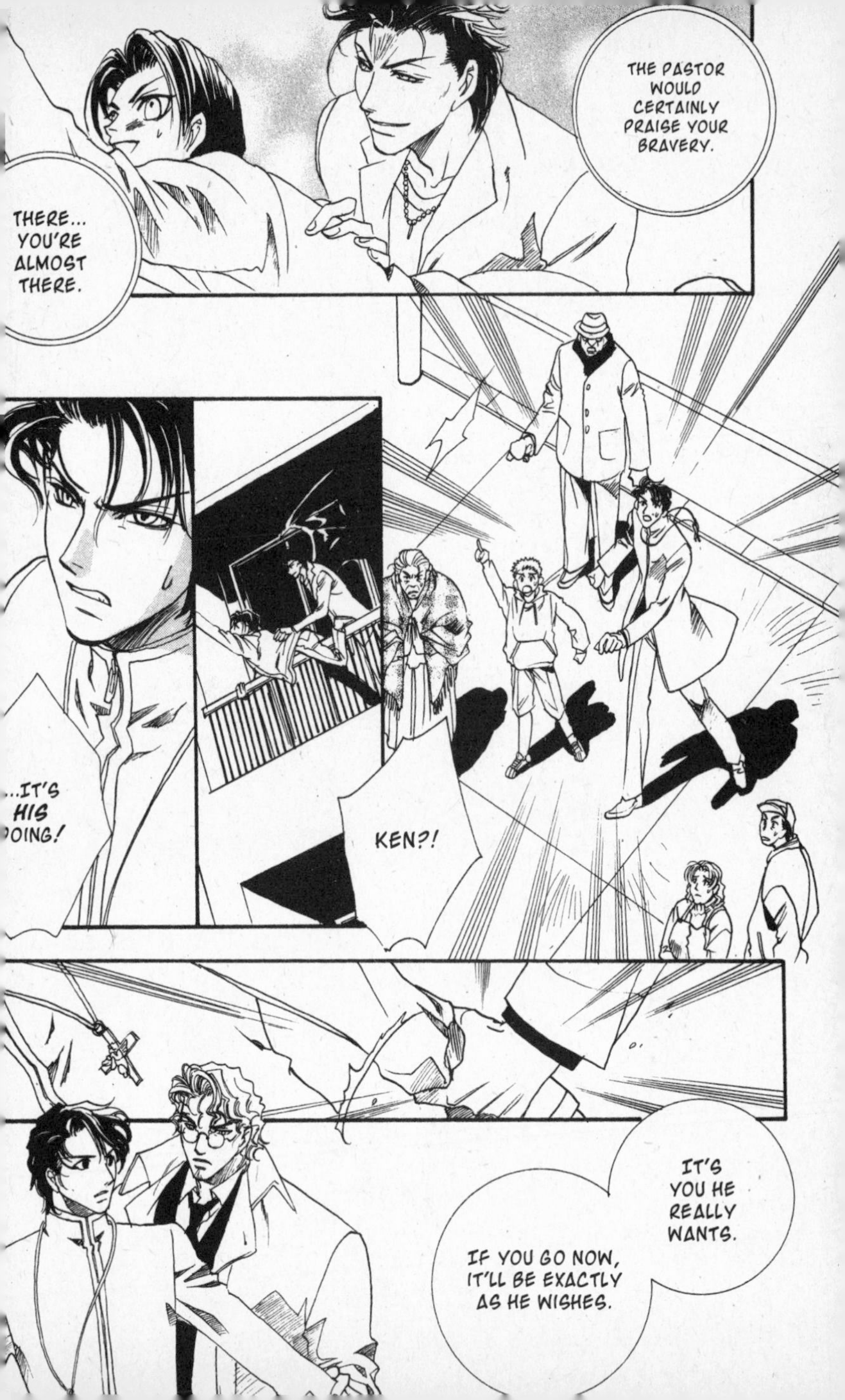
THE PASTOR WOULD CERTAINLY PRAISE YOUR BRAVERY.
THERE... YOU'RE ALMOST THERE.
KEN?!
...IT'S HIS DOING!
IT'S YOU HE REALLY WANTS.
IF YOU GO NOW, IT'LL BE EXACTLY AS HE WISHES.

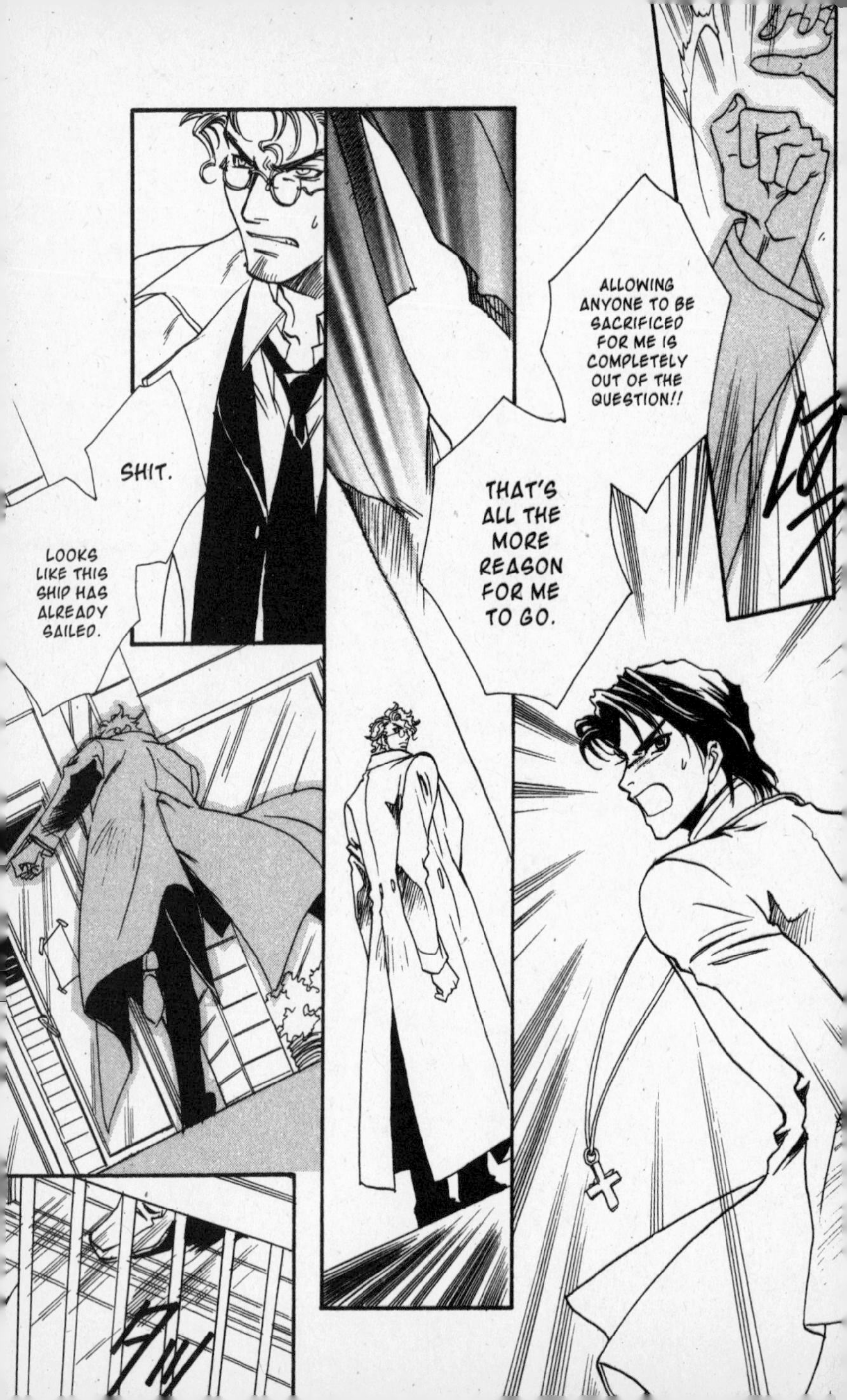
ALLOWING ANYONE TO BE SACRIFICED FOR ME IS COMPLETELY OUT OF THE QUESTION!!
THAT'S ALL THE MORE REASON FOR ME TO GO.
SHIT.
LOOKS LIKE THIS SHIP HAS ALREADY SAILED.

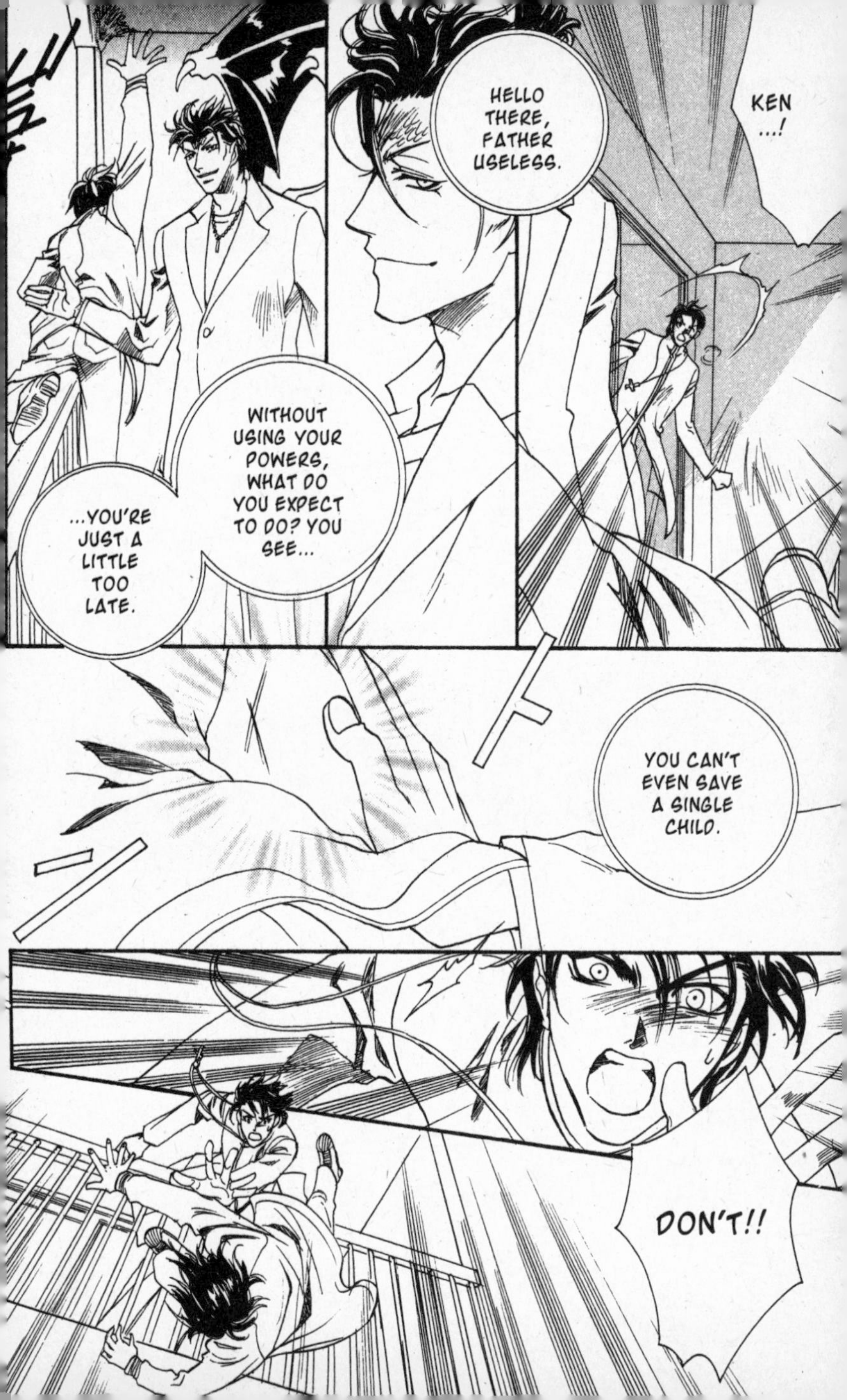
KEN ...!
HELLO THERE, FATHER USELESS.
WITHOUT USING YOUR POWERS, WHAT DO YOU EXPECT TO DO? YOU SEE...
...YOU'RE JUST A LITTLE TOO LATE.
YOU CAN'T EVEN SAVE A SINGLE CHILD.
DON'T!!

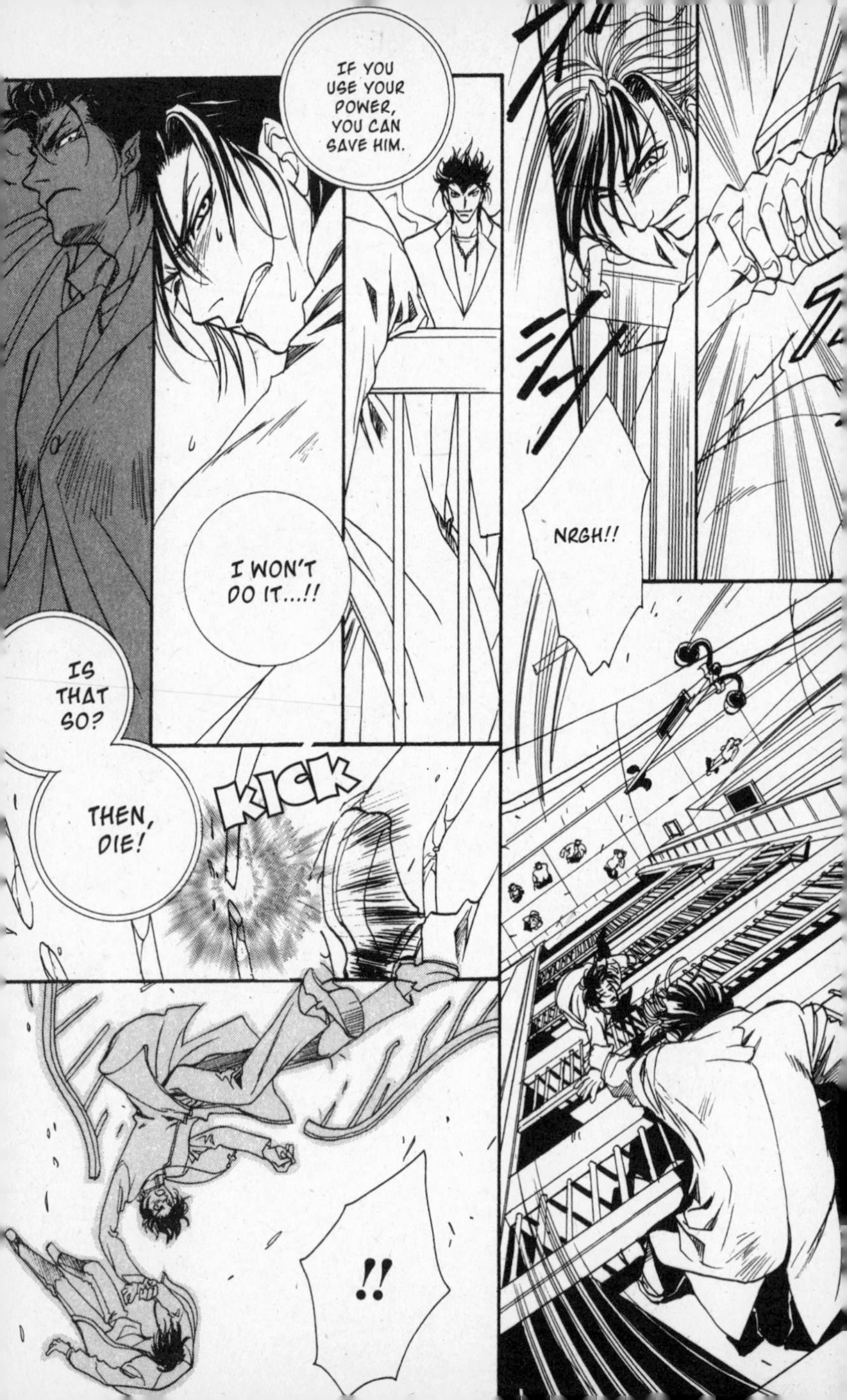
NRGH!!
IF YOU USE YOUR POWER, YOU CAN SAVE HIM.
I WON'T DO IT...!!
IS THAT SO?
THEN, DIE!
KICK
!!

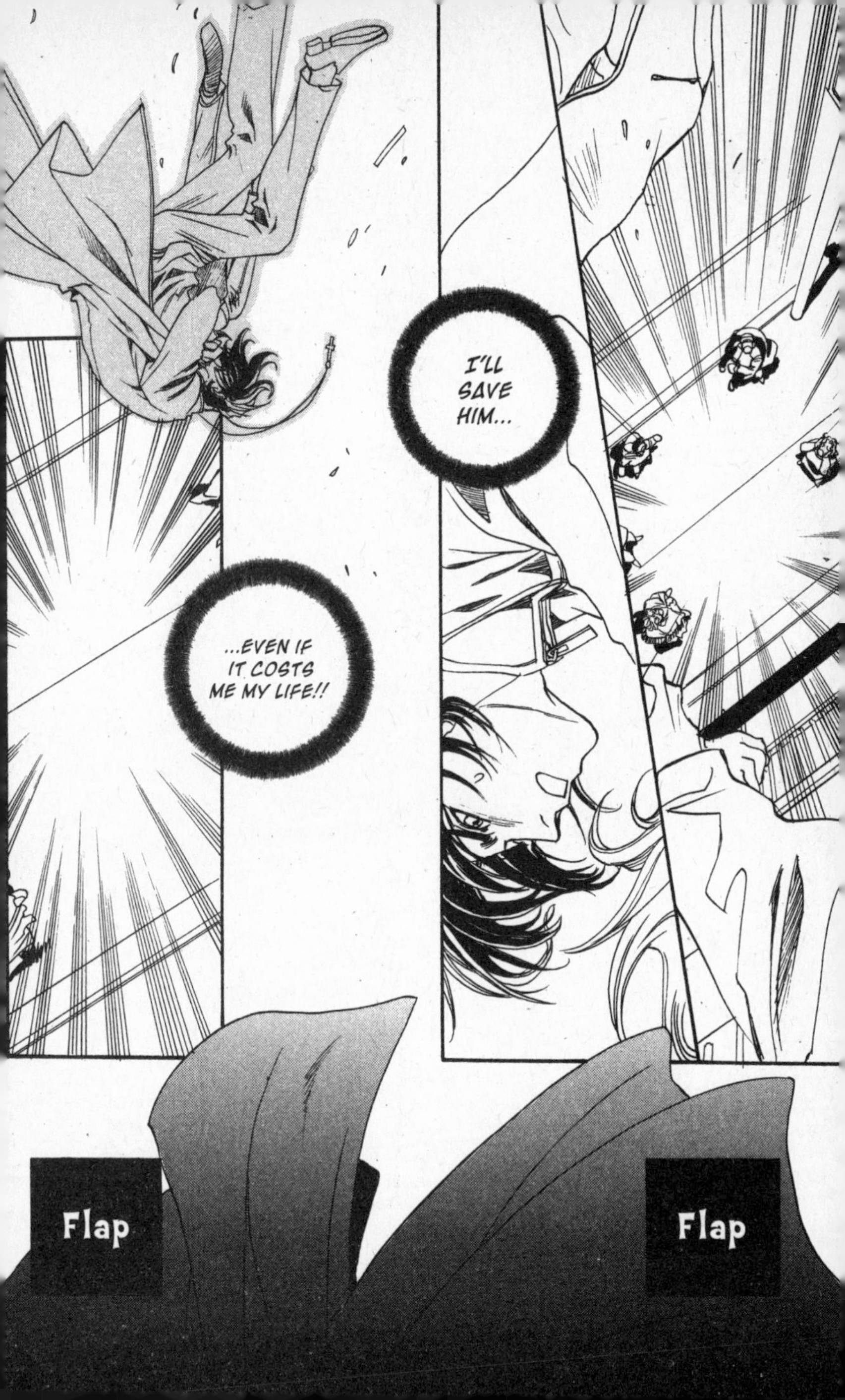
I'LL SAVE HIM...
...EVEN IF IT COSTS ME MY LIFE!!
Flap
Flap

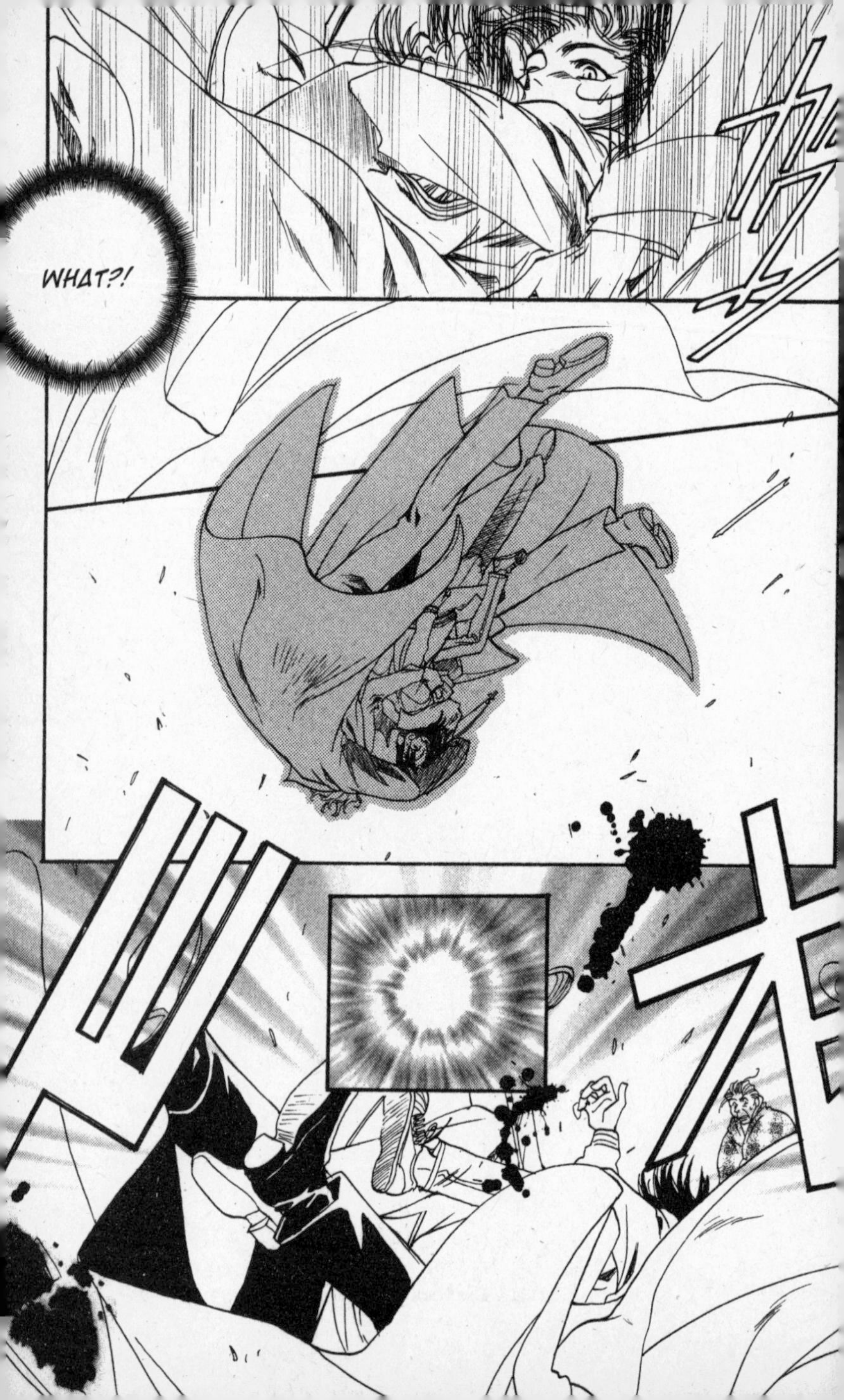
WHAT?!

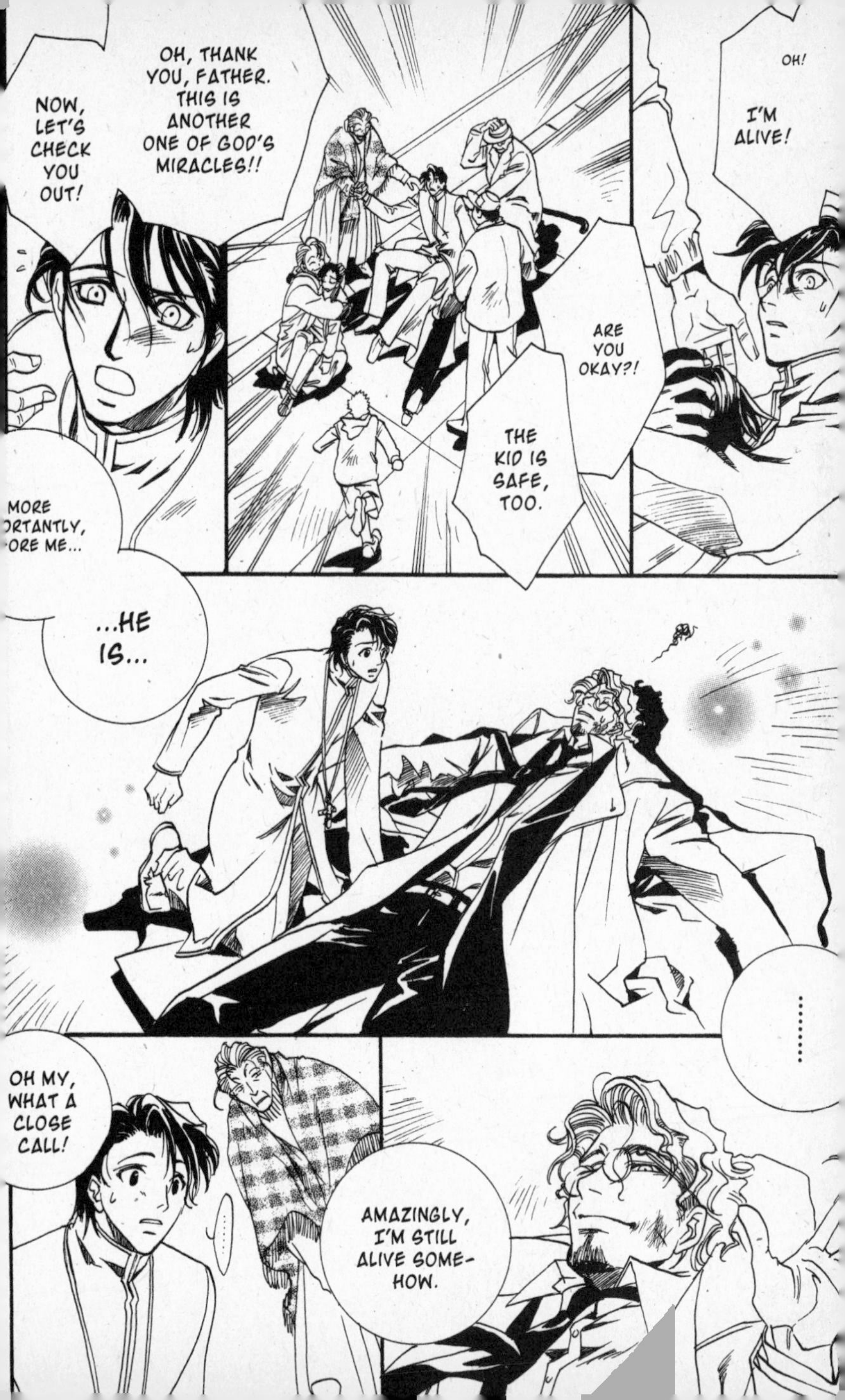
OH!
I'M ALIVE!
ARE YOU OKAY?!
THE KID IS SAFE, TOO.
OH, THANK YOU, FATHER. THIS IS ANOTHER ONE OF GOD'S MIRACLES!!
NOW, LET'S CHECK YOU OUT!
MORE ORTANTLY, ORE ME...
...HE IS...
......
AMAZINGLY, I'M STILL ALIVE SOME-HOW.
OH MY, WHAT A CLOSE CALL!
......

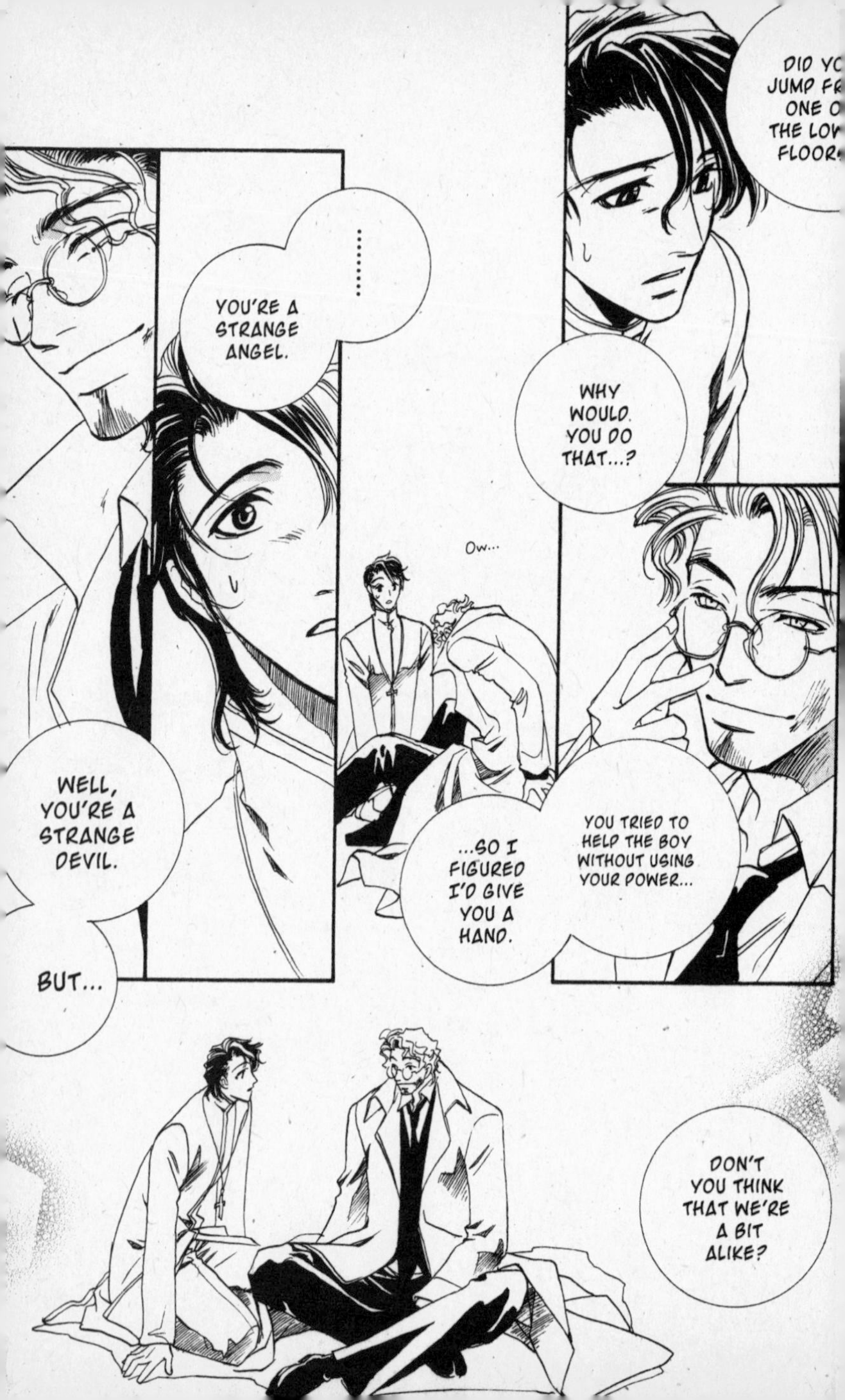

DID YO JUMP FR ONE O THE LOW FLOOR
WHY WOULD YOU DO THAT...?
YOU TRIED TO HELP THE BOY WITHOUT USING YOUR POWER...
...SO I FIGURED I'D GIVE YOU A HAND.
Ow...
......
YOU'RE A STRANGE ANGEL.
WELL, YOU'RE A STRANGE DEVIL.
BUT...
DON'T YOU THINK THAT WE'RE A BIT ALIKE?

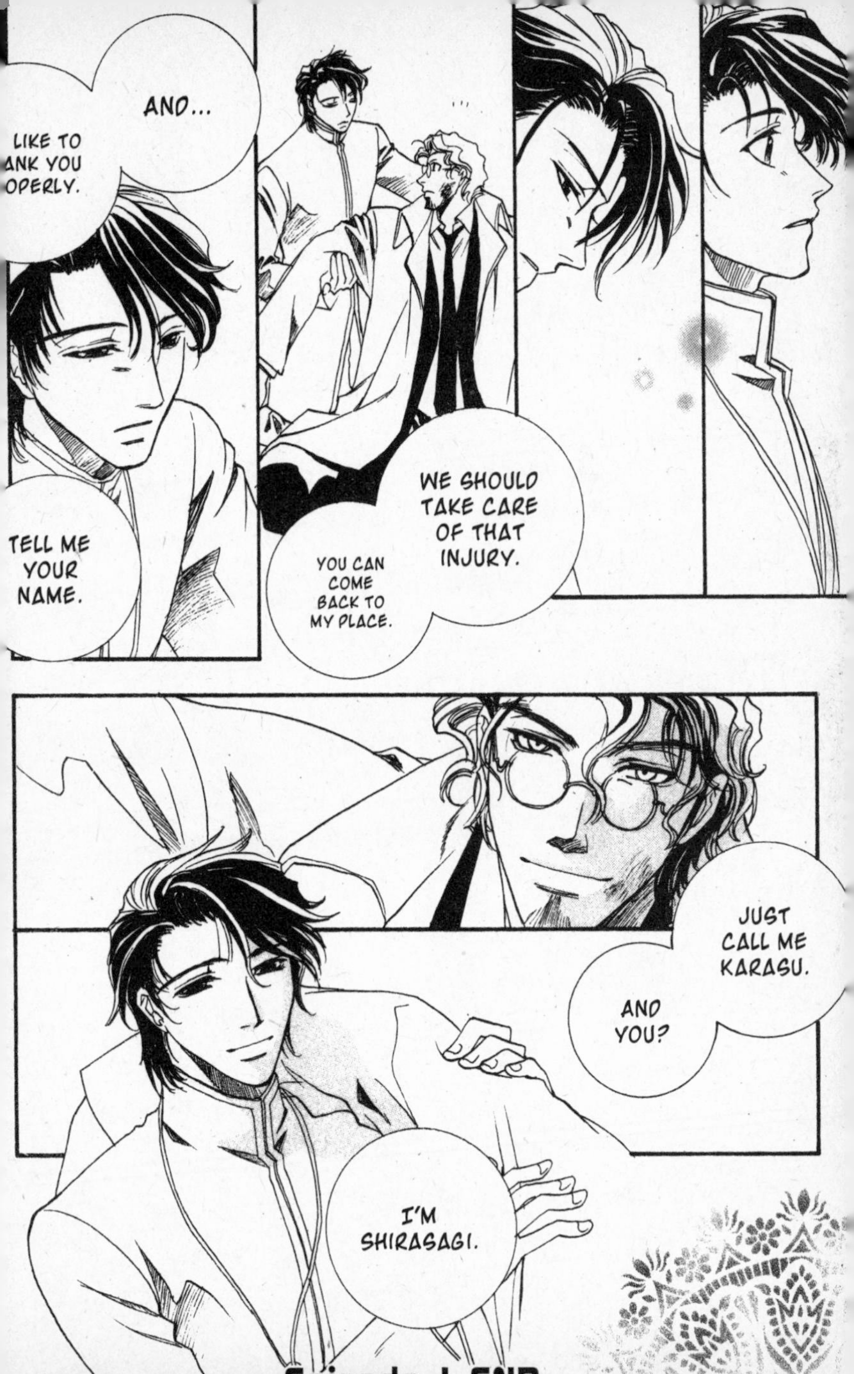
WE SHOULD TAKE CARE OF THAT INJURY.
YOU CAN COME BACK TO MY PLACE.
AND...
LIKE TO ANK YOU OPERLY.
TELL ME YOUR NAME.
JUST CALL ME KARASU.
AND YOU?
I'M SHIRASAGI.

Episode 1 END

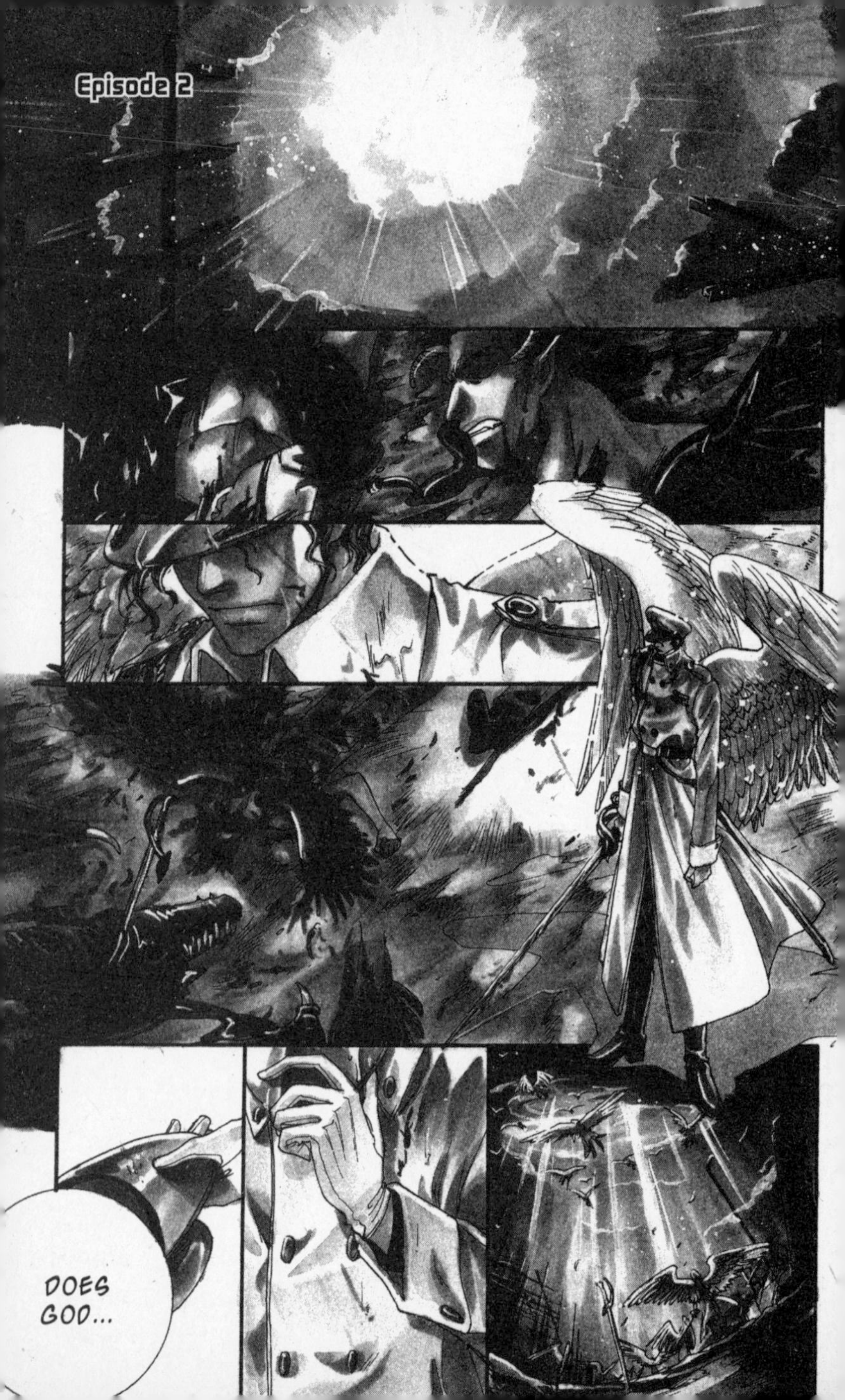
Episode 2
DOES GOD...

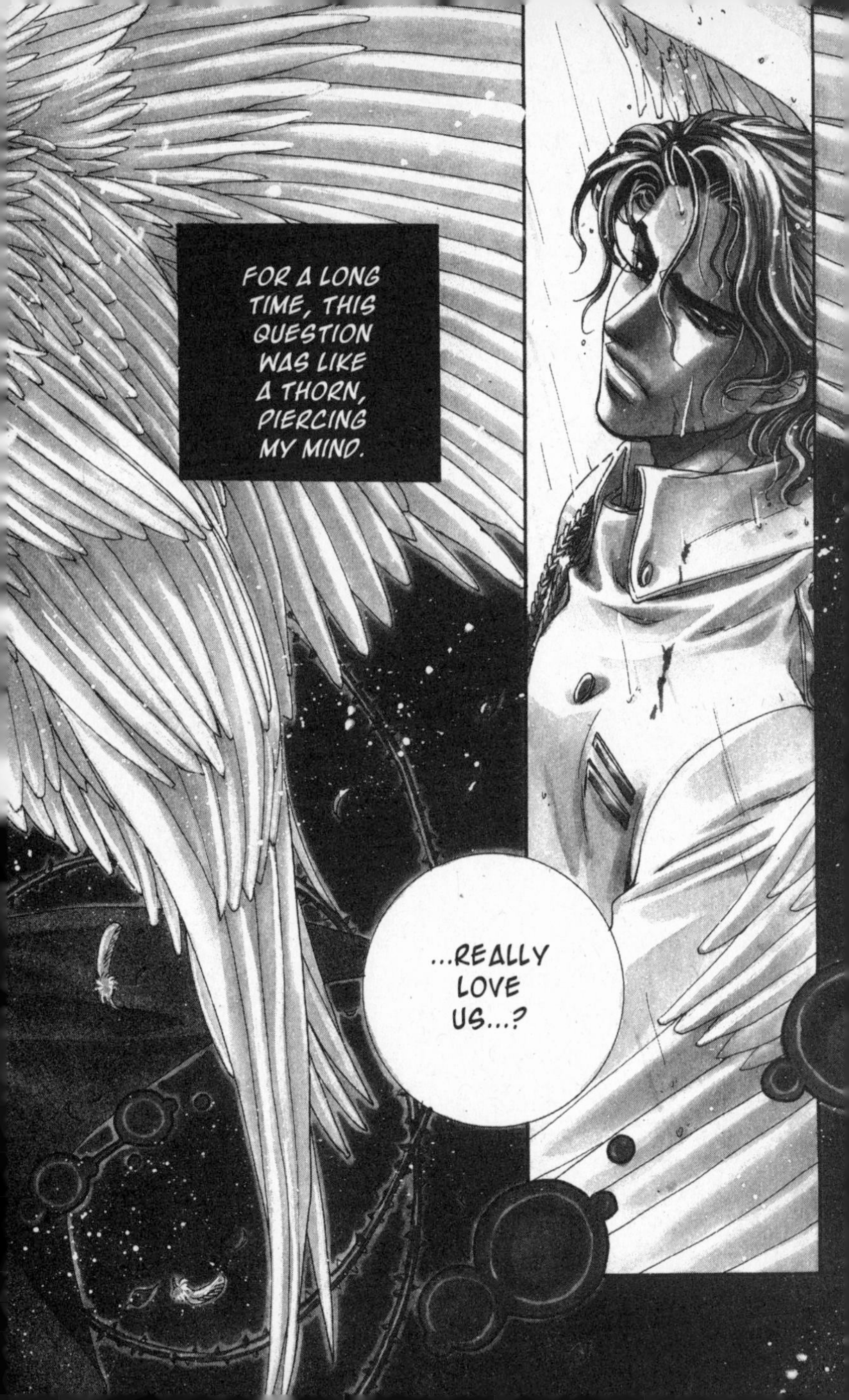
FOR A LONG TIME, THIS QUESTION WAS LIKE A THORN, PIERCING MY MIND.
...REALLY LOVE US...?

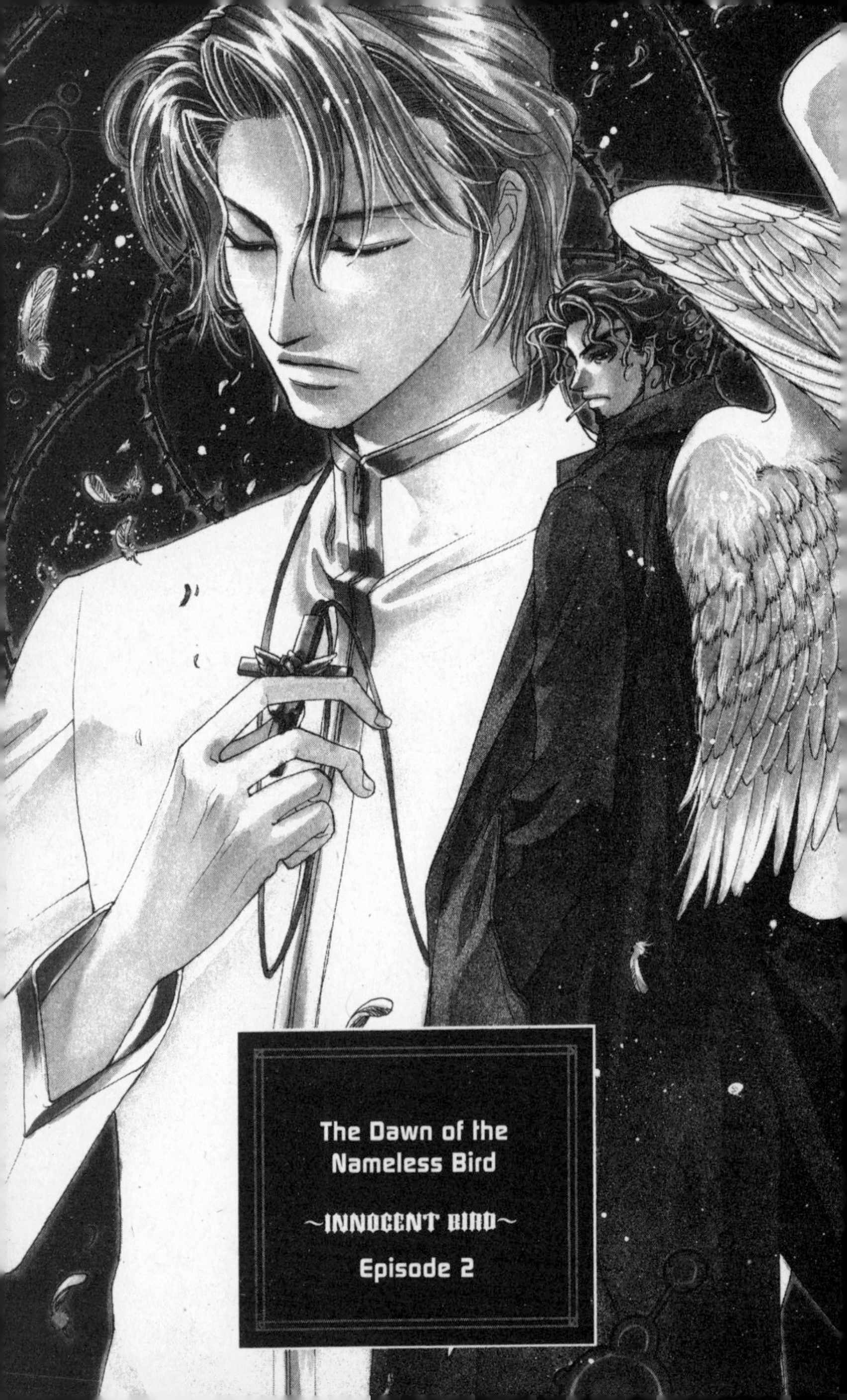
The Dawn of the
Nameless Bird
~INNOCENT BIRD~
Episode 2

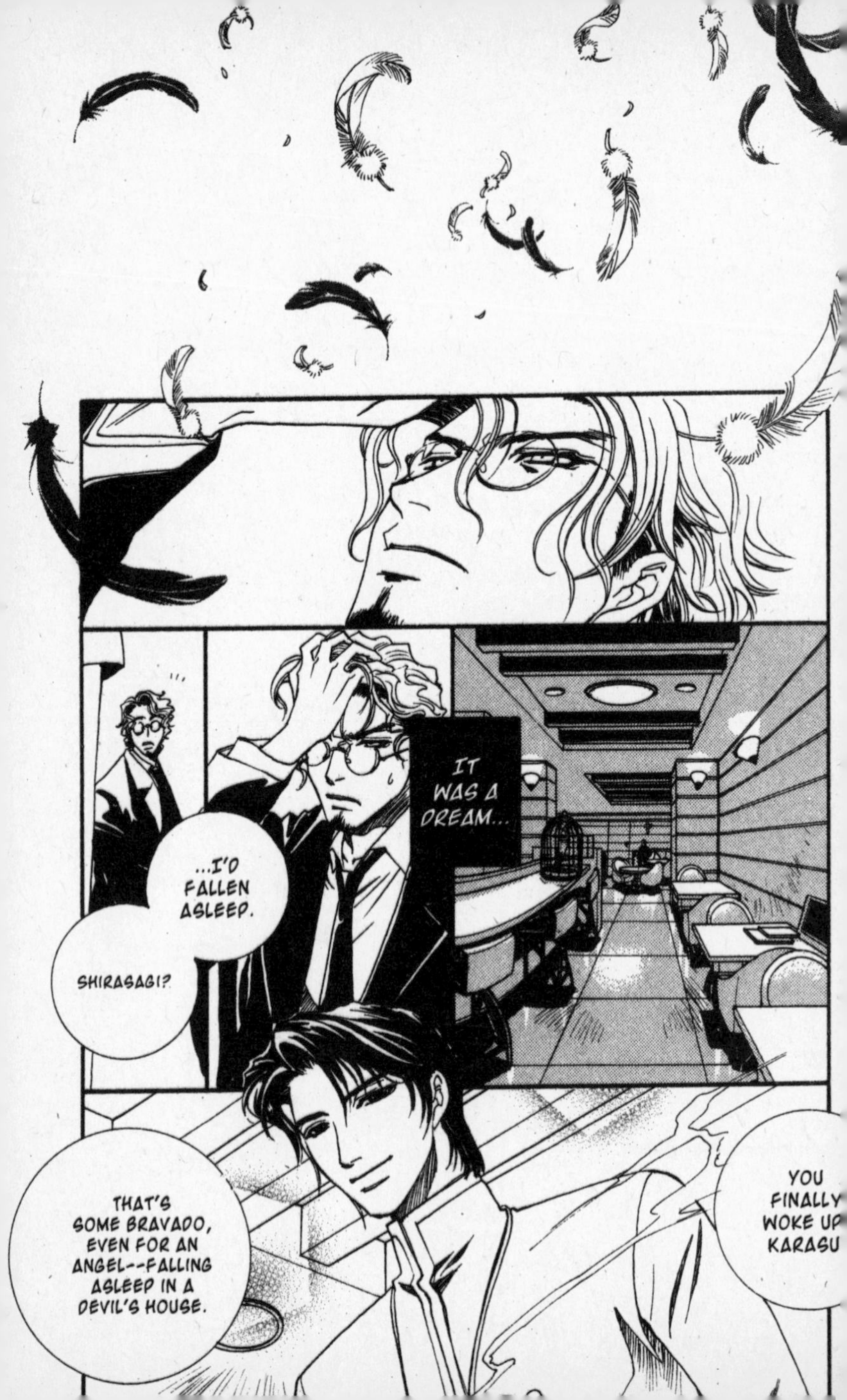

IT WAS A DREAM...
...I'D FALLEN ASLEEP.
SHIRASAGI?
YOU FINALLY WOKE UP KARASU
THAT'S SOME BRAVADO, EVEN FOR AN ANGEL--FALLING ASLEEP IN A DEVIL'S HOUSE.

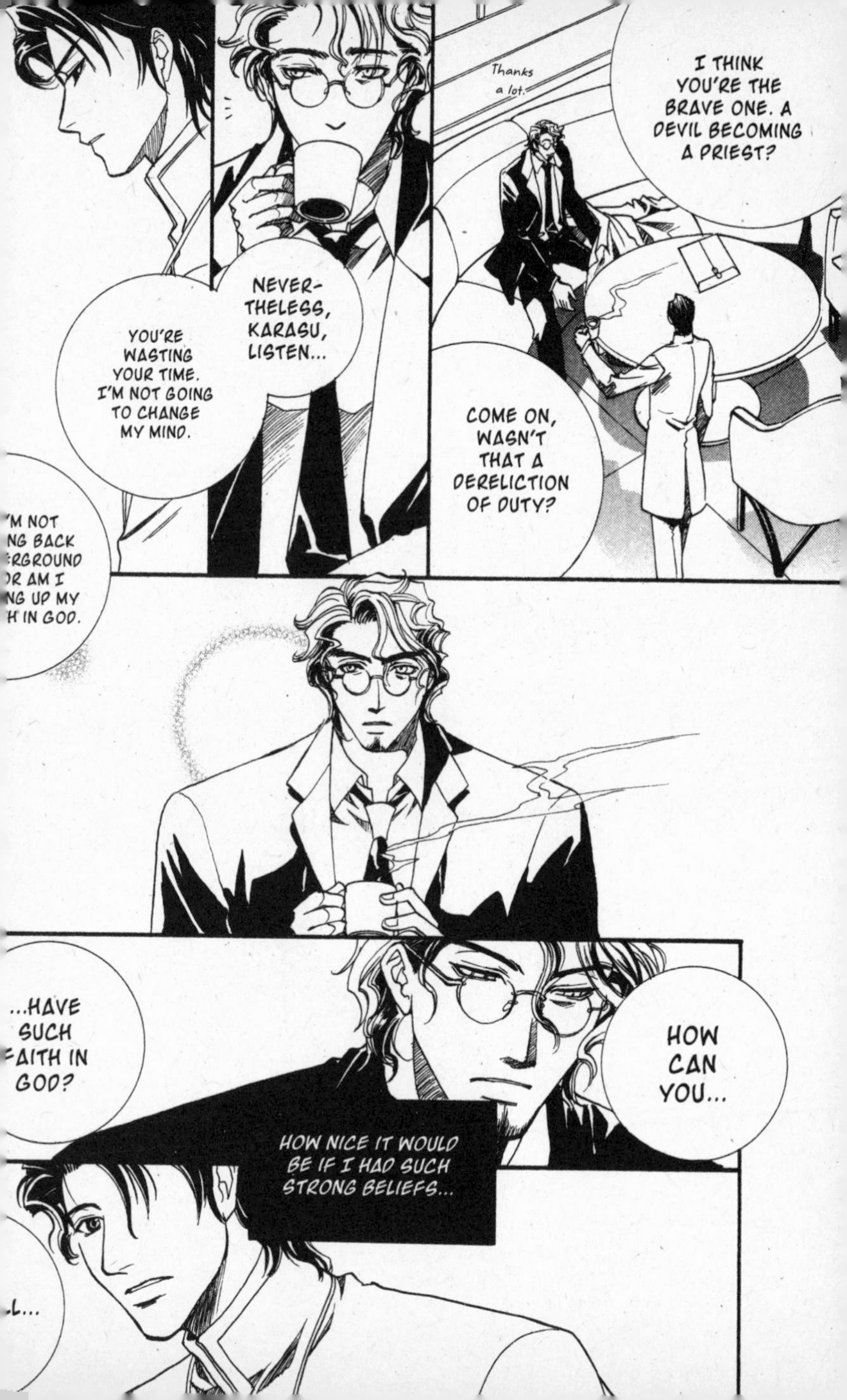
I THINK YOU'RE THE BRAVE ONE. A DEVIL BECOMING A PRIEST?
Thanks a lot.
COME ON, WASN'T THAT A DERELICTION OF DUTY?
NEVER-THELESS, KARASU, LISTEN...
YOU'RE WASTING YOUR TIME. I'M NOT GOING TO CHANGE MY MIND.
'M NOT NG BACK ERGROUND OR AM I NG UP MY H IN GOD.
HOW CAN YOU...
...HAVE SUCH FAITH IN GOD?
HOW NICE IT WOULD BE IF I HAD SUCH STRONG BELIEFS...
L...

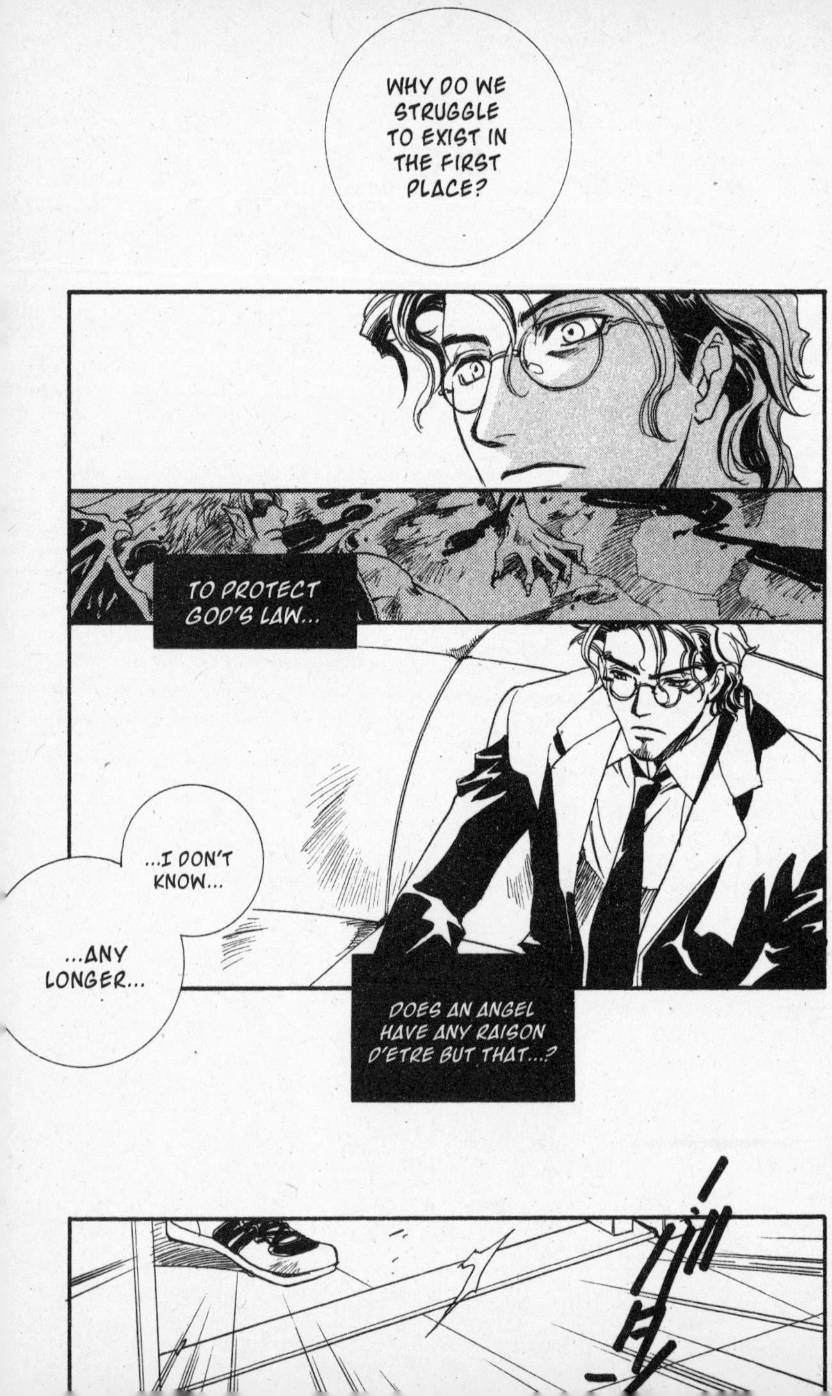
WHY DO WE STRUGGLE TO EXIST IN THE FIRST PLACE?
TO PROTECT GOD'S LAW...
DOES AN ANGEL HAVE ANY RAISON D'ETRE BUT THAT...?
...I DON'T KNOW...
...ANY LONGER...

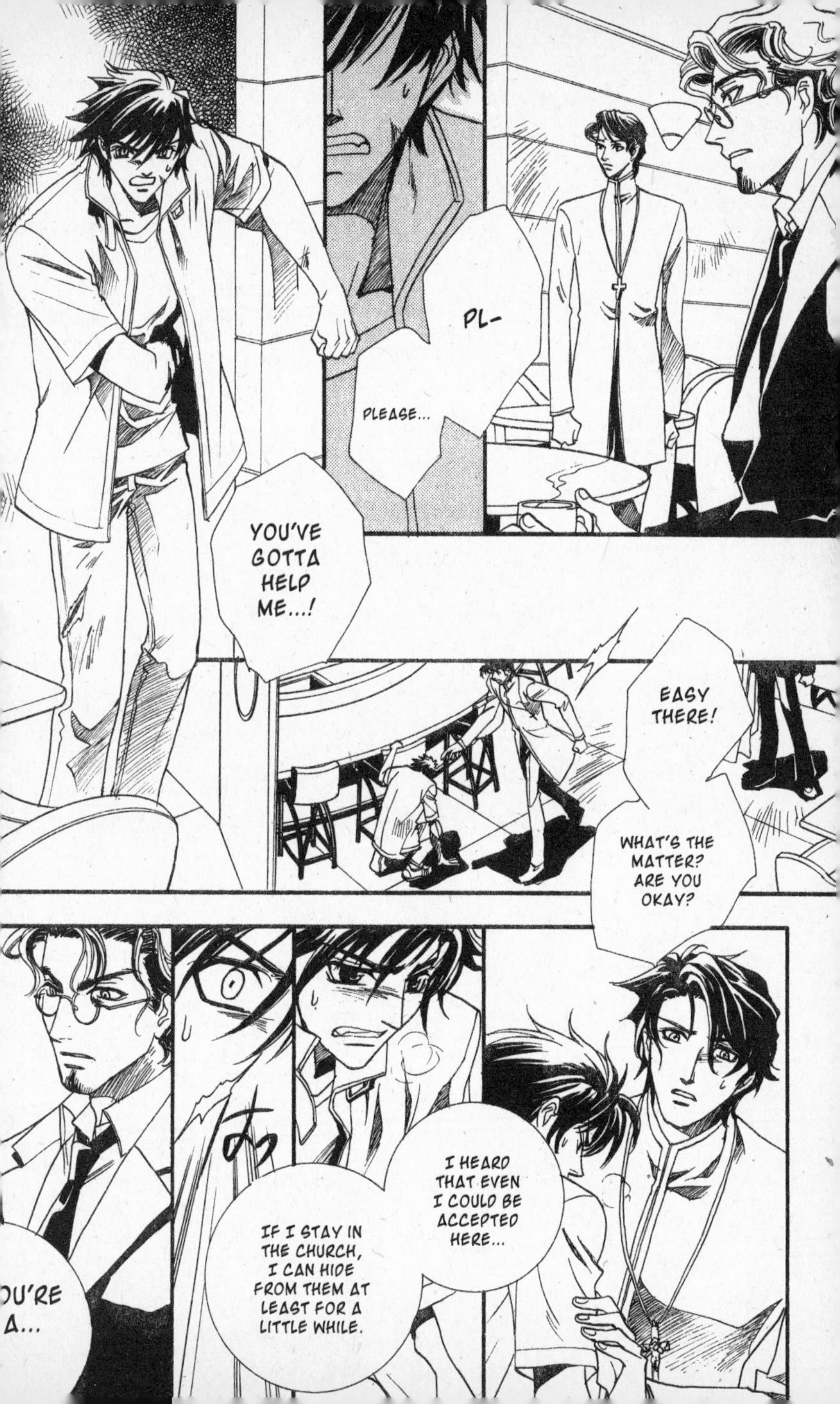
PL-
PLEASE...
YOU'VE GOTTA HELP ME...!
EASY THERE!
WHAT'S THE MATTER? ARE YOU OKAY?
I HEARD THAT EVEN I COULD BE ACCEPTED HERE...
IF I STAY IN THE CHURCH, I CAN HIDE FROM THEM AT LEAST FOR A LITTLE WHILE.
OU'RE A...

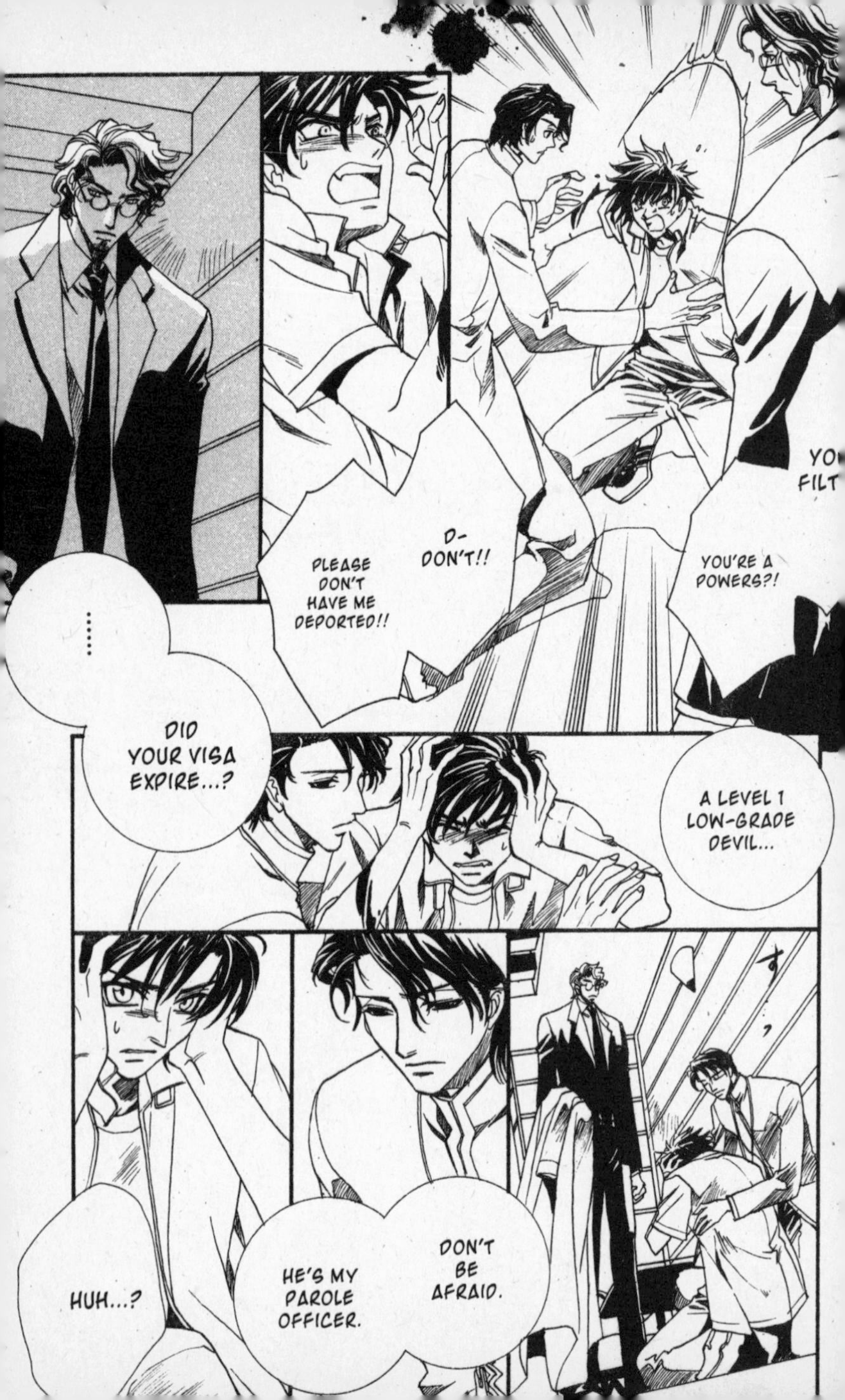
YO
FILT
YOU'RE A POWERS?!
D-DON'T!!
PLEASE DON'T HAVE ME DEPORTED!!
......
A LEVEL 1 LOW-GRADE DEVIL...
DID YOUR VISA EXPIRE...?
す
DON'T BE AFRAID.
HE'S MY PAROLE OFFICER.
HUH...?

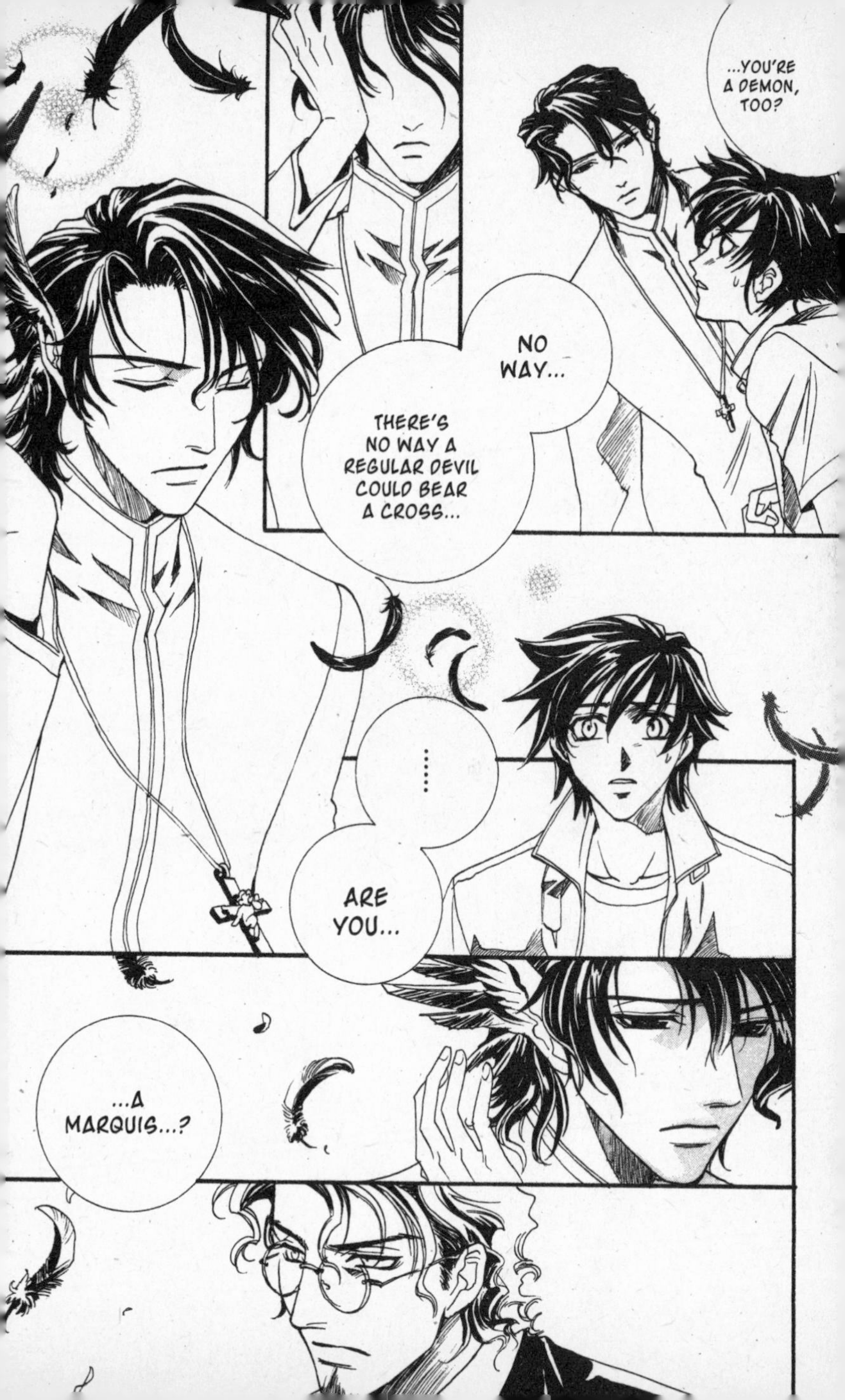
...YOU'RE A DEMON, TOO?
NO WAY...
THERE'S NO WAY A REGULAR DEVIL COULD BEAR A CROSS...
......
ARE YOU...
...A MARQUIS...?

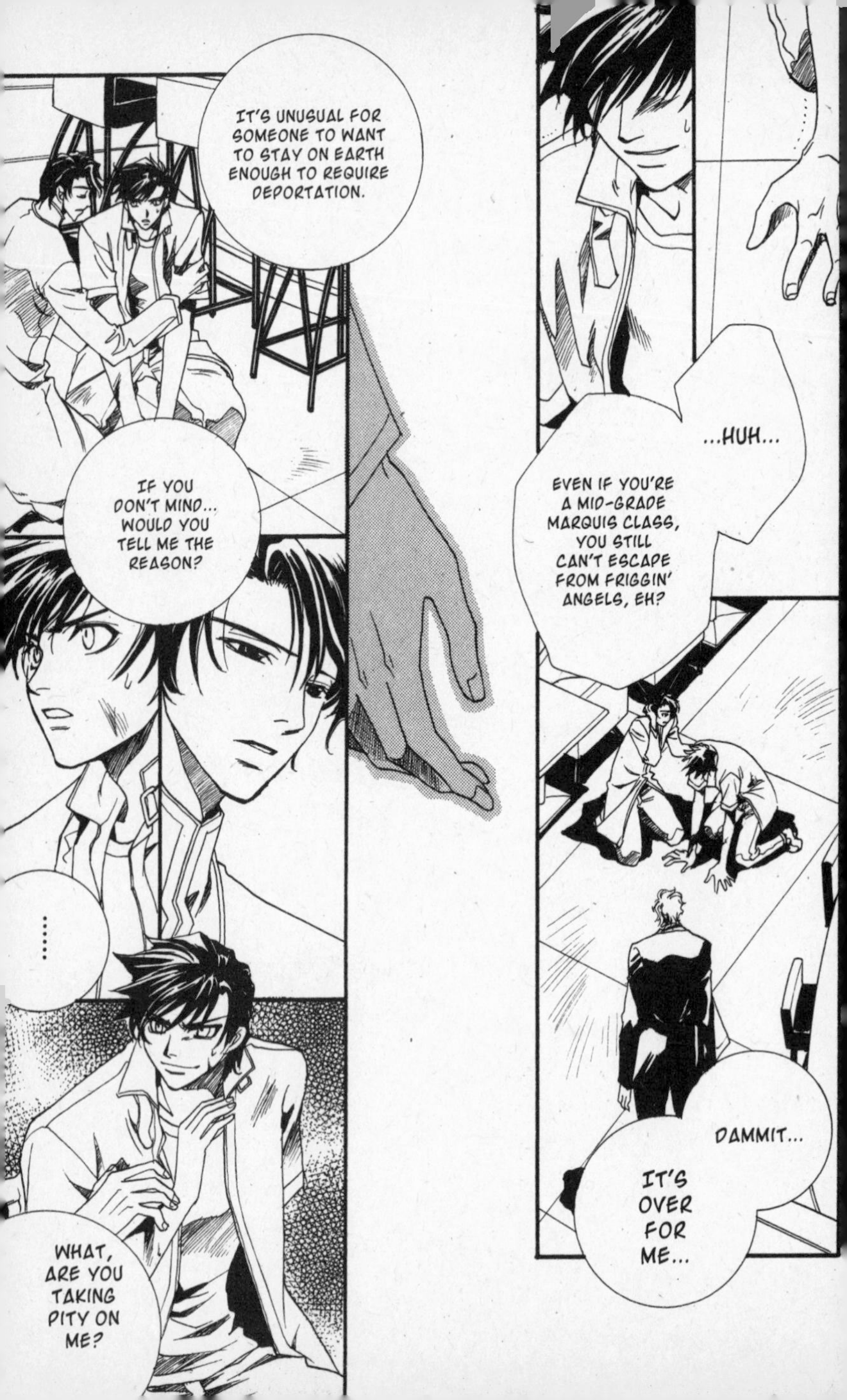
...HUH...
EVEN IF YOU'RE A MID-GRADE MARQUIS CLASS, YOU STILL CAN'T ESCAPE FROM FRIGGIN' ANGELS, EH?
DAMMIT...
IT'S OVER FOR ME...
IT'S UNUSUAL FOR SOMEONE TO WANT TO STAY ON EARTH ENOUGH TO REQUIRE DEPORTATION.
IF YOU DON'T MIND... WOULD YOU TELL ME THE REASON?
......
WHAT, ARE YOU TAKING PITY ON ME?

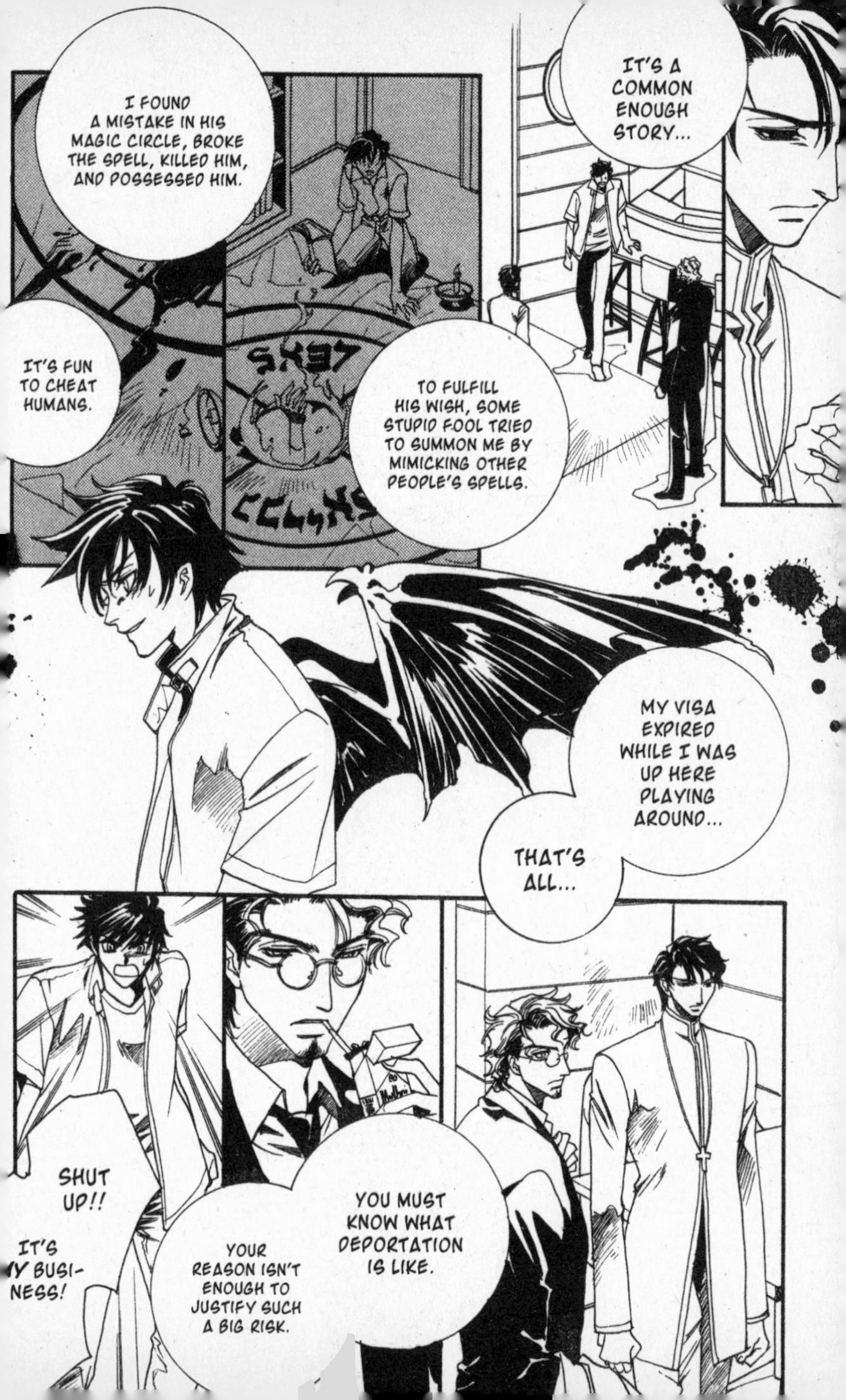
IT'S A COMMON ENOUGH STORY...
TO FULFILL HIS WISH, SOME STUPID FOOL TRIED TO SUMMON ME BY MIMICKING OTHER PEOPLE'S SPELLS.
I FOUND A MISTAKE IN HIS MAGIC CIRCLE, BROKE THE SPELL, KILLED HIM, AND POSSESSED HIM.
IT'S FUN TO CHEAT HUMANS.
MY VISA EXPIRED WHILE I WAS UP HERE PLAYING AROUND...
THAT'S ALL...
YOU MUST KNOW WHAT DEPORTATION IS LIKE.
YOUR REASON ISN'T ENOUGH TO JUSTIFY SUCH A BIG RISK.
SHUT UP!!
IT'S Y BUSI- NESS!

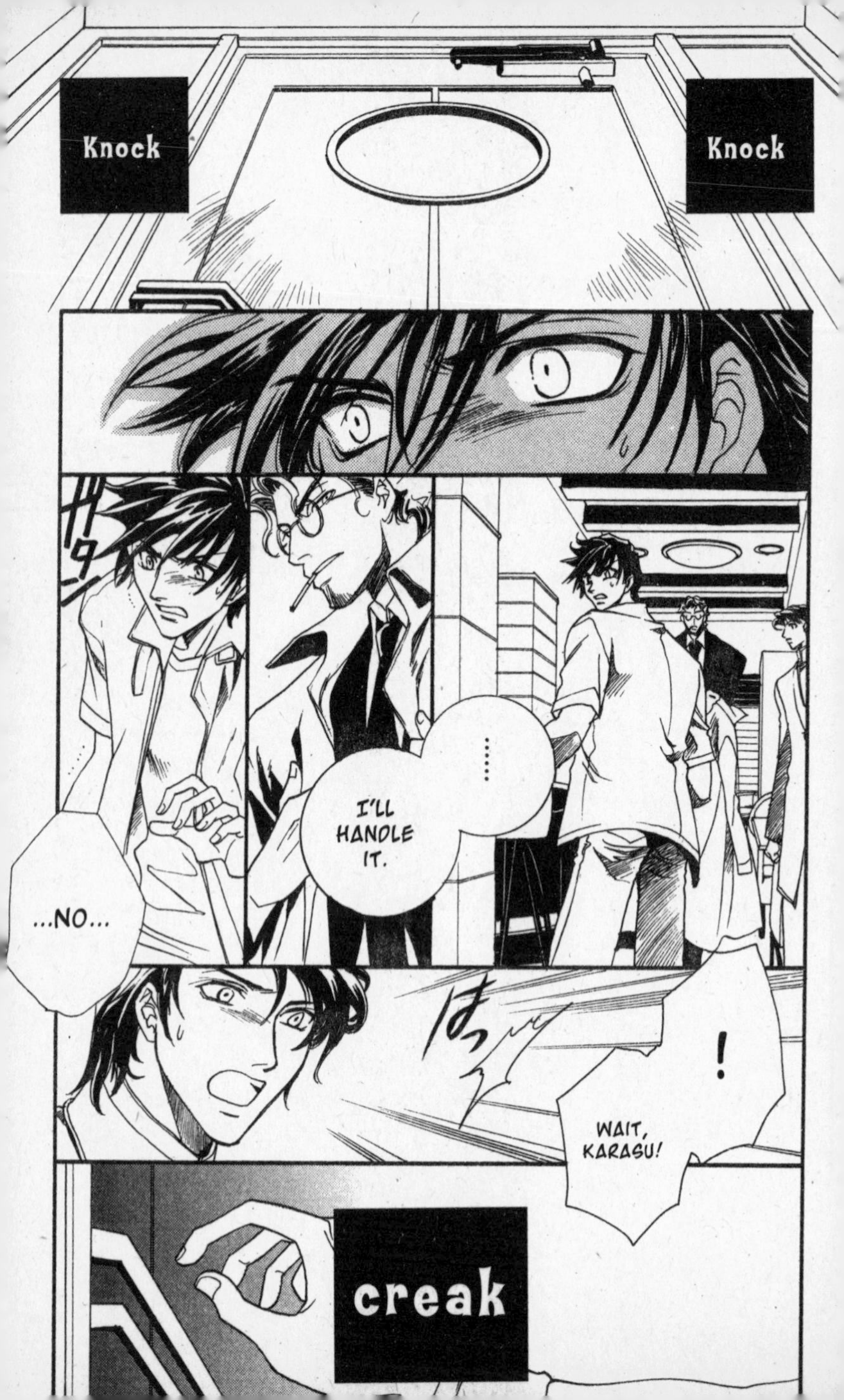

Knock
Knock
......
I'LL HANDLE IT.
...NO...
!
WAIT, KARASU!
はっ
creak

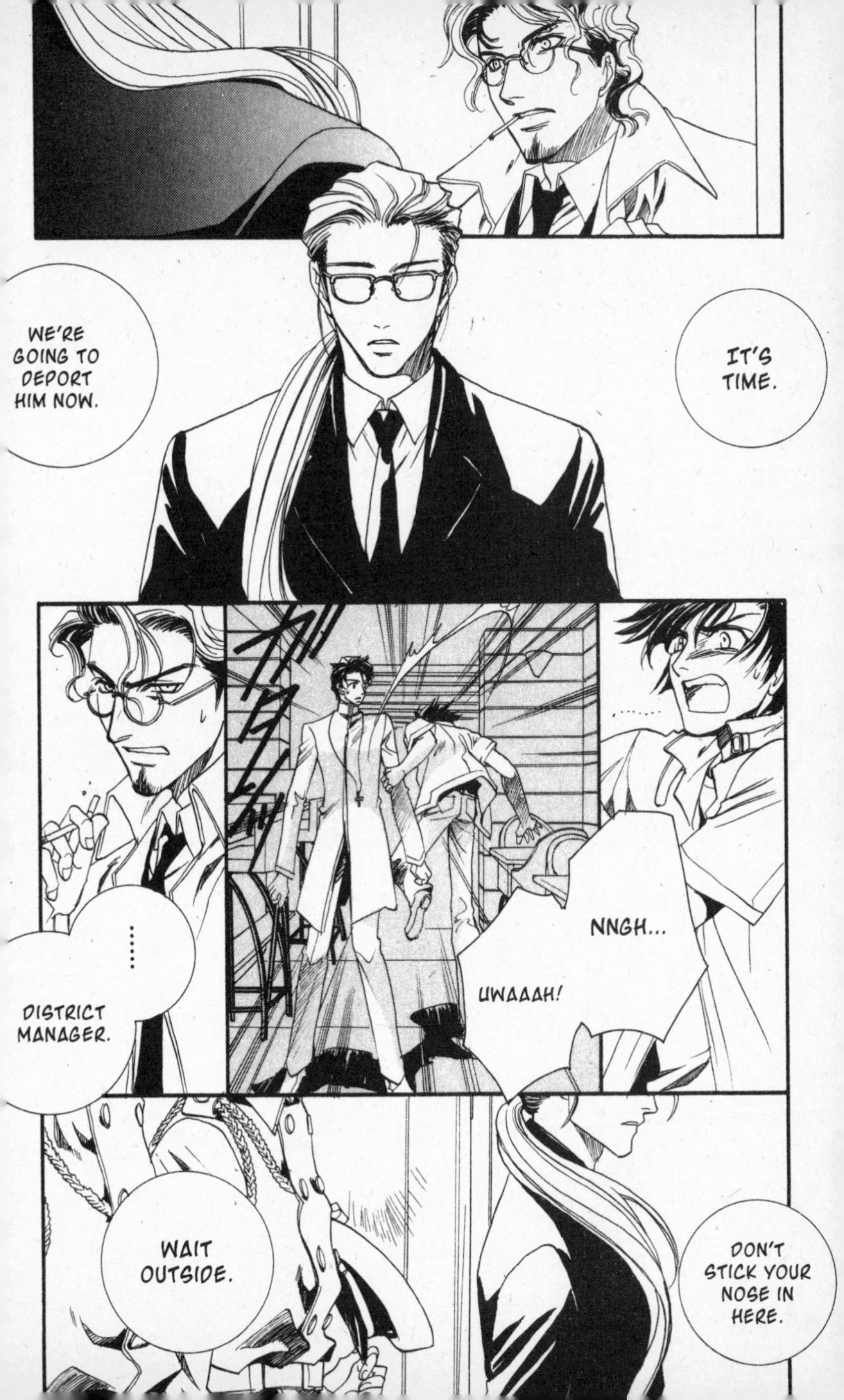
IT'S TIME.
WE'RE GOING TO DEPORT HIM NOW.
......
NNGH...
UWAAAH!
......
DISTRICT MANAGER.
DON'T STICK YOUR NOSE IN HERE.
WAIT OUTSIDE.

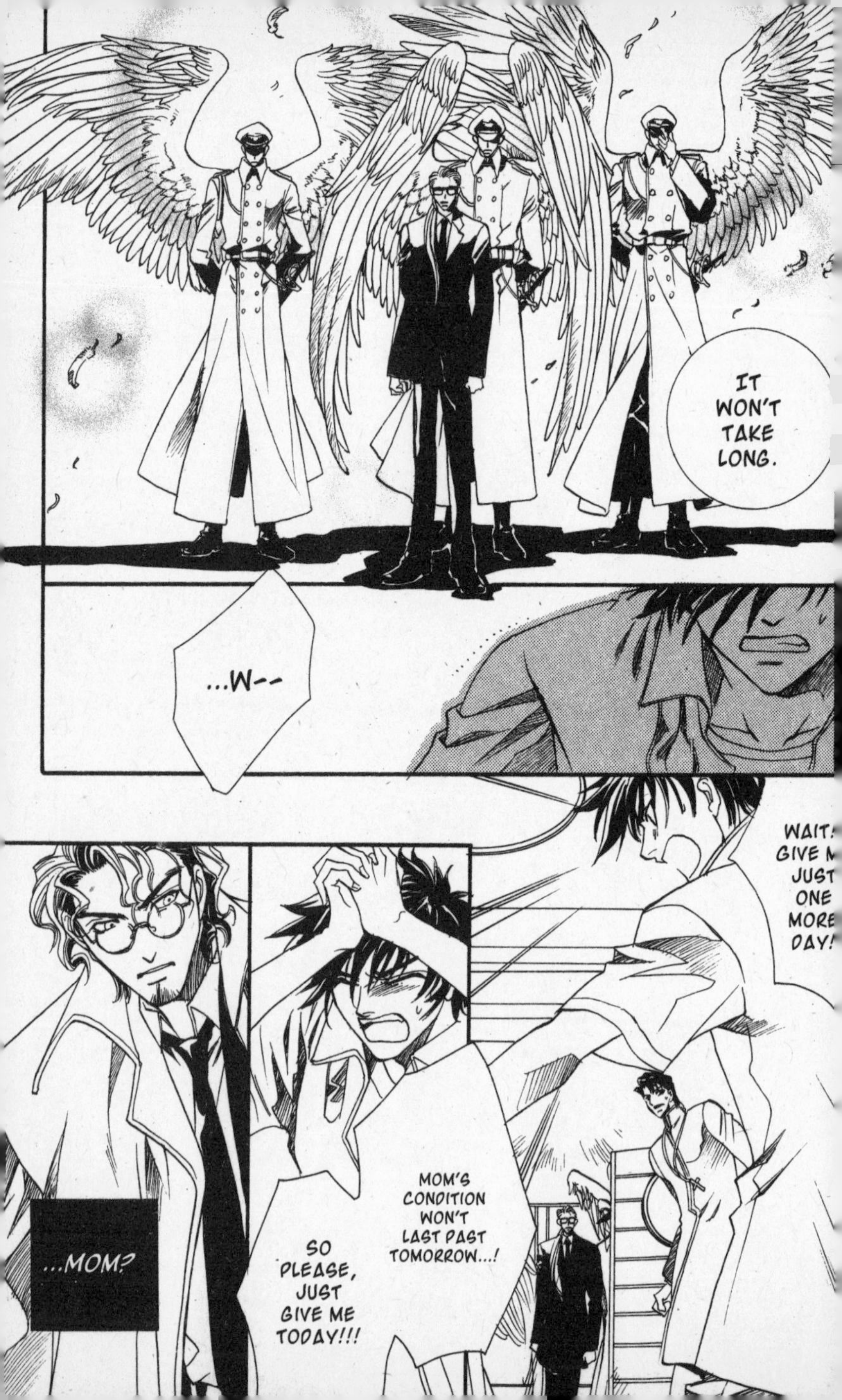
IT WON'T TAKE LONG.
...W--
WAIT! GIVE M JUST ONE MORE DAY!
MOM'S CONDITION WON'T LAST PAST TOMORROW...!
SO PLEASE, JUST GIVE ME TODAY!!!
...MOM?

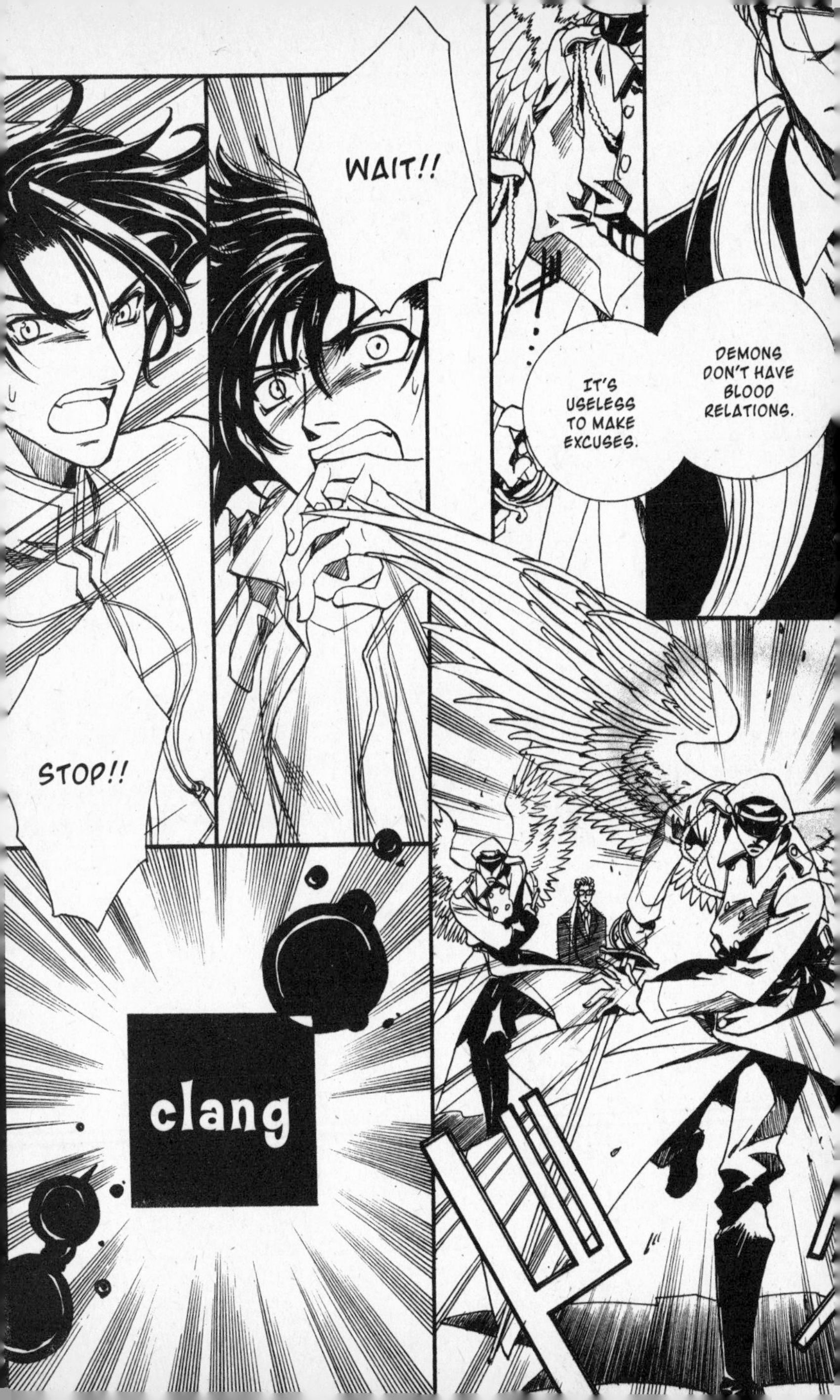
DEMONS DON'T HAVE BLOOD RELATIONS.
IT'S USELESS TO MAKE EXCUSES.
WAIT!!
STOP!!
clang

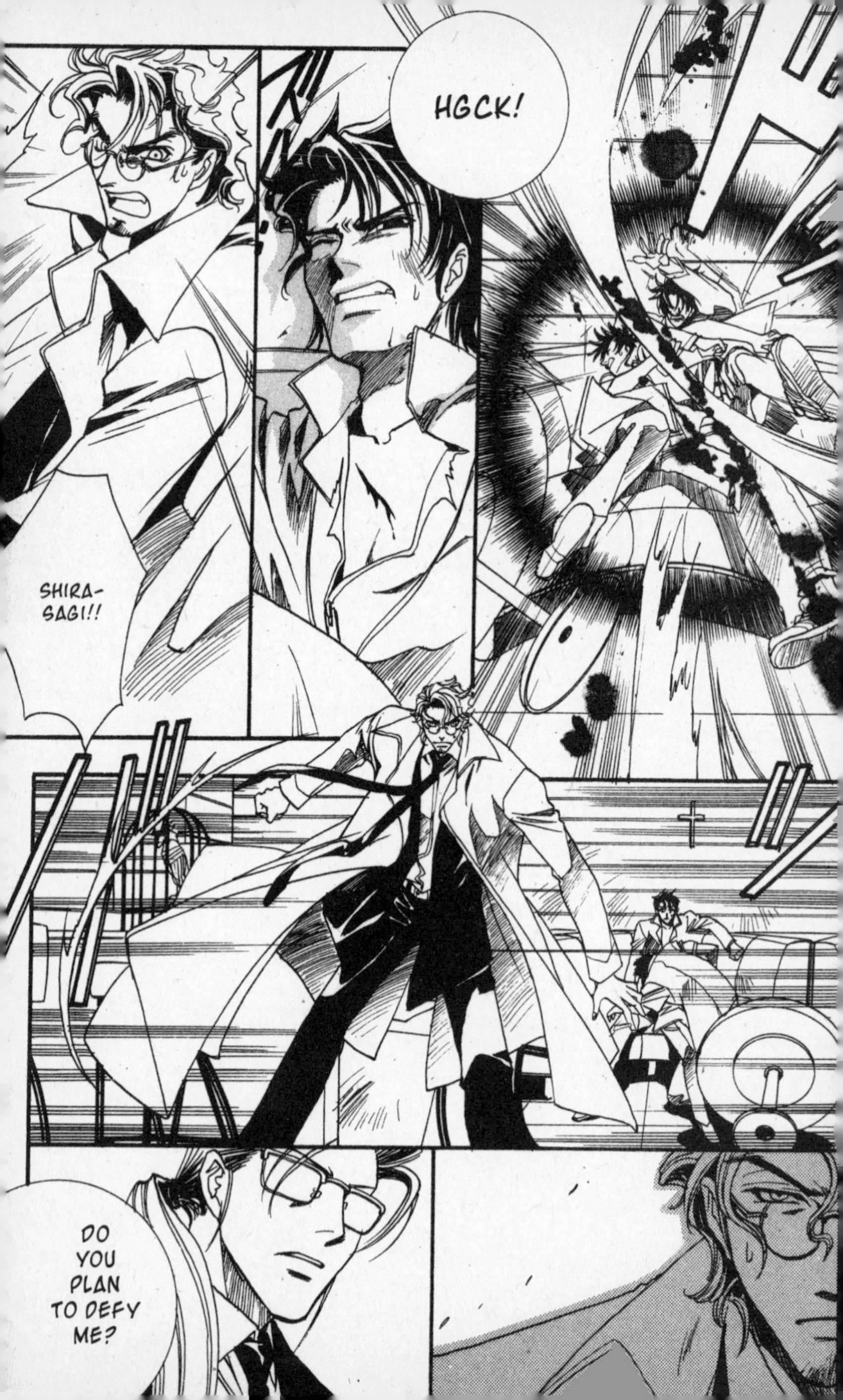
HGCK!
SHIRA-SAGI!!
DO YOU PLAN TO DEFY ME?

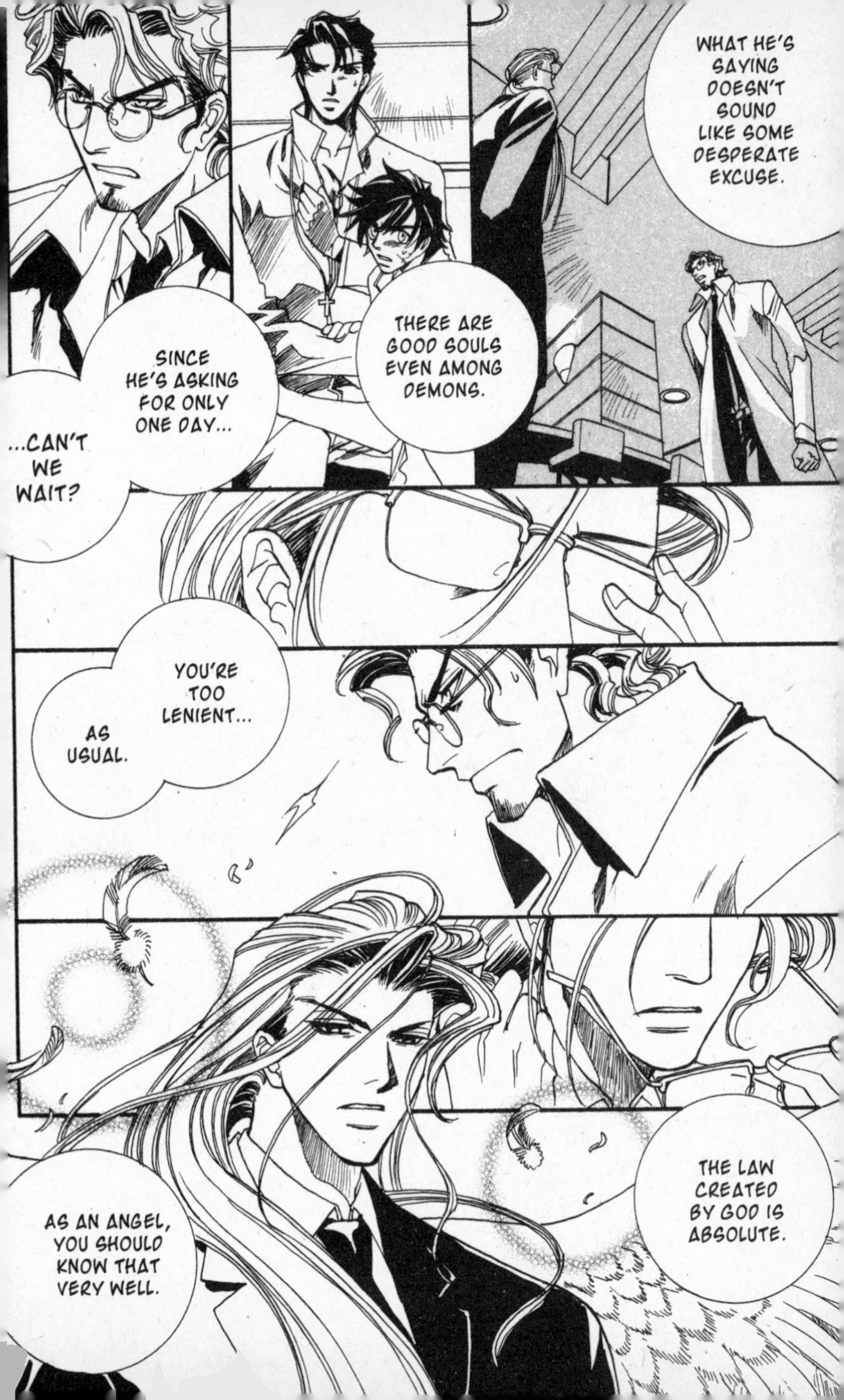
WHAT HE'S SAYING DOESN'T SOUND LIKE SOME DESPERATE EXCUSE.
THERE ARE GOOD SOULS EVEN AMONG DEMONS.
SINCE HE'S ASKING FOR ONLY ONE DAY...
...CAN'T WE WAIT?
YOU'RE TOO LENIENT...
AS USUAL.
THE LAW CREATED BY GOD IS ABSOLUTE.
AS AN ANGEL, YOU SHOULD KNOW THAT VERY WELL.

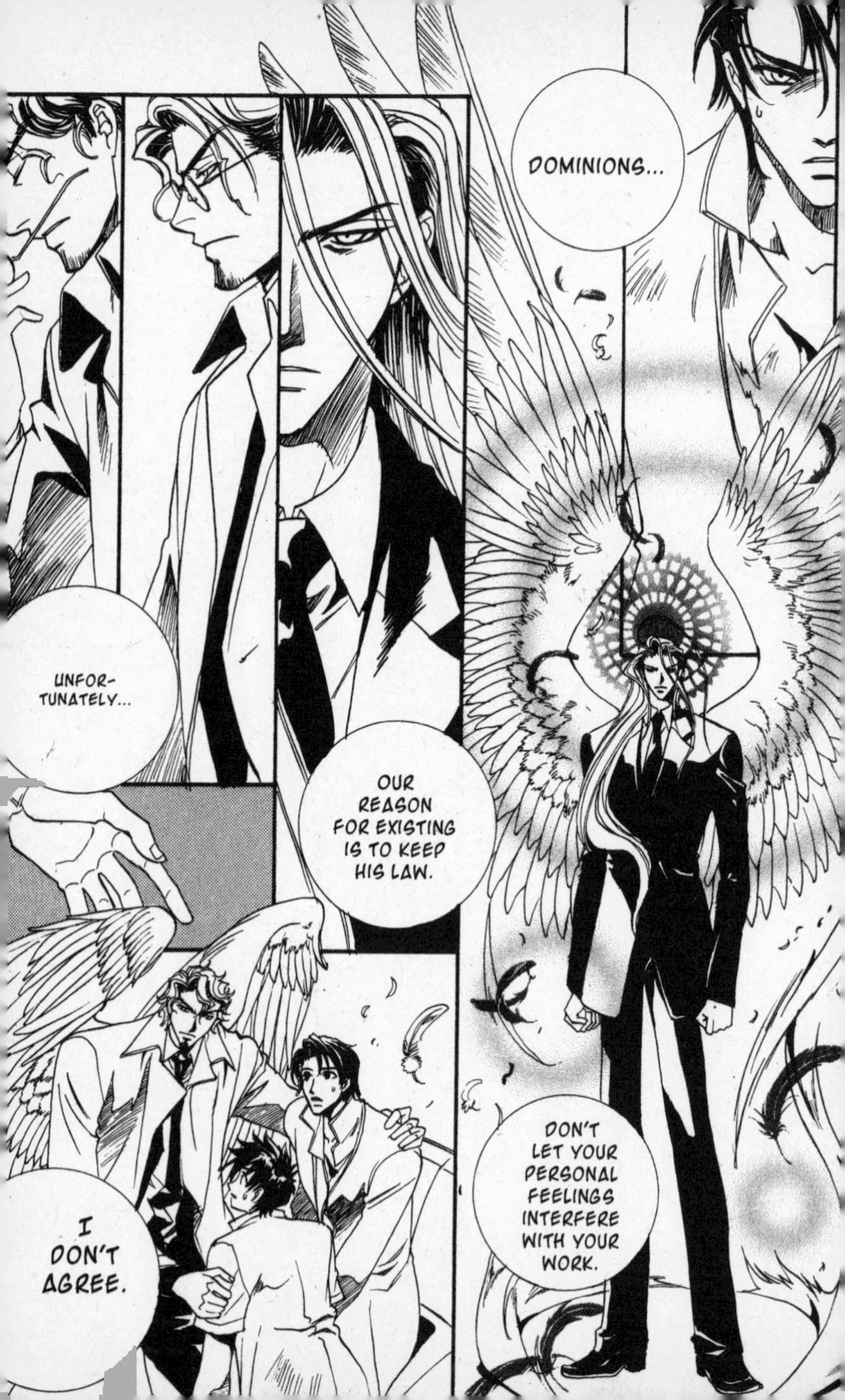
DOMINIONS...
DON'T LET YOUR PERSONAL FEELINGS INTERFERE WITH YOUR WORK.
UNFOR-TUNATELY...
OUR REASON FOR EXISTING IS TO KEEP HIS LAW.
I DON'T AGREE.

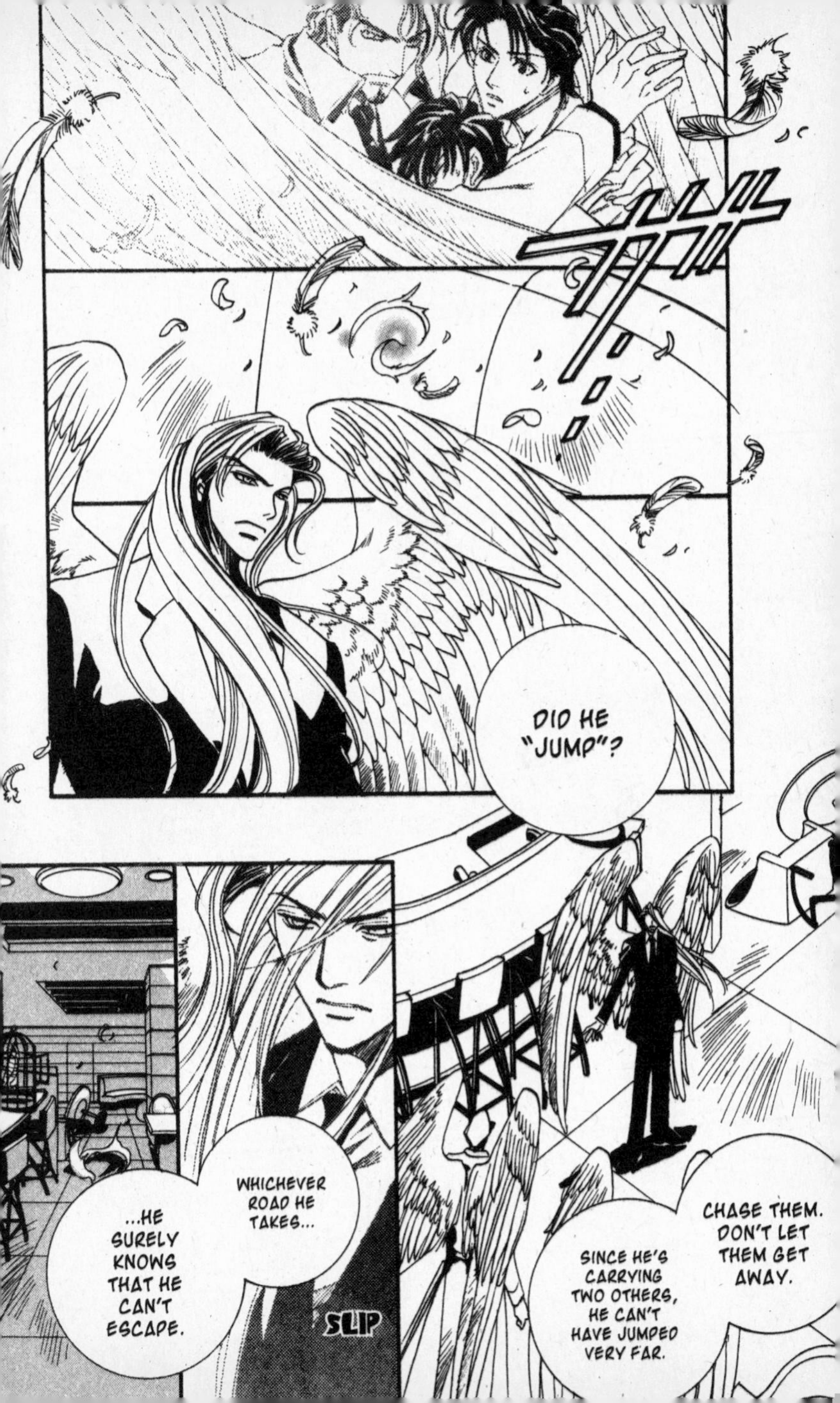
DID HE "JUMP"?
CHASE THEM. DON'T LET THEM GET AWAY.
SINCE HE'S CARRYING TWO OTHERS, HE CAN'T HAVE JUMPED VERY FAR.
WHICHEVER ROAD HE TAKES...
...HE SURELY KNOWS THAT HE CAN'T ESCAPE.
SLIP

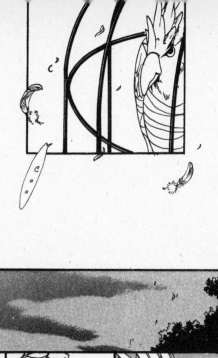

SWOOSH

Huff

GUESS I HAVEN'T BEEN WORKING OUT ENOUGH LATELY.

I CAN'T TELEPORT ANY FARTHER.

CAN YOU RUN?

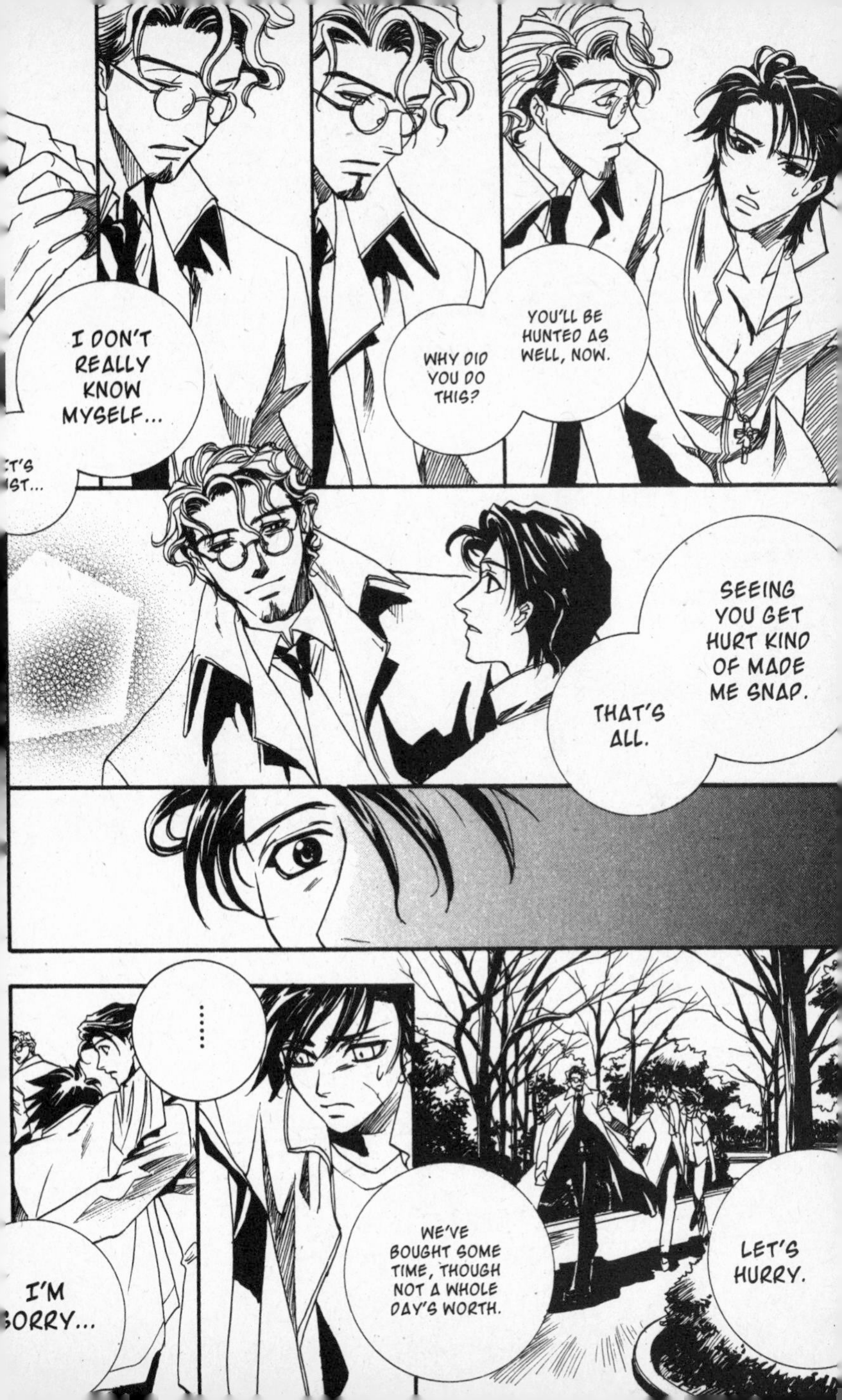
YOU'LL BE HUNTED AS WELL, NOW.
WHY DID YOU DO THIS?
I DON'T REALLY KNOW MYSELF...
SEEING YOU GET HURT KIND OF MADE ME SNAP.
THAT'S ALL.
LET'S HURRY.
WE'VE BOUGHT SOME TIME, THOUGH NOT A WHOLE DAY'S WORTH.
......
I'M SORRY...

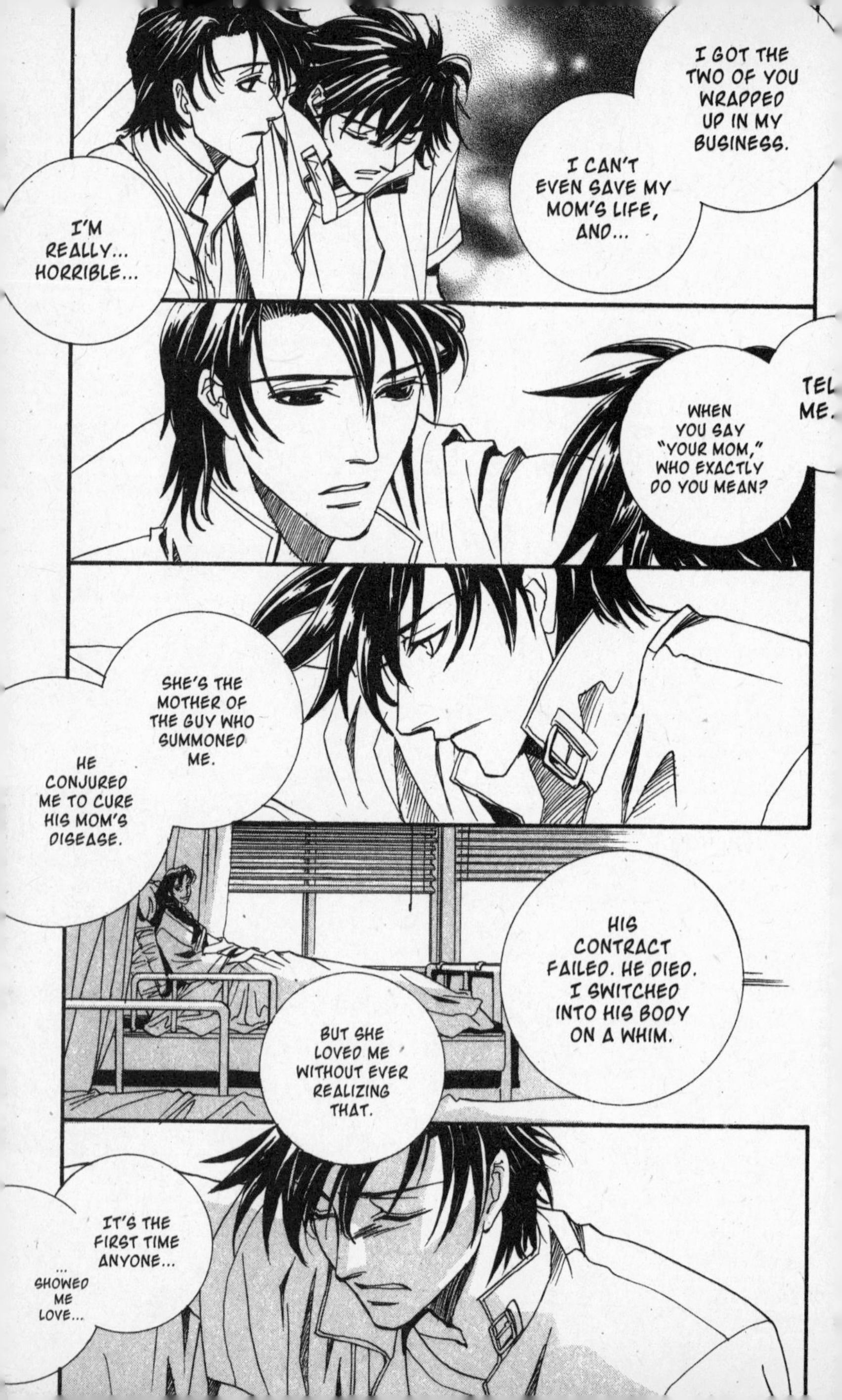
I GOT THE TWO OF YOU WRAPPED UP IN MY BUSINESS.
I CAN'T EVEN SAVE MY MOM'S LIFE, AND...
I'M REALLY... HORRIBLE...
TEL ME.
WHEN YOU SAY "YOUR MOM," WHO EXACTLY DO YOU MEAN?
SHE'S THE MOTHER OF THE GUY WHO SUMMONED ME.
HE CONJURED ME TO CURE HIS MOM'S DISEASE.
HIS CONTRACT FAILED. HE DIED. I SWITCHED INTO HIS BODY ON A WHIM.
BUT SHE LOVED ME WITHOUT EVER REALIZING THAT.
IT'S THE FIRST TIME ANYONE...
...SHOWED ME LOVE...

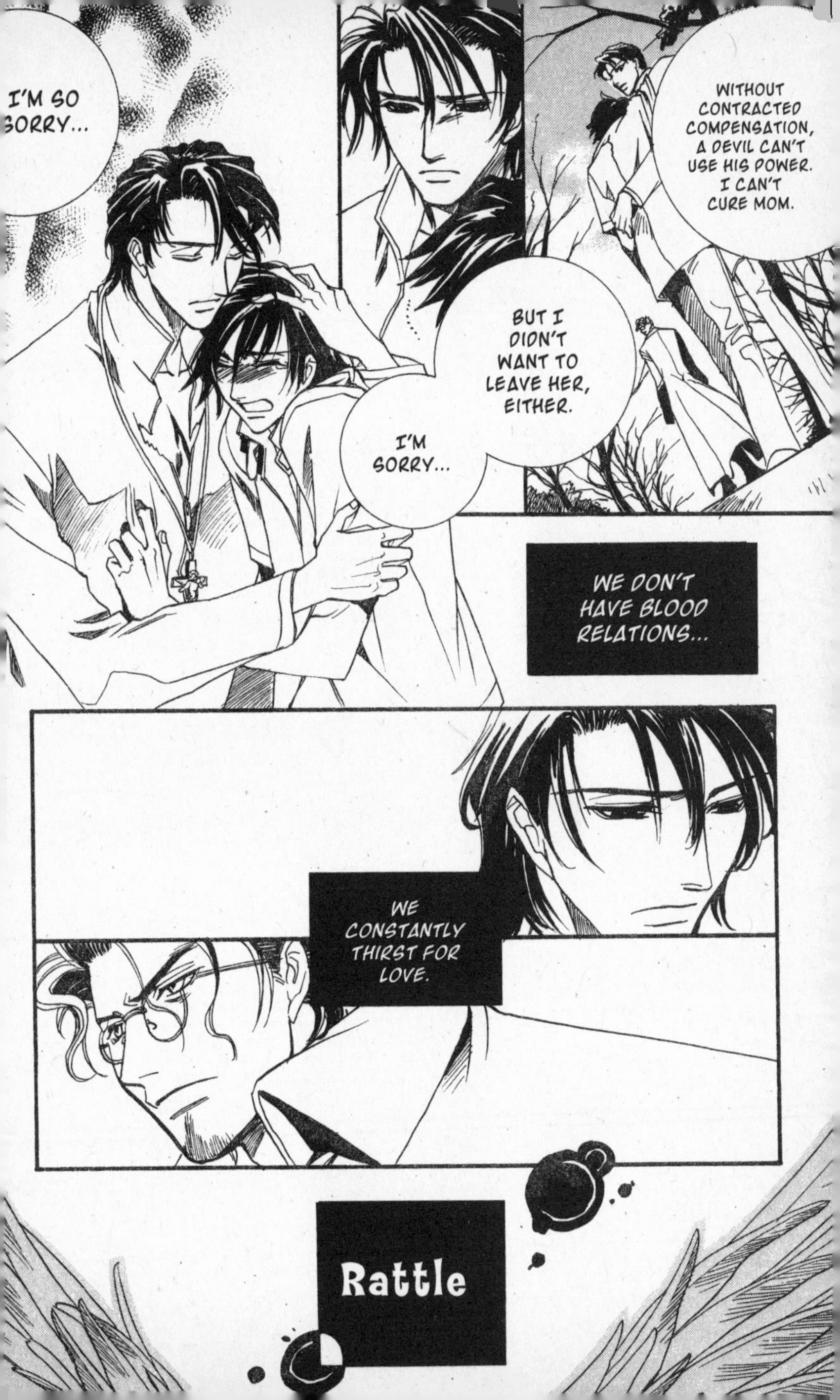
WITHOUT CONTRACTED COMPENSATION, A DEVIL CAN'T USE HIS POWER. I CAN'T CURE MOM.
BUT I DIDN'T WANT TO LEAVE HER, EITHER.
I'M SORRY...
I'M SO SORRY...
WE DON'T HAVE BLOOD RELATIONS...
WE CONSTANTLY THIRST FOR LOVE.
Rattle

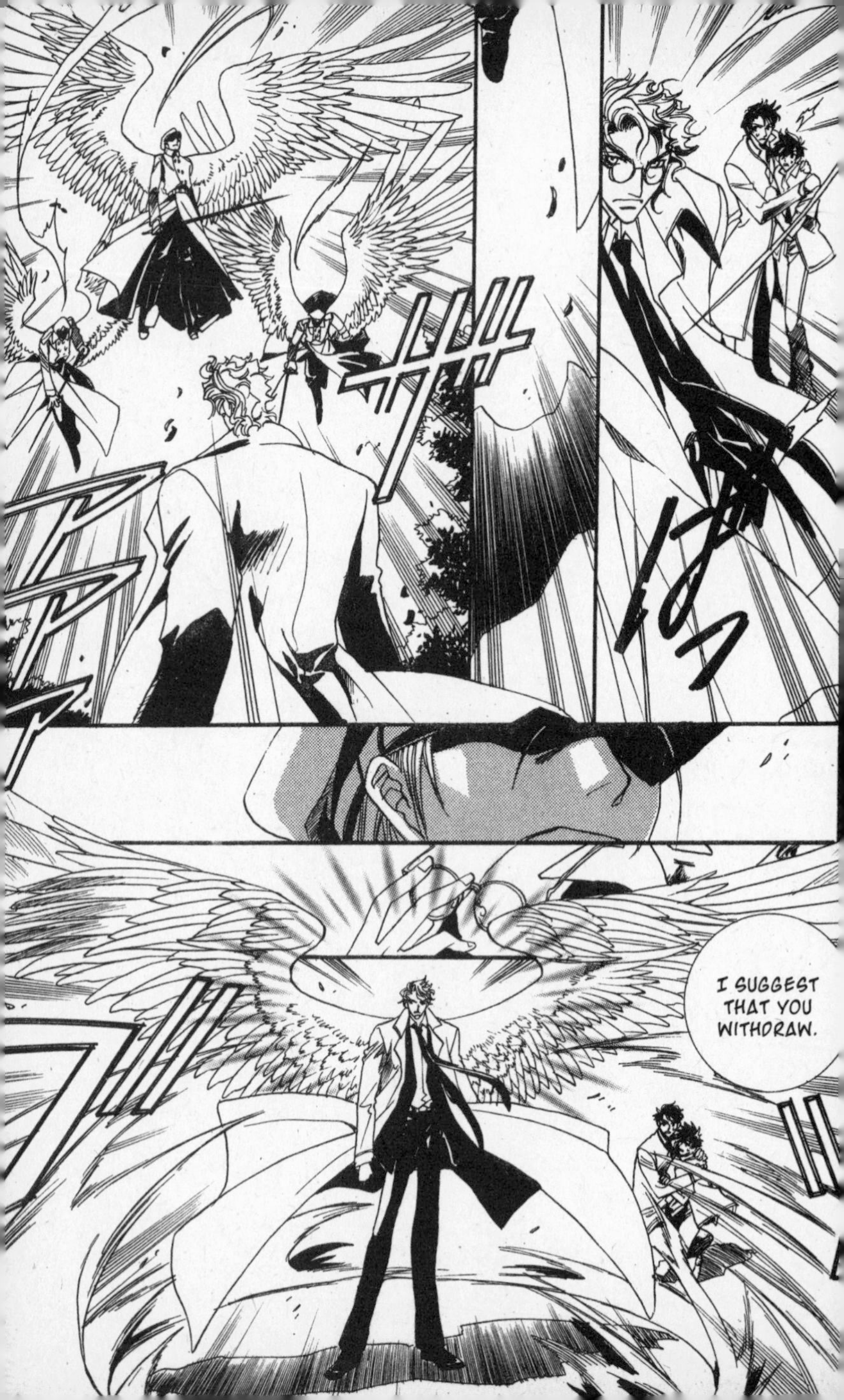
I SUGGEST THAT YOU WITHDRAW.

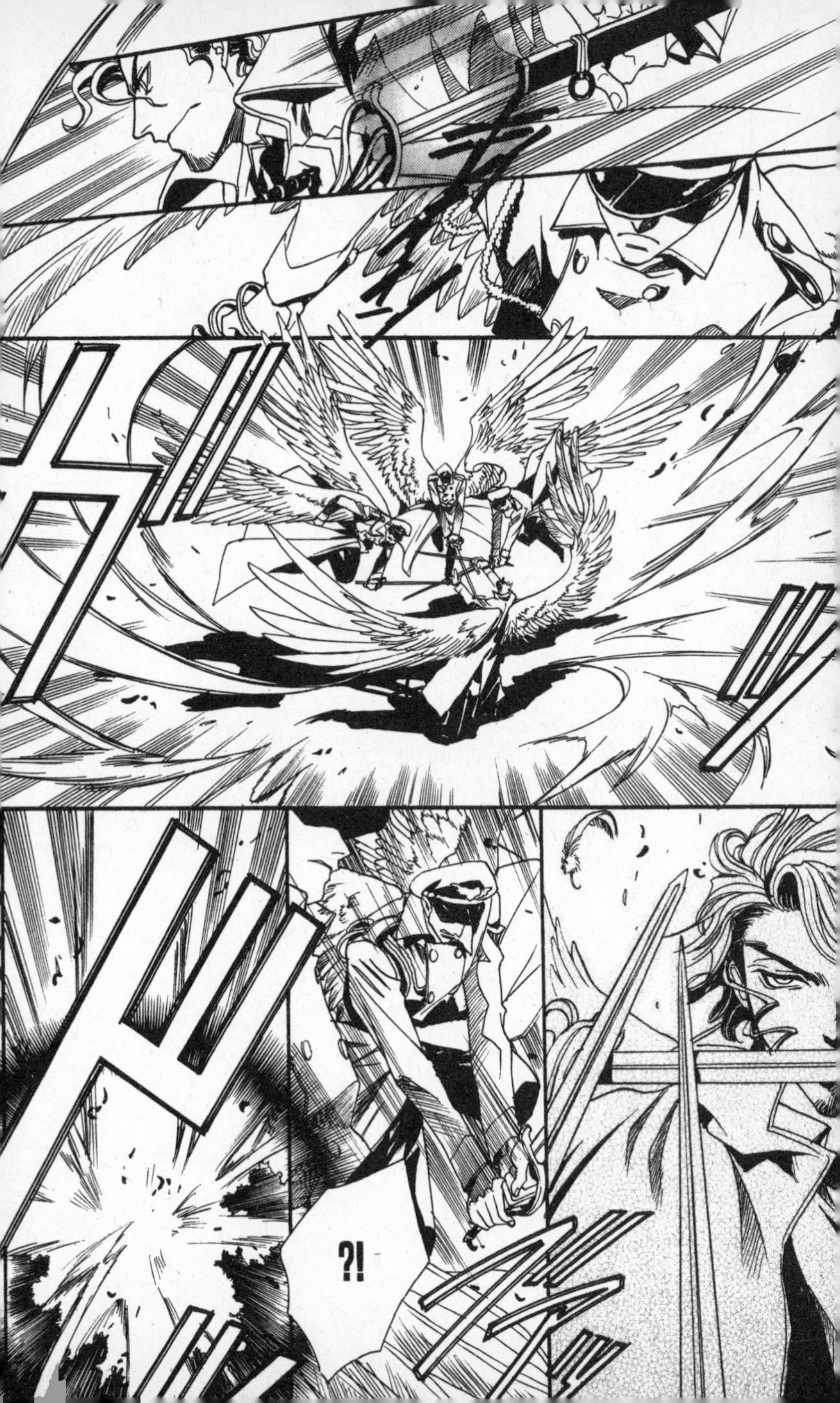
?!

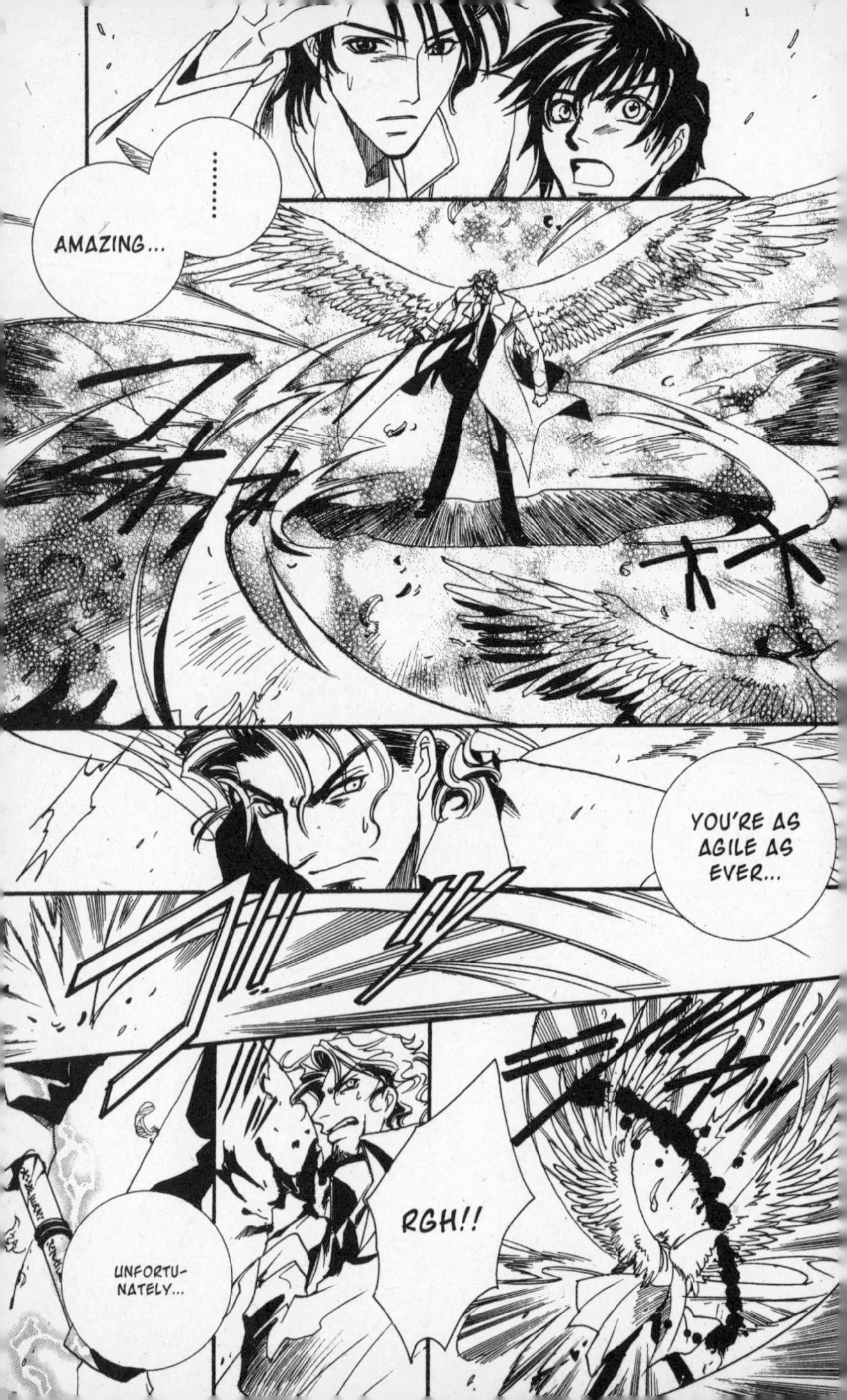
......
AMAZING...
YOU'RE AS AGILE AS EVER...
RGH!!
UNFORTUNATELY...

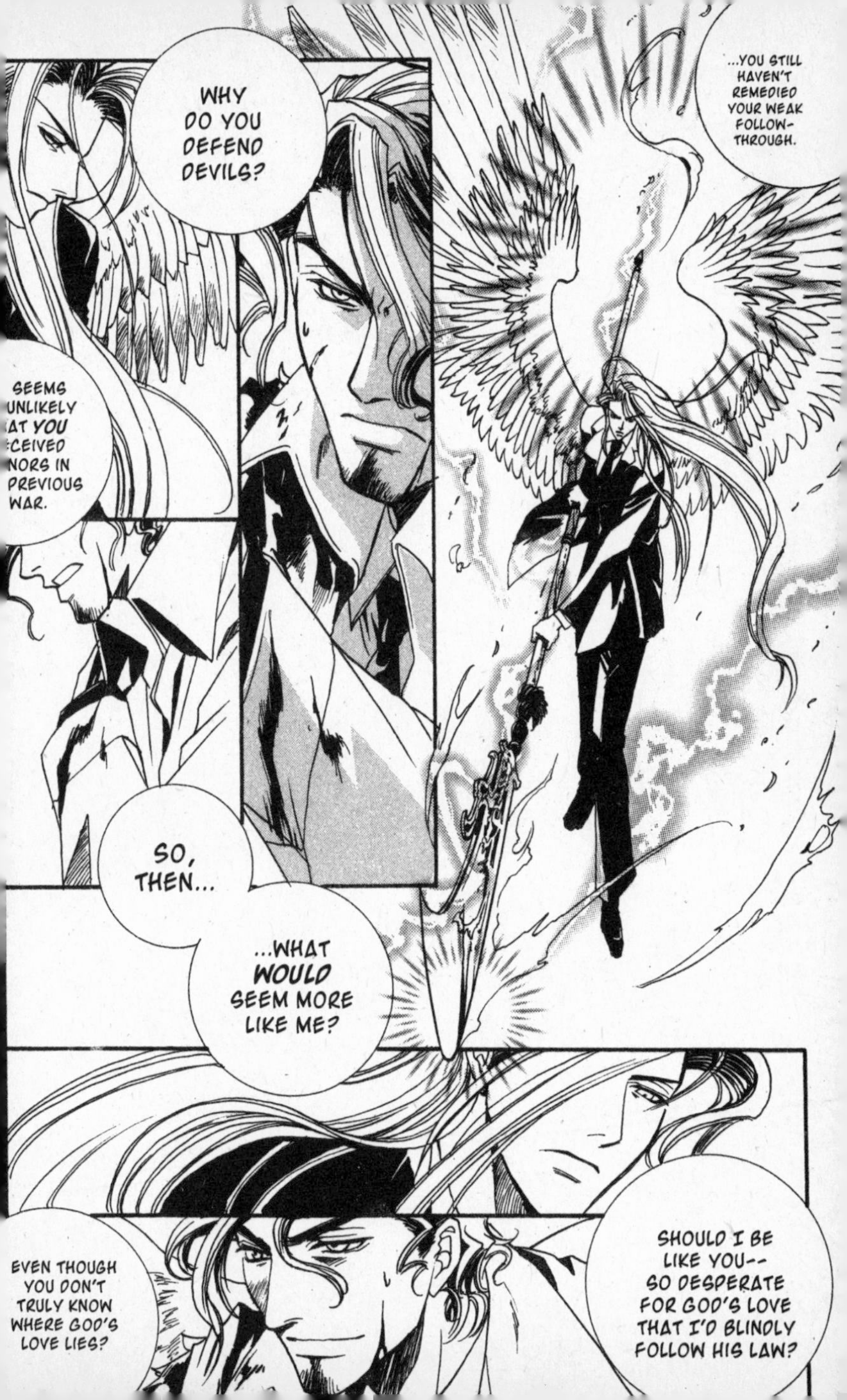
...YOU STILL HAVEN'T REMEDIED YOUR WEAK FOLLOW-THROUGH.
WHY DO YOU DEFEND DEVILS?
SEEMS UNLIKELY AT *YOU* CEIVED NORS IN PREVIOUS WAR.
SO, THEN...
...WHAT *WOULD* SEEM MORE LIKE ME?
SHOULD I BE LIKE YOU-- SO DESPERATE FOR GOD'S LOVE THAT I'D BLINDLY FOLLOW HIS LAW?
EVEN THOUGH YOU DON'T TRULY KNOW WHERE GOD'S LOVE LIES?

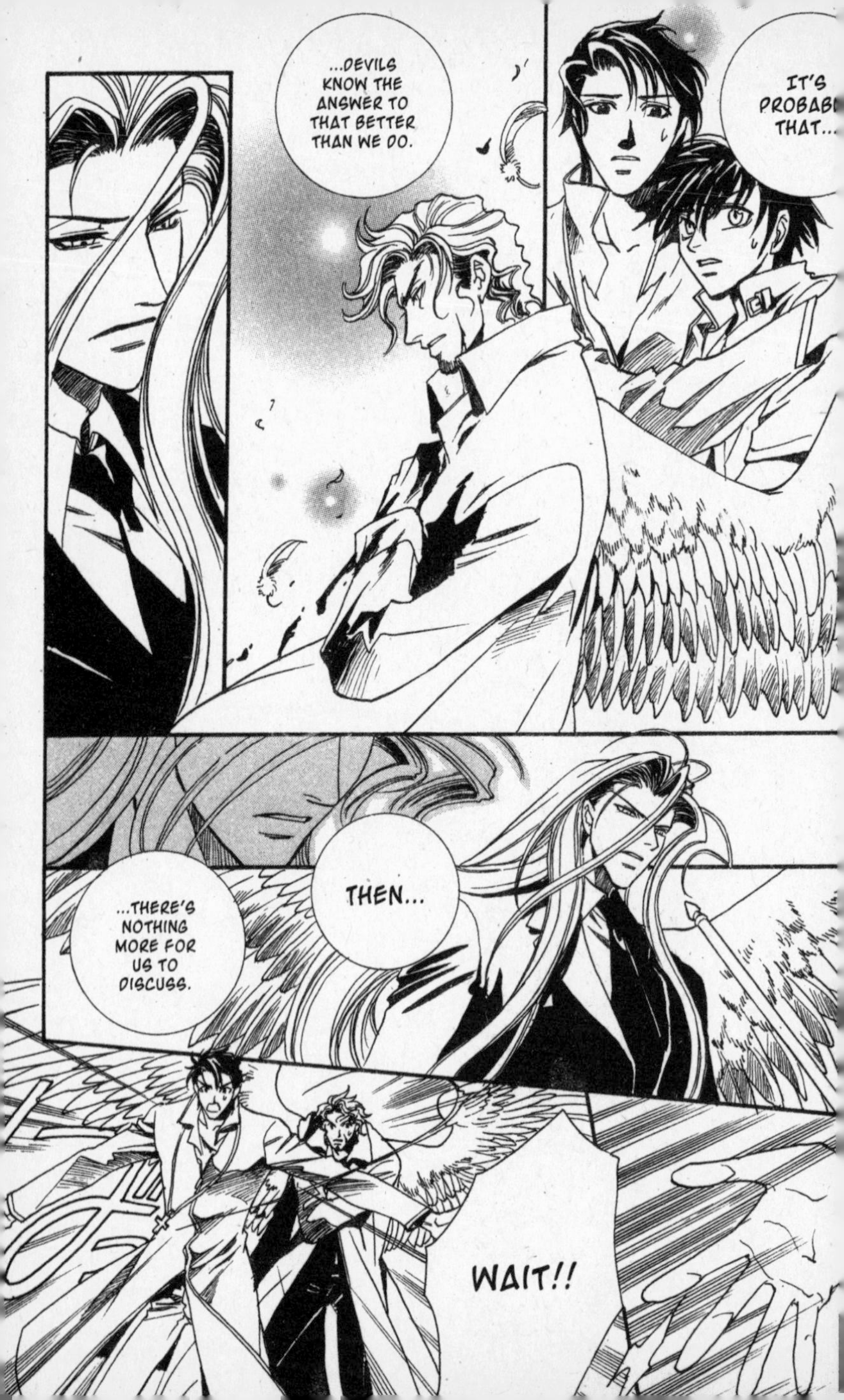
IT'S PROBABL THAT...
...DEVILS KNOW THE ANSWER TO THAT BETTER THAN WE DO.
THEN...
...THERE'S NOTHING MORE FOR US TO DISCUSS.
WAIT!!

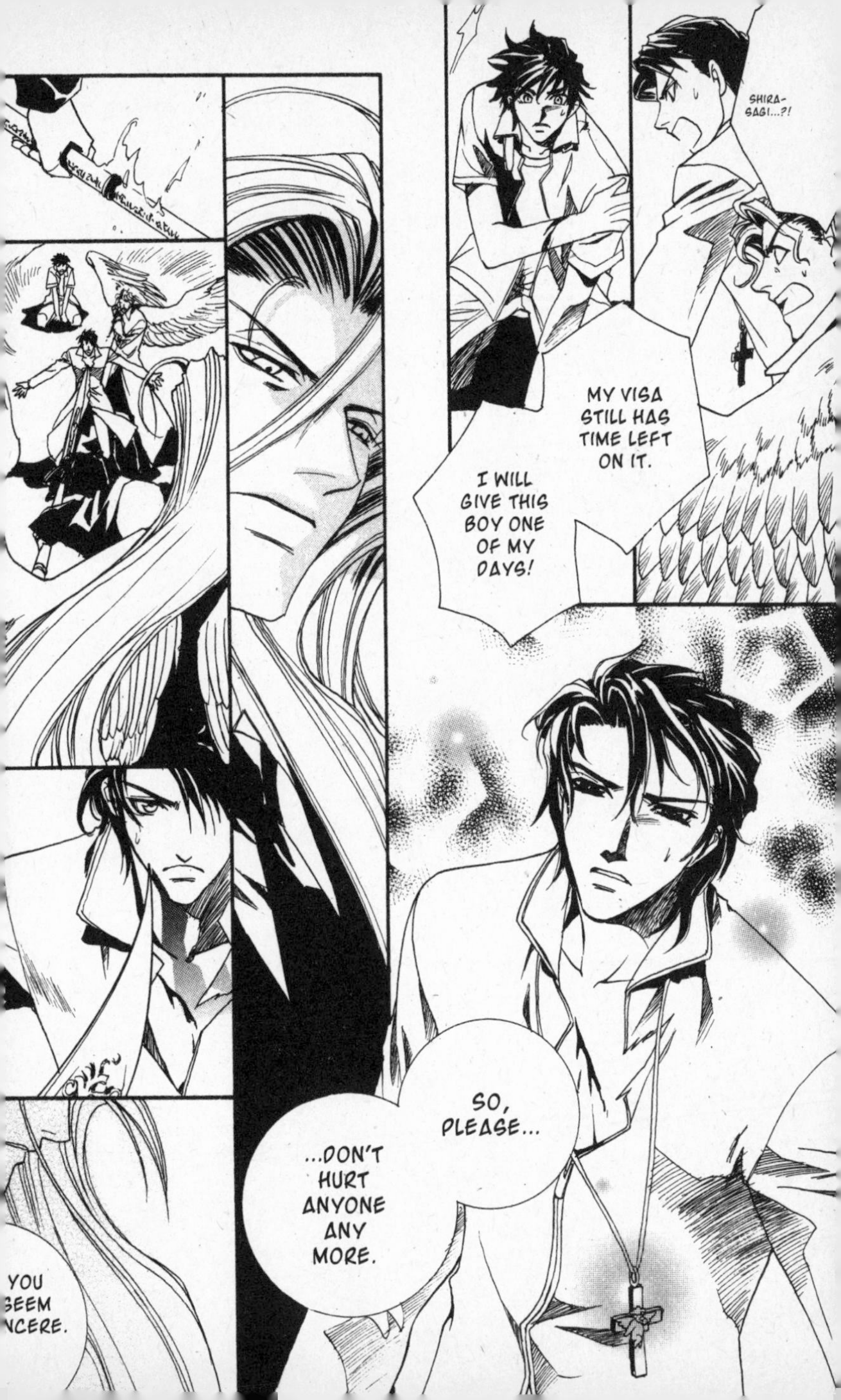
SHIRA-SAGI...?!
MY VISA STILL HAS TIME LEFT ON IT.
I WILL GIVE THIS BOY ONE OF MY DAYS!
SO, PLEASE...
...DON'T HURT ANYONE ANY MORE.
YOU SEEM NCERE.

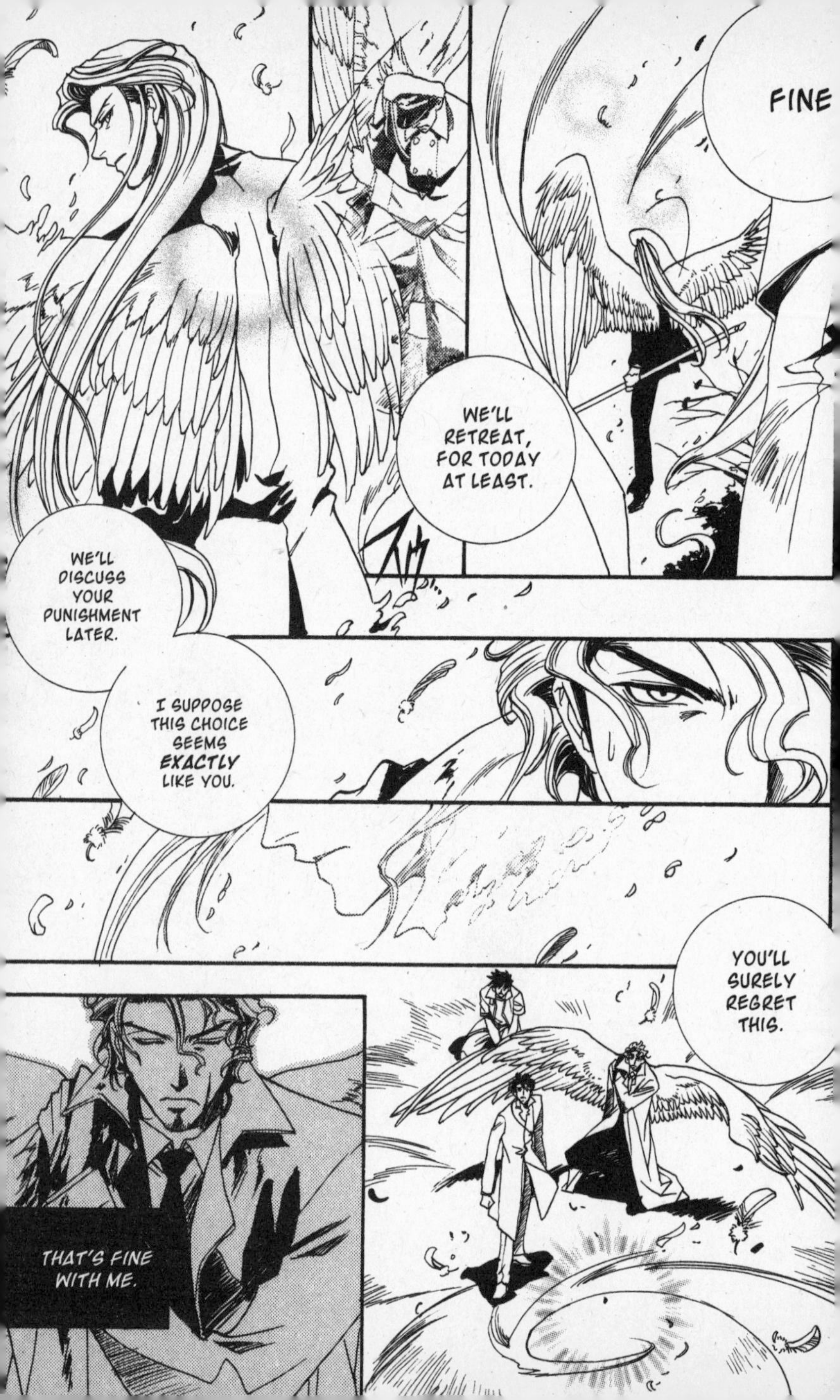
FINE
WE'LL RETREAT, FOR TODAY AT LEAST.
WE'LL DISCUSS YOUR PUNISHMENT LATER.
I SUPPOSE THIS CHOICE SEEMS **EXACTLY** LIKE YOU.
YOU'LL SURELY REGRET THIS.
THAT'S FINE WITH ME.

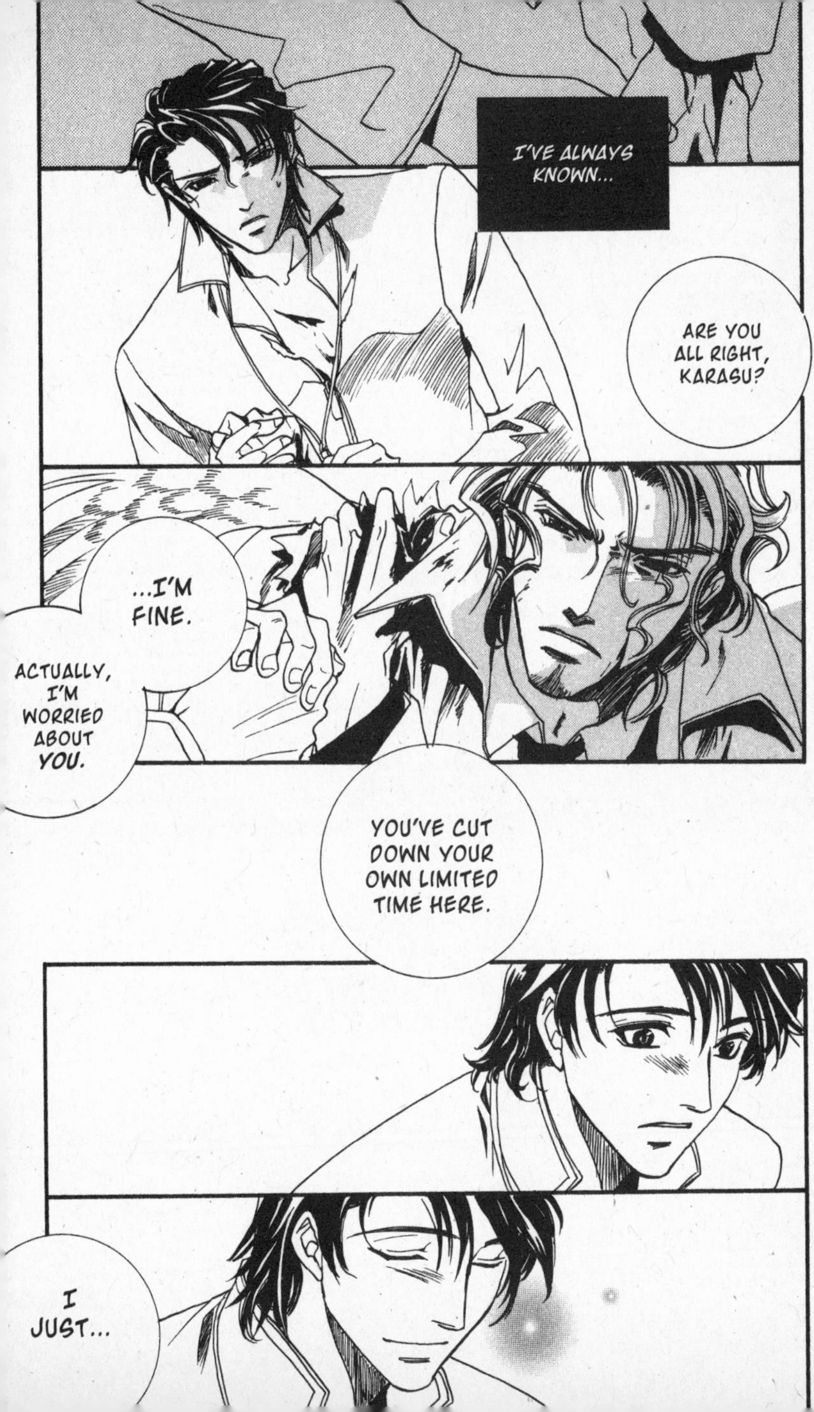
I'VE ALWAYS KNOWN...
ARE YOU ALL RIGHT, KARASU?
...I'M FINE.
ACTUALLY, I'M WORRIED ABOUT *YOU.*
YOU'VE CUT DOWN YOUR OWN LIMITED TIME HERE.
I JUST...

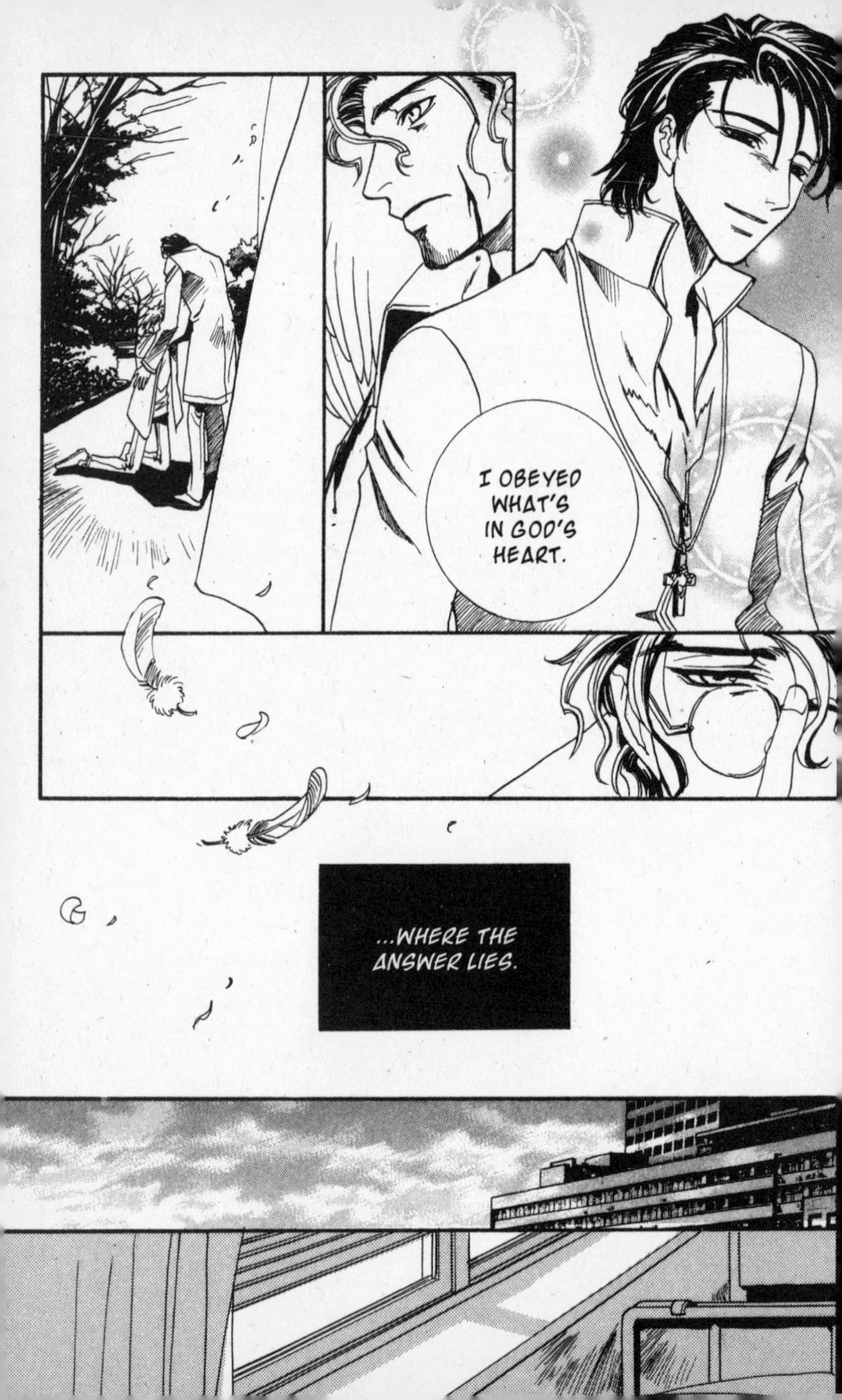
I OBEYED WHAT'S IN GOD'S HEART.
...WHERE THE ANSWER LIES.

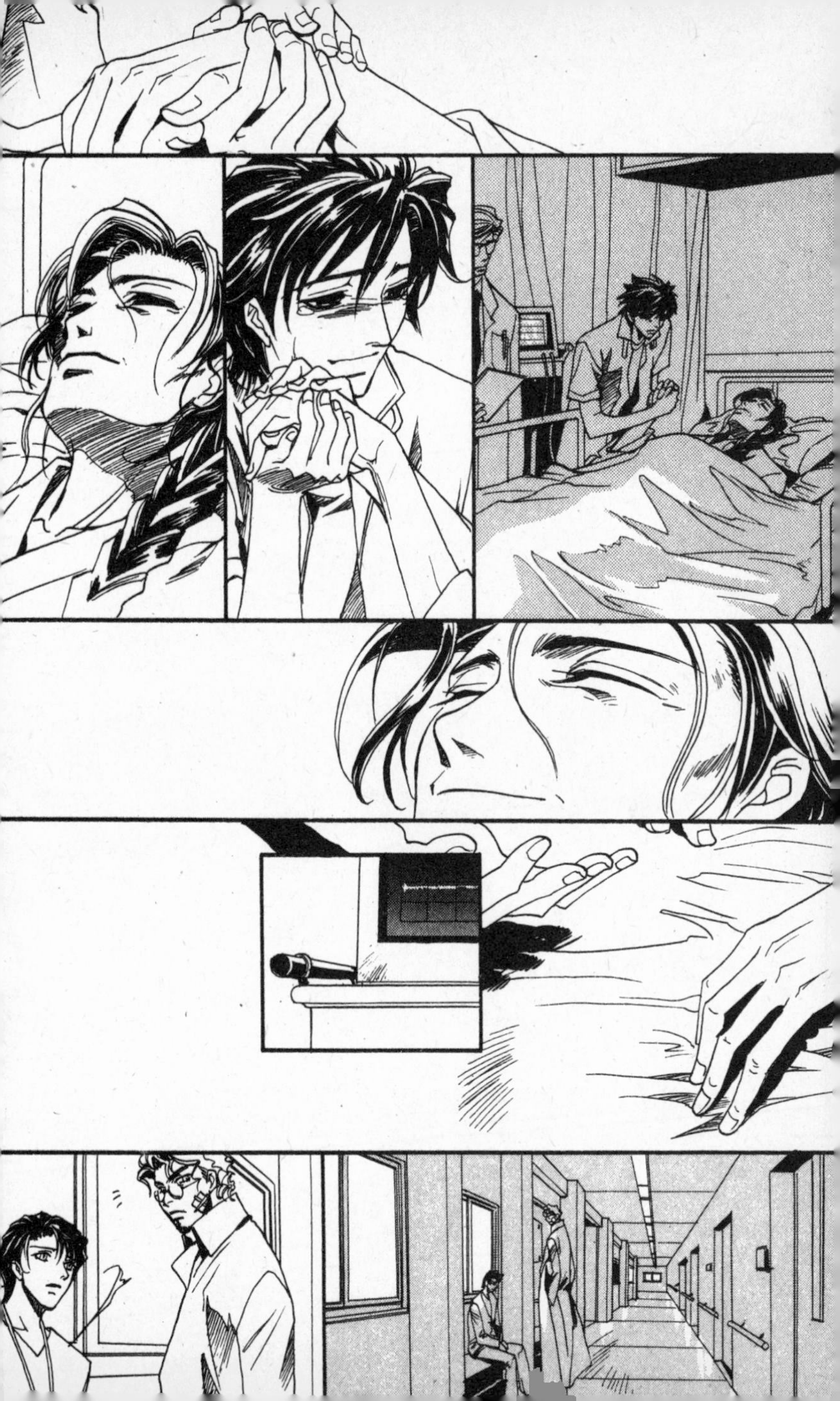

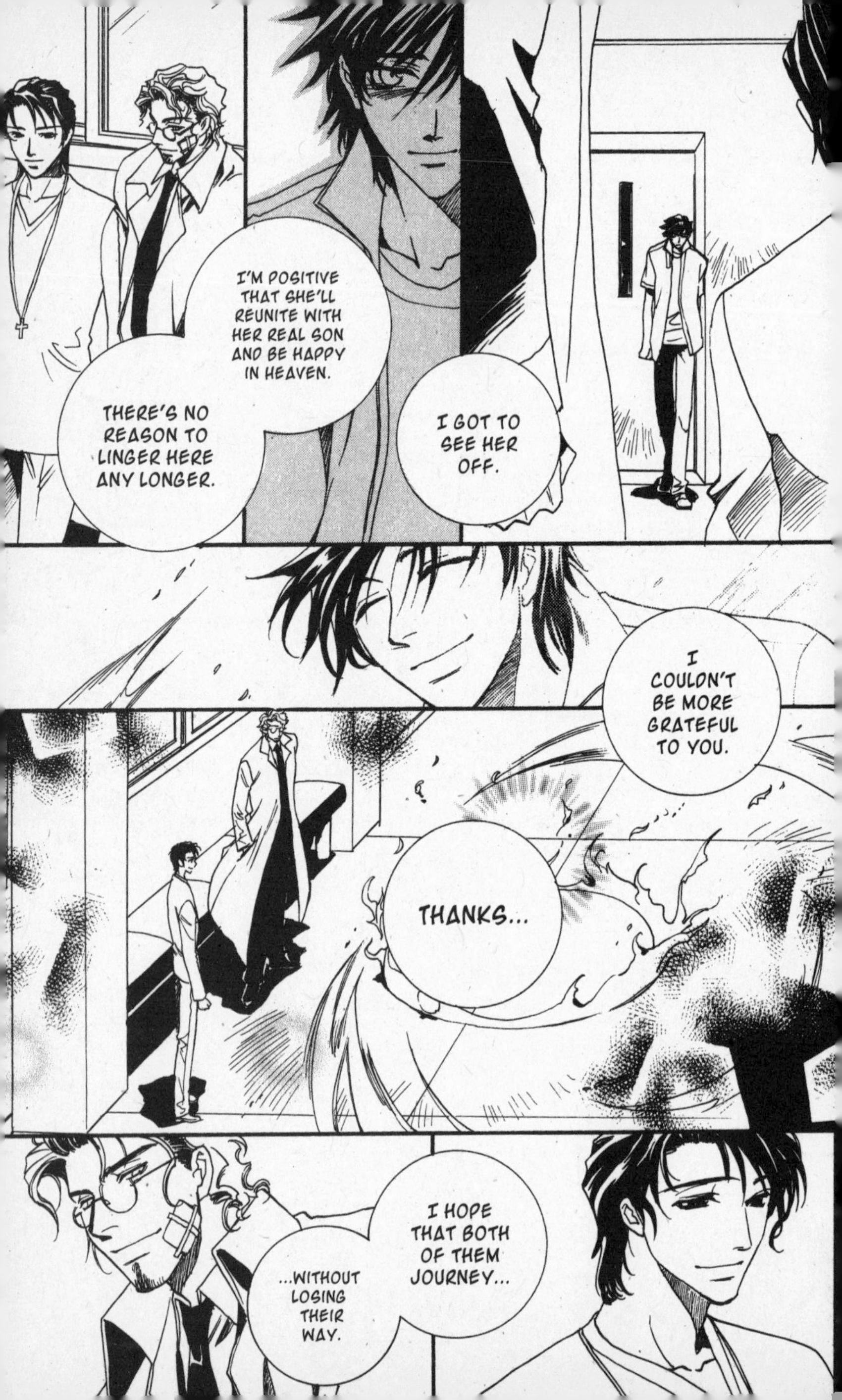
I GOT TO SEE HER OFF.
I'M POSITIVE THAT SHE'LL REUNITE WITH HER REAL SON AND BE HAPPY IN HEAVEN.
THERE'S NO REASON TO LINGER HERE ANY LONGER.
I COULDN'T BE MORE GRATEFUL TO YOU.
THANKS...
I HOPE THAT BOTH OF THEM JOURNEY...
...WITHOUT LOSING THEIR WAY.

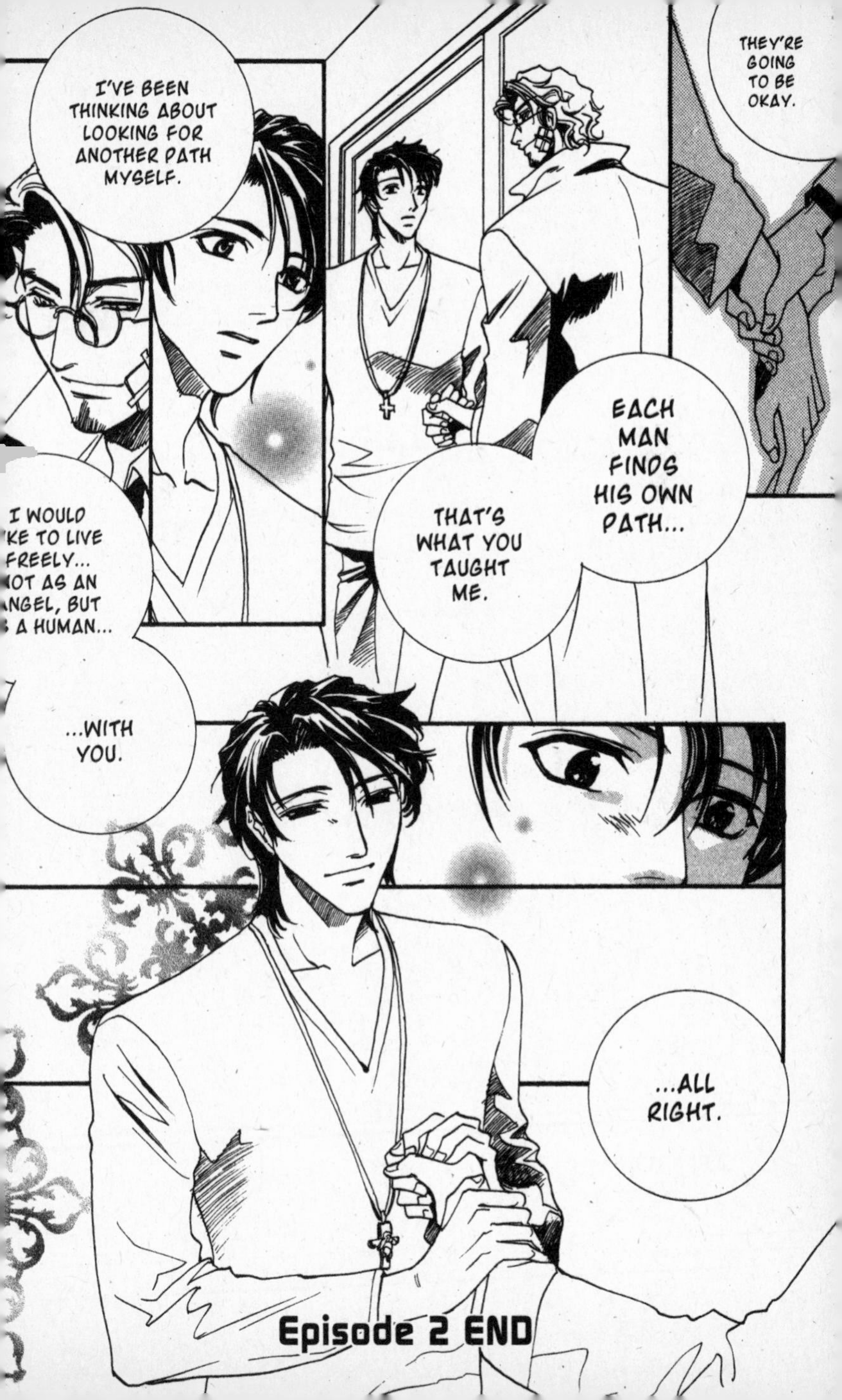
THEY'RE GOING TO BE OKAY.
I'VE BEEN THINKING ABOUT LOOKING FOR ANOTHER PATH MYSELF.
EACH MAN FINDS HIS OWN PATH...
THAT'S WHAT YOU TAUGHT ME.
I WOULD KE TO LIVE FREELY... IOT AS AN NGEL, BUT A HUMAN...
...WITH YOU.
...ALL RIGHT.
Episode 2 END

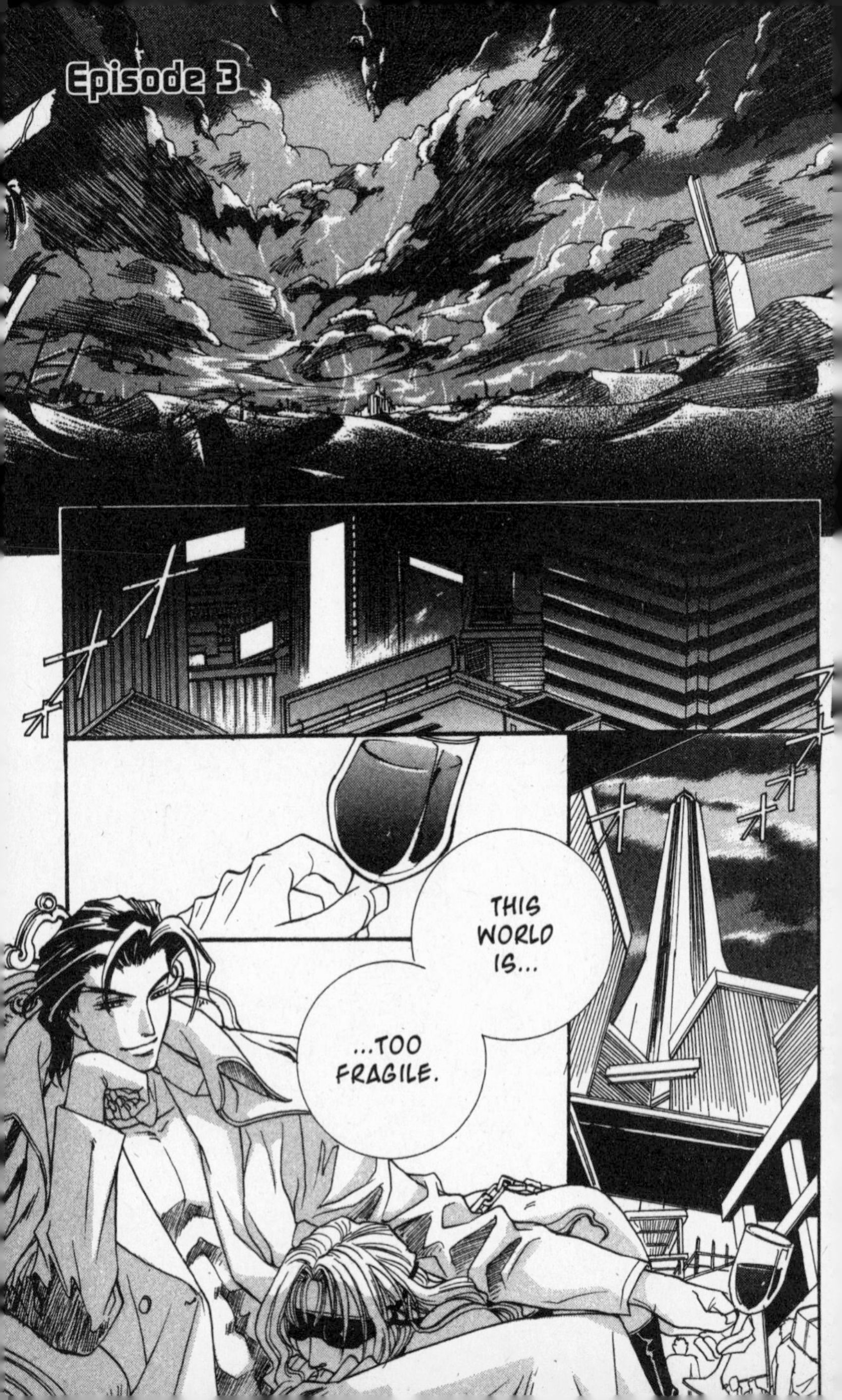
Episode 3
THIS WORLD IS...
...TOO FRAGILE.

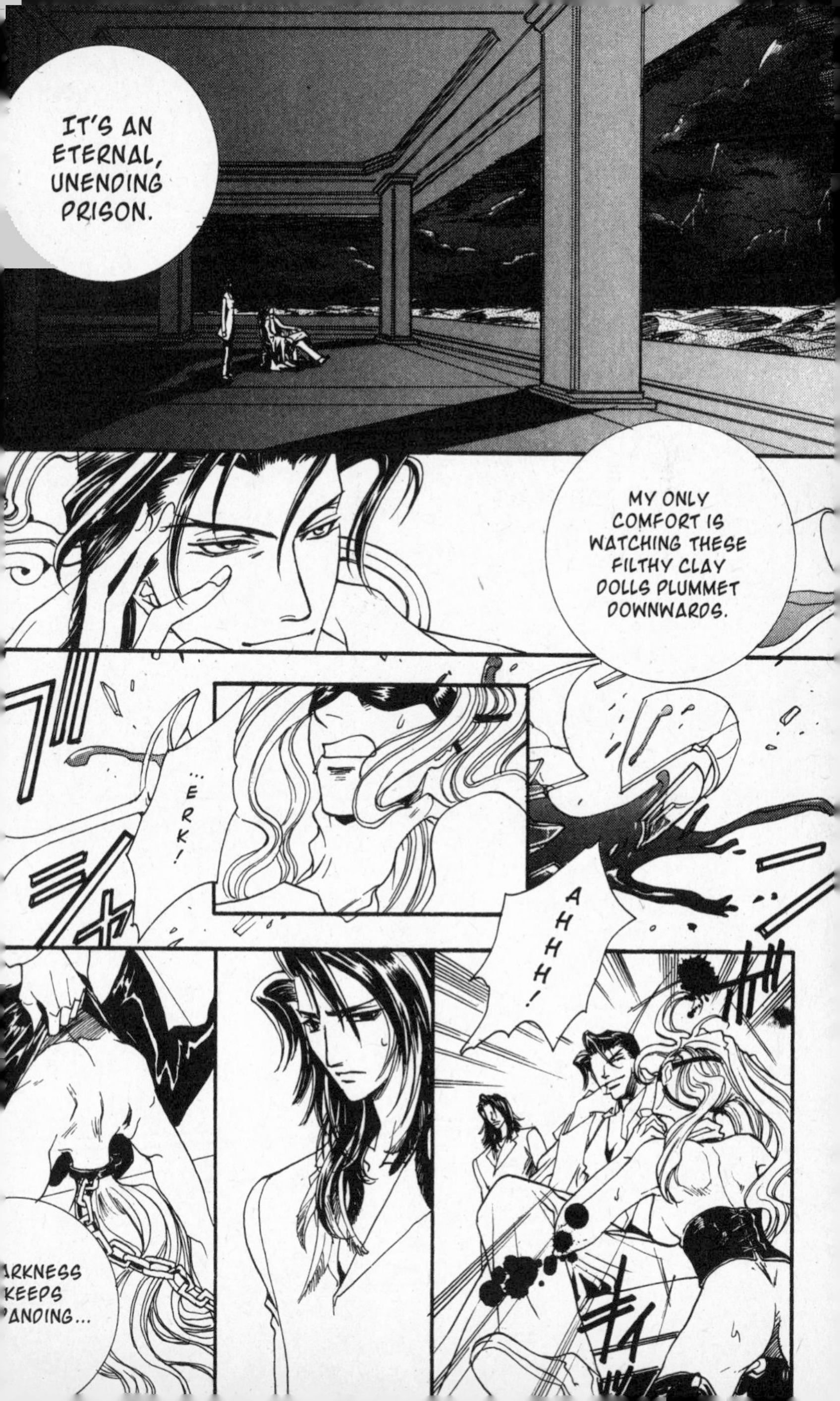
IT'S AN ETERNAL, UNENDING PRISON.
MY ONLY COMFORT IS WATCHING THESE FILTHY CLAY DOLLS PLUMMET DOWNWARDS.
...ERK!
AHHHH!
ARKNESS KEEPS ANDING...

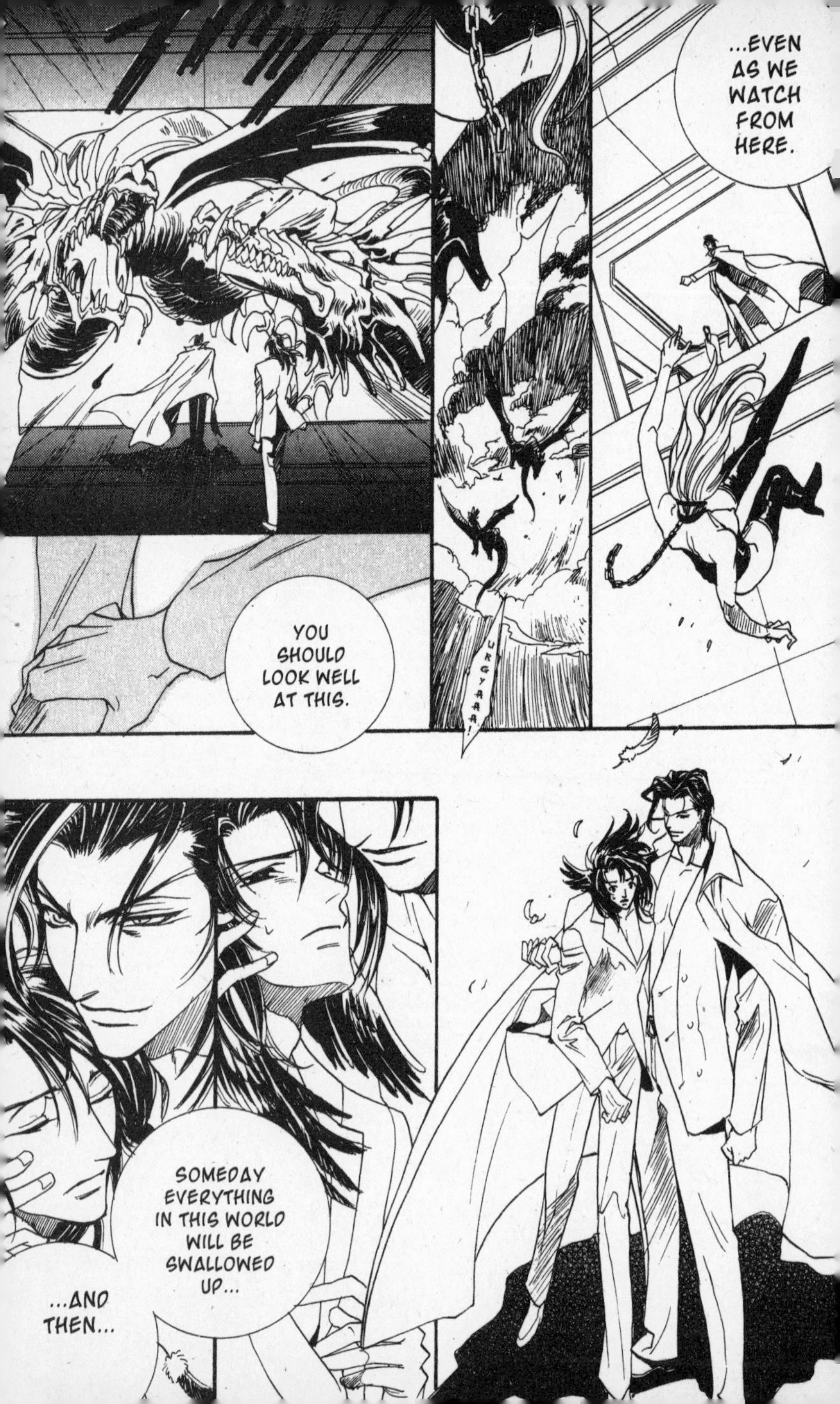
...EVEN AS WE WATCH FROM HERE.
URGYAAA!
YOU SHOULD LOOK WELL AT THIS.
SOMEDAY EVERYTHING IN THIS WORLD WILL BE SWALLOWED UP...
...AND THEN...

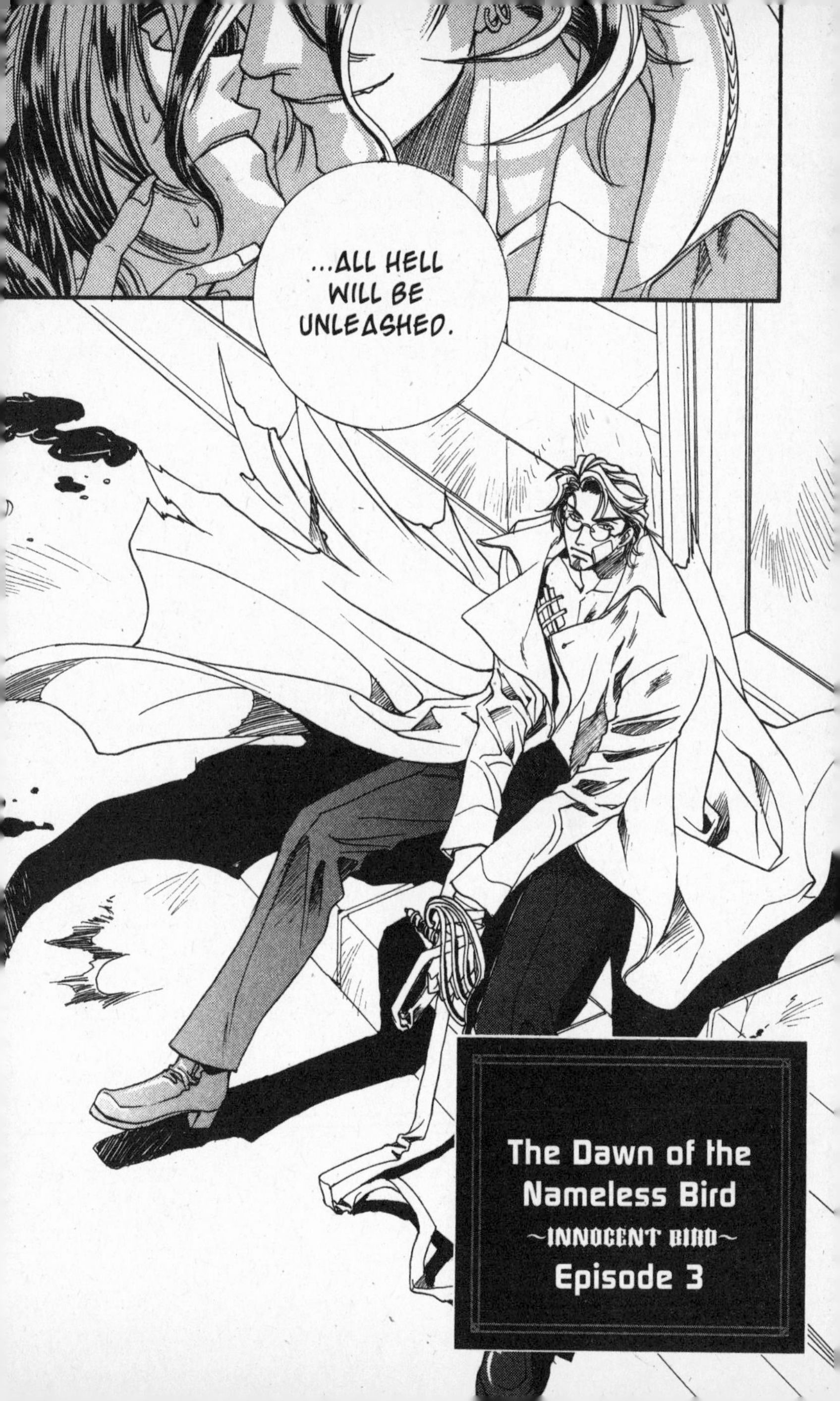
...ALL HELL WILL BE UNLEASHED.
The Dawn of the Nameless Bird
~INNOCENT BIRD~
Episode 3

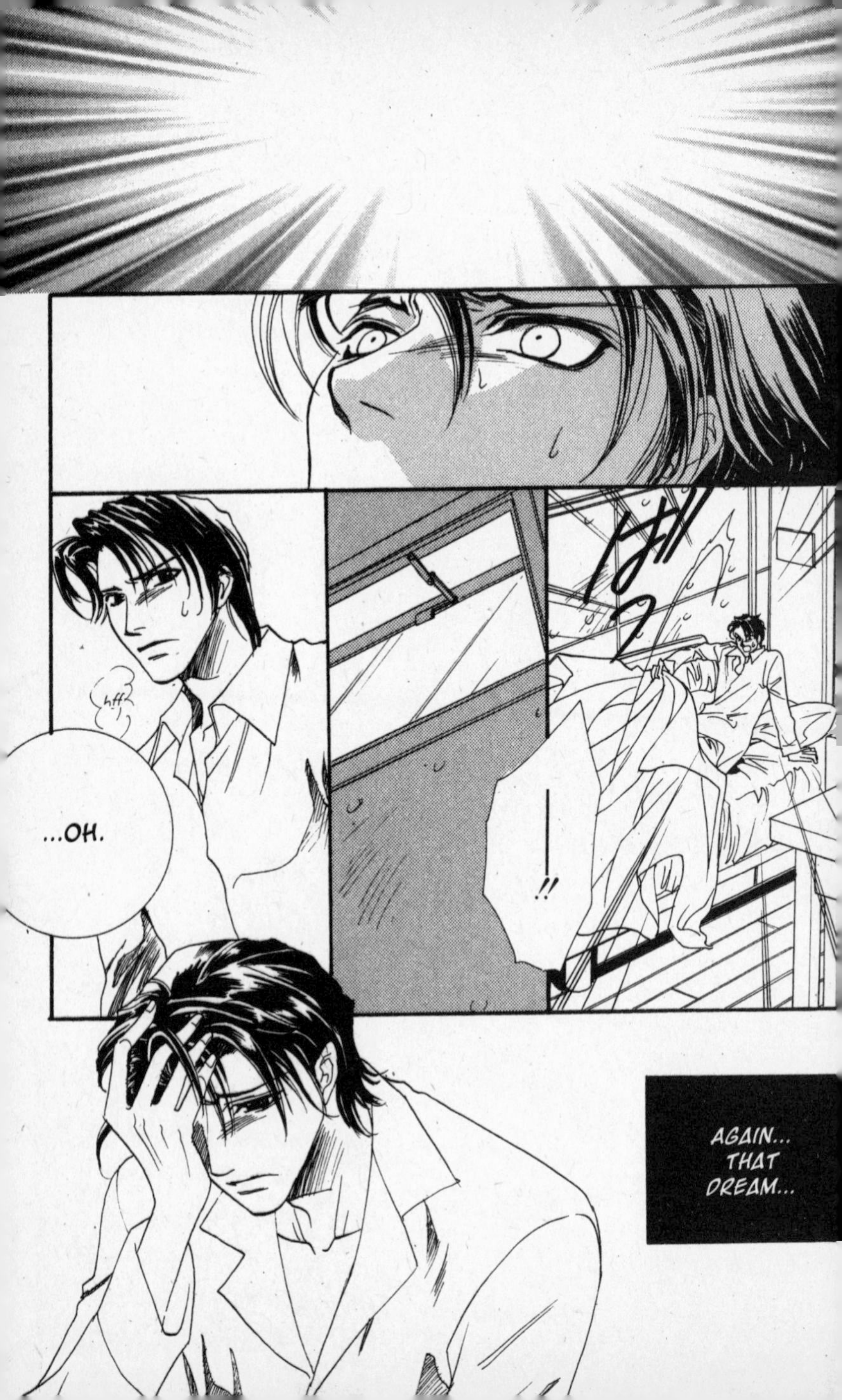
はっ
!!
hff
...OH.
AGAIN... THAT DREAM...

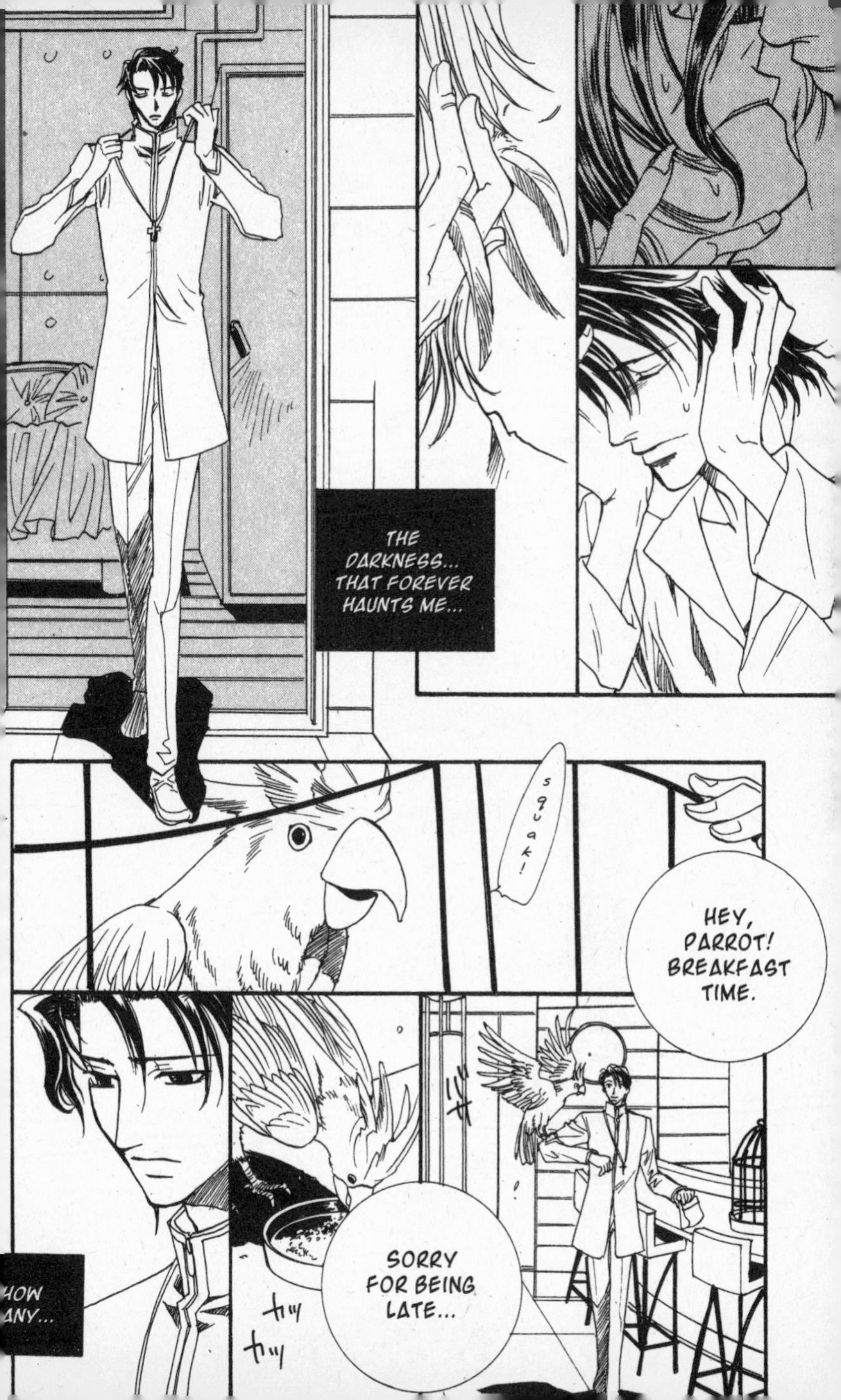
THE DARKNESS... THAT FOREVER HAUNTS ME...
HEY, PARROT! BREAKFAST TIME.
squak!
SORRY FOR BEING LATE...
HOW
ANY...

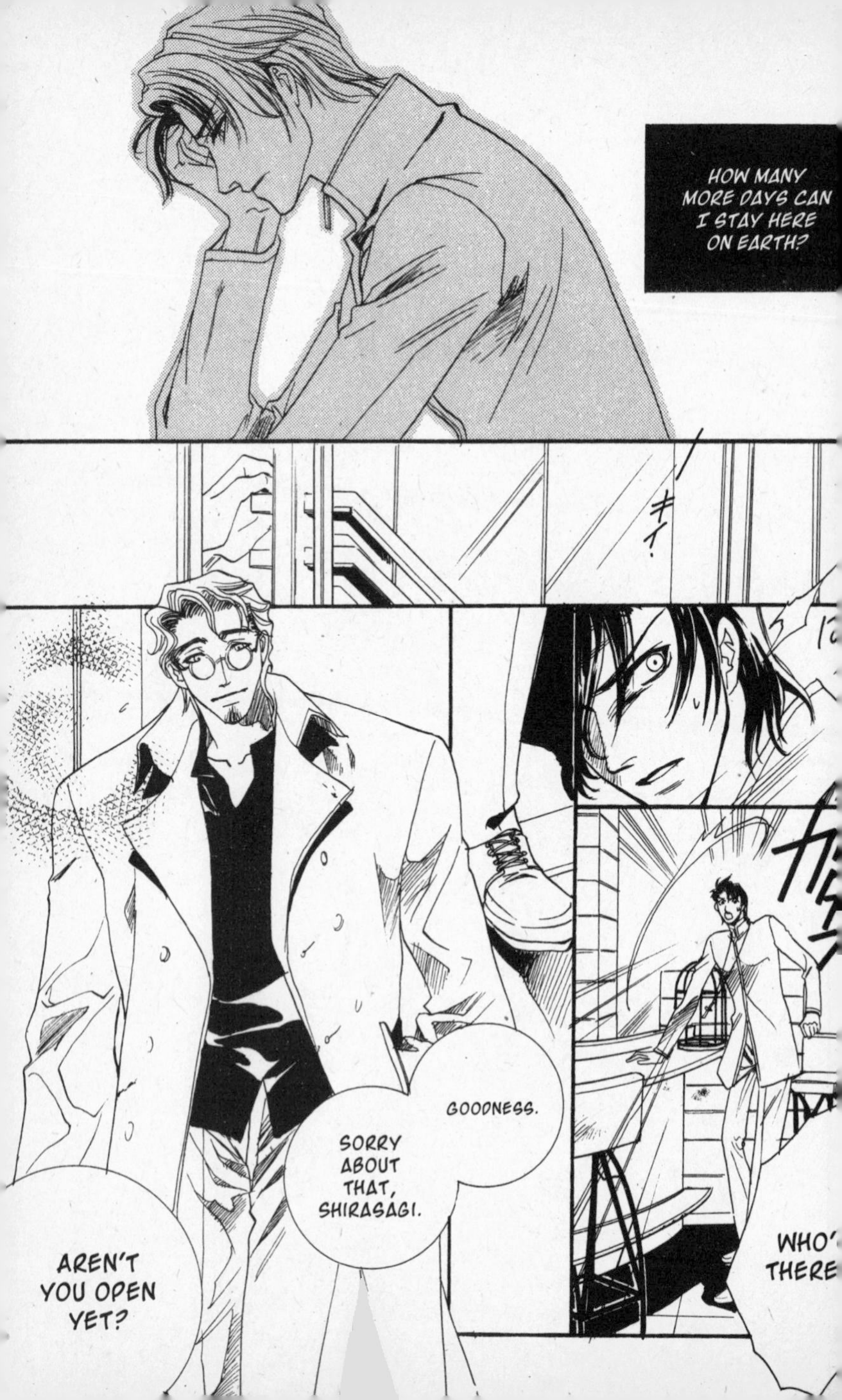

HOW MANY MORE DAYS CAN I STAY HERE ON EARTH?
WHO'
THERE
GOODNESS.
SORRY ABOUT THAT, SHIRASAGI.
AREN'T YOU OPEN YET?

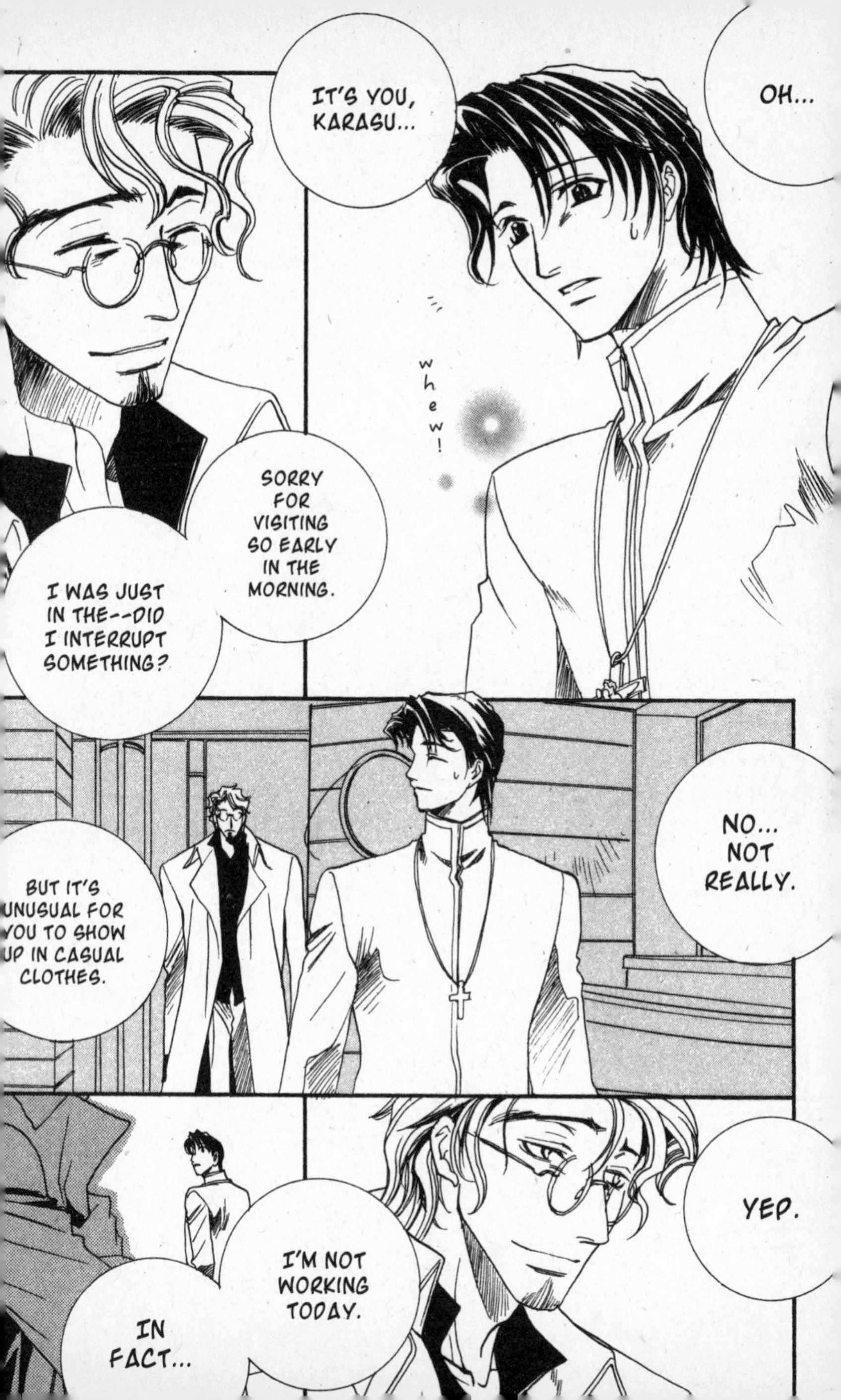
OH...
IT'S YOU, KARASU...
whew!
SORRY FOR VISITING SO EARLY IN THE MORNING.
I WAS JUST IN THE--DID I INTERRUPT SOMETHING?
NO... NOT REALLY.
BUT IT'S UNUSUAL FOR YOU TO SHOW UP IN CASUAL CLOTHES.
YEP.
I'M NOT WORKING TODAY.
IN FACT...

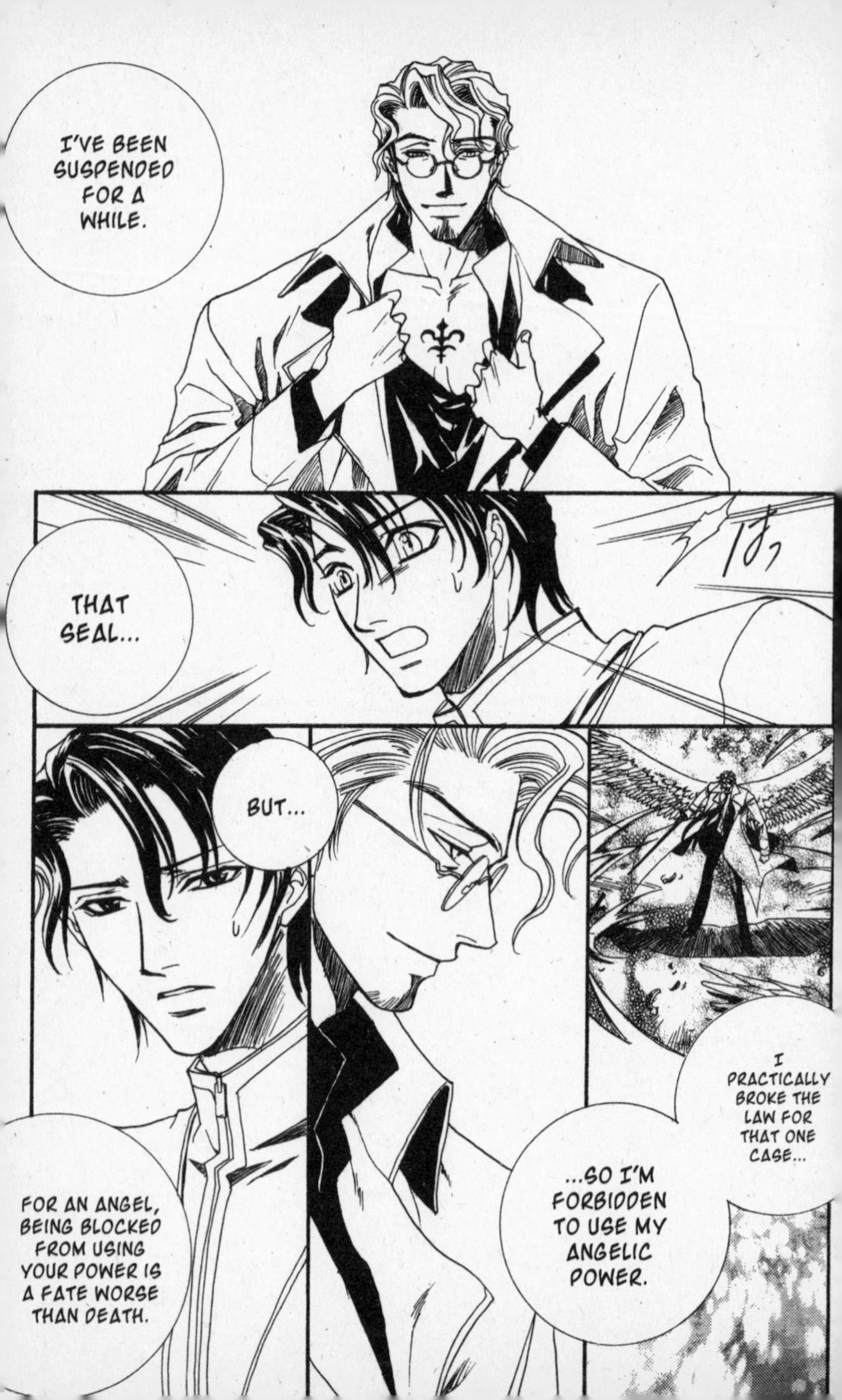
I'VE BEEN SUSPENDED FOR A WHILE.
はっ
THAT SEAL...
I PRACTICALLY BROKE THE LAW FOR THAT ONE CASE...
...SO I'M FORBIDDEN TO USE MY ANGELIC POWER.
BUT...
FOR AN ANGEL, BEING BLOCKED FROM USING YOUR POWER IS A FATE WORSE THAN DEATH.

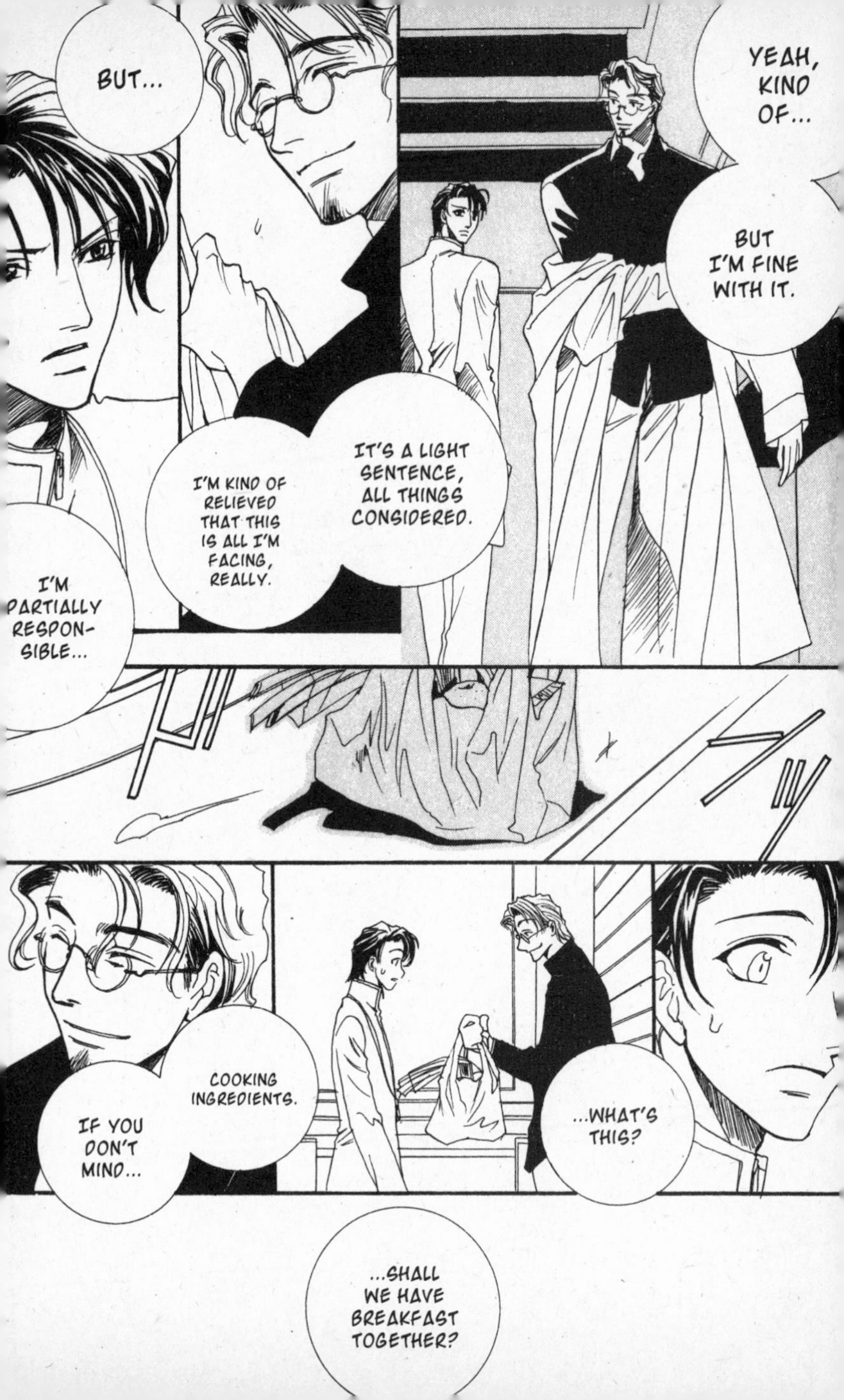
YEAH, KIND OF...
BUT I'M FINE WITH IT.
IT'S A LIGHT SENTENCE, ALL THINGS CONSIDERED.
BUT...
I'M KIND OF RELIEVED THAT THIS IS ALL I'M FACING, REALLY.
I'M PARTIALLY RESPON-SIBLE...
...WHAT'S THIS?
COOKING INGREDIENTS.
IF YOU DON'T MIND...
...SHALL WE HAVE BREAKFAST TOGETHER?

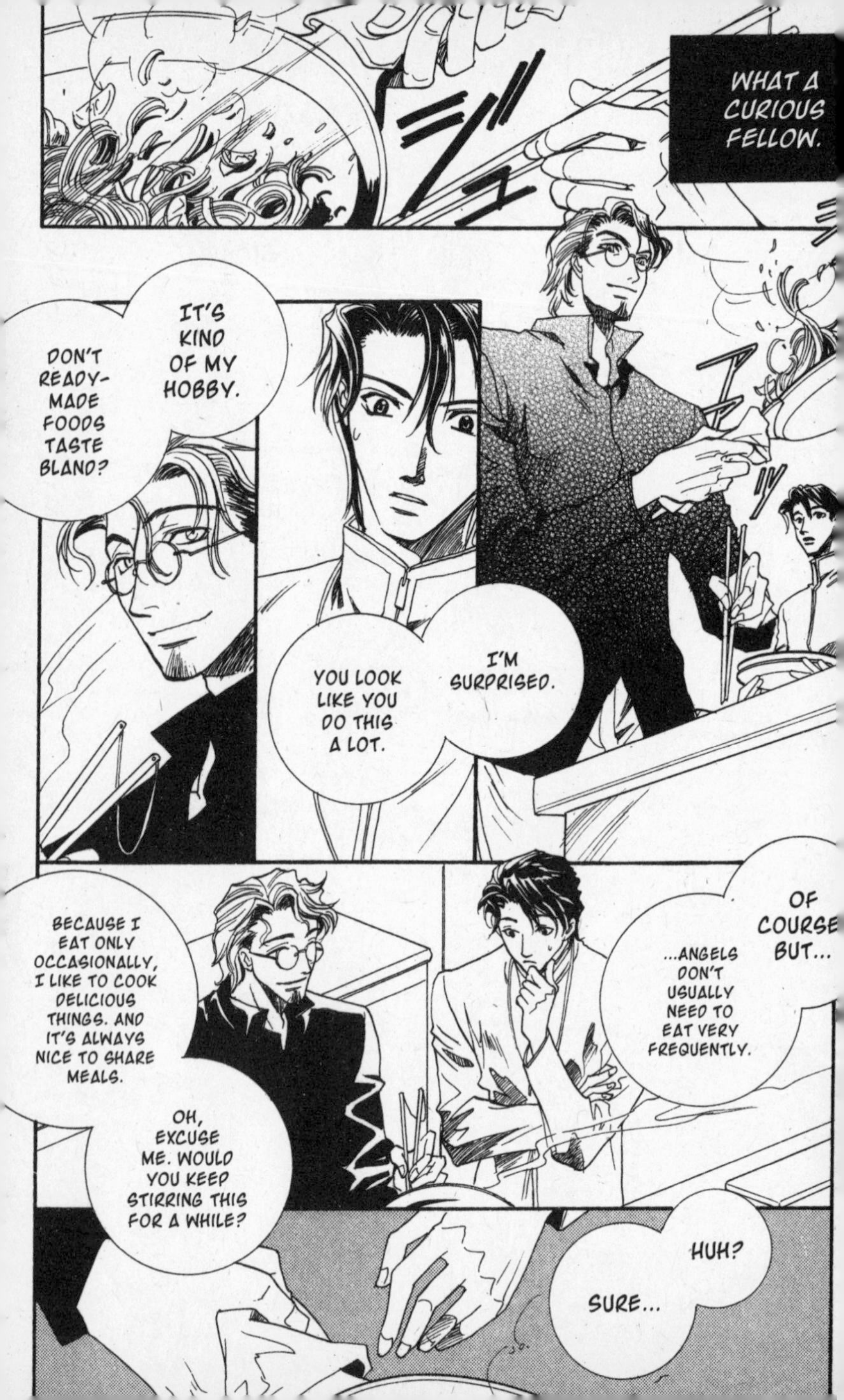

WHAT A CURIOUS FELLOW.
I'M SURPRISED.
YOU LOOK LIKE YOU DO THIS A LOT.
IT'S KIND OF MY HOBBY.
DON'T READY-MADE FOODS TASTE BLAND?
OF COURSE BUT...
...ANGELS DON'T USUALLY NEED TO EAT VERY FREQUENTLY.
BECAUSE I EAT ONLY OCCASIONALLY, I LIKE TO COOK DELICIOUS THINGS. AND IT'S ALWAYS NICE TO SHARE MEALS.
OH, EXCUSE ME. WOULD YOU KEEP STIRRING THIS FOR A WHILE?
HUH?
SURE...

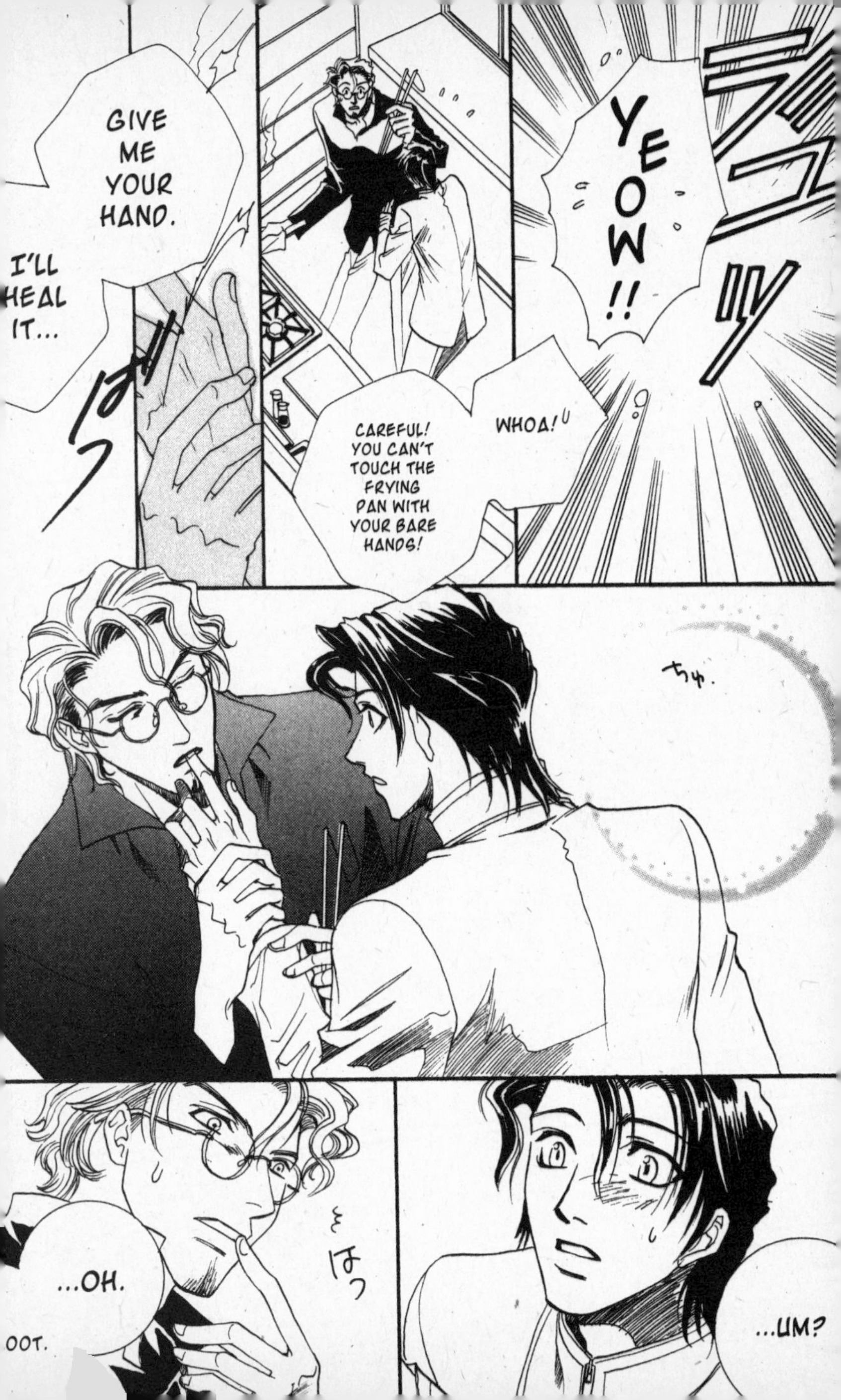
YEOW!!
WHOA!
CAREFUL! YOU CAN'T TOUCH THE FRYING PAN WITH YOUR BARE HANDS!
GIVE ME YOUR HAND.
I'LL HEAL IT...
ちゅ.
...UM?
はっ
...OH.
OOT.

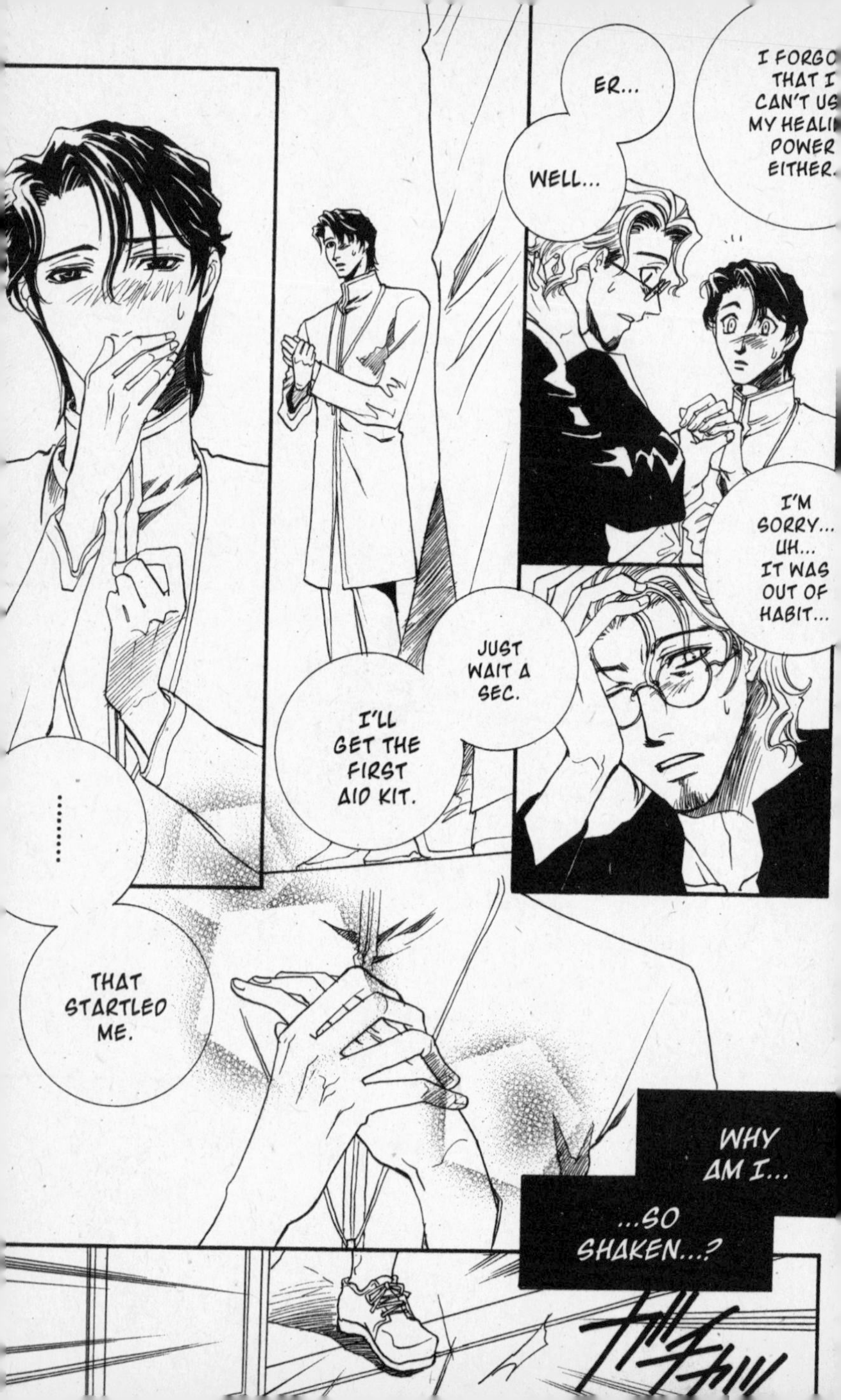
I FORGO THAT I CAN'T US MY HEALI POWER EITHER.
ER...
WELL...
I'M SORRY... UH... IT WAS OUT OF HABIT...
JUST WAIT A SEC.
I'LL GET THE FIRST AID KIT.
......
THAT STARTLED ME.
WHY AM I...
...SO SHAKEN...?

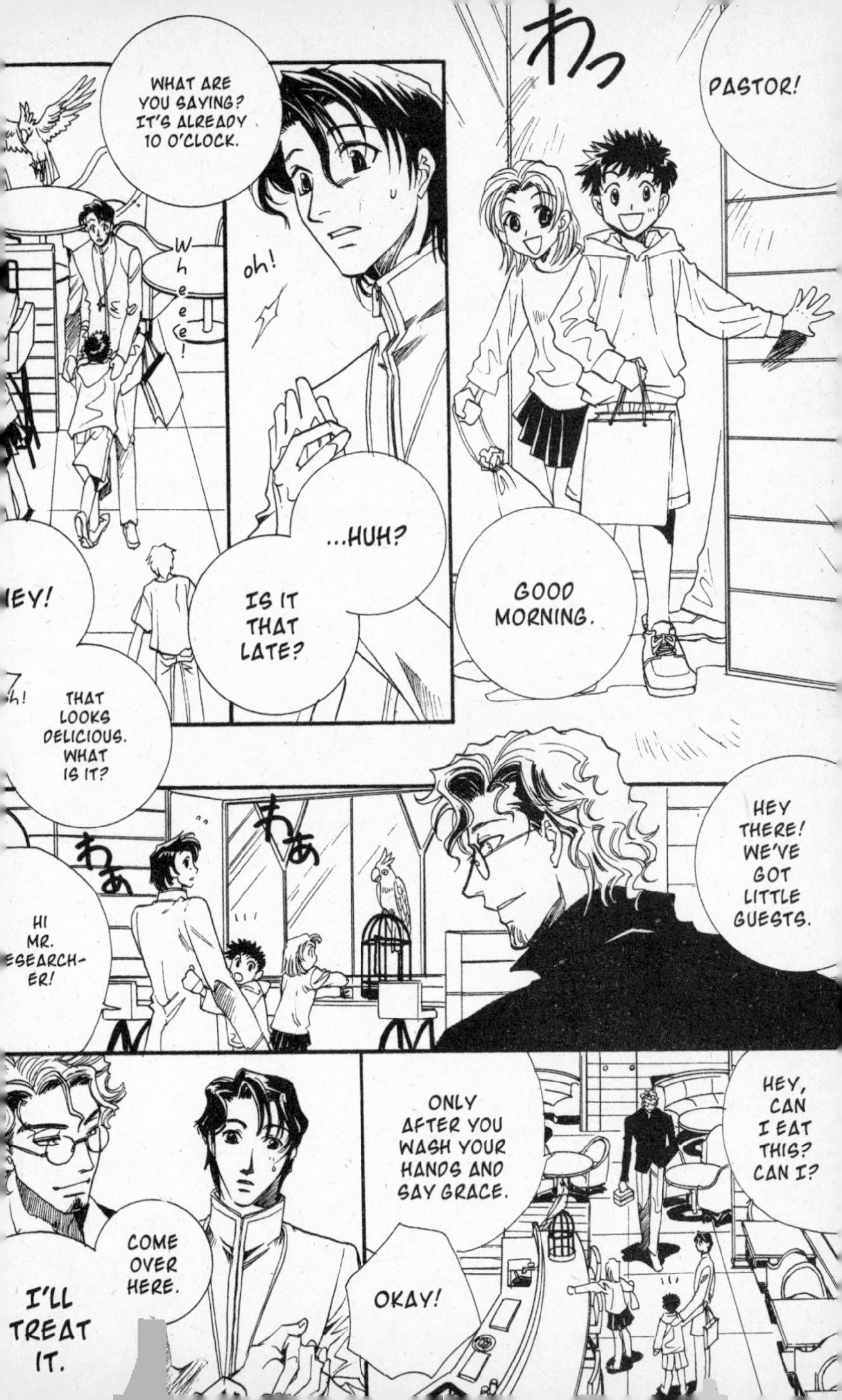
わっ
PASTOR!
GOOD MORNING.
WHAT ARE YOU SAYING? IT'S ALREADY 10 O'CLOCK.
oh!
...HUH?
IS IT THAT LATE?
Wheeee!
EY!
h!
THAT LOOKS DELICIOUS. WHAT IS IT?
HEY THERE! WE'VE GOT LITTLE GUESTS.
わあ
わあ
HI MR. ESEARCH-ER!
HEY, CAN I EAT THIS? CAN I?
ONLY AFTER YOU WASH YOUR HANDS AND SAY GRACE.
OKAY!
COME OVER HERE.
I'LL TREAT IT.

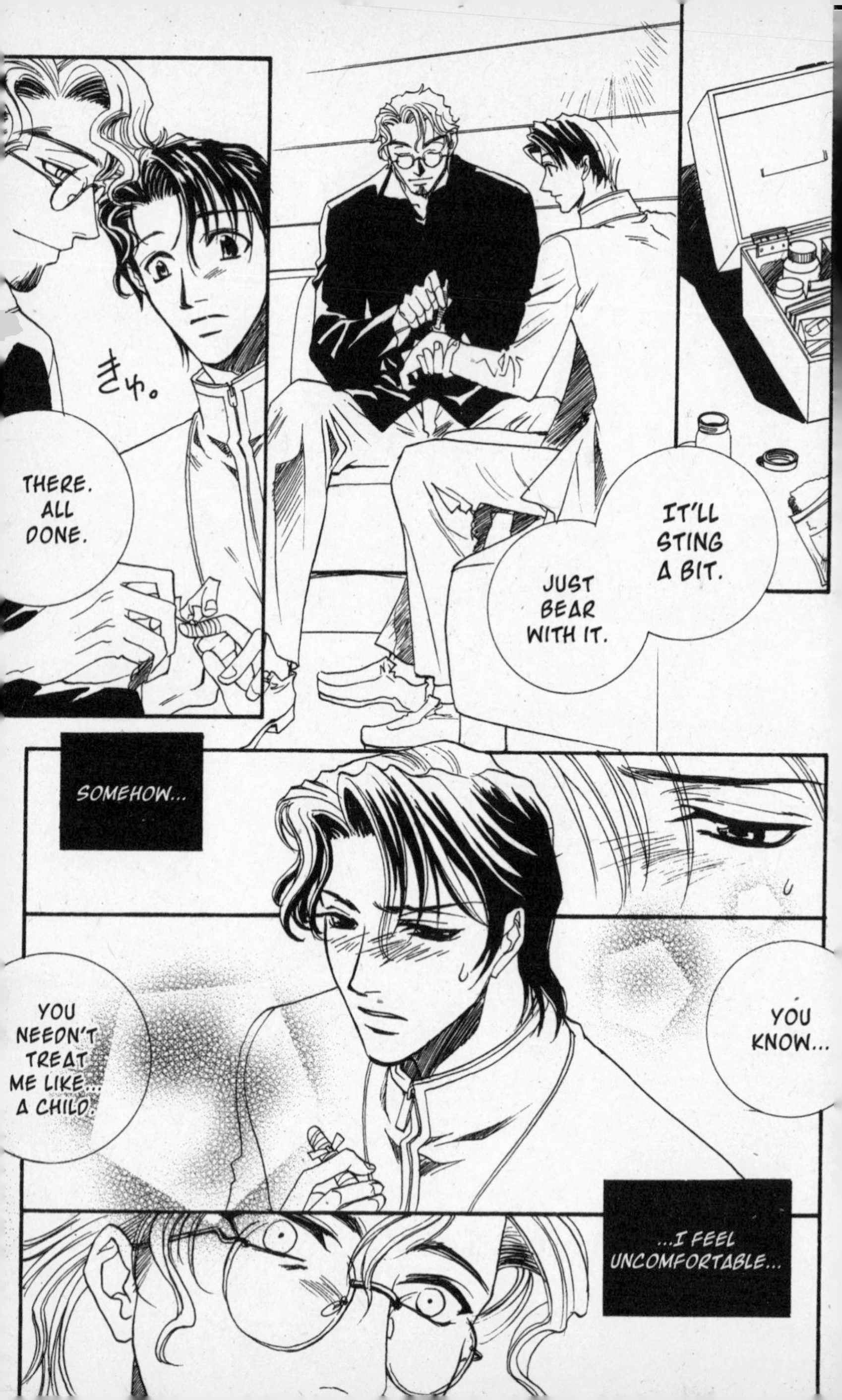
IT'LL STING A BIT.
JUST BEAR WITH IT.
きゅ。
THERE. ALL DONE.
SOMEHOW...
YOU KNOW...
YOU NEEDN'T TREAT ME LIKE... A CHILD.
...I FEEL UNCOMFORTABLE...

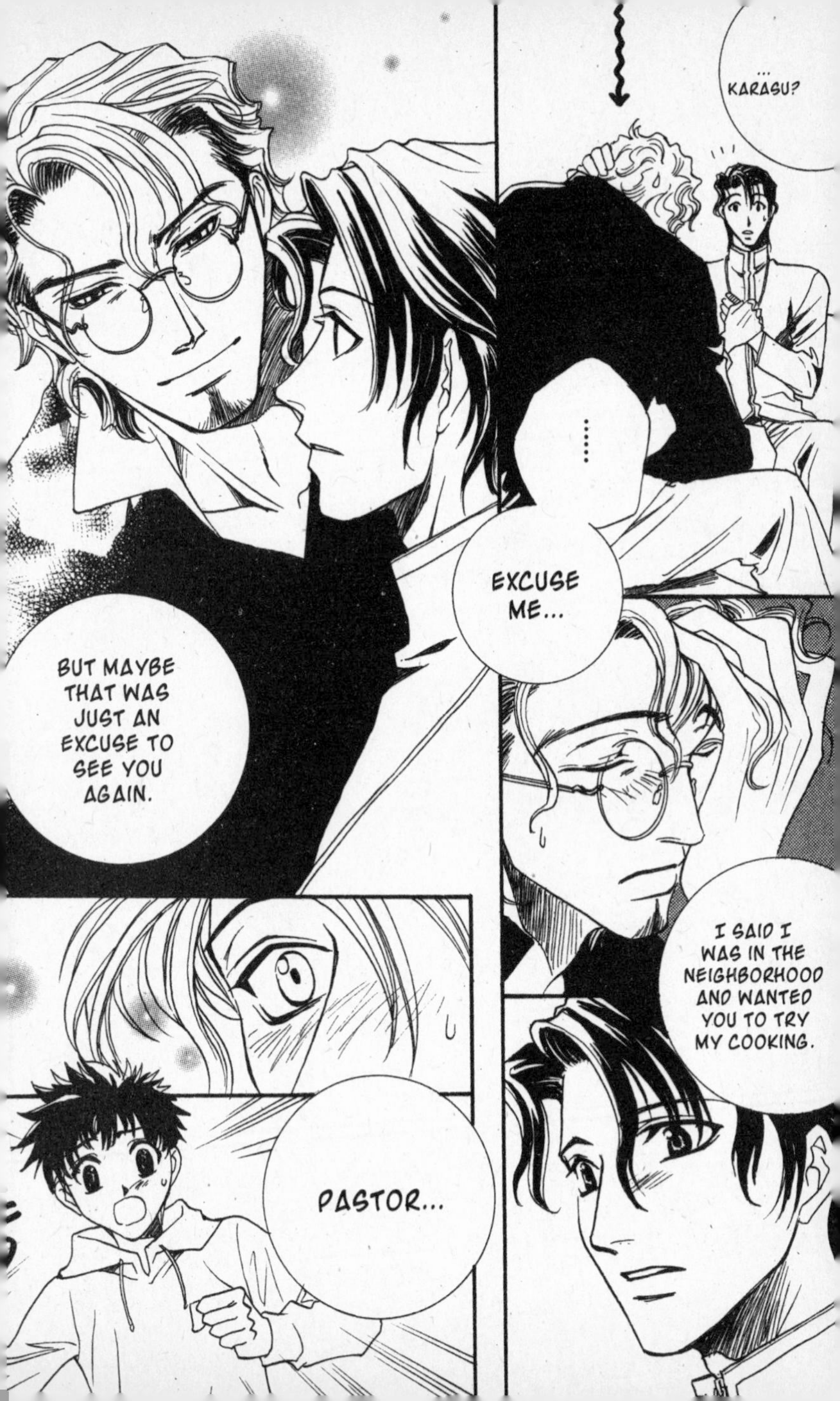

... KARASU?
......
EXCUSE ME...
I SAID I WAS IN THE NEIGHBORHOOD AND WANTED YOU TO TRY MY COOKING.
BUT MAYBE THAT WAS JUST AN EXCUSE TO SEE YOU AGAIN.
PASTOR...

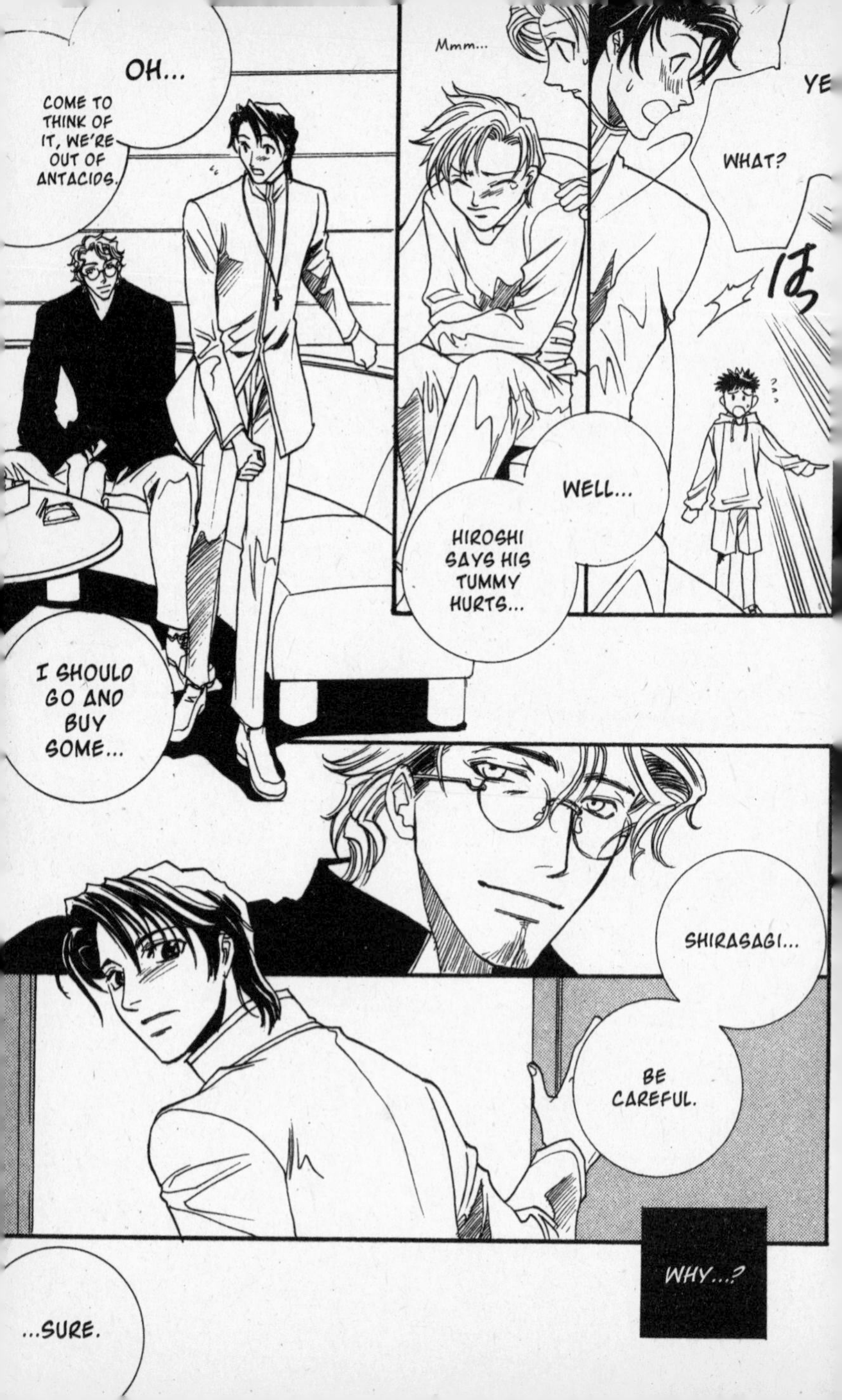
YE
WHAT?
は
Mmm...
WELL...
HIROSHI SAYS HIS TUMMY HURTS...
OH...
COME TO THINK OF IT, WE'RE OUT OF ANTACIDS.
I SHOULD GO AND BUY SOME...
SHIRASAGI...
BE CAREFUL.
WHY...?
...SURE.

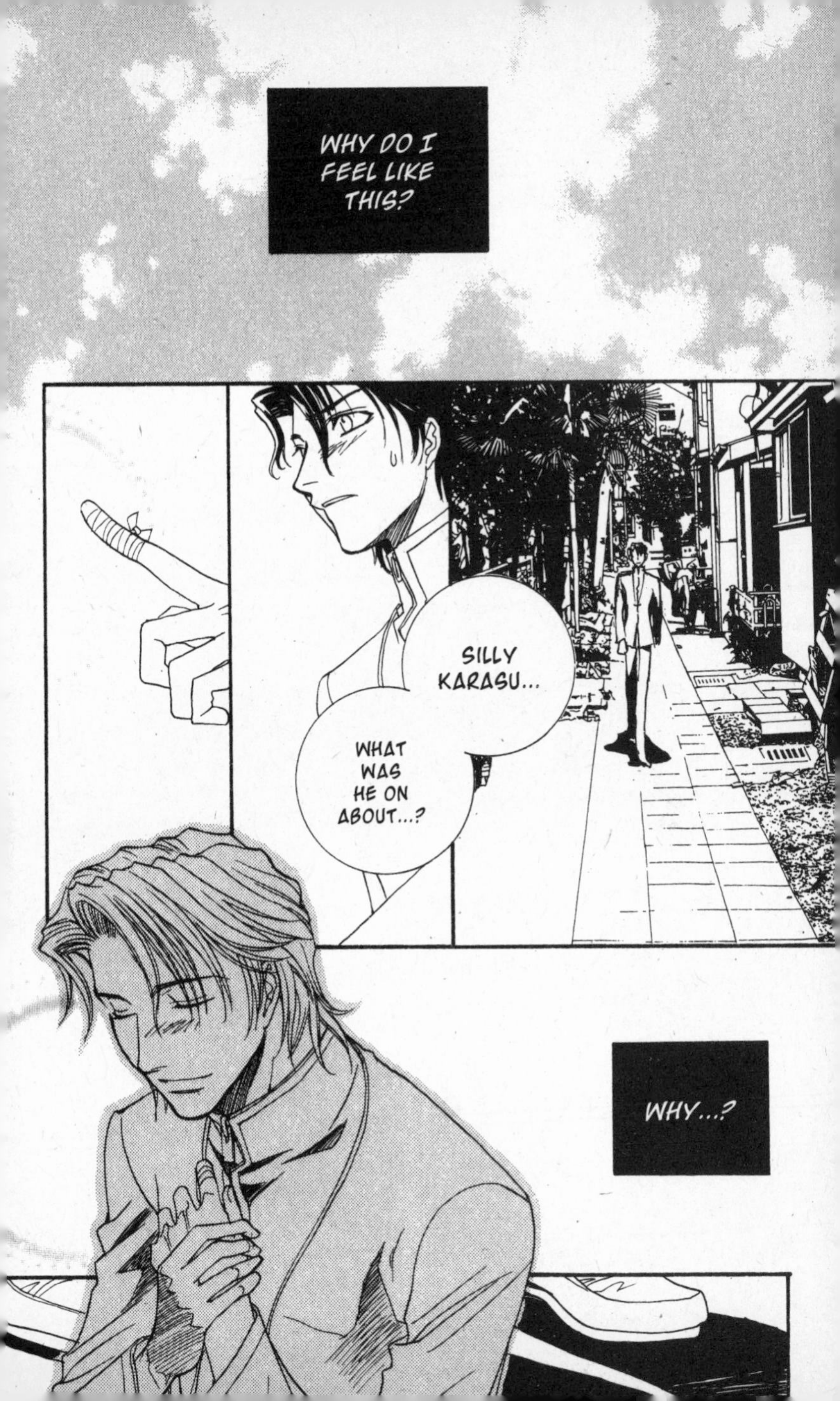
WHY DO I FEEL LIKE THIS?
SILLY KARASU...
WHAT WAS HE ON ABOUT...?
WHY...?

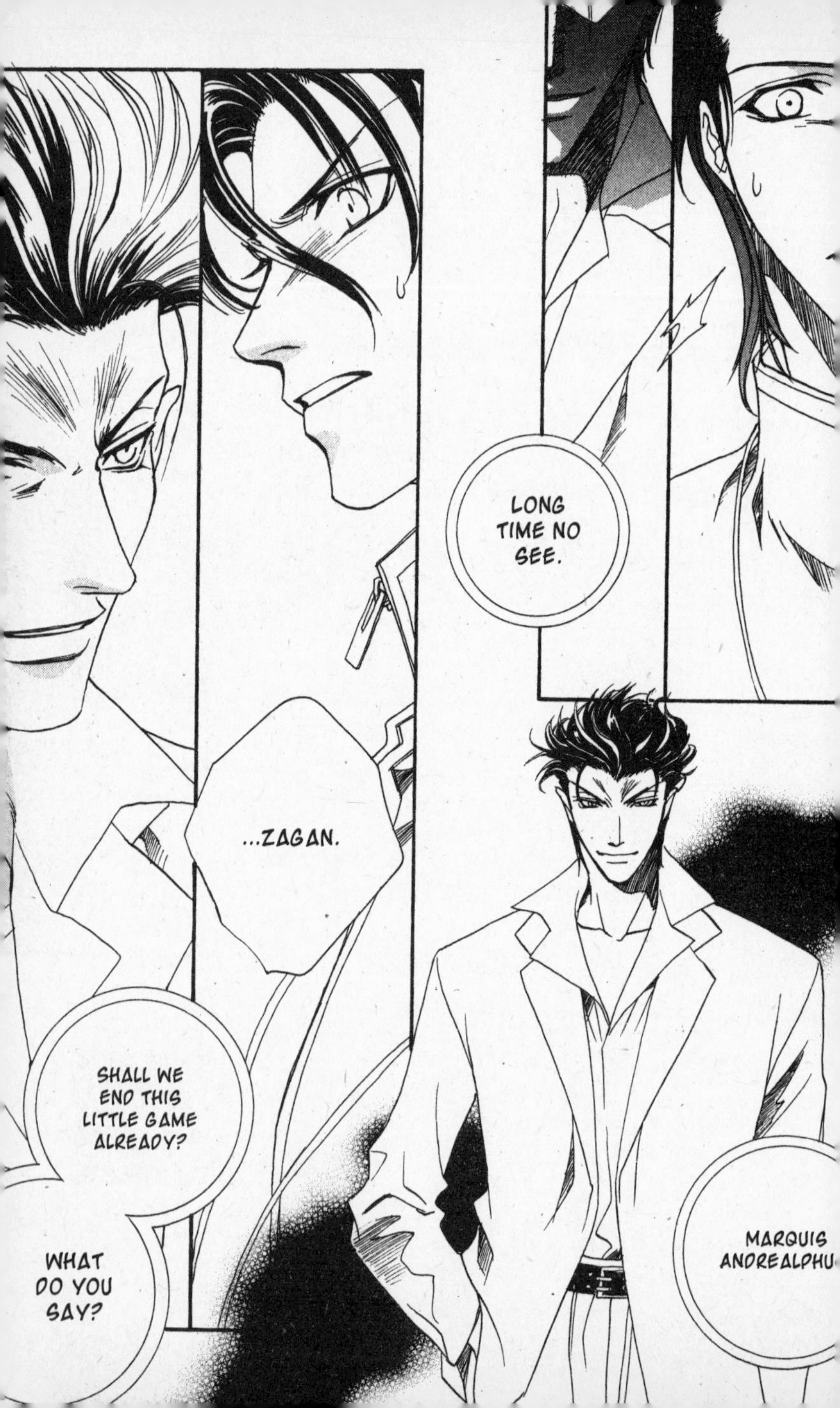
LONG TIME NO SEE.
MARQUIS ANDREALPHU
...ZAGAN.
SHALL WE END THIS LITTLE GAME ALREADY?
WHAT DO YOU SAY?

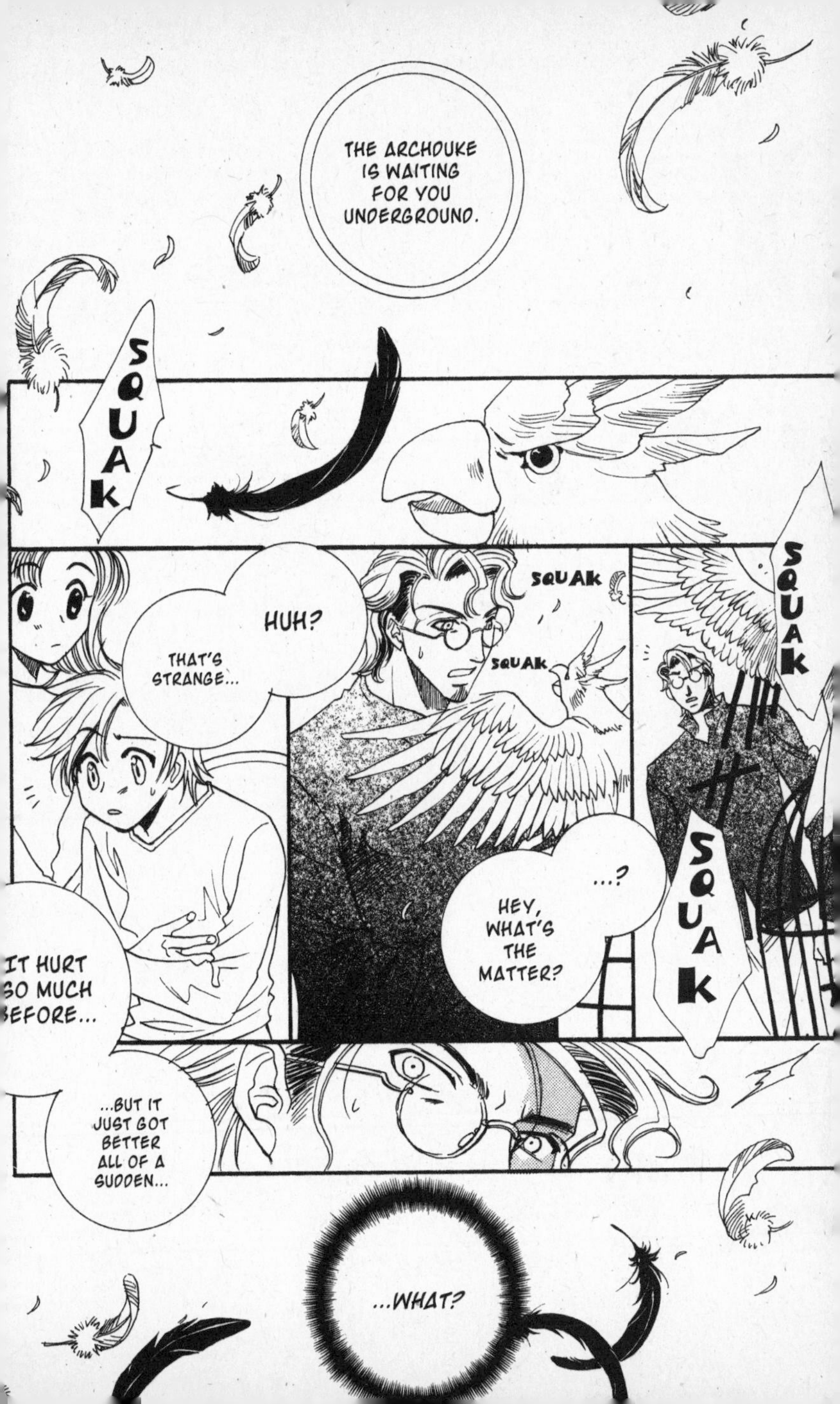
THE ARCHDUKE IS WAITING FOR YOU UNDERGROUND.
SQUAK
SQUAK
SQUAK
SQUAK
SQUAK
...?
HEY, WHAT'S THE MATTER?
HUH?
THAT'S STRANGE...
IT HURT SO MUCH BEFORE...
...BUT IT JUST GOT BETTER ALL OF A SUDDEN...
...WHAT?

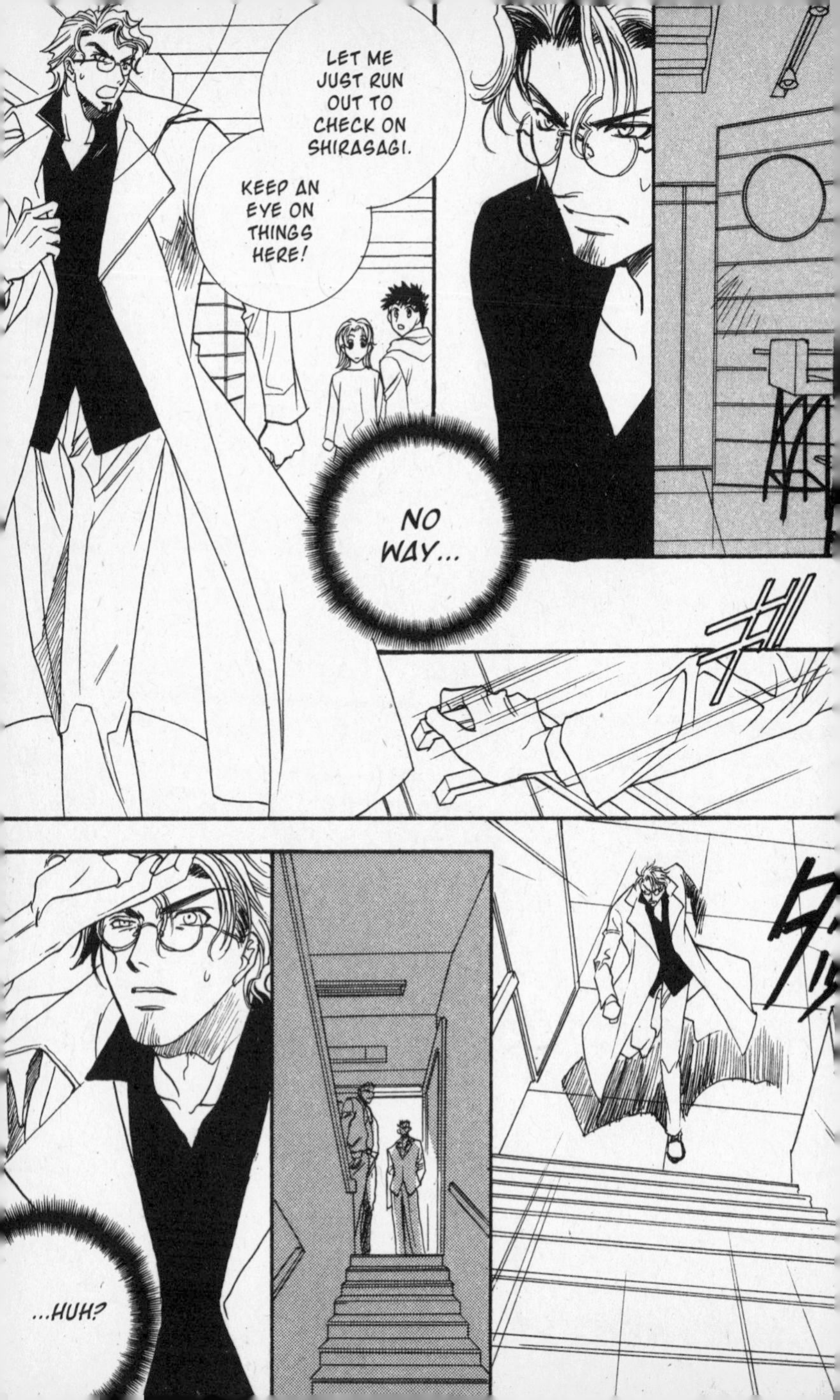
LET ME JUST RUN OUT TO CHECK ON SHIRASAGI.
KEEP AN EYE ON THINGS HERE!
NO WAY...
...HUH?

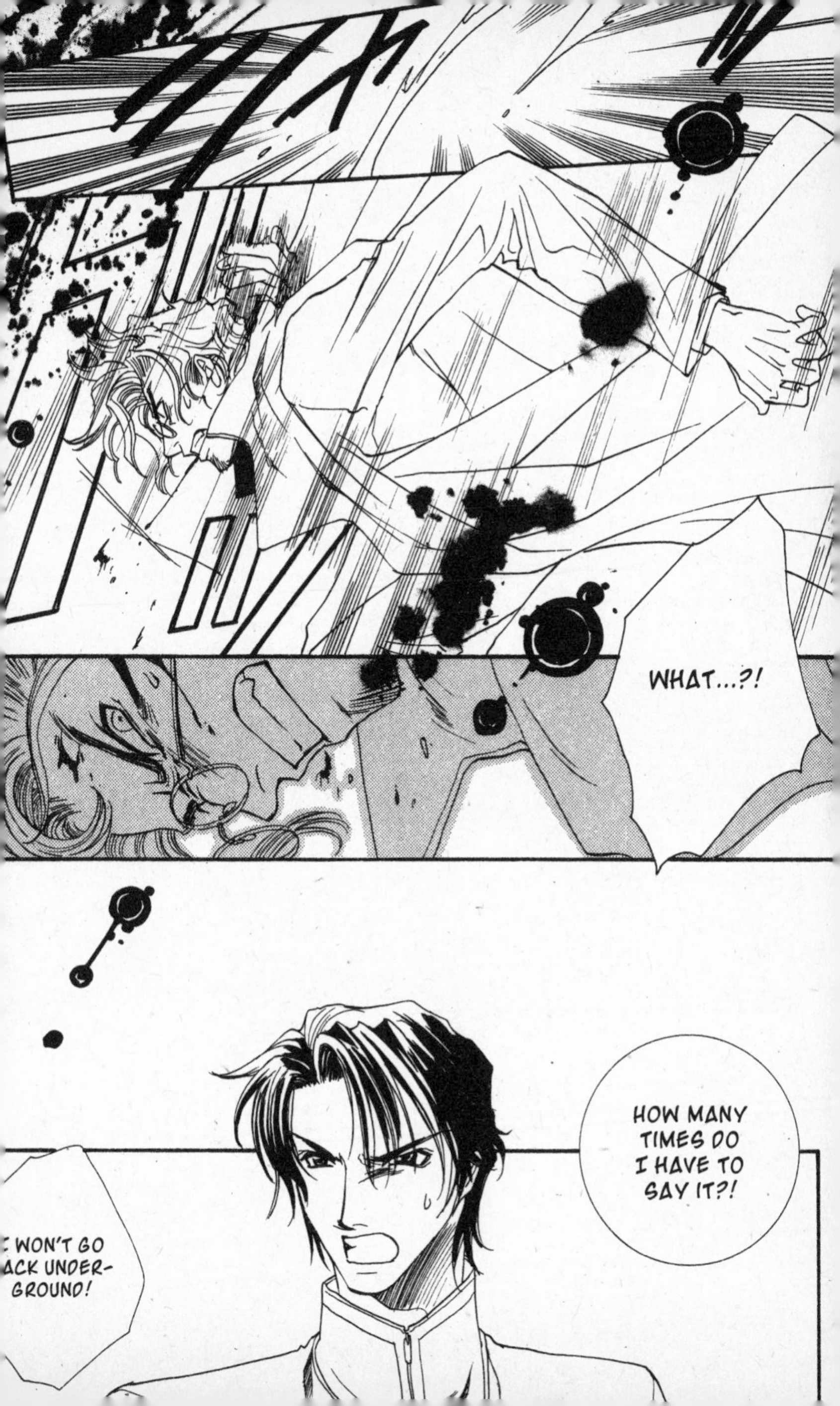
WHAT...?!
HOW MANY TIMES DO I HAVE TO SAY IT?!
WON'T GO ACK UNDER-GROUND!

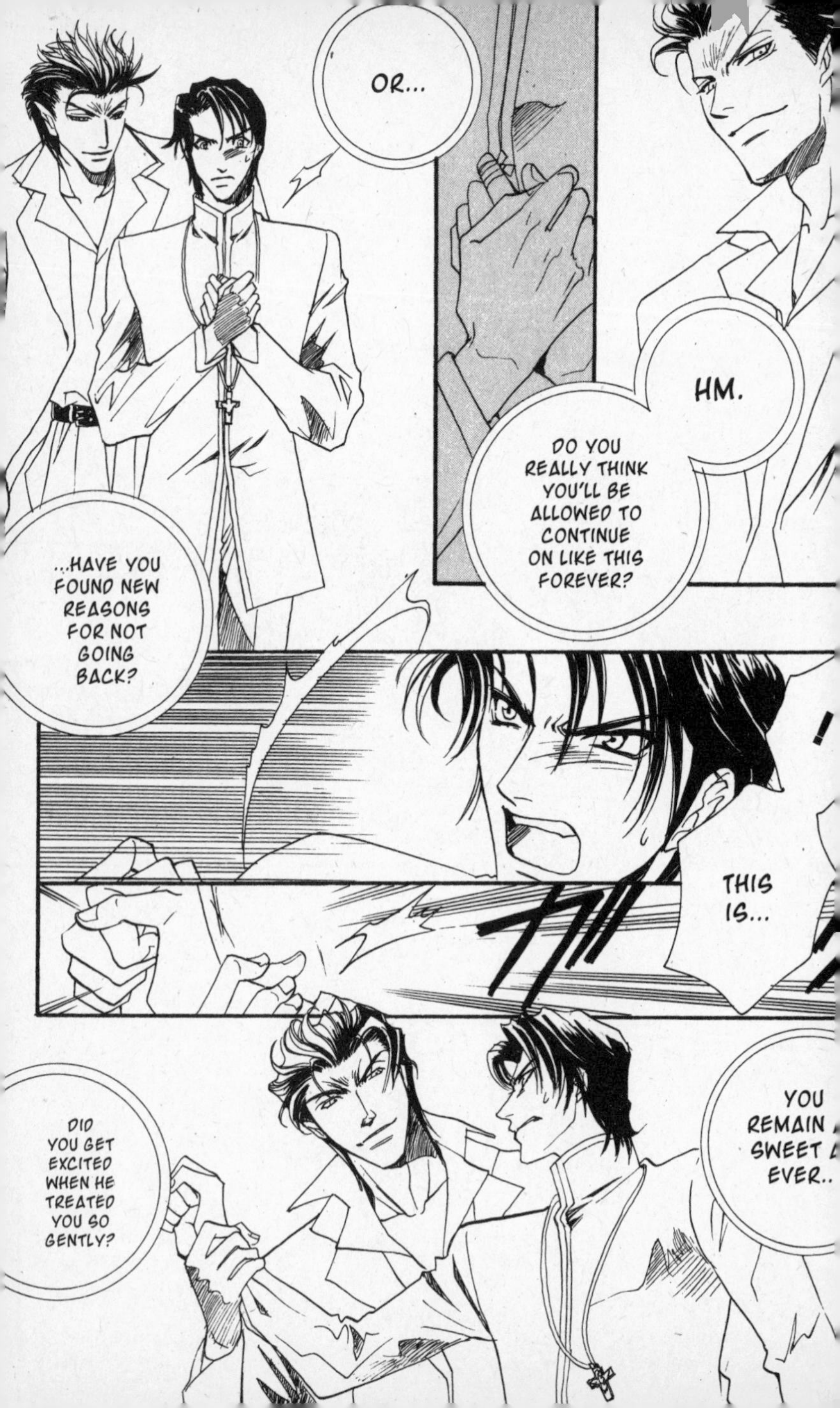
HM.
DO YOU REALLY THINK YOU'LL BE ALLOWED TO CONTINUE ON LIKE THIS FOREVER?
OR...
...HAVE YOU FOUND NEW REASONS FOR NOT GOING BACK?
!
THIS IS...
YOU REMAIN SWEET EVER..
DID YOU GET EXCITED WHEN HE TREATED YOU SO GENTLY?

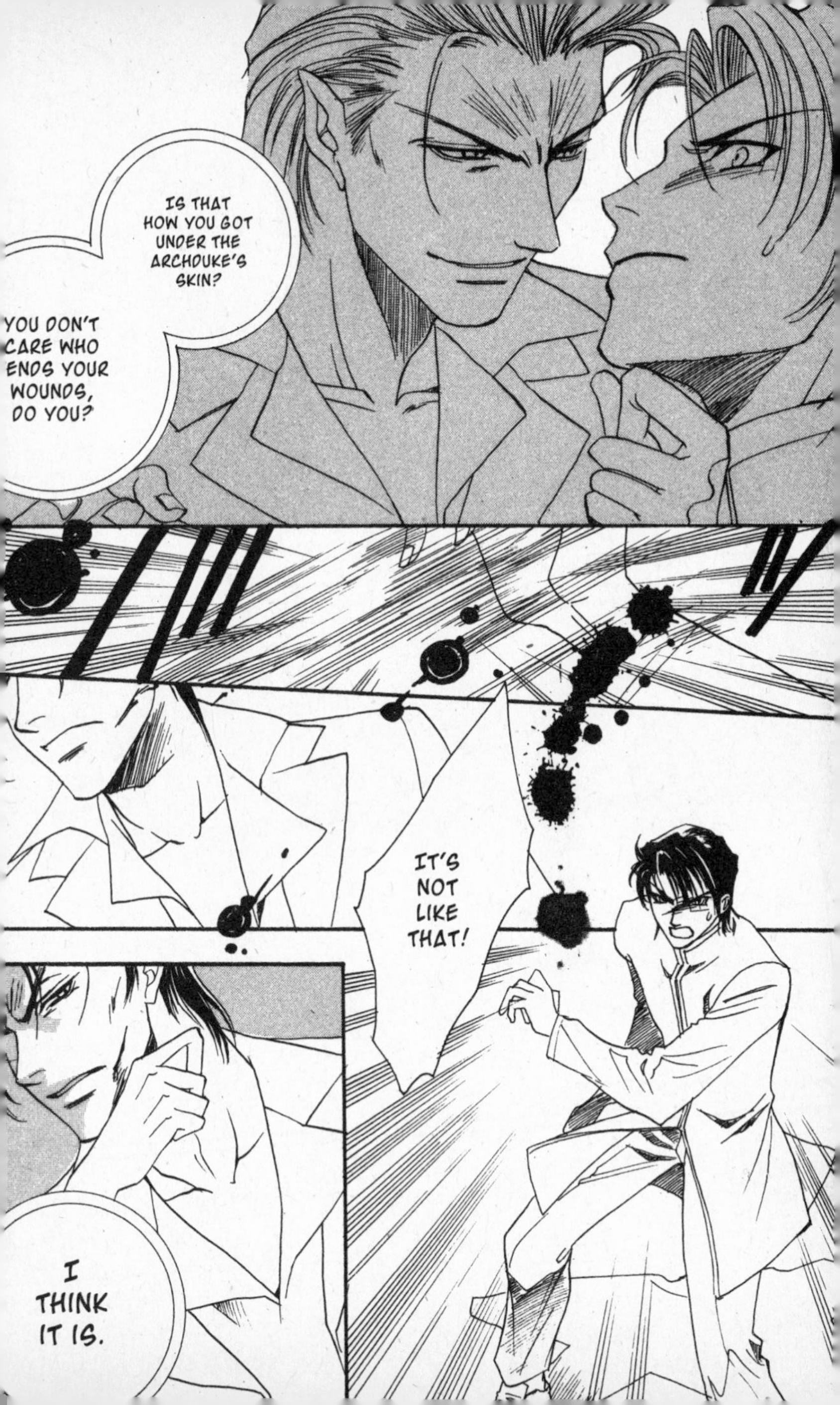
IS THAT HOW YOU GOT UNDER THE ARCHDUKE'S SKIN?
YOU DON'T CARE WHO ENDS YOUR WOUNDS, DO YOU?
IT'S NOT LIKE THAT!
I THINK IT IS.

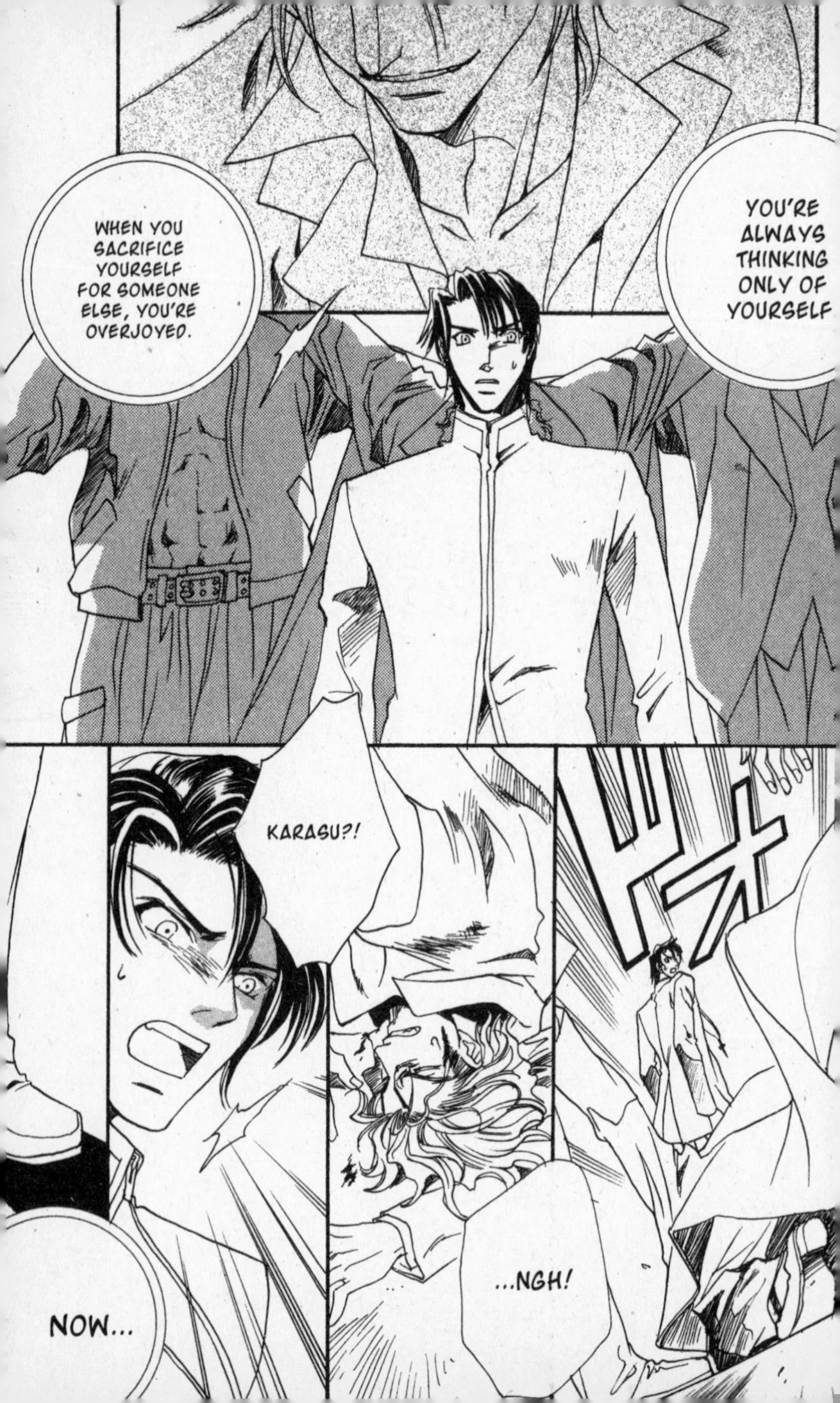
YOU'RE ALWAYS THINKING ONLY OF YOURSELF
WHEN YOU SACRIFICE YOURSELF FOR SOMEONE ELSE, YOU'RE OVERJOYED.
...NGH!
KARASU?!
NOW...

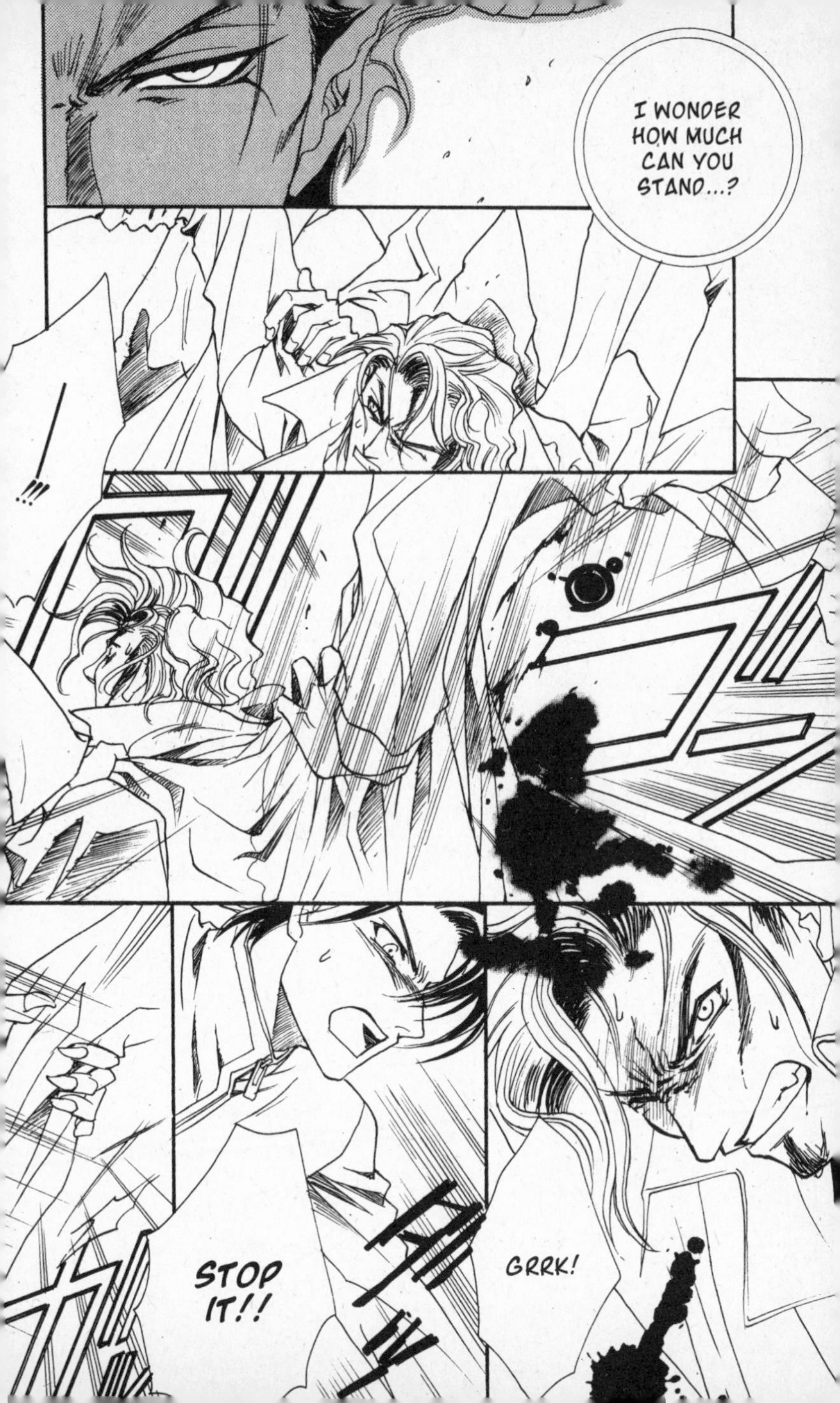
I WONDER HOW MUCH CAN YOU STAND...?
!!!
GRRK!
STOP IT!!

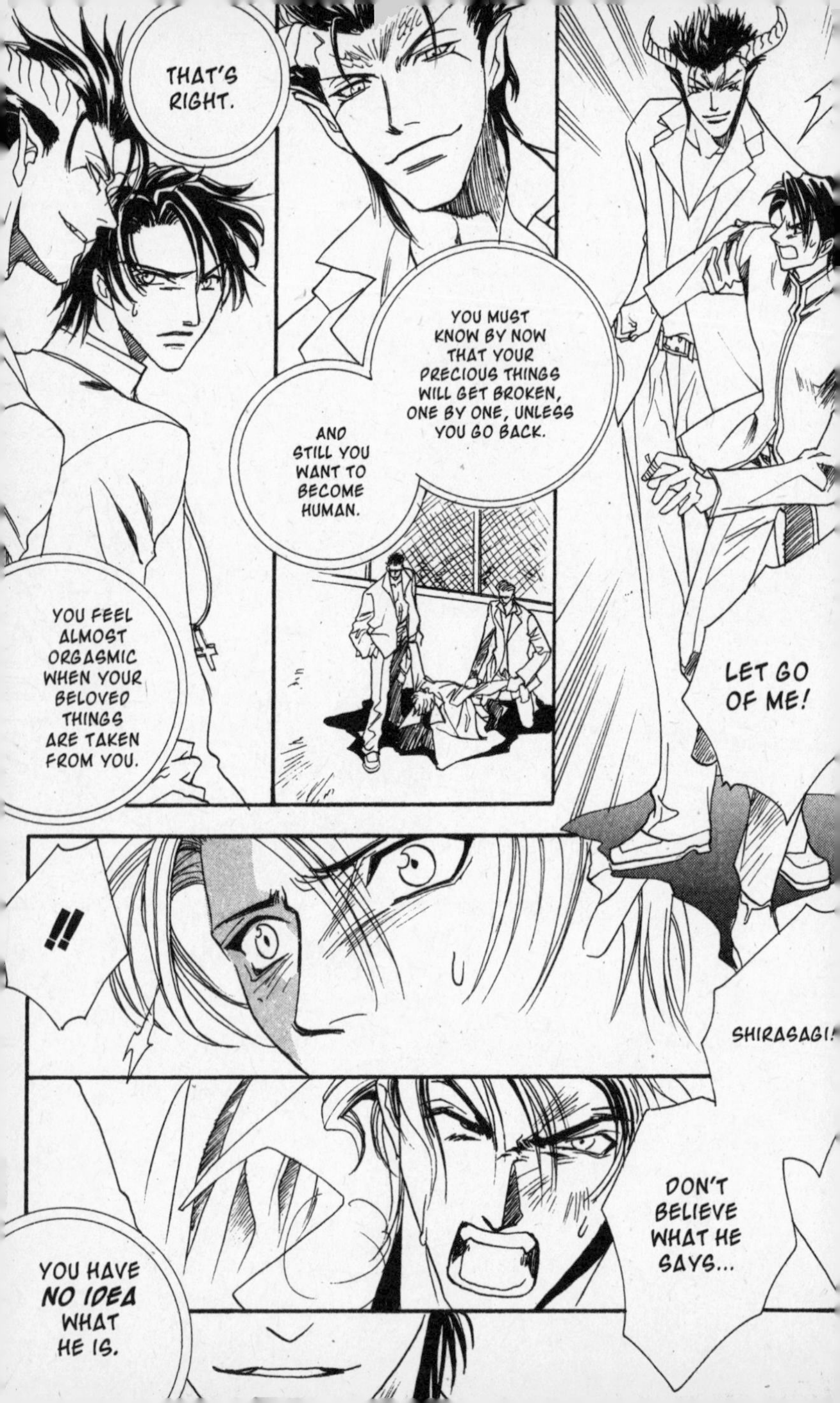
LET GO OF ME!
SHIRASAGI!
YOU MUST KNOW BY NOW THAT YOUR PRECIOUS THINGS WILL GET BROKEN, ONE BY ONE, UNLESS YOU GO BACK.
AND STILL YOU WANT TO BECOME HUMAN.
THAT'S RIGHT.
YOU FEEL ALMOST ORGASMIC WHEN YOUR BELOVED THINGS ARE TAKEN FROM YOU.
!!
DON'T BELIEVE WHAT HE SAYS...
YOU HAVE **NO IDEA** WHAT HE IS.

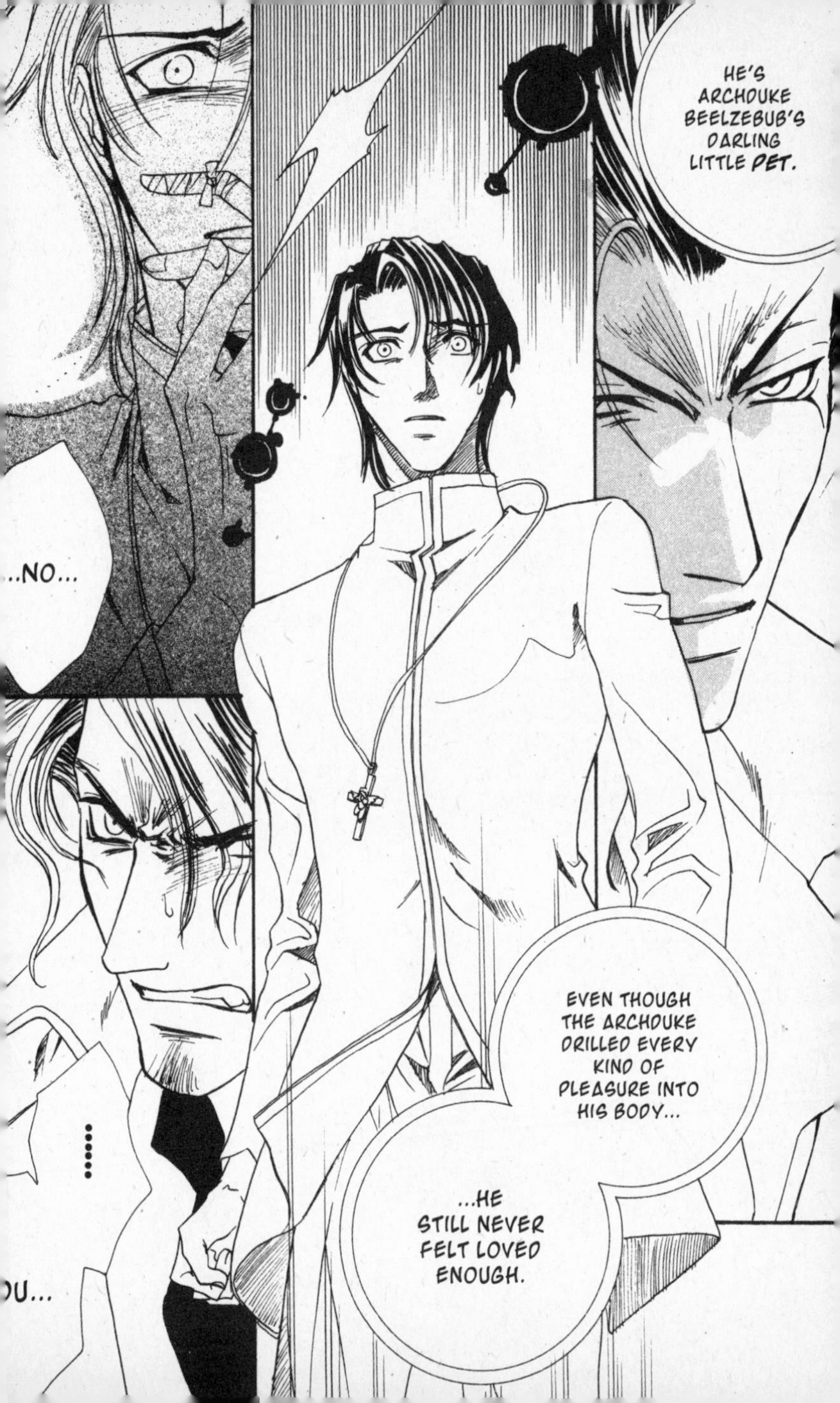
HE'S ARCHDUKE BEELZEBUB'S DARLING LITTLE PET.
EVEN THOUGH THE ARCHDUKE DRILLED EVERY KIND OF PLEASURE INTO HIS BODY...
...HE STILL NEVER FELT LOVED ENOUGH.
..NO...
......
OU...

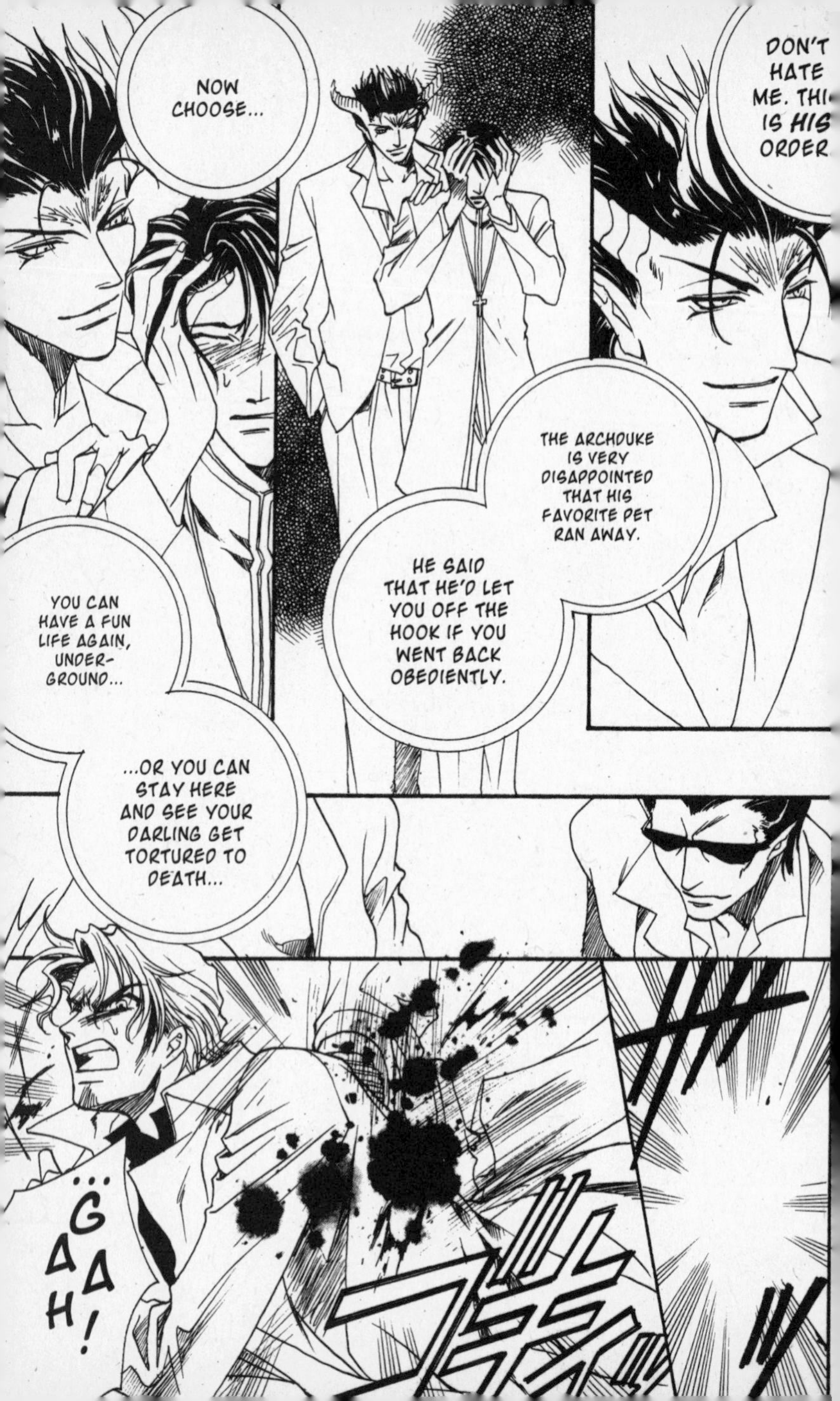
DON'T HATE ME. THI IS HIS ORDER
THE ARCHDUKE IS VERY DISAPPOINTED THAT HIS FAVORITE PET RAN AWAY.
HE SAID THAT HE'D LET YOU OFF THE HOOK IF YOU WENT BACK OBEDIENTLY.
NOW CHOOSE...
YOU CAN HAVE A FUN LIFE AGAIN, UNDER-GROUND...
...OR YOU CAN STAY HERE AND SEE YOUR DARLING GET TORTURED TO DEATH...
...GAAH!

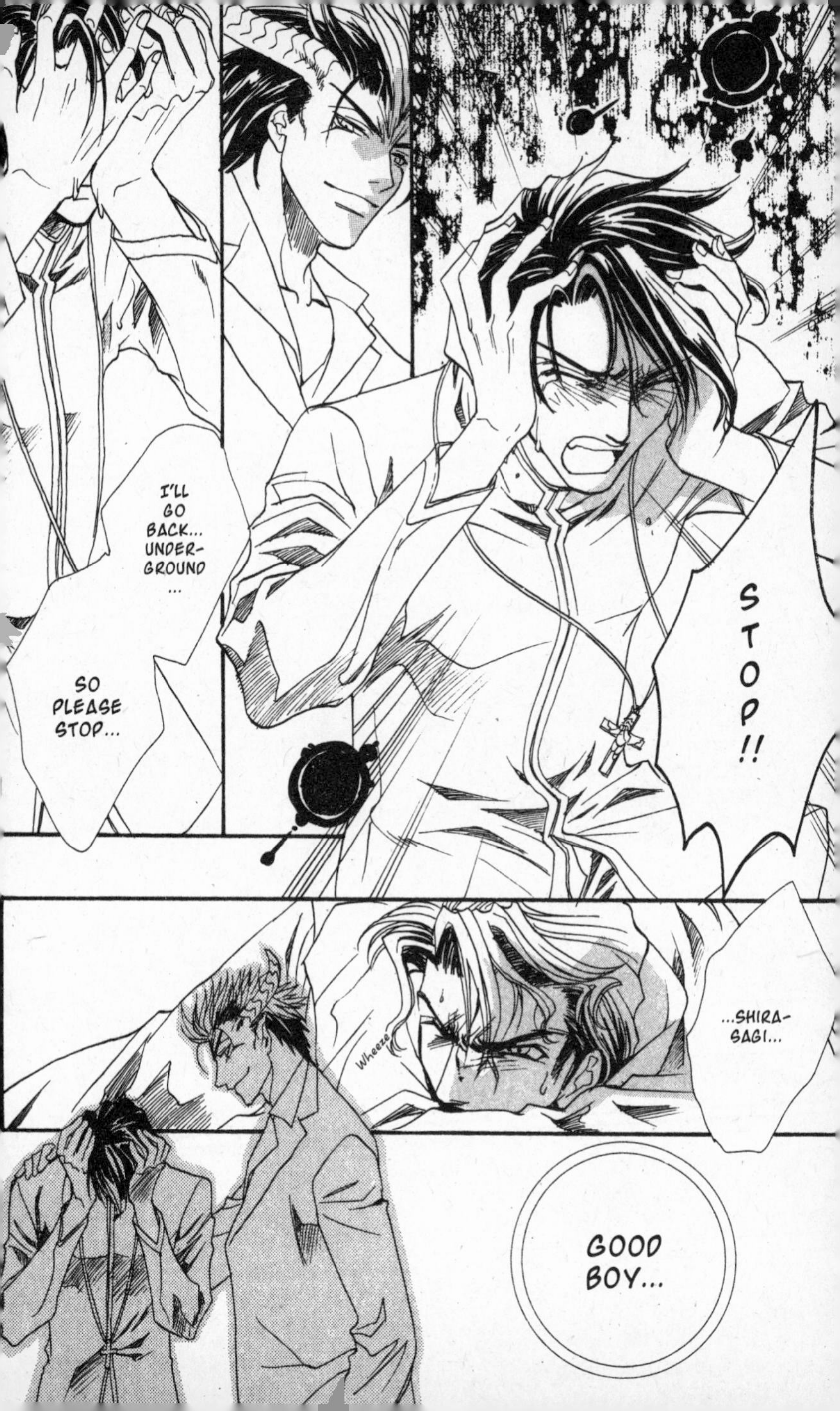
STOP!!
I'LL GO BACK... UNDER-GROUND...
SO PLEASE STOP...
Wheeze
...SHIRA-SAGI...
GOOD BOY...

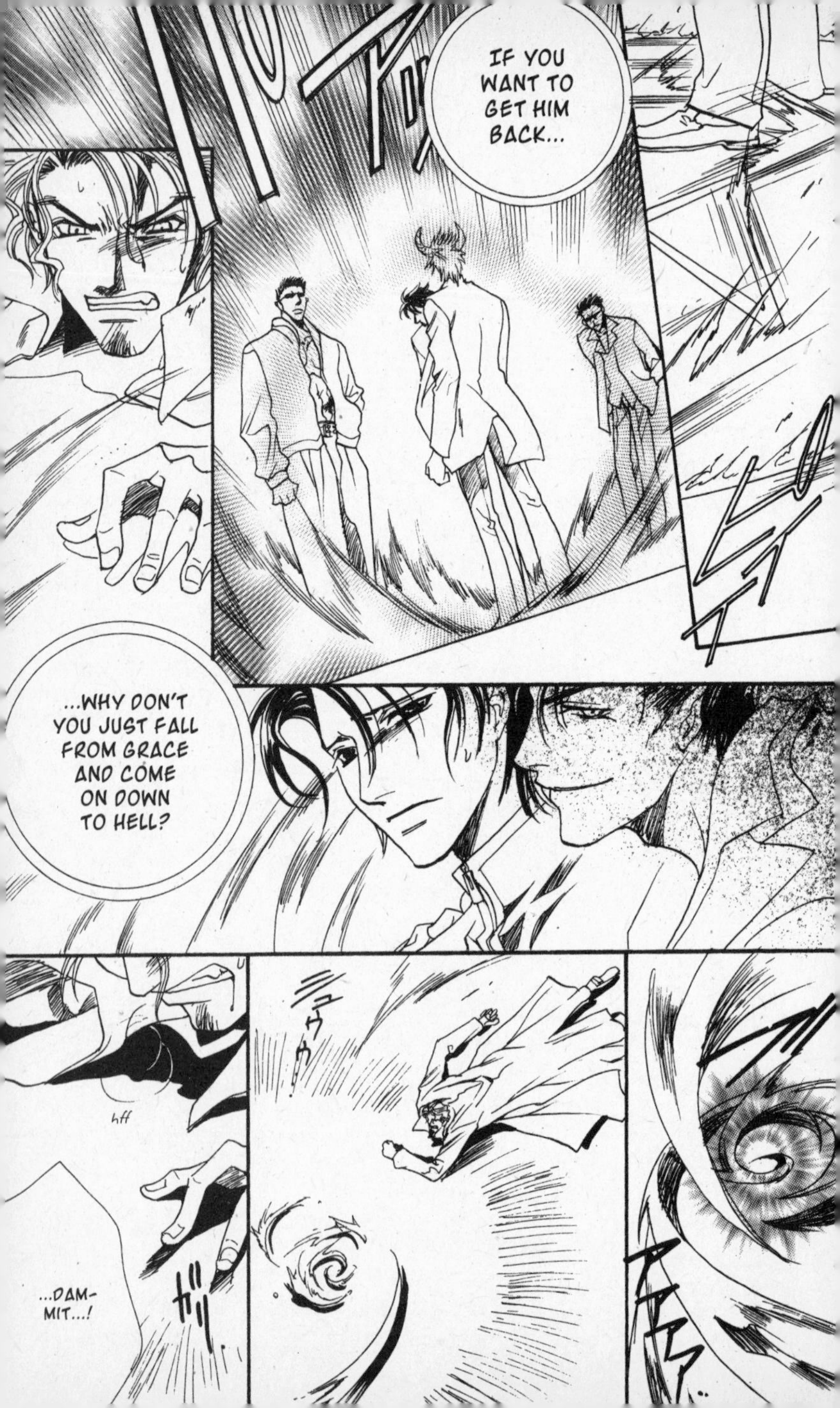
IF YOU WANT TO GET HIM BACK...
...WHY DON'T YOU JUST FALL FROM GRACE AND COME ON DOWN TO HELL?
hff
...DAM-
MIT...!

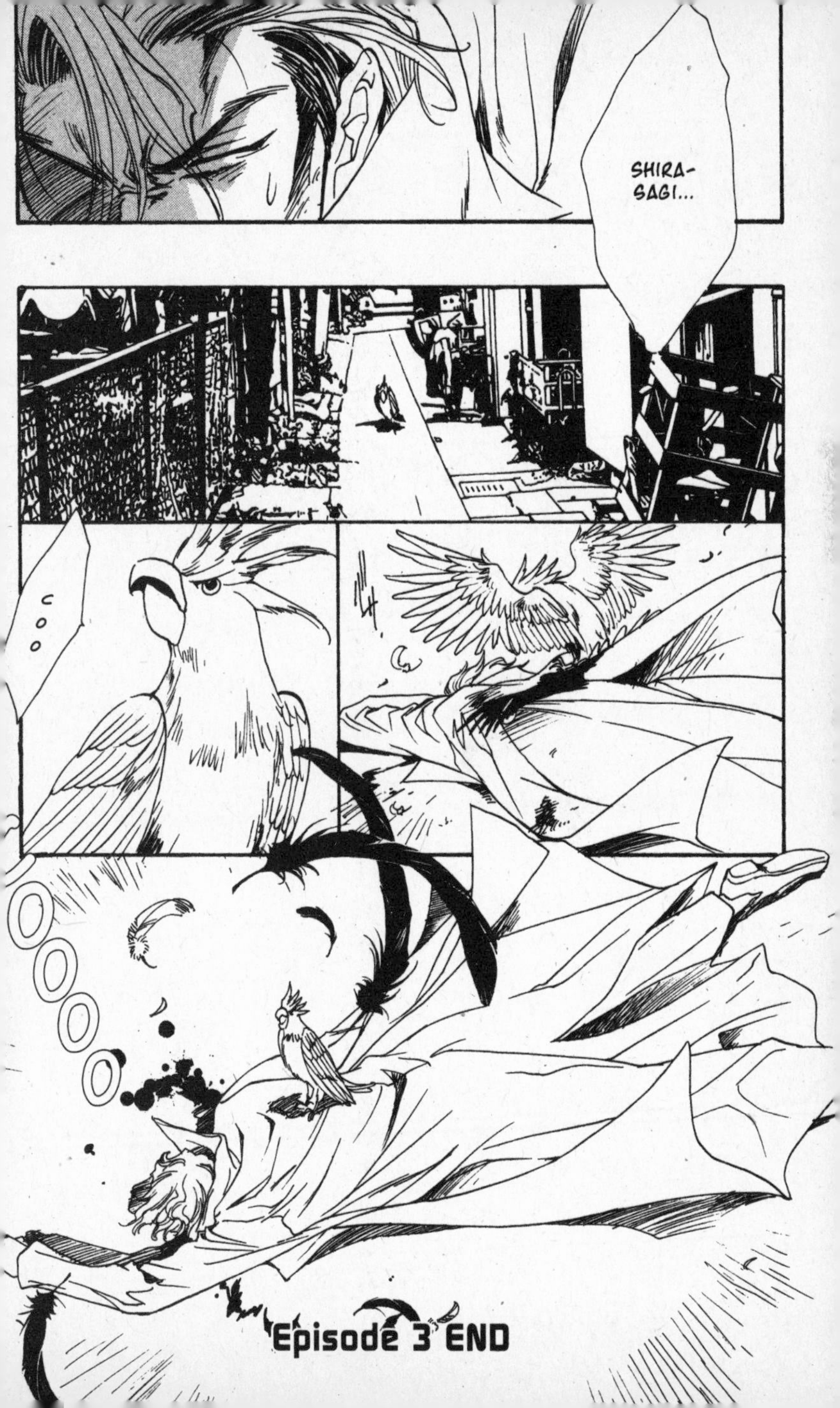
SHIRA-
SAGI...
...
Episode 3 END

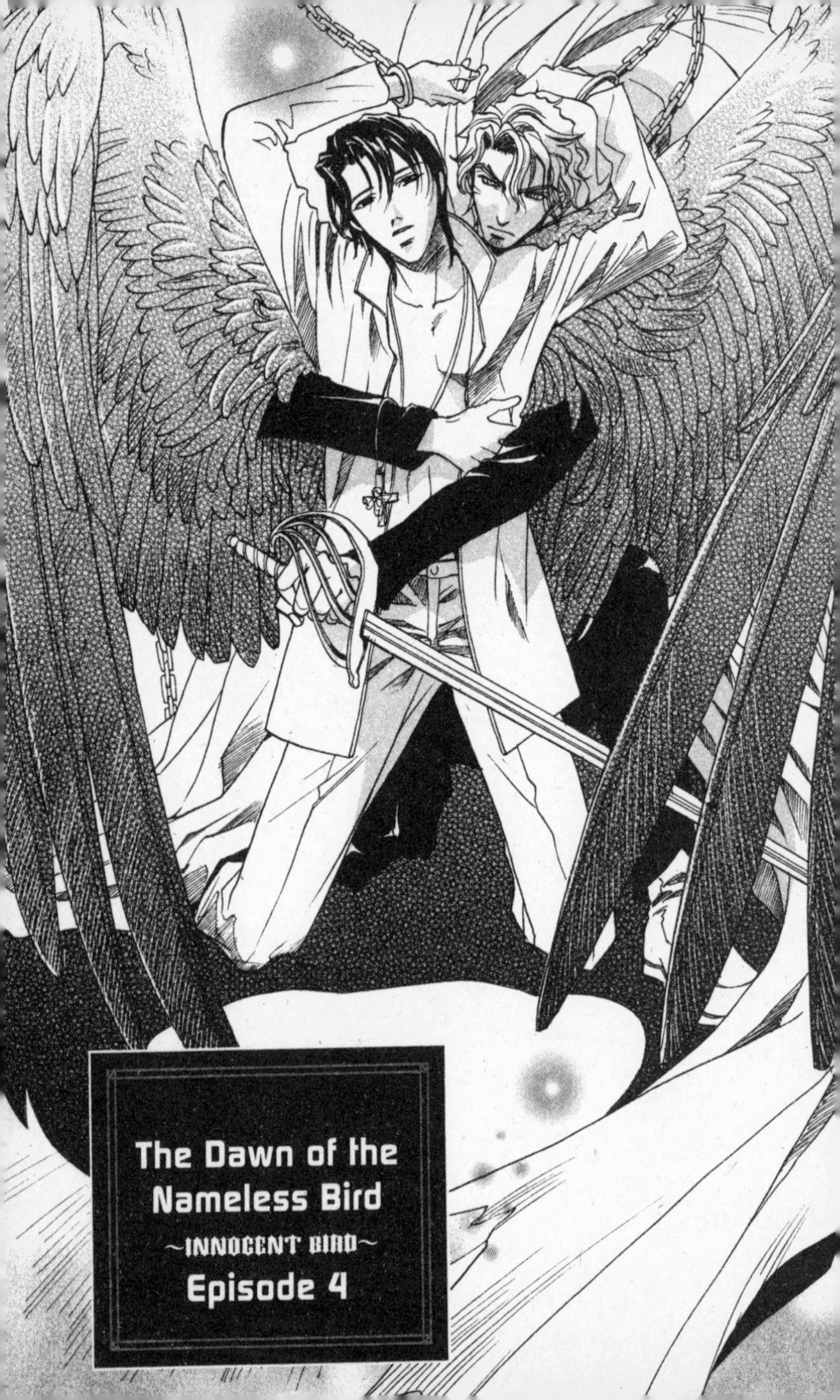

The Dawn of the
Nameless Bird
~INNOCENT BIRD~
Episode 4

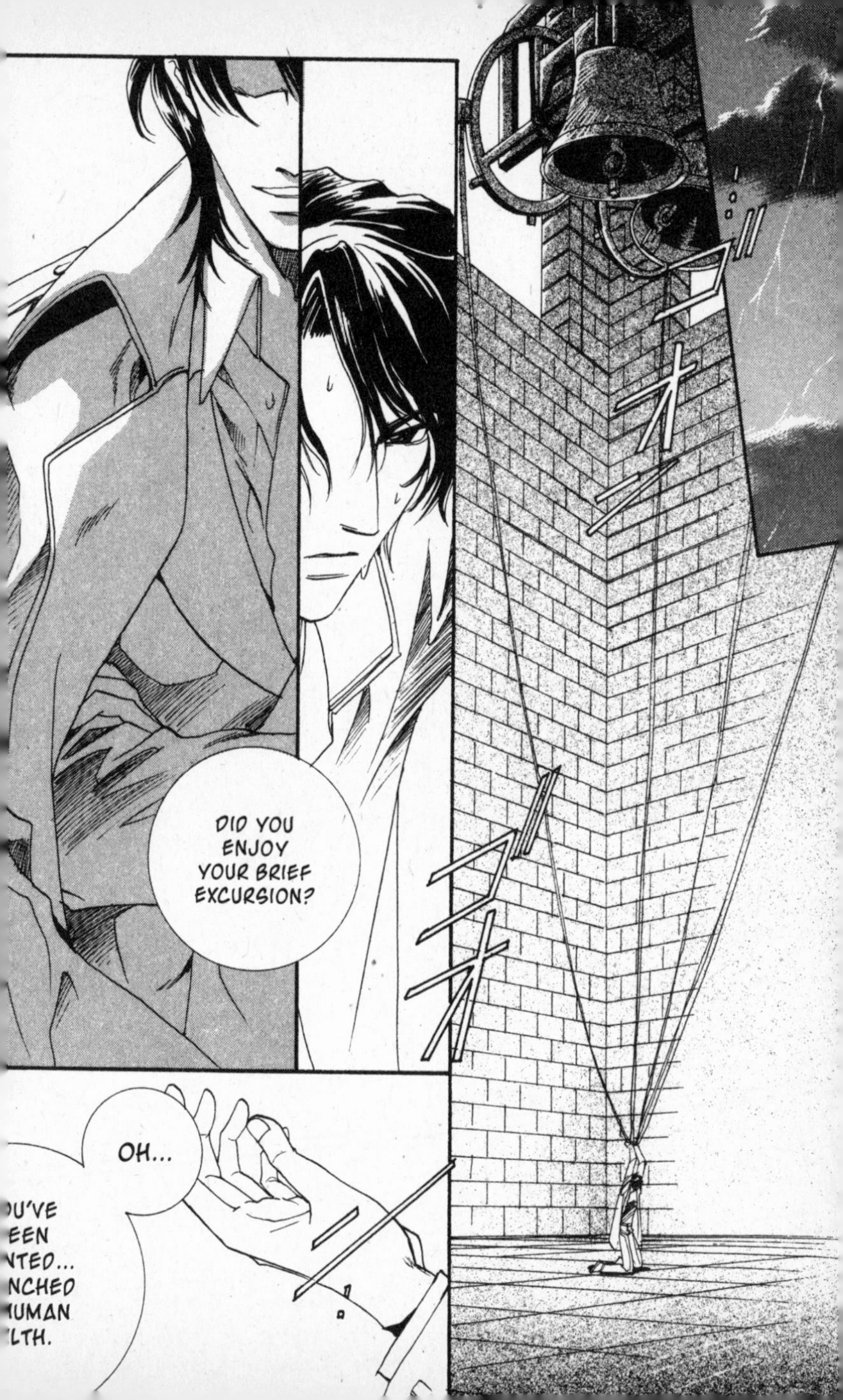
DID YOU ENJOY YOUR BRIEF EXCURSION?
OH...

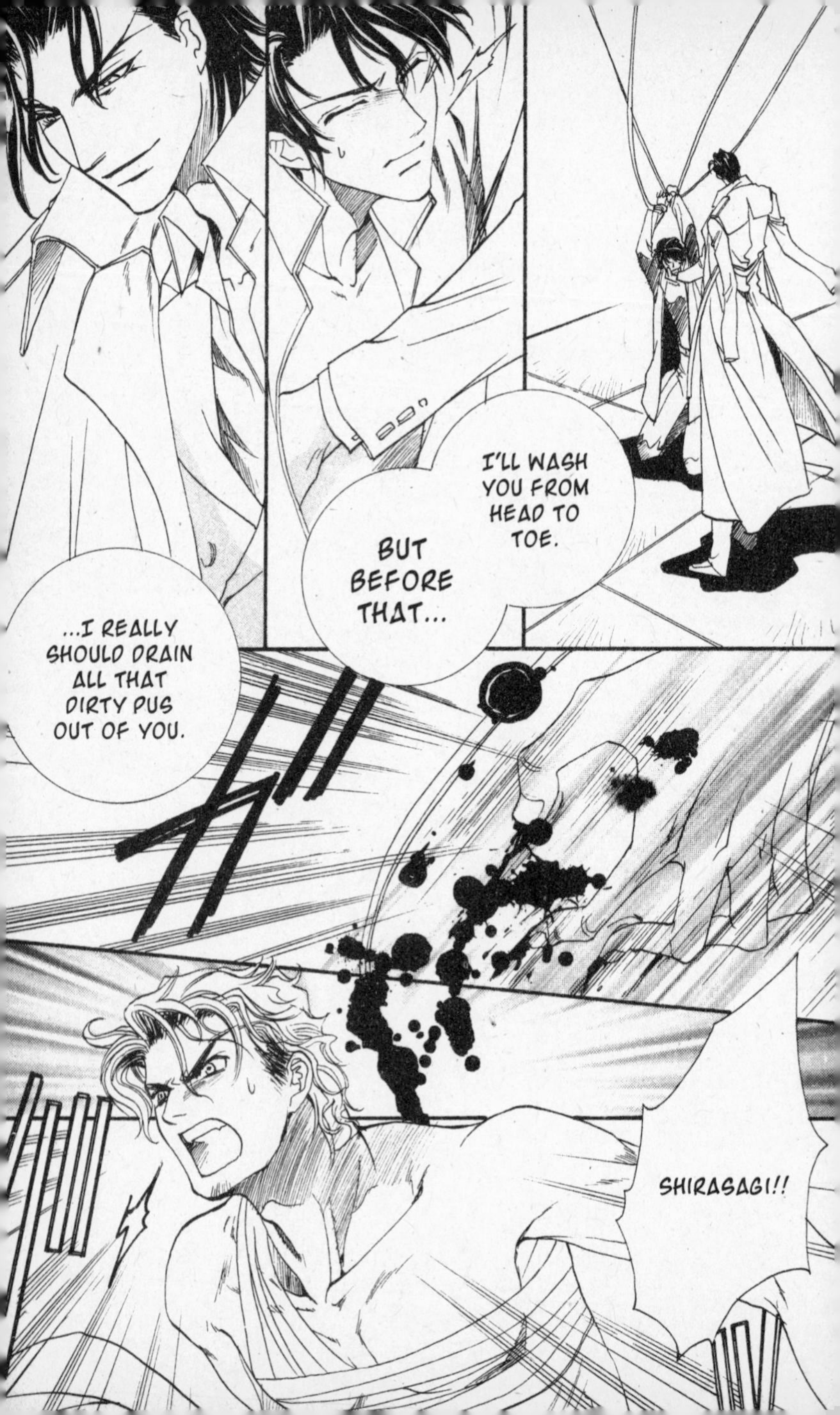
I'LL WASH YOU FROM HEAD TO TOE.
BUT BEFORE THAT...
...I REALLY SHOULD DRAIN ALL THAT DIRTY PUS OUT OF YOU.
SHIRASAGI!!

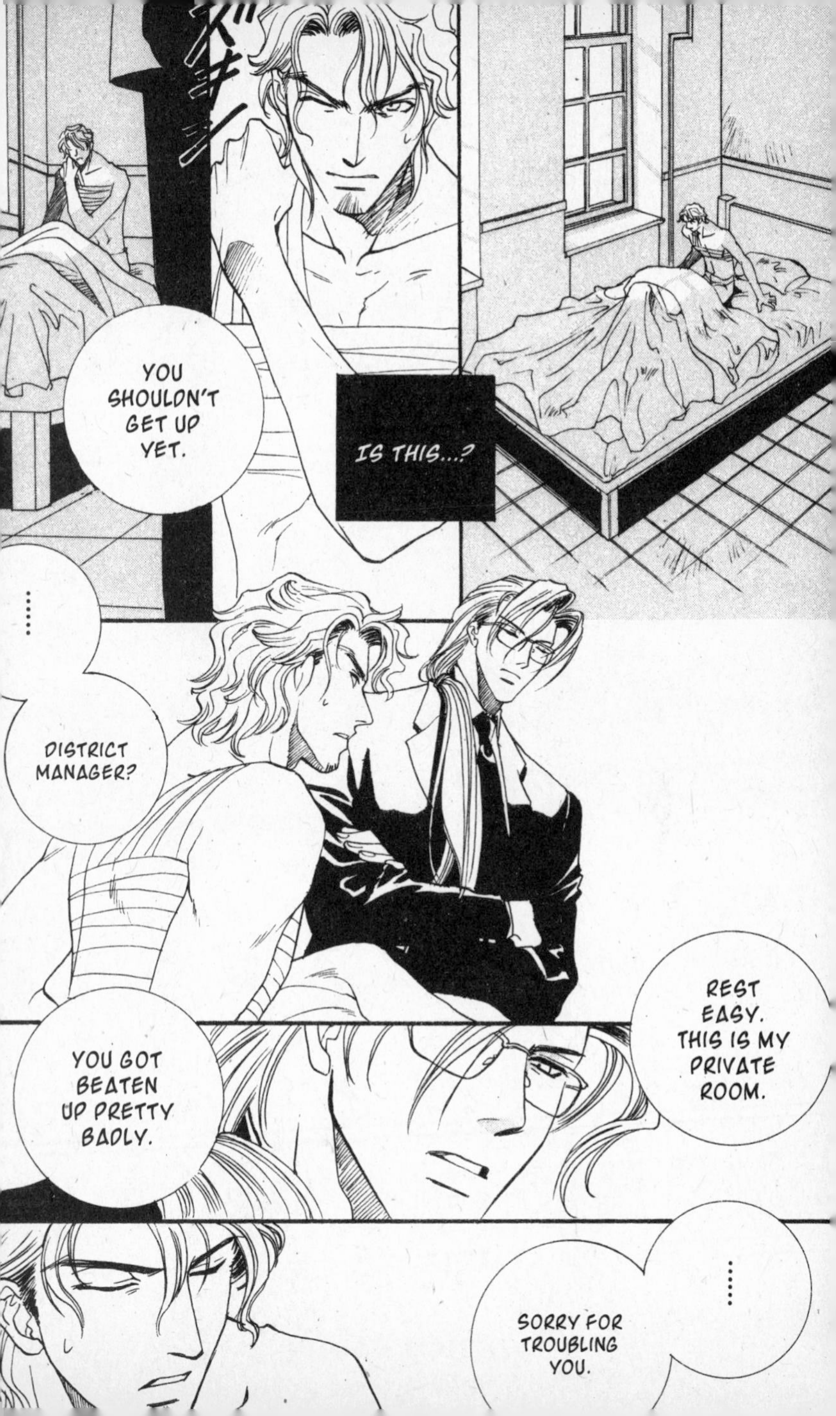
IS THIS...?
YOU SHOULDN'T GET UP YET.
......
DISTRICT MANAGER?
REST EASY. THIS IS MY PRIVATE ROOM.
YOU GOT BEATEN UP PRETTY BADLY.
......
SORRY FOR TROUBLING YOU.

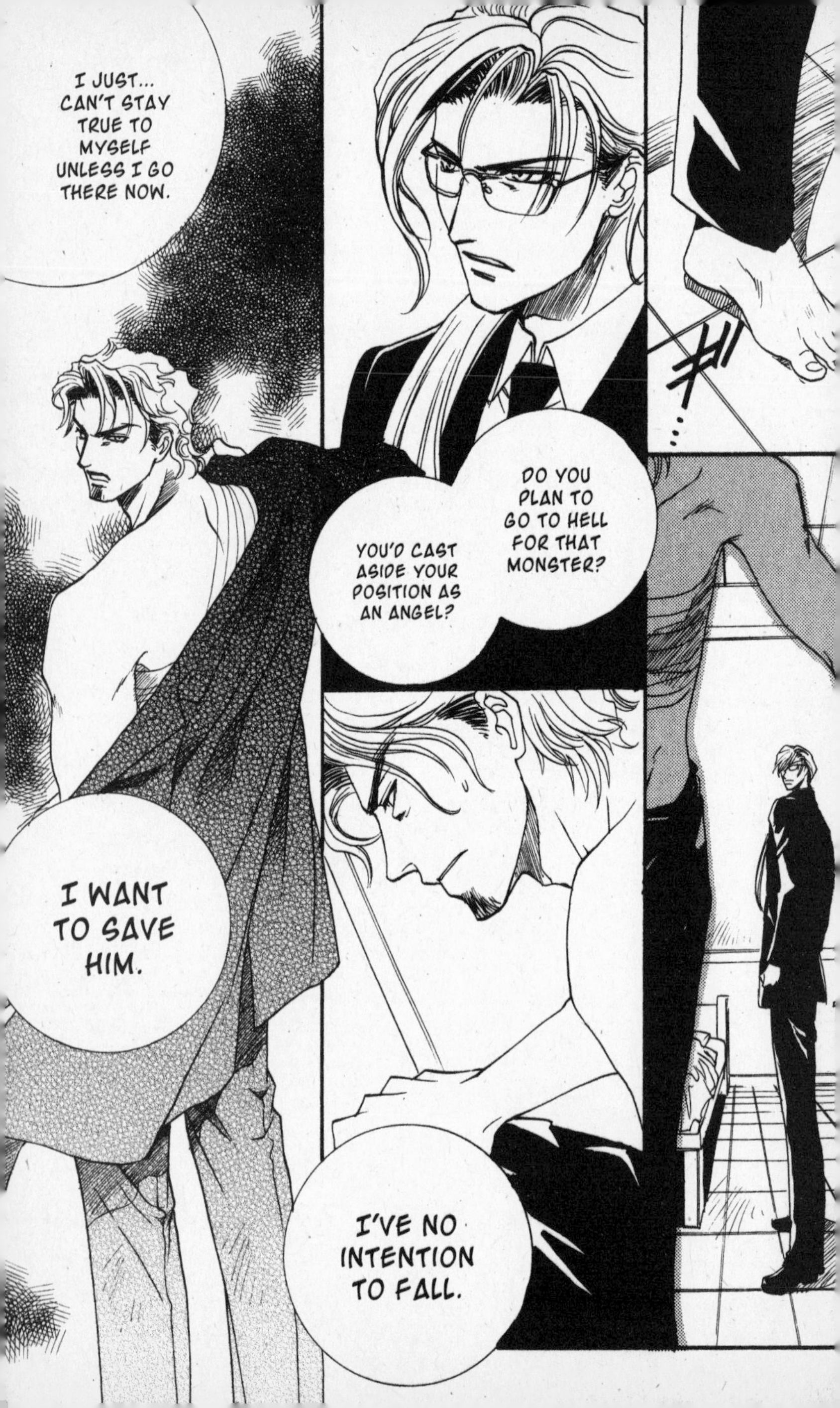
DO YOU PLAN TO GO TO HELL FOR THAT MONSTER?
YOU'D CAST ASIDE YOUR POSITION AS AN ANGEL?
I'VE NO INTENTION TO FALL.
I JUST... CAN'T STAY TRUE TO MYSELF UNLESS I GO THERE NOW.
I WANT TO SAVE HIM.

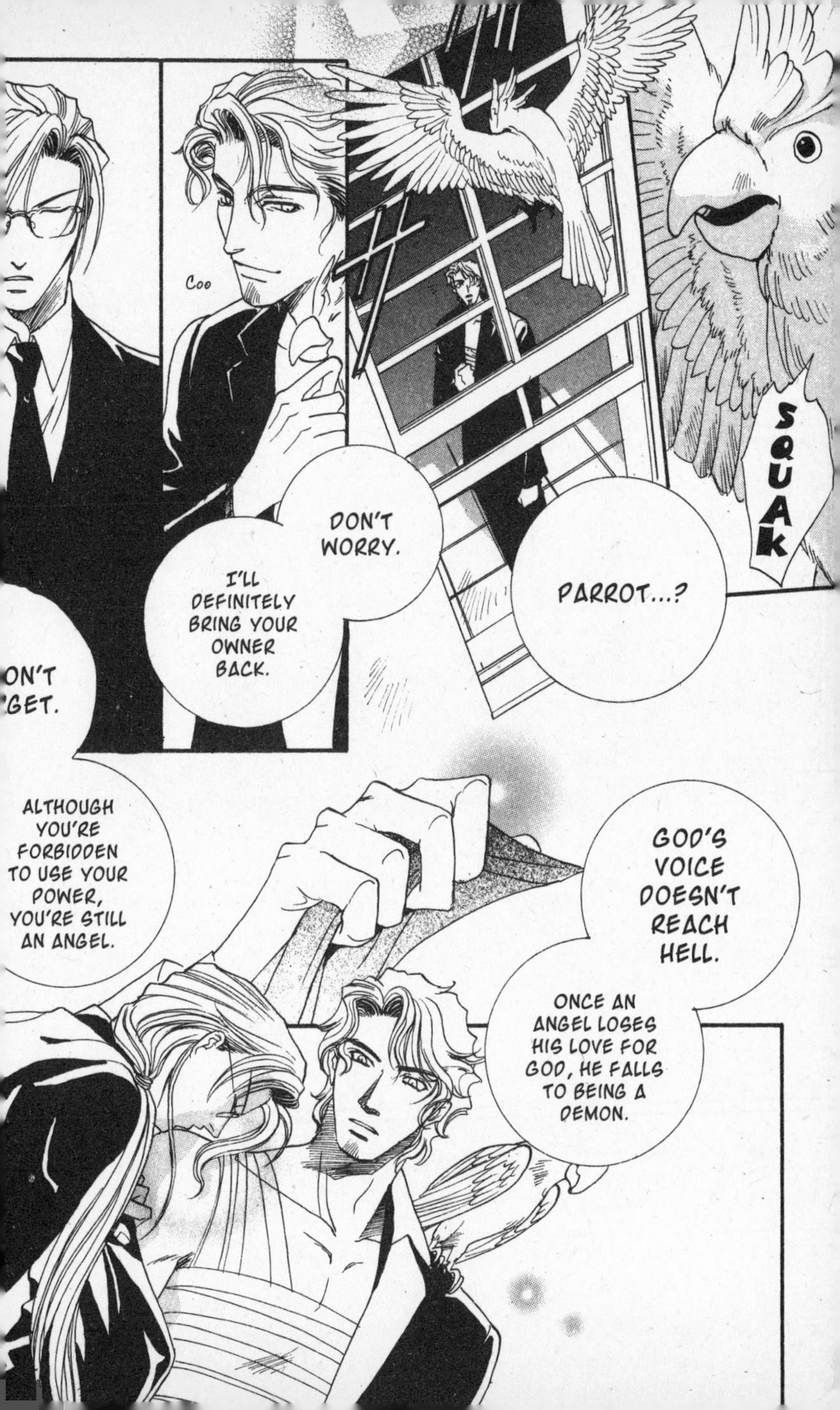
SQUAK
PARROT...?
DON'T WORRY.
Coo
I'LL DEFINITELY BRING YOUR OWNER BACK.
ON'T GET.
GOD'S VOICE DOESN'T REACH HELL.
ONCE AN ANGEL LOSES HIS LOVE FOR GOD, HE FALLS TO BEING A DEMON.
ALTHOUGH YOU'RE FORBIDDEN TO USE YOUR POWER, YOU'RE STILL AN ANGEL.

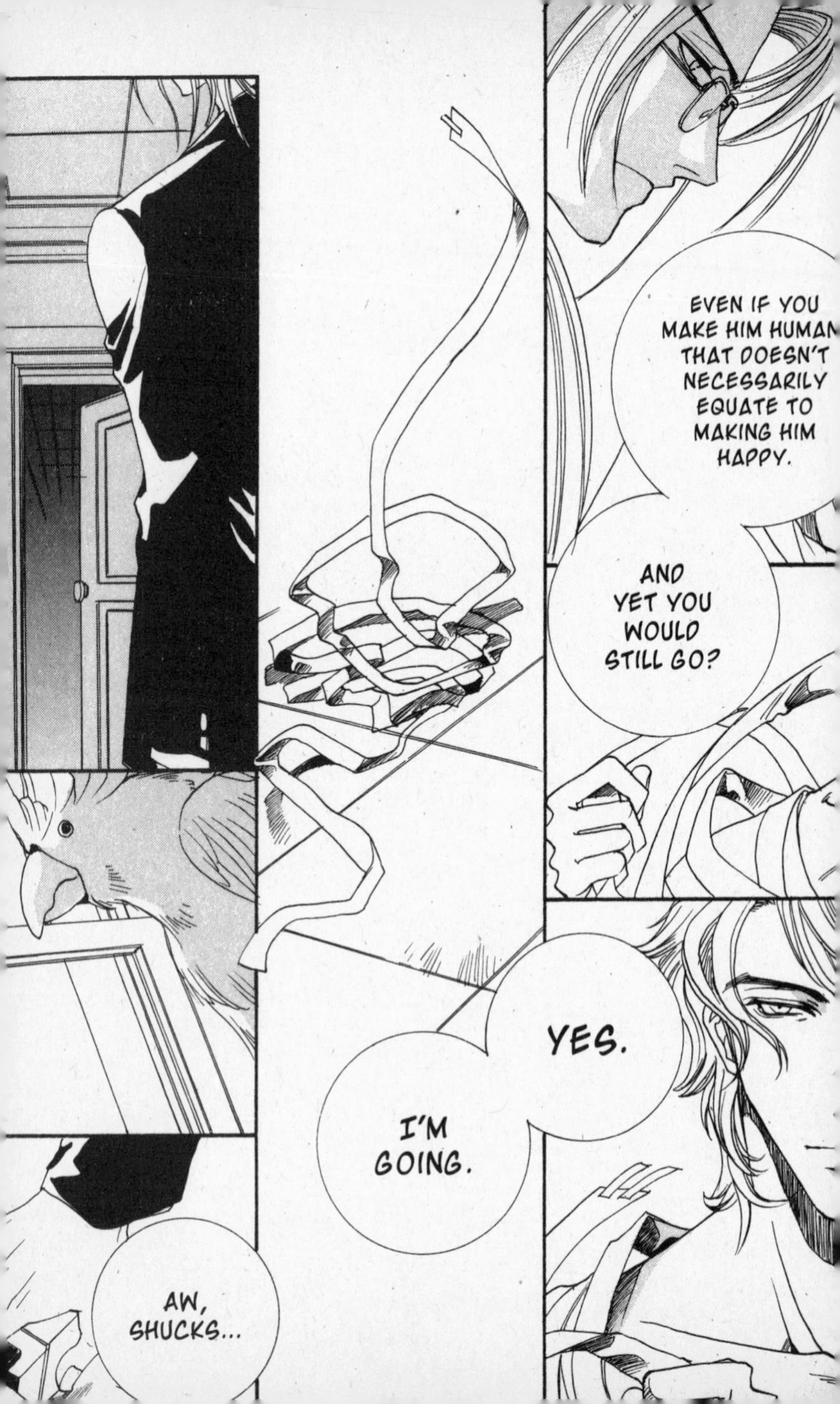
EVEN IF YOU MAKE HIM HUMAN THAT DOESN'T NECESSARILY EQUATE TO MAKING HIM HAPPY.
AND YET YOU WOULD STILL GO?
YES.
I'M GOING.
AW, SHUCKS...

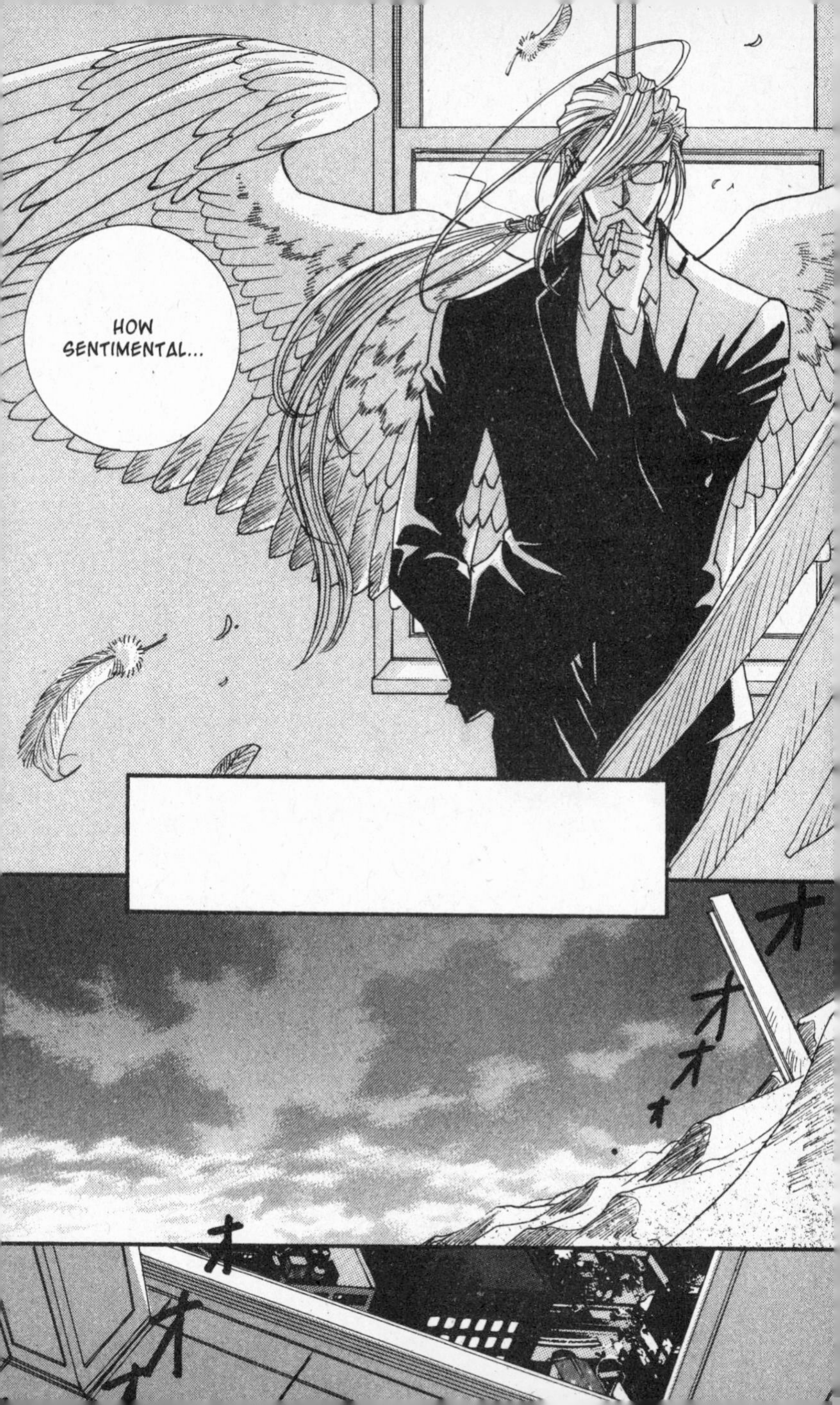

HOW SENTIMENTAL...
オオオオ
オオオ

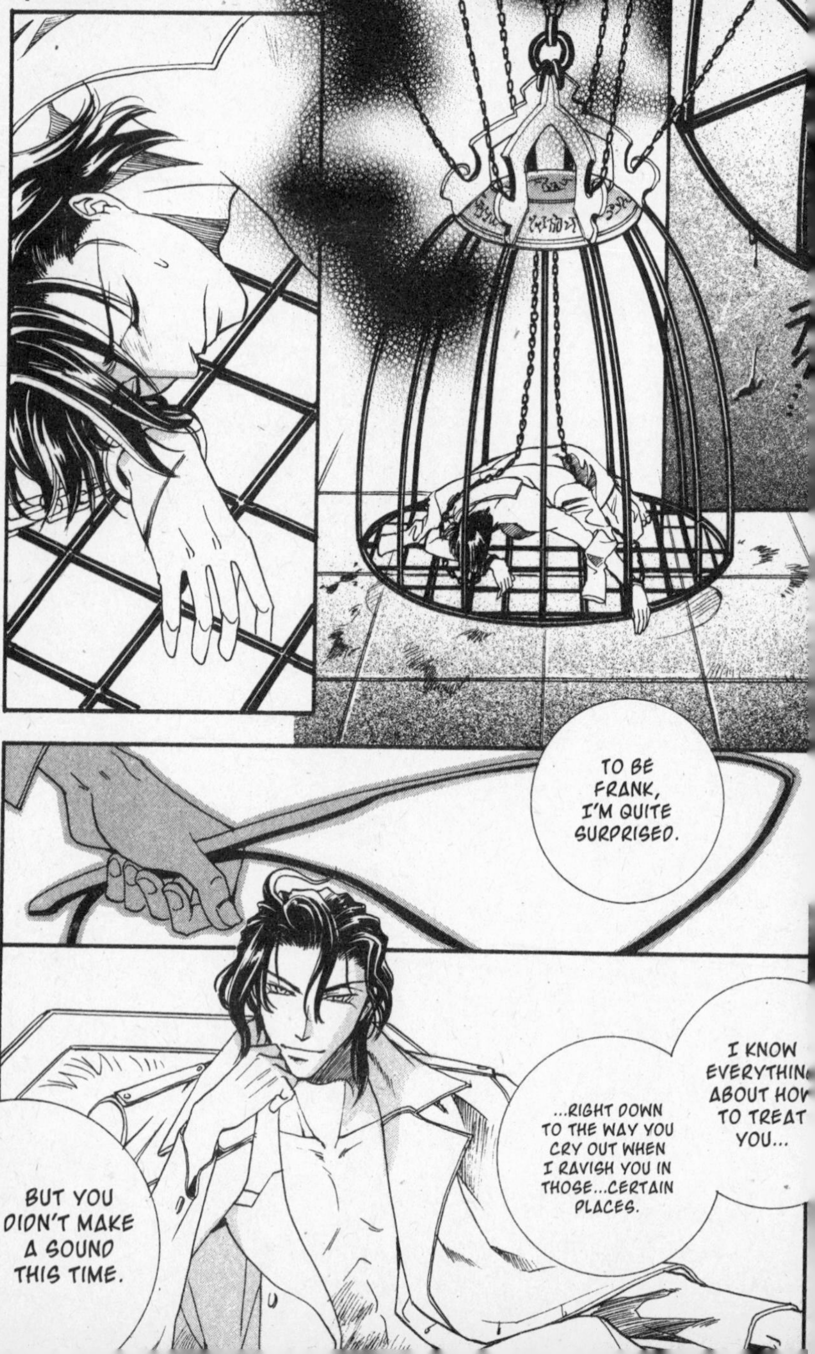
TO BE FRANK, I'M QUITE SURPRISED.
I KNOW EVERYTHIN ABOUT HOV TO TREAT YOU...
...RIGHT DOWN TO THE WAY YOU CRY OUT WHEN I RAVISH YOU IN THOSE...CERTAIN PLACES.
BUT YOU DIDN'T MAKE A SOUND THIS TIME.

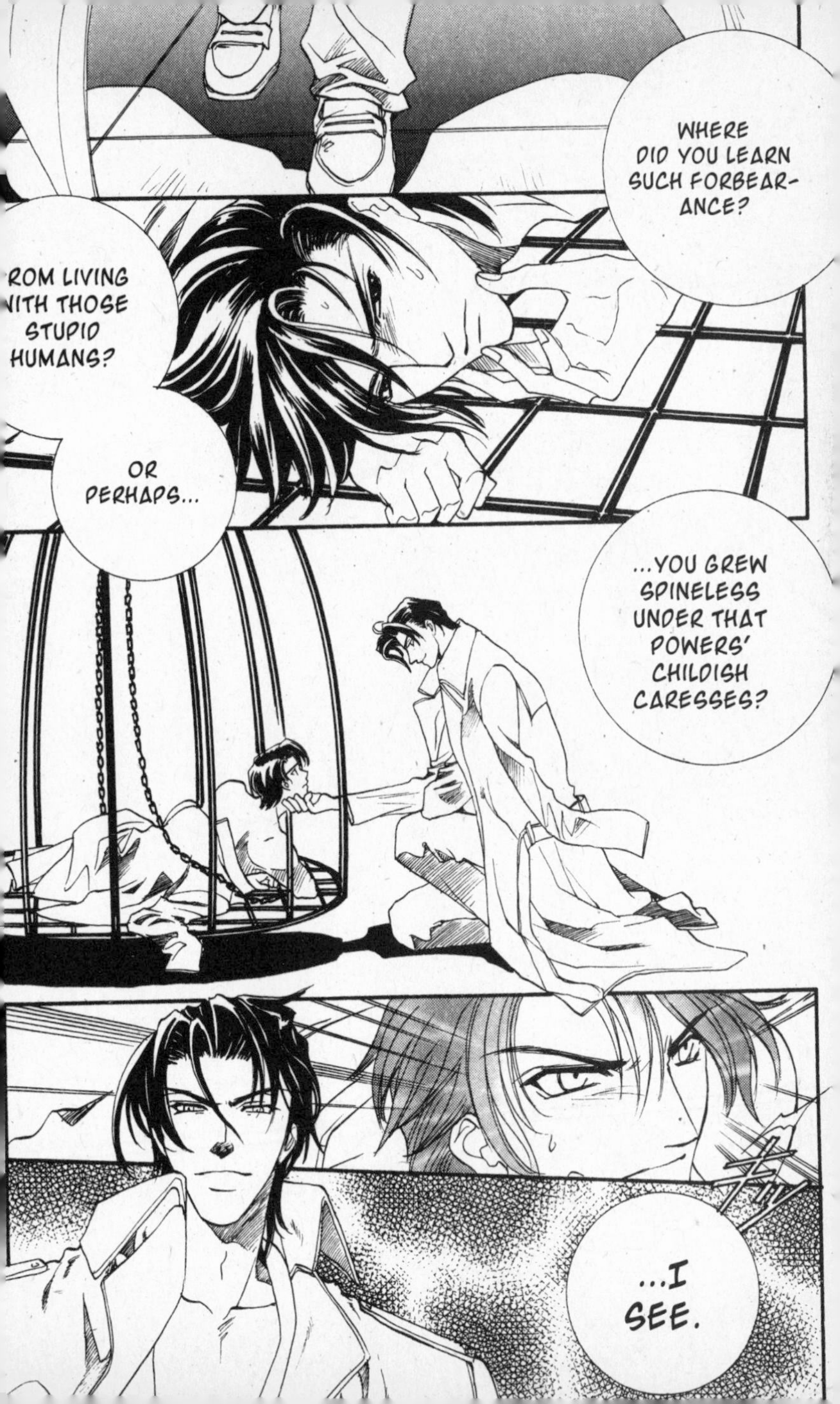
WHERE DID YOU LEARN SUCH FORBEAR-ANCE?
ROM LIVING ITH THOSE STUPID HUMANS?
OR PERHAPS...
...YOU GREW SPINELESS UNDER THAT POWERS' CHILDISH CARESSES?
...I SEE.

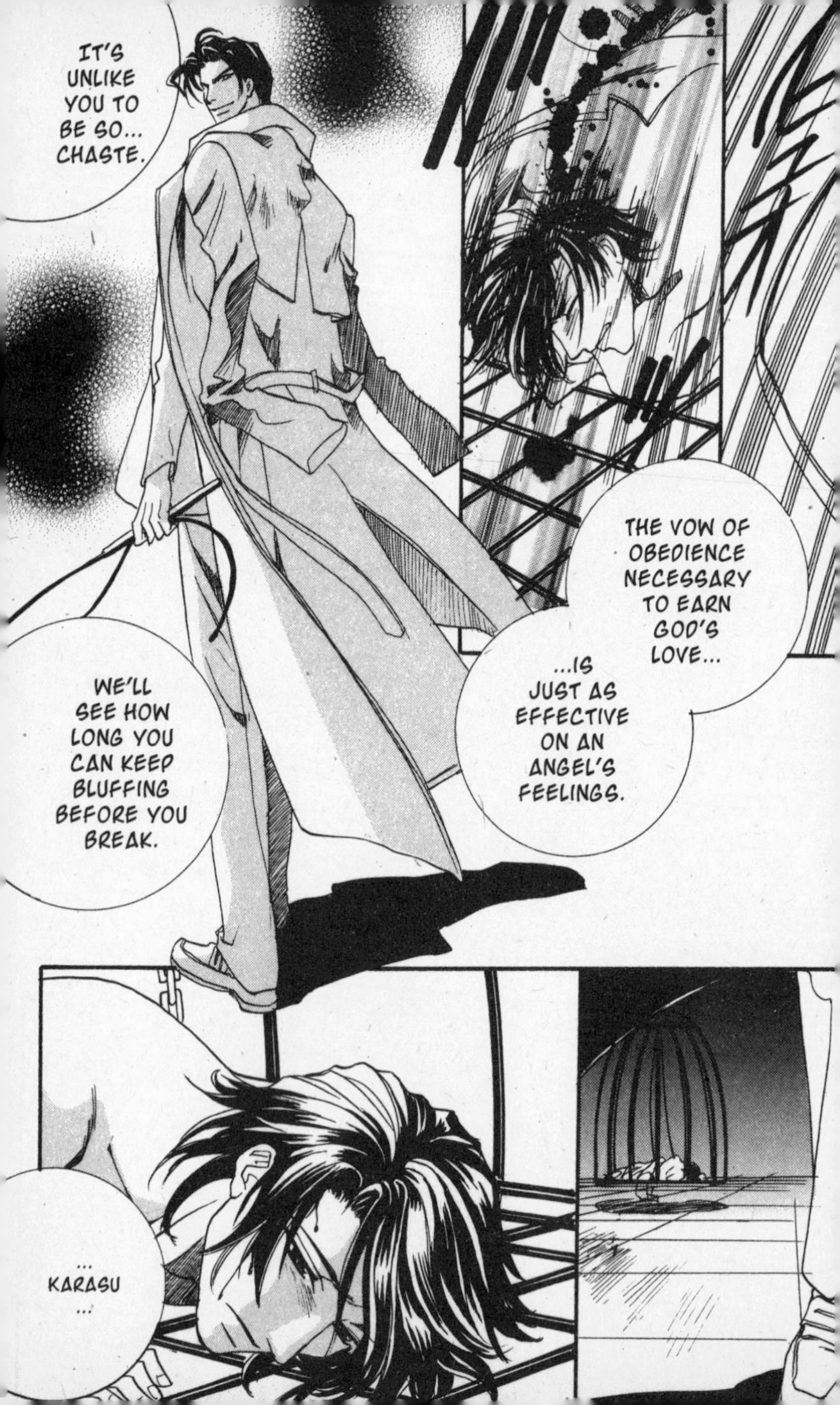
THE VOW OF OBEDIENCE NECESSARY TO EARN GOD'S LOVE...
...IS JUST AS EFFECTIVE ON AN ANGEL'S FEELINGS.
IT'S UNLIKE YOU TO BE SO... CHASTE.
WE'LL SEE HOW LONG YOU CAN KEEP BLUFFING BEFORE YOU BREAK.
... KARASU ...

IT'S
HEAVY...

オ
オ

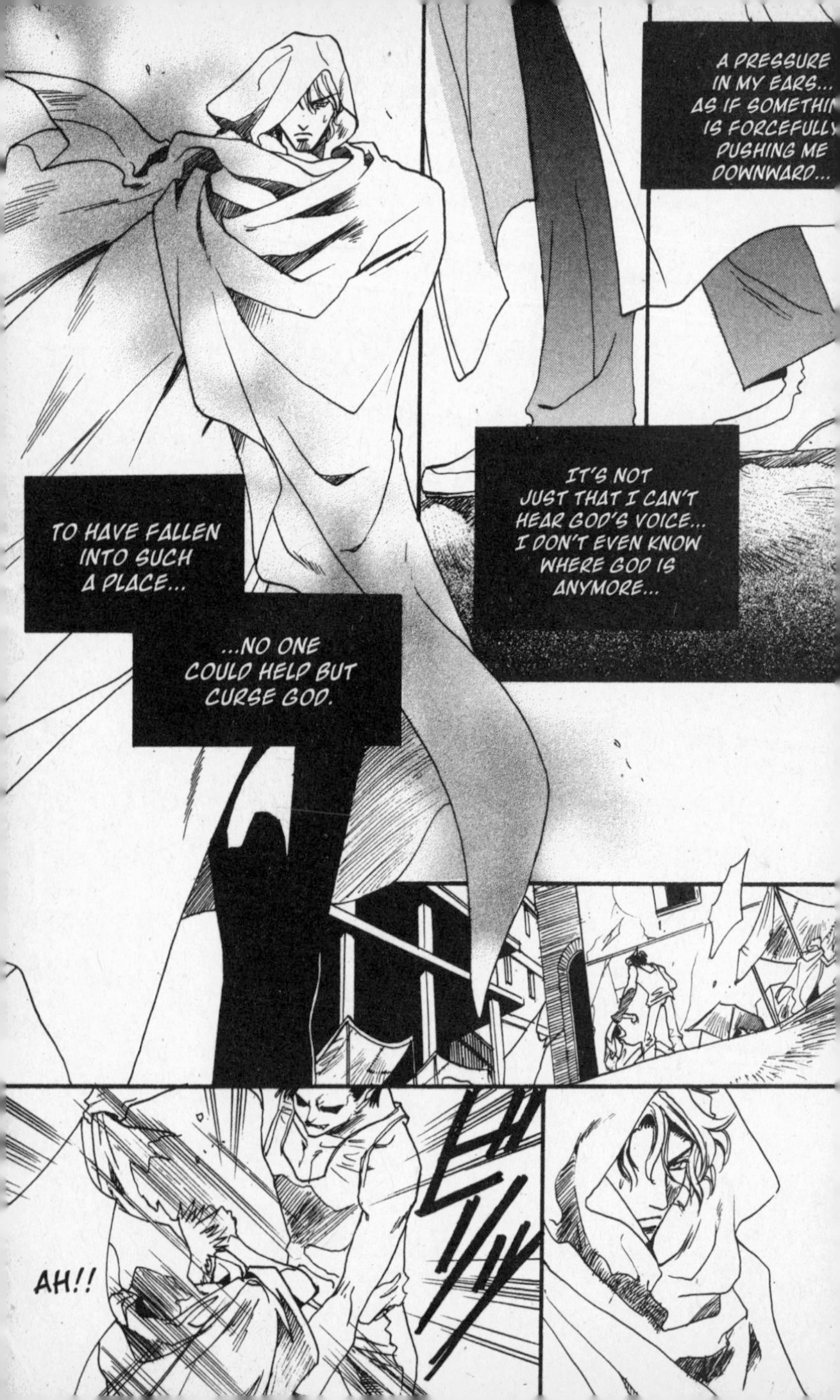
A PRESSURE IN MY EARS... AS IF SOMETHI IS FORCEFULLY PUSHING ME DOWNWARD...
IT'S NOT JUST THAT I CAN'T HEAR GOD'S VOICE... I DON'T EVEN KNOW WHERE GOD IS ANYMORE...
TO HAVE FALLEN INTO SUCH A PLACE...
...NO ONE COULD HELP BUT CURSE GOD.
AH!!

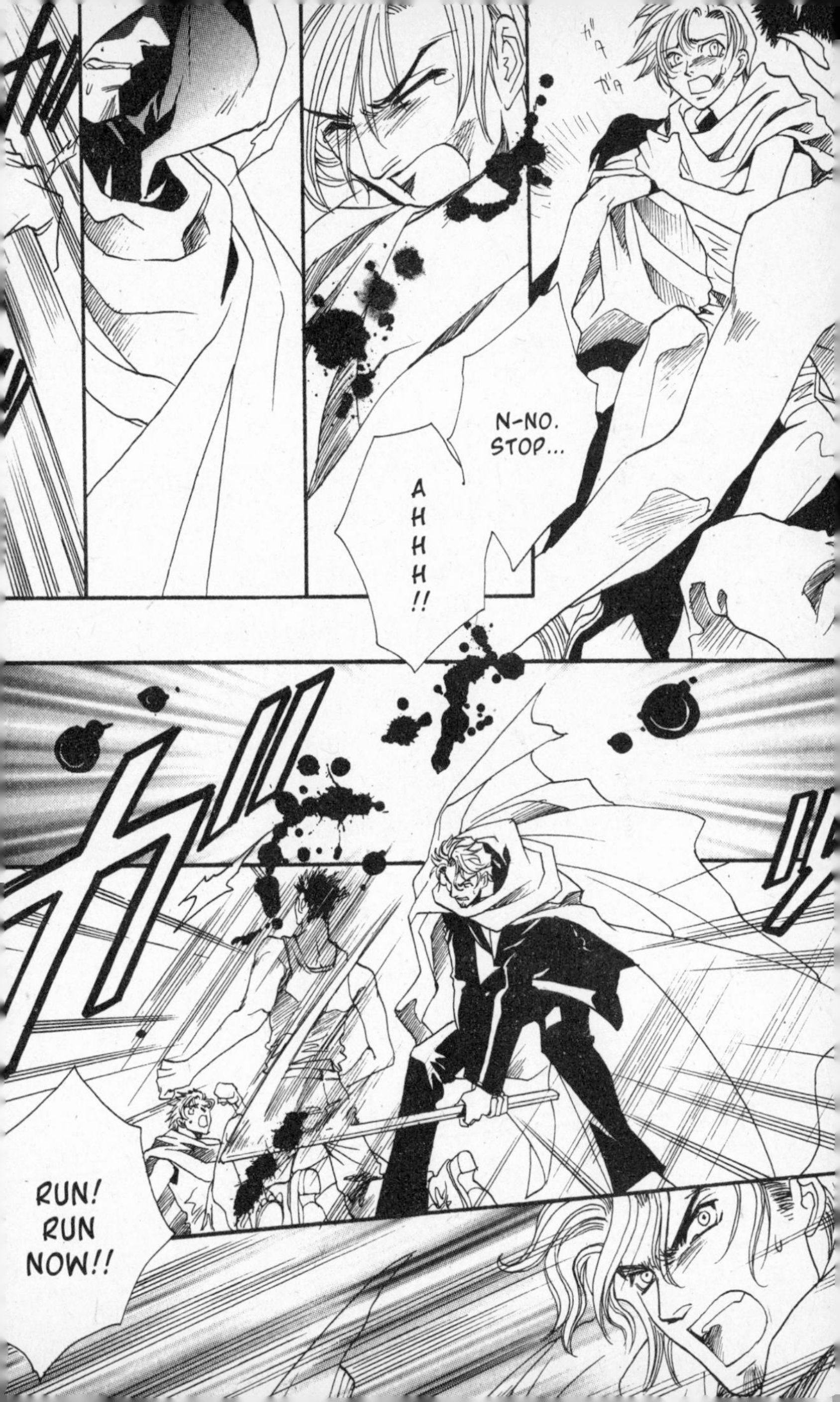
ガタガタ
N-NO. STOP...
AHHHH!!
RUN! RUN NOW!!

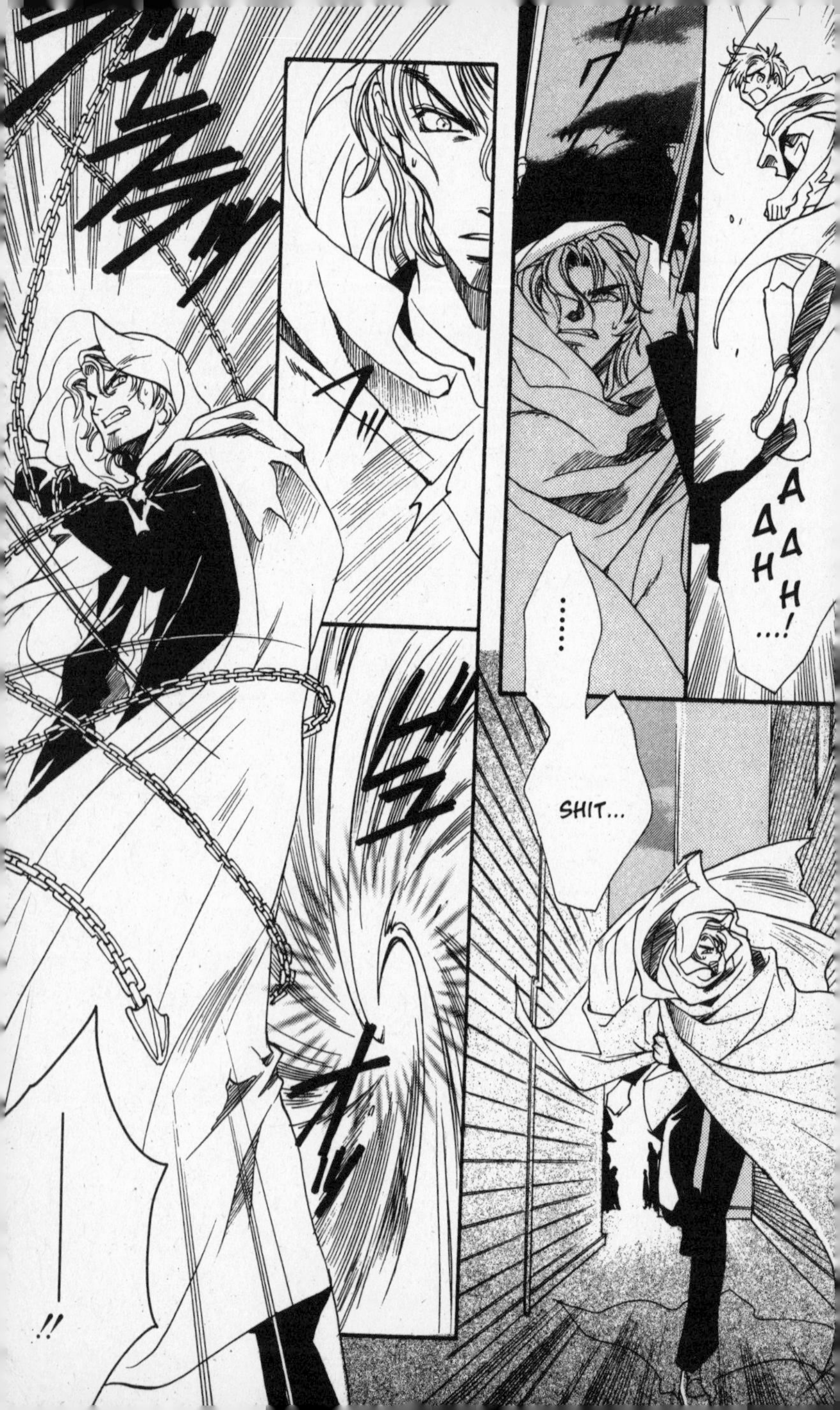
AAAH...!
......
SHIT...
!!

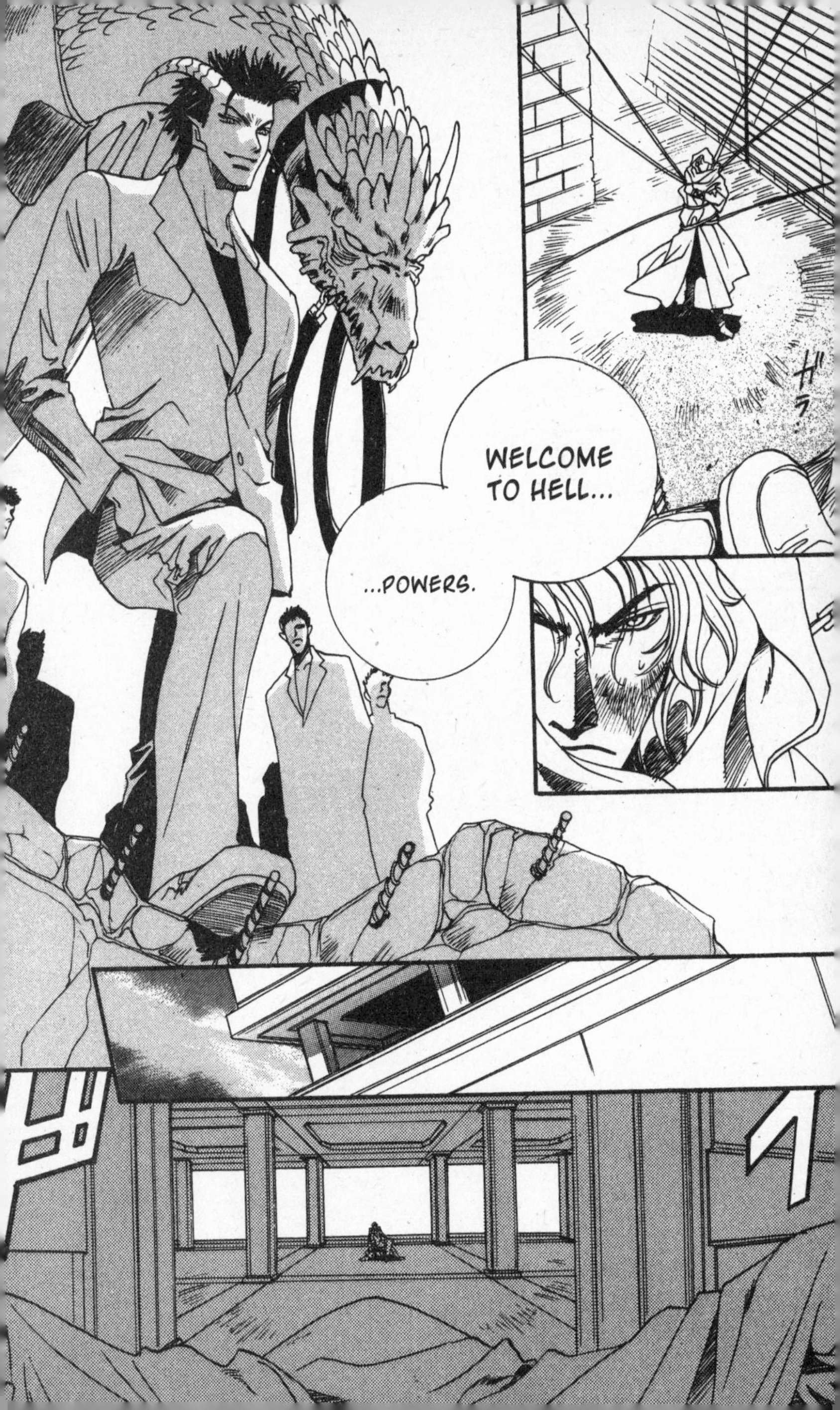
ガラ
WELCOME TO HELL...
...POWERS.

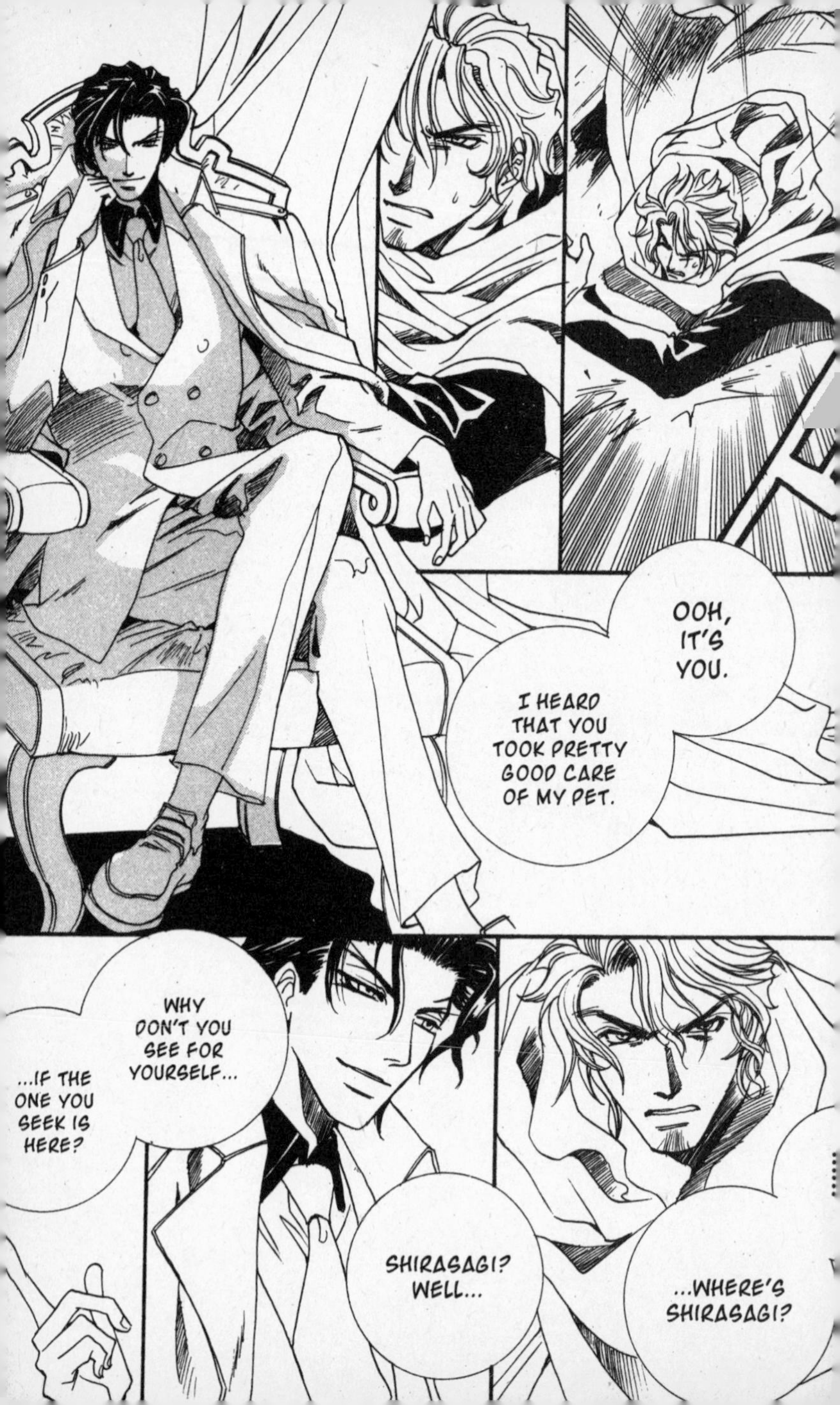
OOH, IT'S YOU.
I HEARD THAT YOU TOOK PRETTY GOOD CARE OF MY PET.
...WHERE'S SHIRASAGI?
SHIRASAGI? WELL...
WHY DON'T YOU SEE FOR YOURSELF...
...IF THE ONE YOU SEEK IS HERE?

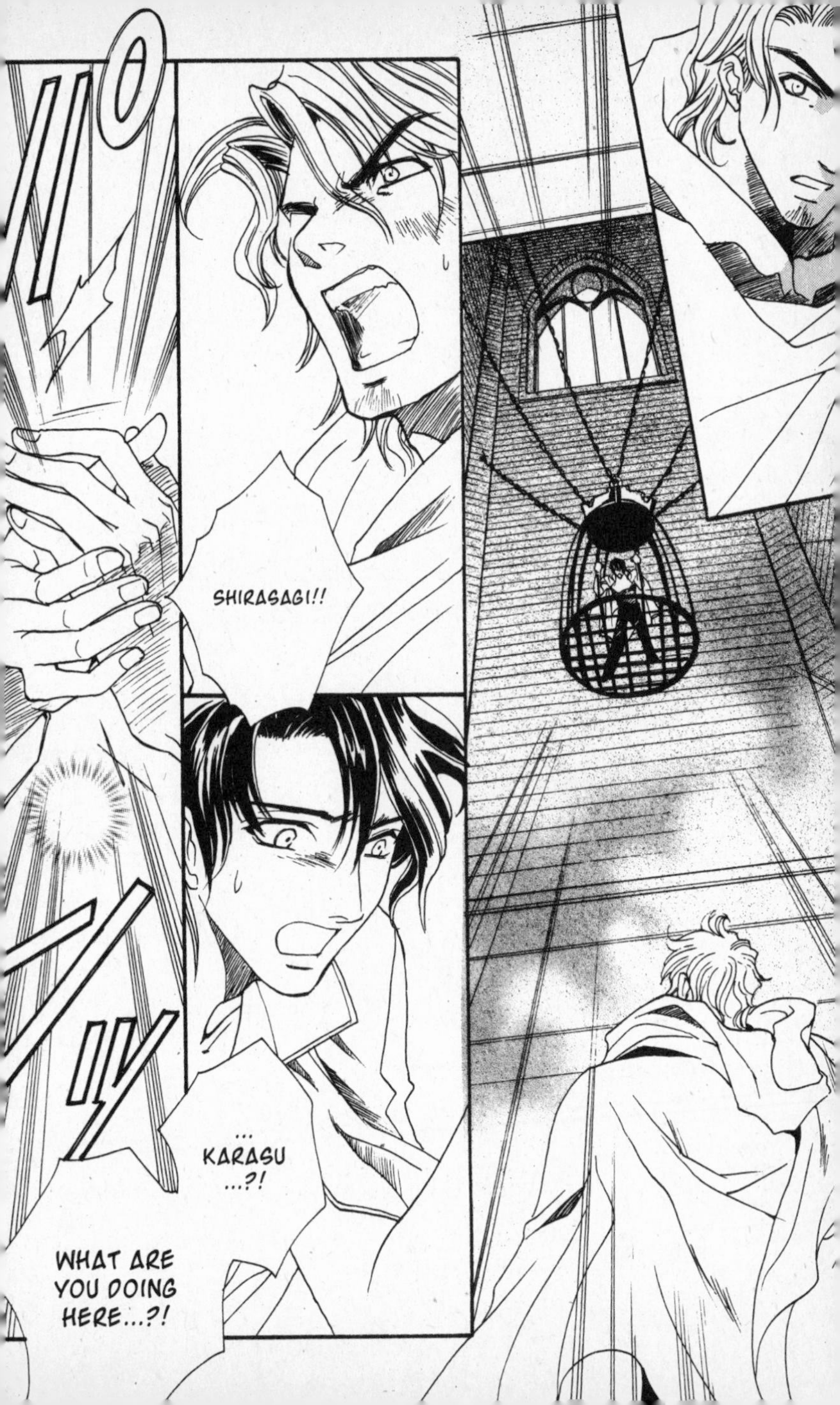
SHIRASAGI!!
... KARASU ...?!
WHAT ARE YOU DOING HERE...?!

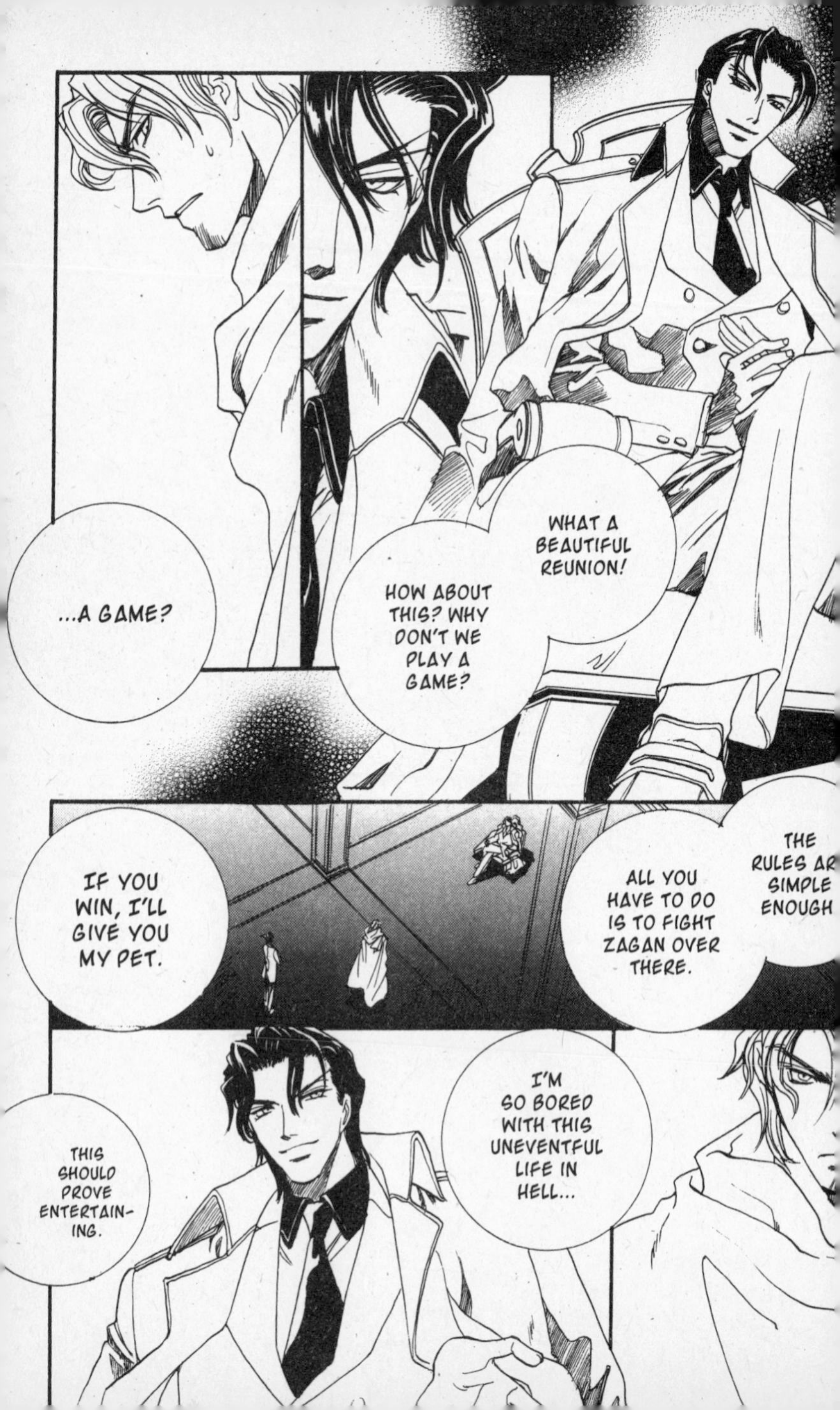
WHAT A BEAUTIFUL REUNION!
HOW ABOUT THIS? WHY DON'T WE PLAY A GAME?
...A GAME?
THE RULES AR SIMPLE ENOUGH
ALL YOU HAVE TO DO IS TO FIGHT ZAGAN OVER THERE.
IF YOU WIN, I'LL GIVE YOU MY PET.
I'M SO BORED WITH THIS UNEVENTFUL LIFE IN HELL...
THIS SHOULD PROVE ENTERTAIN-ING.

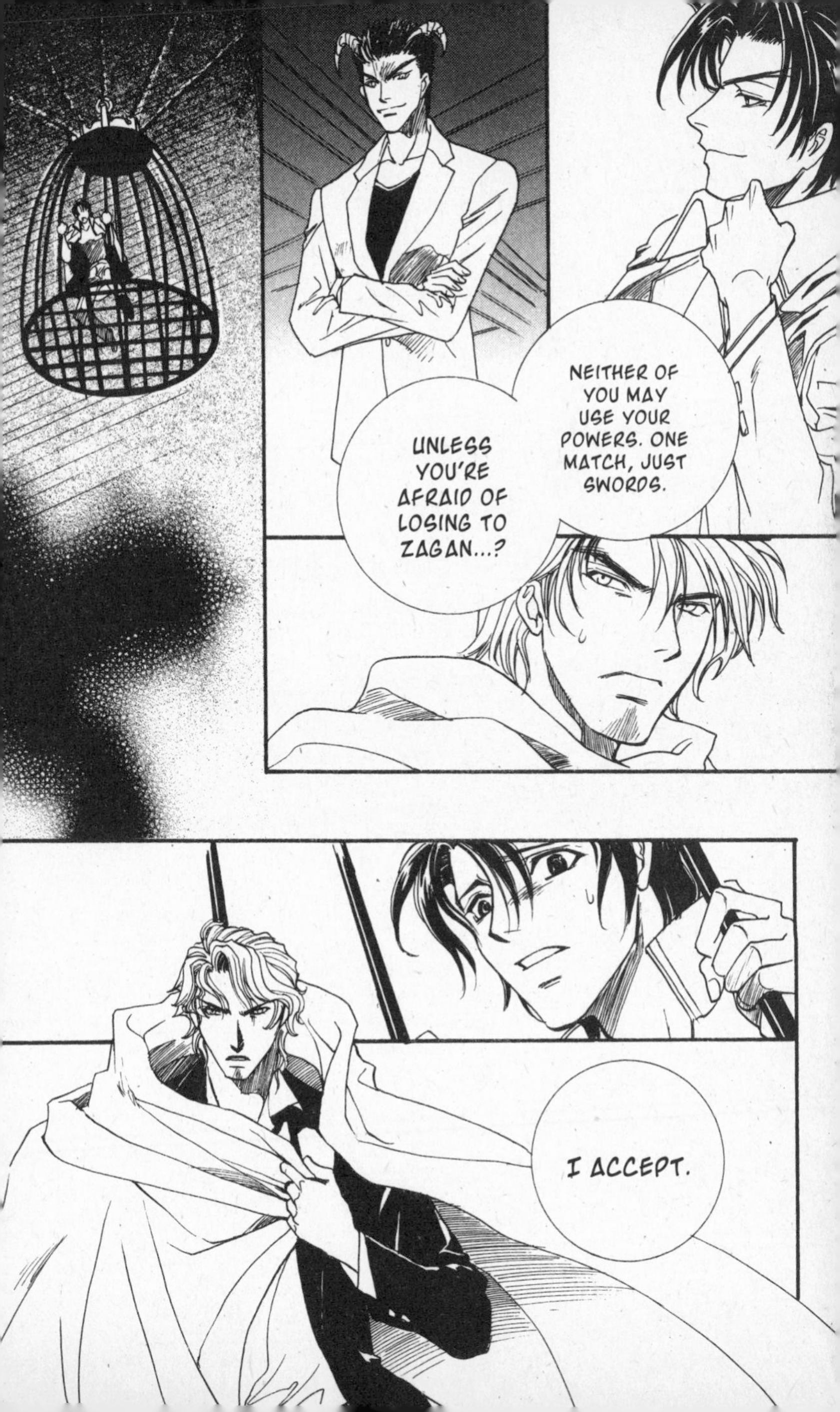
NEITHER OF YOU MAY USE YOUR POWERS. ONE MATCH, JUST SWORDS.
UNLESS YOU'RE AFRAID OF LOSING TO ZAGAN...?
I ACCEPT.

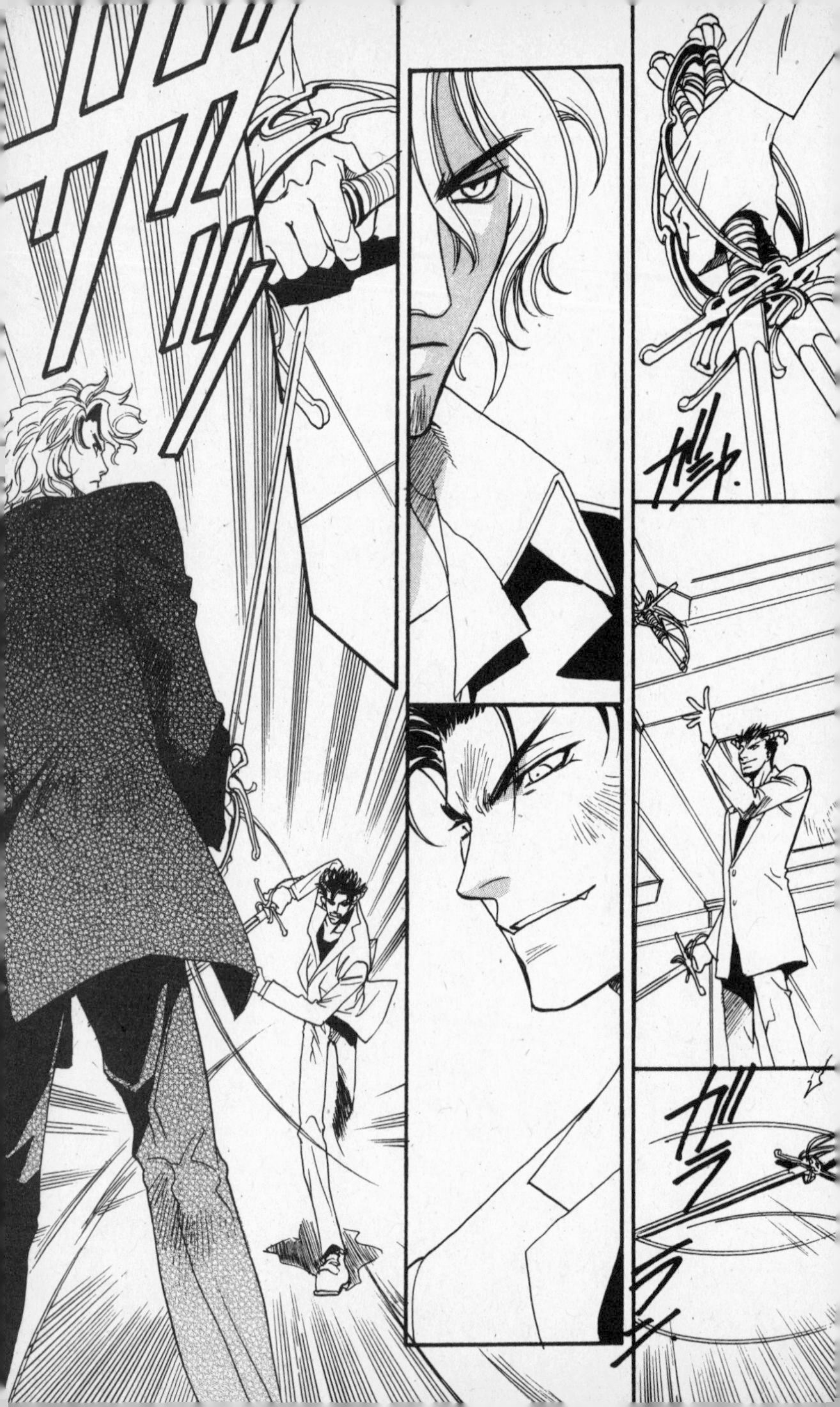
ガシャ.

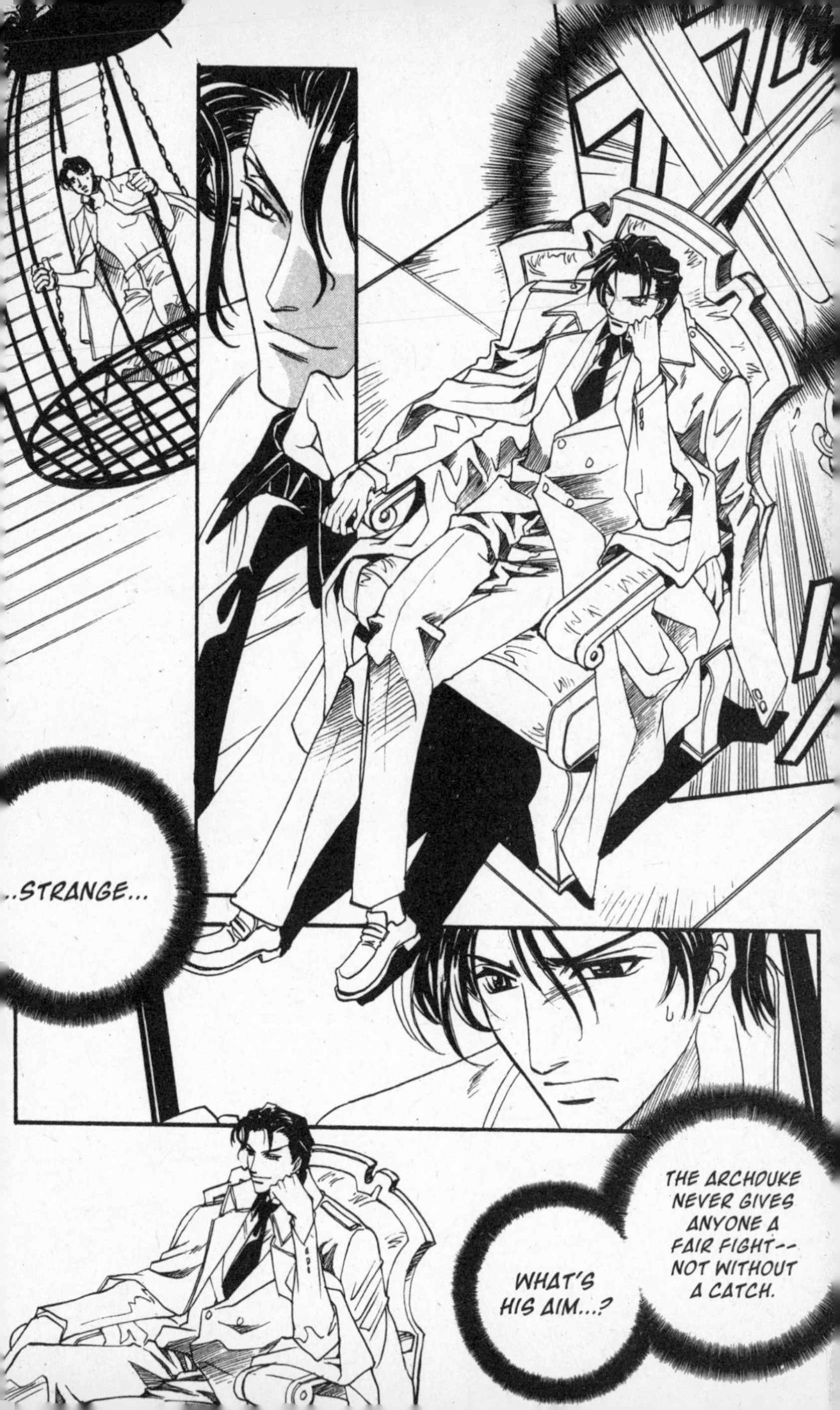
..STRANGE...
THE ARCHDUKE NEVER GIVES ANYONE A FAIR FIGHT-- NOT WITHOUT A CATCH.
WHAT'S HIS AIM...?

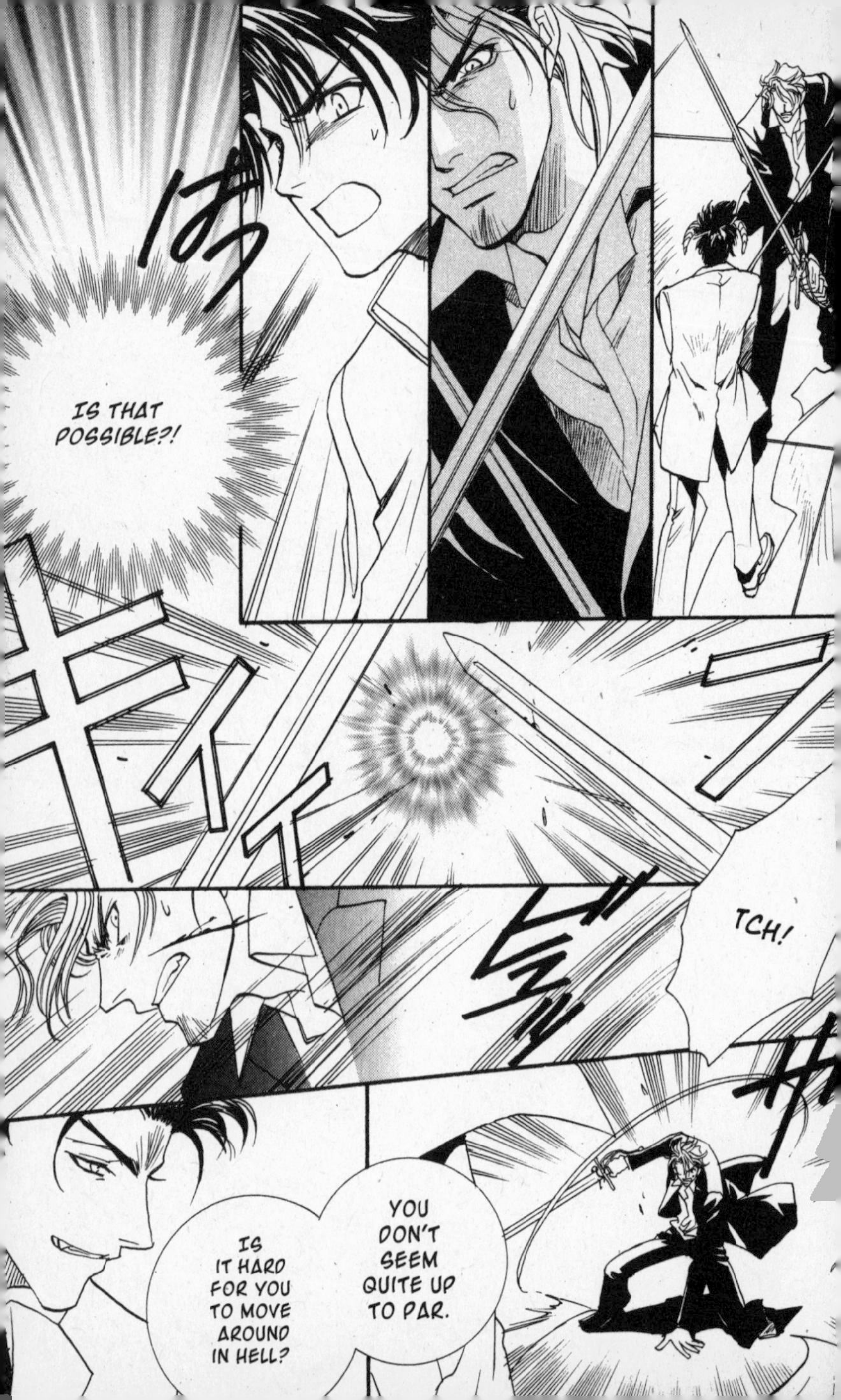
ばっ
IS THAT POSSIBLE?!
TCH!
YOU DON'T SEEM QUITE UP TO PAR.
IS IT HARD FOR YOU TO MOVE AROUND IN HELL?

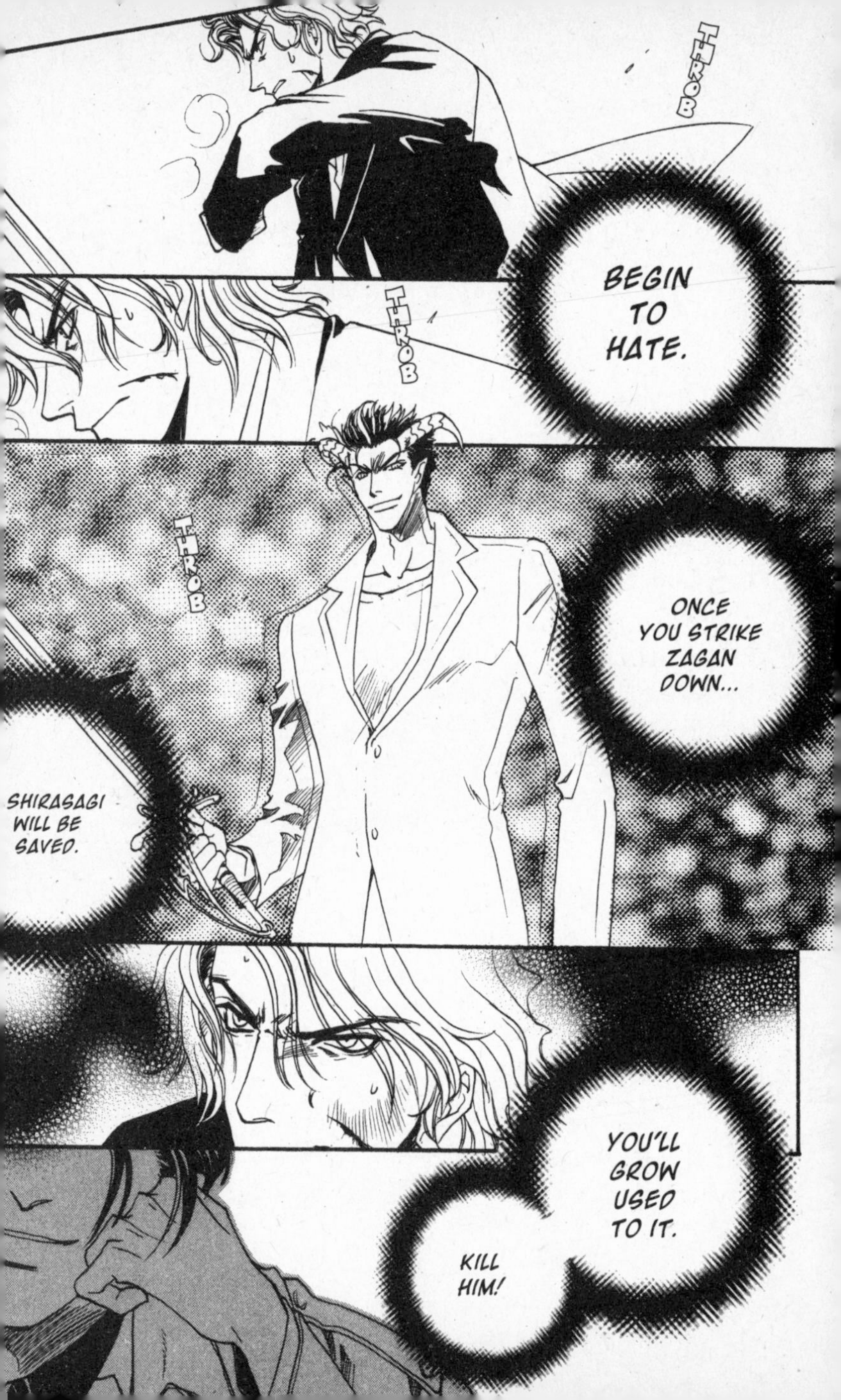
THROB
BEGIN TO HATE.
THROB
THROB
ONCE YOU STRIKE ZAGAN DOWN...
SHIRASAGI WILL BE SAVED.
YOU'LL GROW USED TO IT.
KILL HIM!

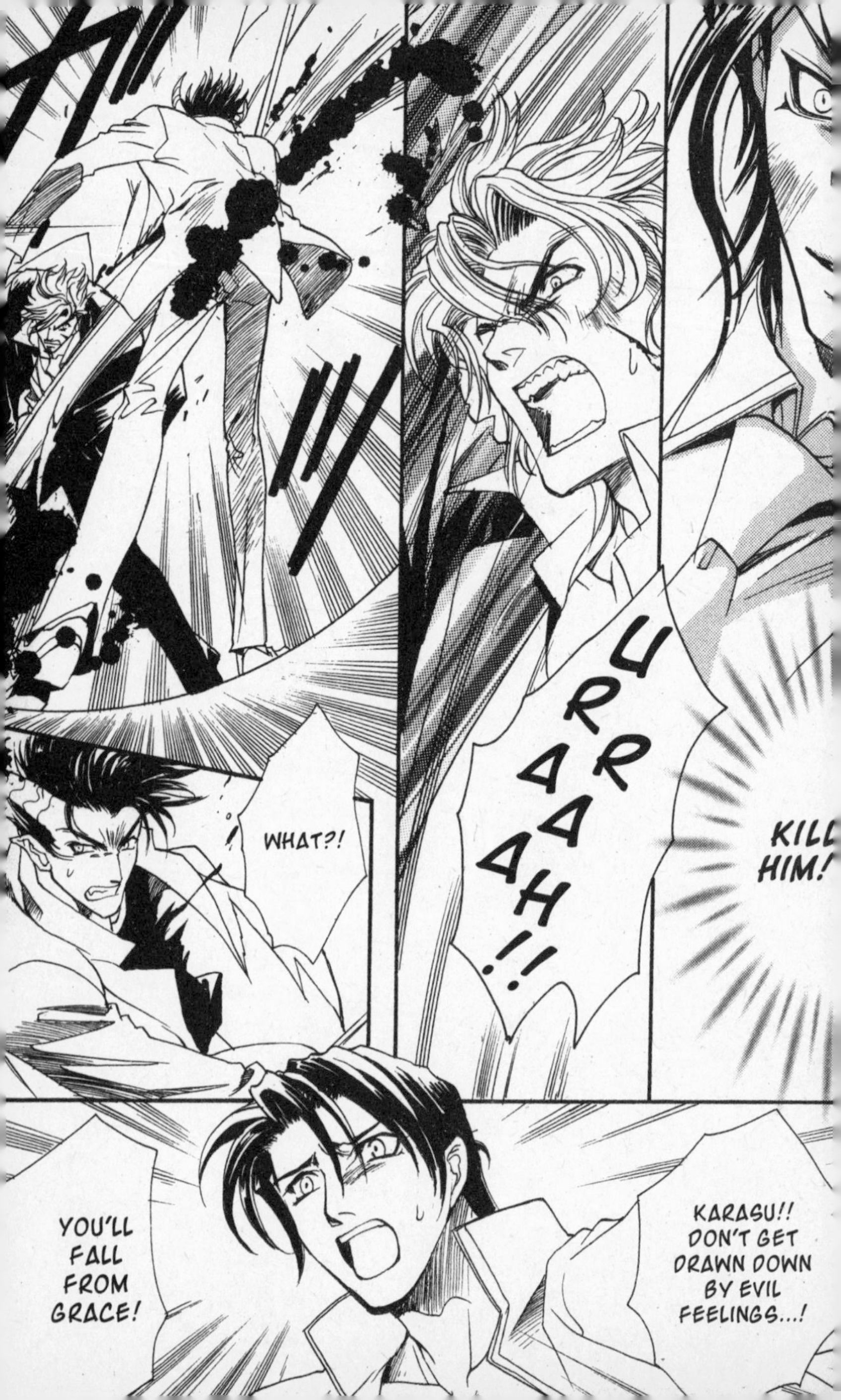
KILL HIM!
URRAAAH!!
WHAT?!
KARASU!! DON'T GET DRAWN DOWN BY EVIL FEELINGS...!
YOU'LL FALL FROM GRACE!

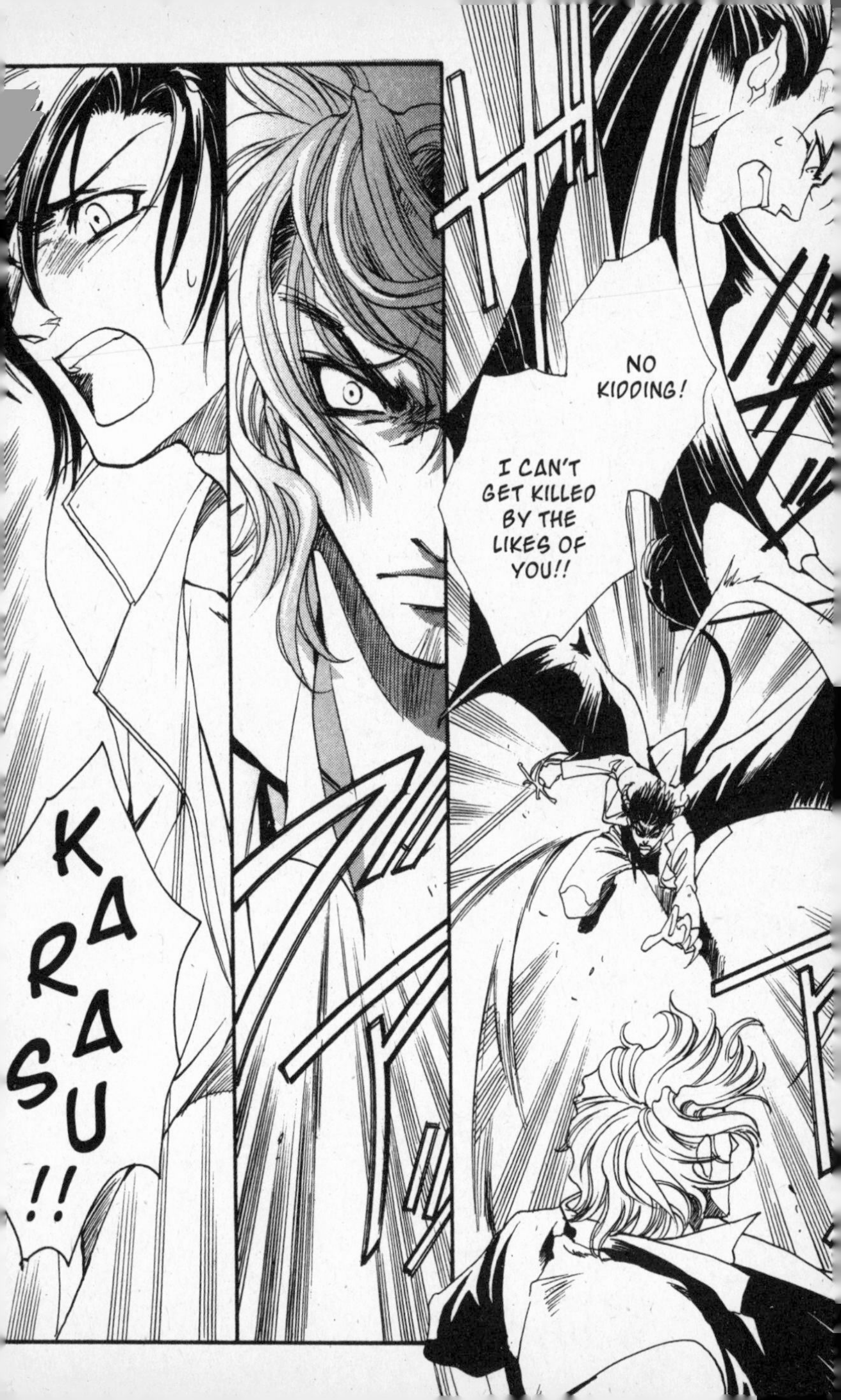
NO KIDDING!
I CAN'T GET KILLED BY THE LIKES OF YOU!!
KARASU!!

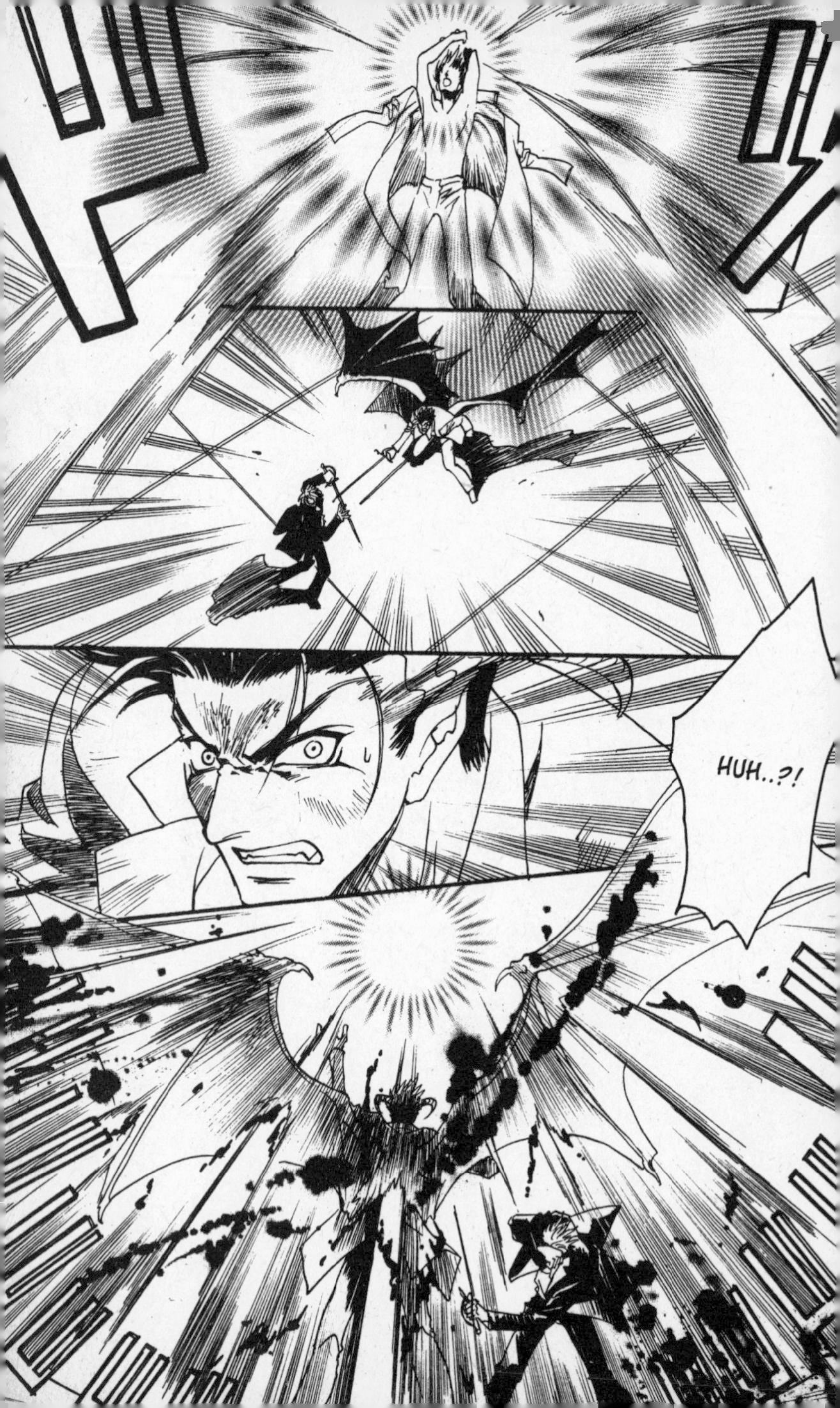
HUH..?!

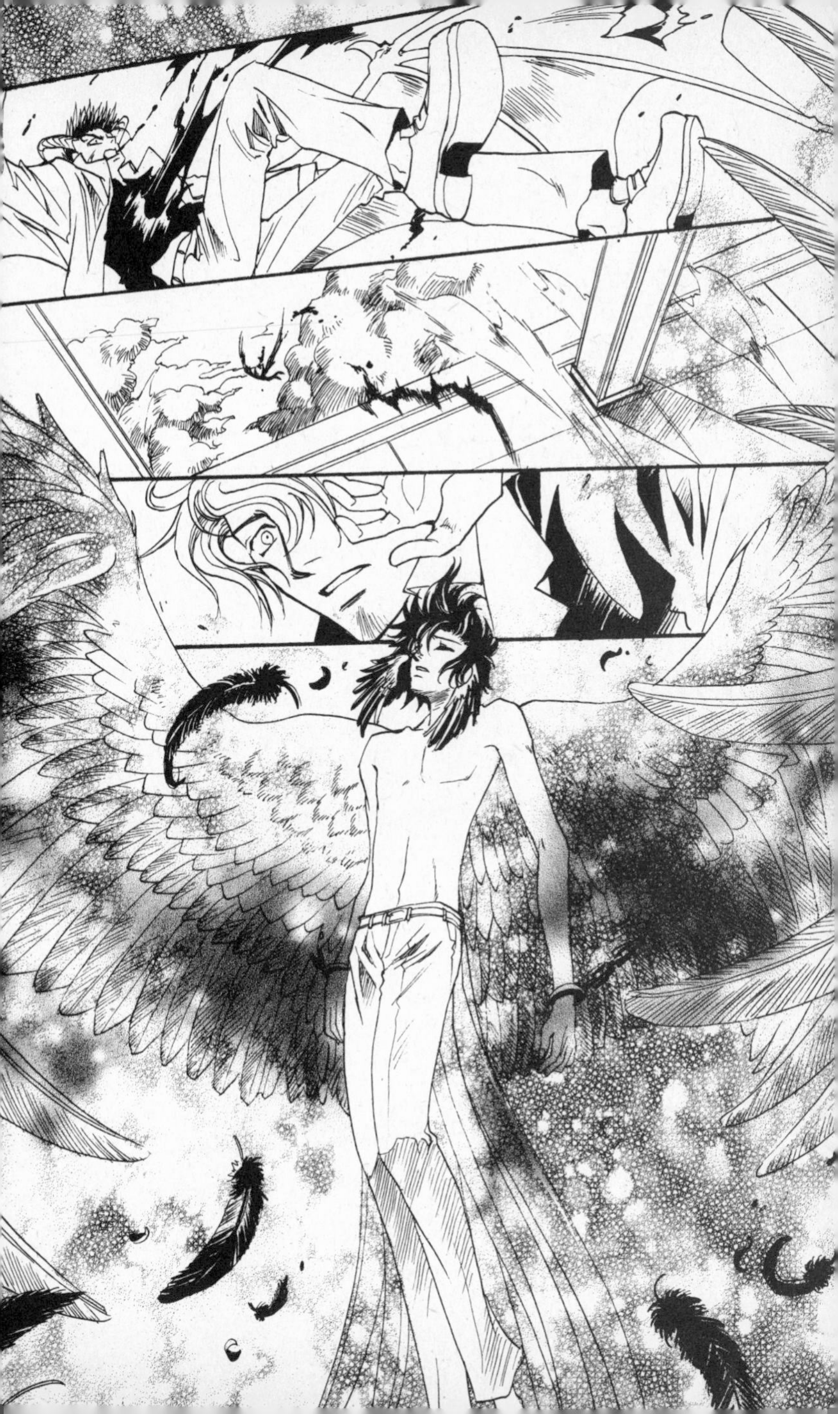

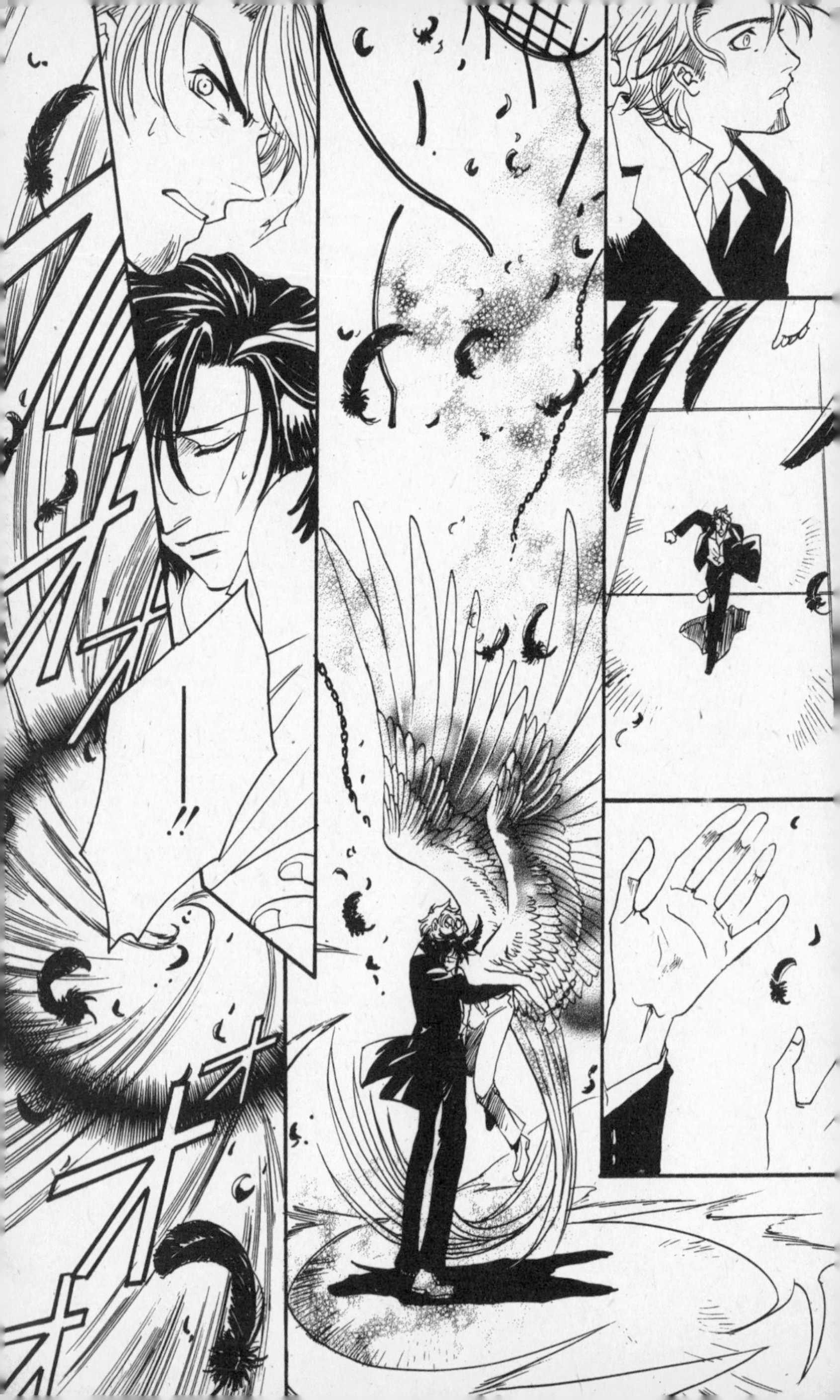
—!!

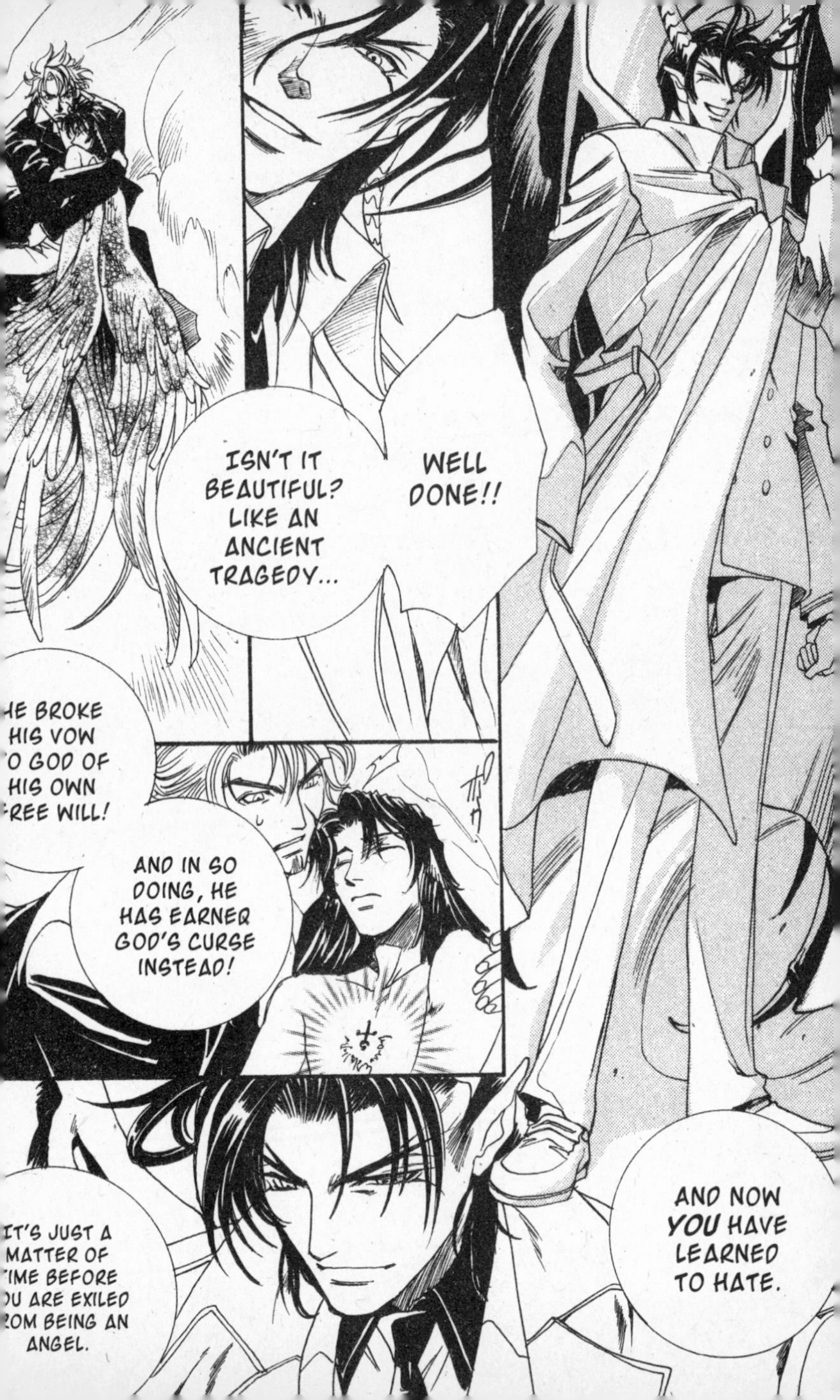
WELL DONE!!
ISN'T IT BEAUTIFUL? LIKE AN ANCIENT TRAGEDY...
HE BROKE HIS VOW TO GOD OF HIS OWN FREE WILL!
AND IN SO DOING, HE HAS EARNED GOD'S CURSE INSTEAD!
AND NOW YOU HAVE LEARNED TO HATE.
IT'S JUST A MATTER OF TIME BEFORE YOU ARE EXILED FROM BEING AN ANGEL.

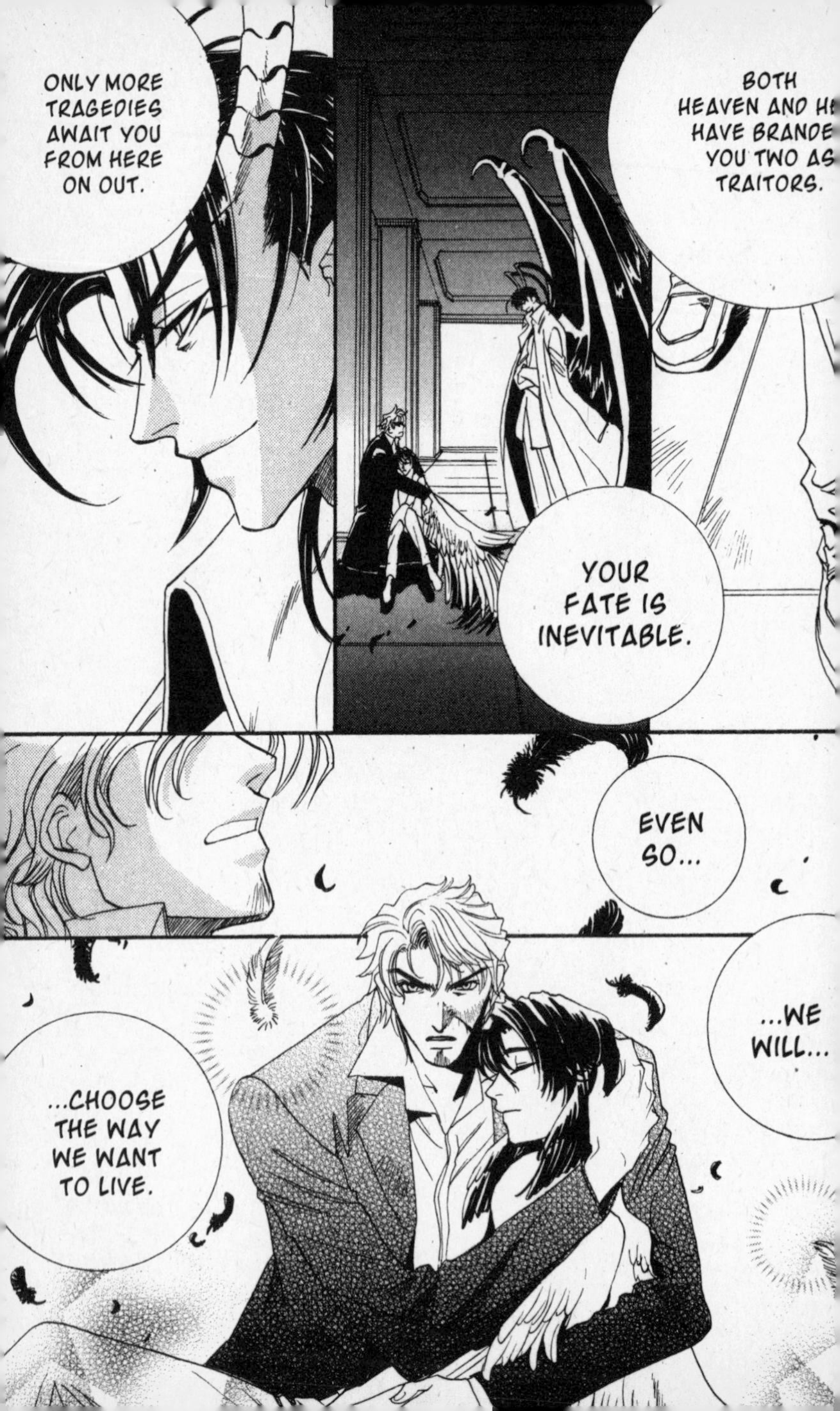

BOTH HEAVEN AND HE HAVE BRANDE YOU TWO AS TRAITORS.
YOUR FATE IS INEVITABLE.
ONLY MORE TRAGEDIES AWAIT YOU FROM HERE ON OUT.
EVEN SO...
...WE WILL...
...CHOOSE THE WAY WE WANT TO LIVE.

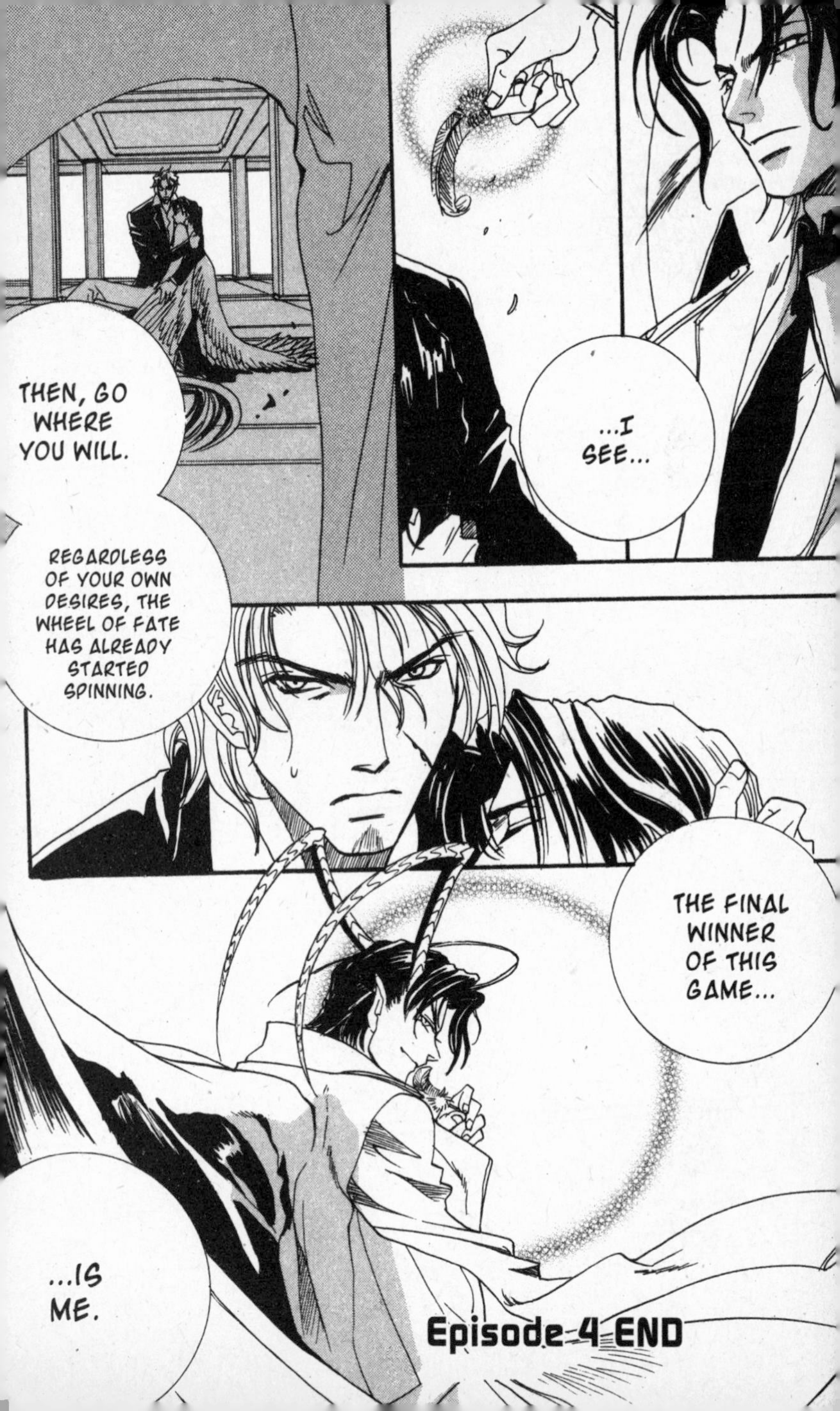
...I SEE...
THEN, GO WHERE YOU WILL.
REGARDLESS OF YOUR OWN DESIRES, THE WHEEL OF FATE HAS ALREADY STARTED SPINNING.
THE FINAL WINNER OF THIS GAME...
...IS ME.

Episode 4 END

The Dawn of the
Nameless Bird
~INNOCENT BIRD~

My Sweet Darling

ONE HOT SUMMER DAY FIVE YEARS AGO, OUR MOTHER GOT A BOYFRIEND AND LEFT HOME.

THIS SPRING, OUR FATHER REMARRIED AND MOVED ABROAD FOR HIS NEW JOB.

FROM THEN ON, THE TWO OF US WERE EXPECTED TO LIVE ON OUR OWN.

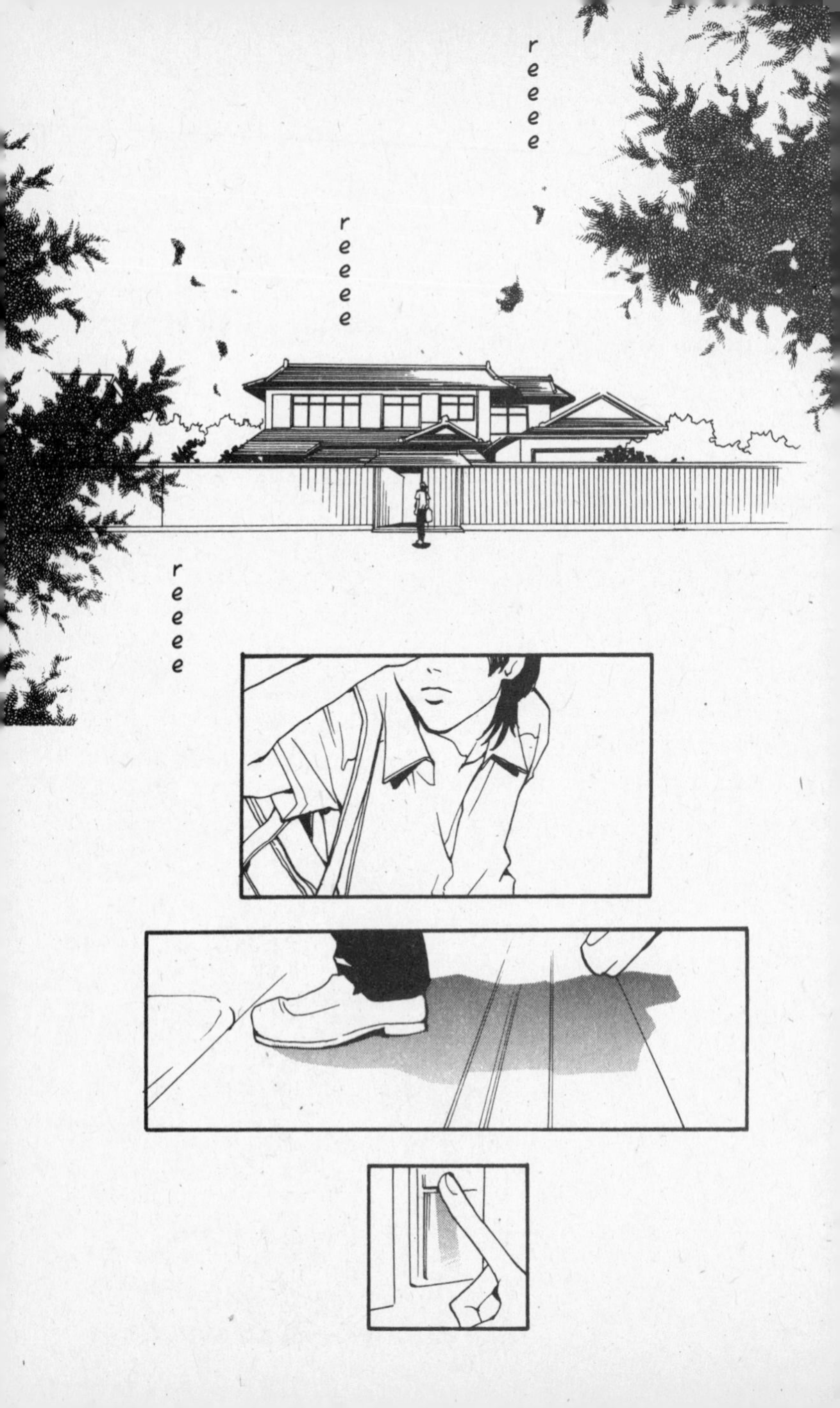
reeee
reeee
reeee

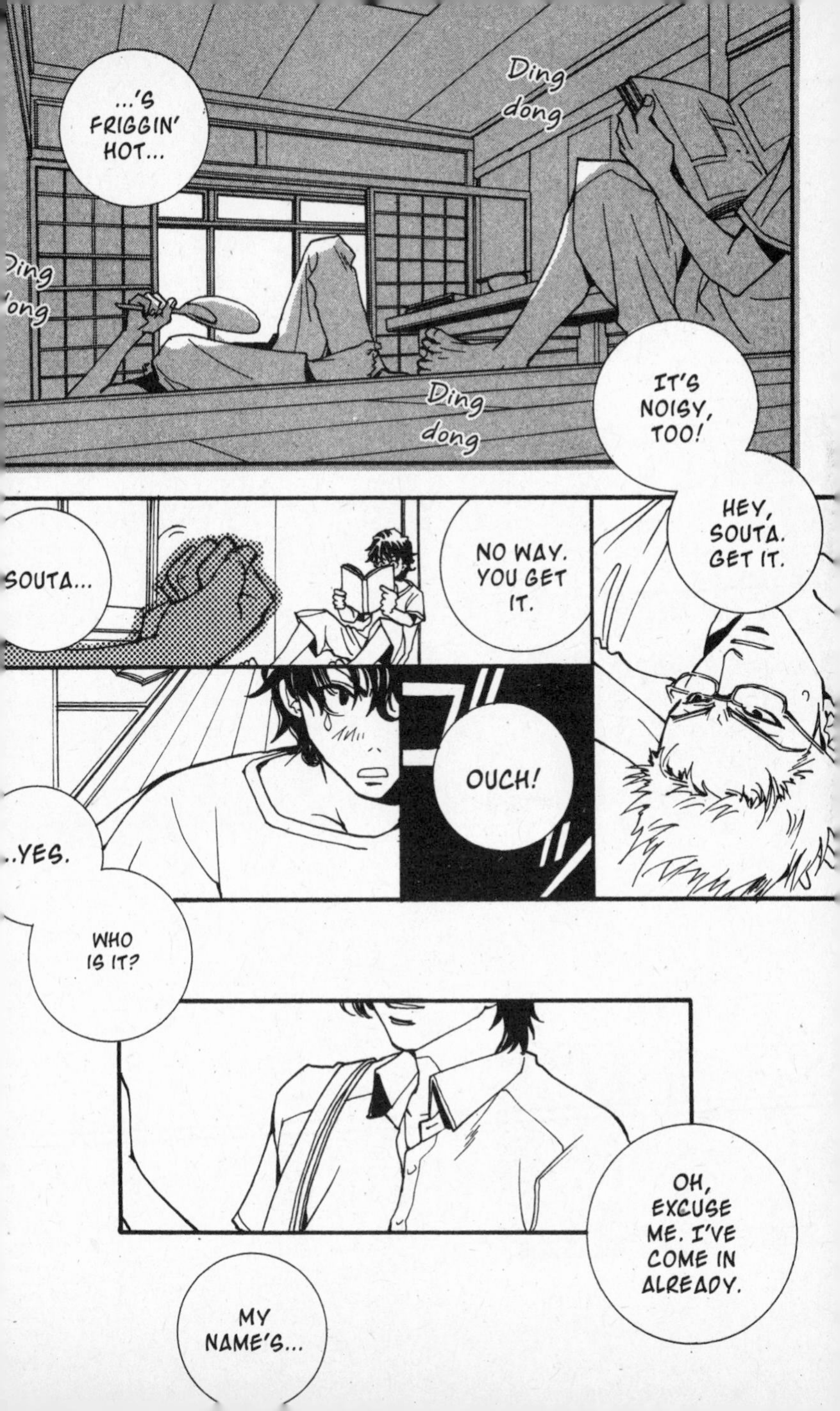
Ding dong
...'S FRIGGIN' HOT...
Ding ong
Ding dong
IT'S NOISY, TOO!
HEY, SOUTA. GET IT.
NO WAY. YOU GET IT.
SOUTA...
OUCH!
..YES.
WHO IS IT?
OH, EXCUSE ME. I'VE COME IN ALREADY.
MY NAME'S...

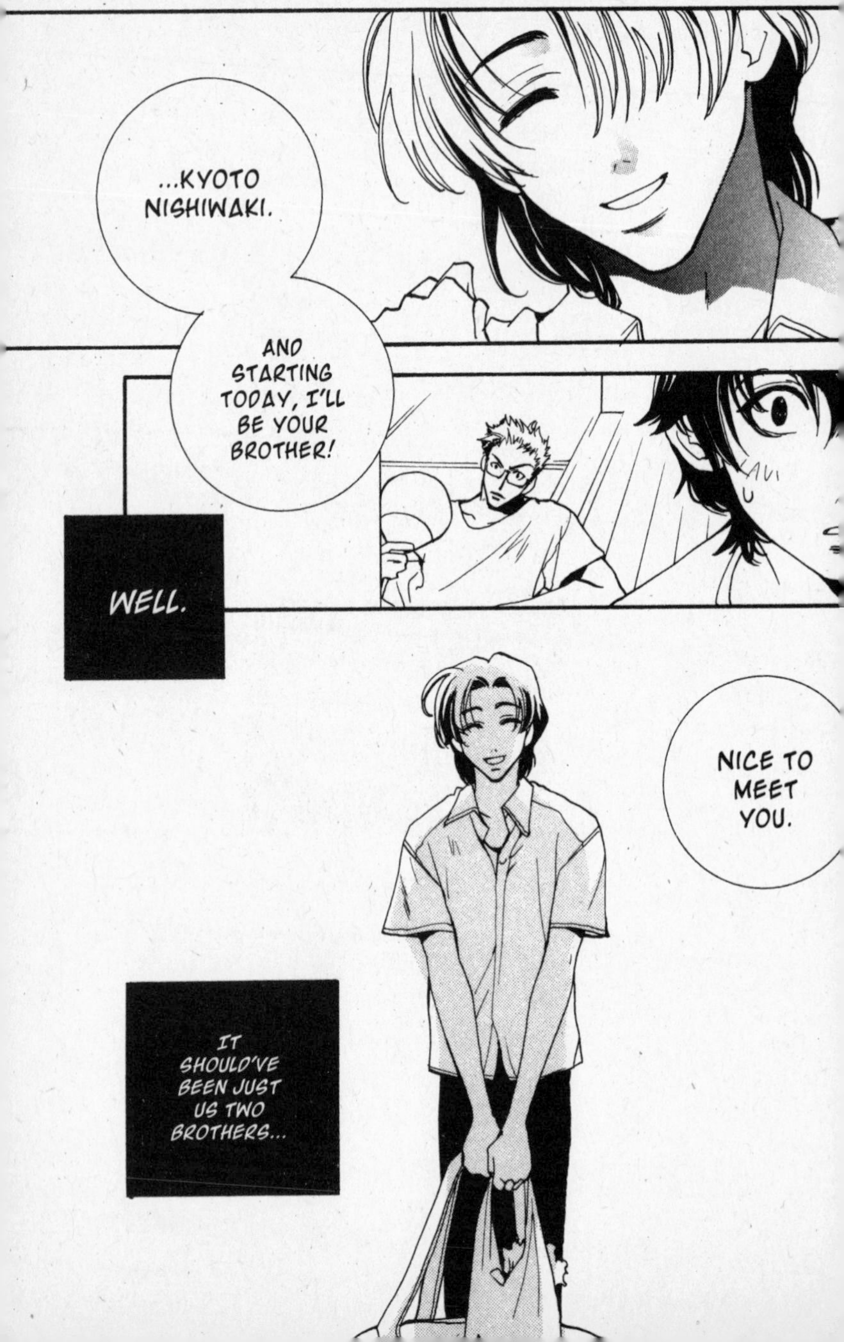
...KYOTO NISHIWAKI.
AND STARTING TODAY, I'LL BE YOUR BROTHER!
WELL.
NICE TO MEET YOU.
IT SHOULD'VE BEEN JUST US TWO BROTHERS...

My Sweet Darling

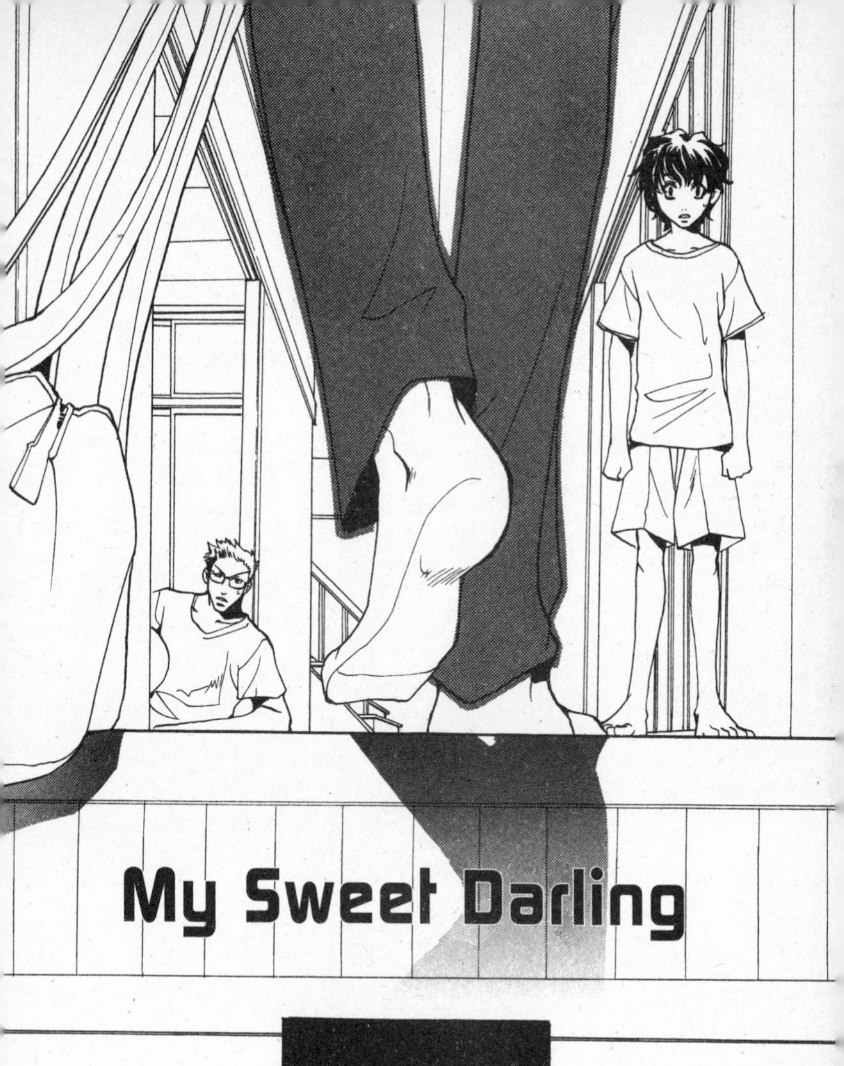
...THEN HE CAME TO OUR HOUSE.

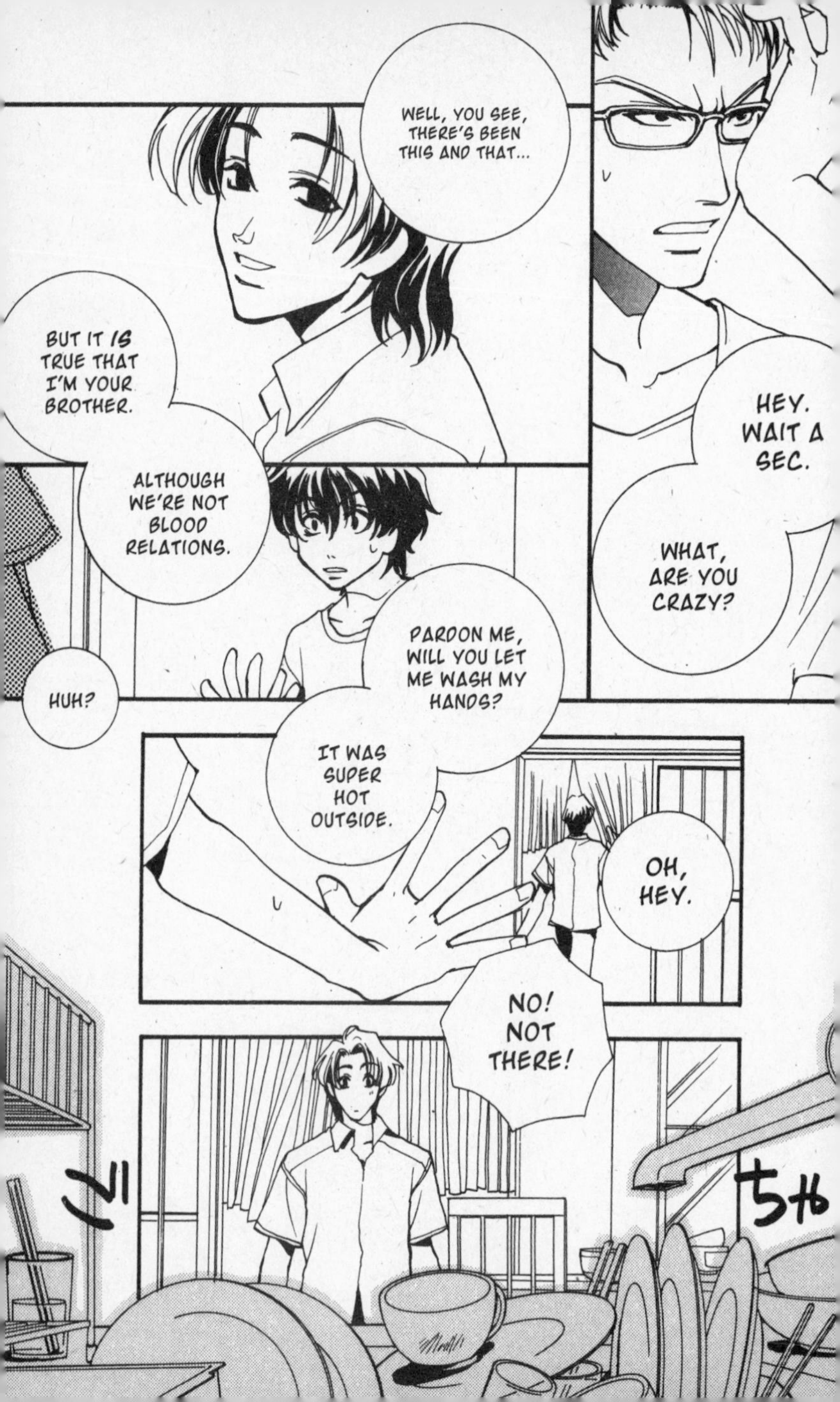
HEY. WAIT A SEC.
WHAT, ARE YOU CRAZY?
WELL, YOU SEE, THERE'S BEEN THIS AND THAT...
BUT IT *IS* TRUE THAT I'M YOUR BROTHER.
ALTHOUGH WE'RE NOT BLOOD RELATIONS.
HUH?
PARDON ME, WILL YOU LET ME WASH MY HANDS?
IT WAS SUPER HOT OUTSIDE.
OH, HEY.
NO! NOT THERE!

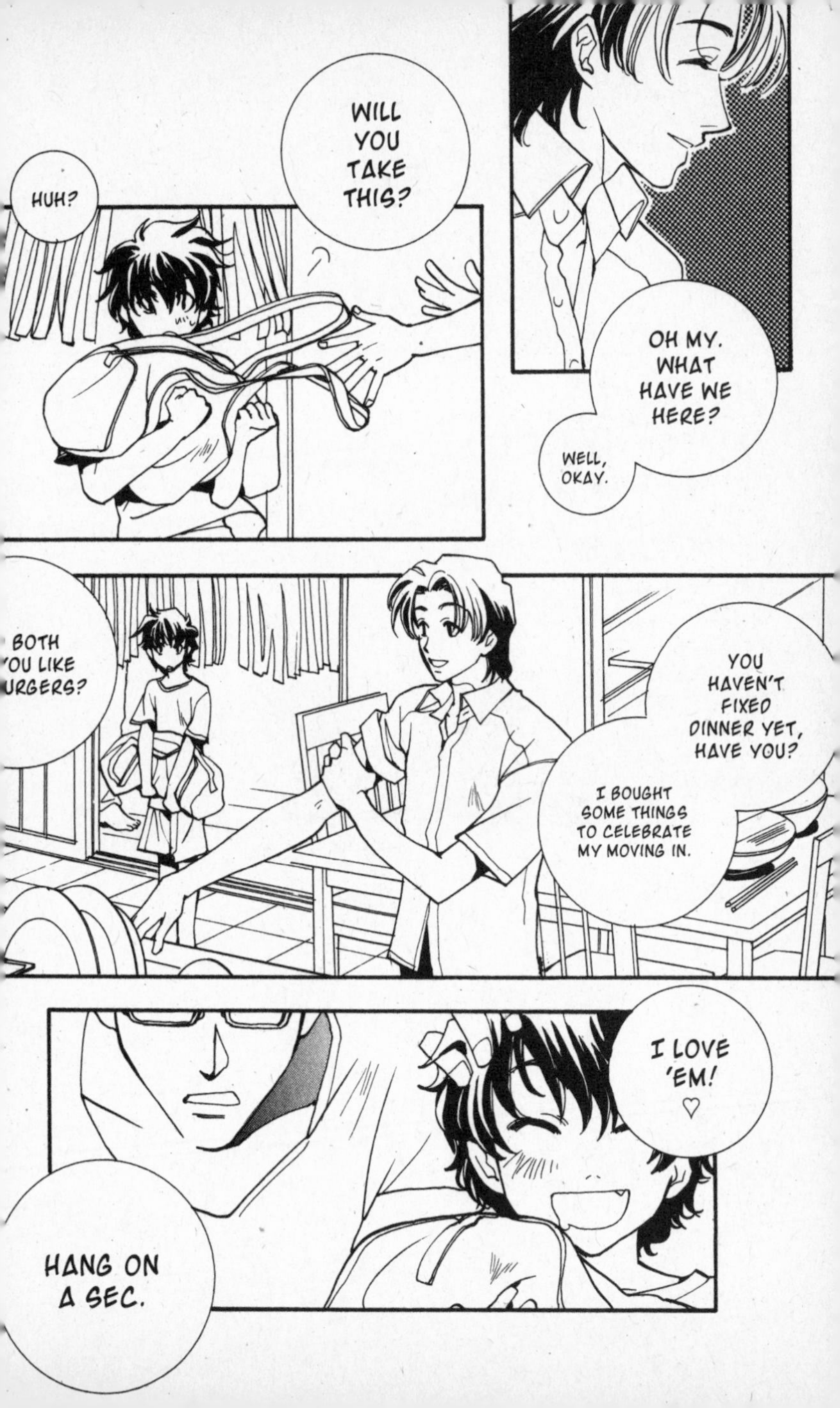
WILL YOU TAKE THIS?
HUH?
OH MY. WHAT HAVE WE HERE?
WELL, OKAY.
YOU HAVEN'T FIXED DINNER YET, HAVE YOU?
I BOUGHT SOME THINGS TO CELEBRATE MY MOVING IN.
BOTH 'OU LIKE URGERS?
I LOVE 'EM! ♡
HANG ON A SEC.

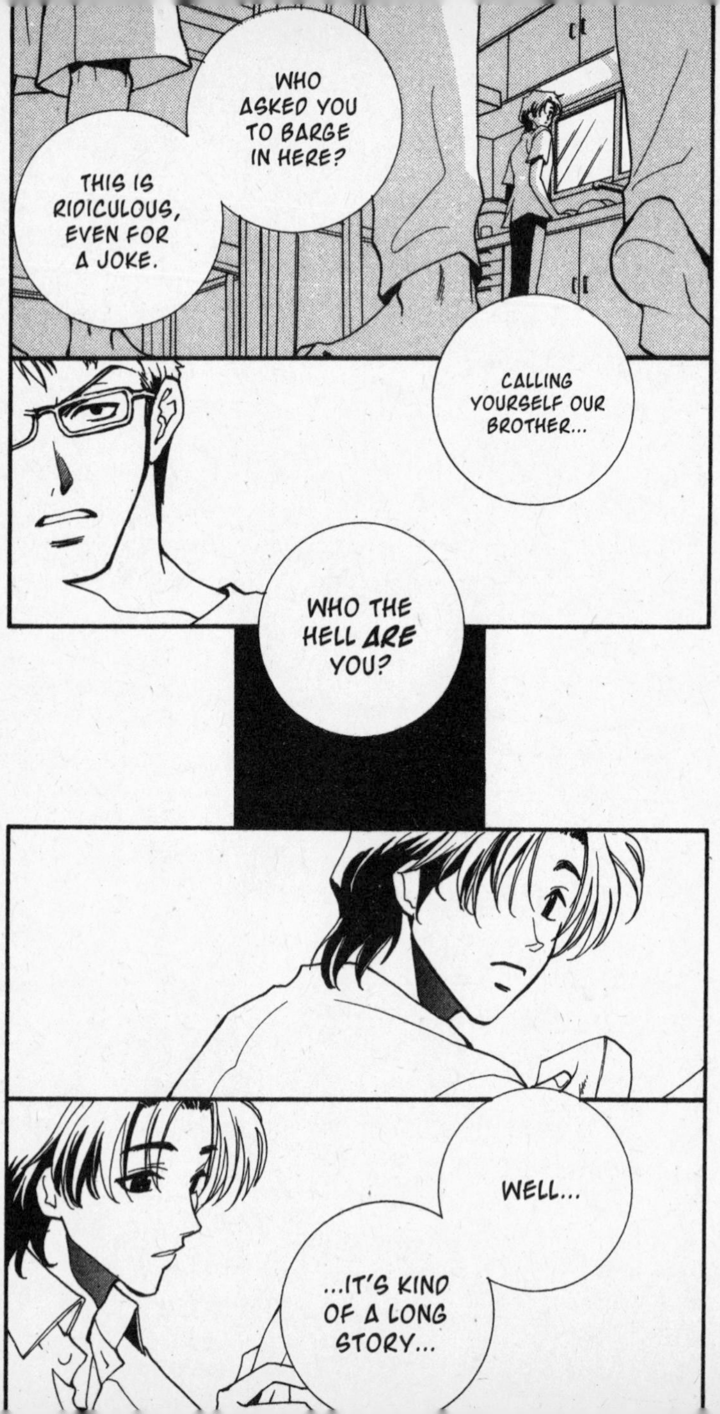
WHO ASKED YOU TO BARGE IN HERE?
THIS IS RIDICULOUS, EVEN FOR A JOKE.
CALLING YOURSELF OUR BROTHER...
WHO THE HELL *ARE* YOU?
WELL...
...IT'S KIND OF A LONG STORY...

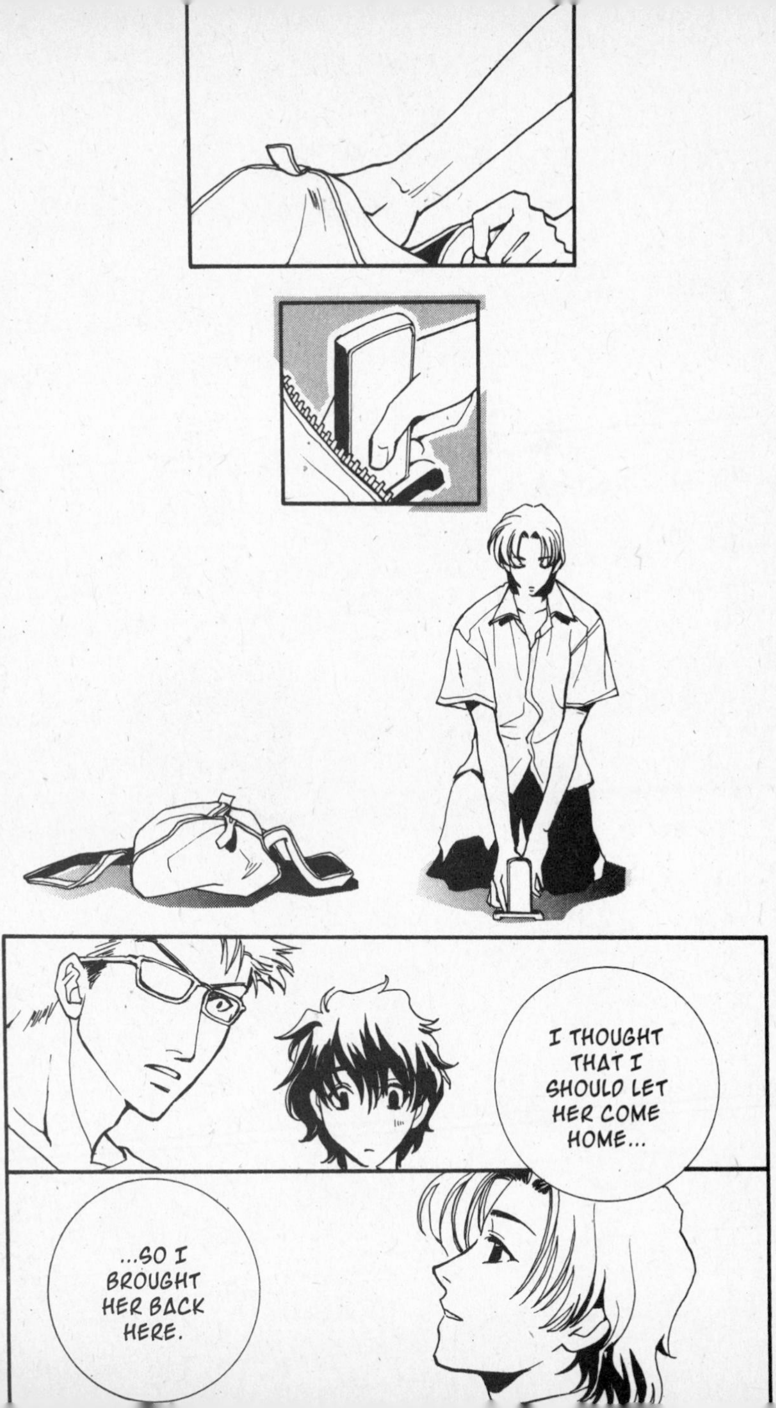
I THOUGHT THAT I SHOULD LET HER COME HOME...
...SO I BROUGHT HER BACK HERE.

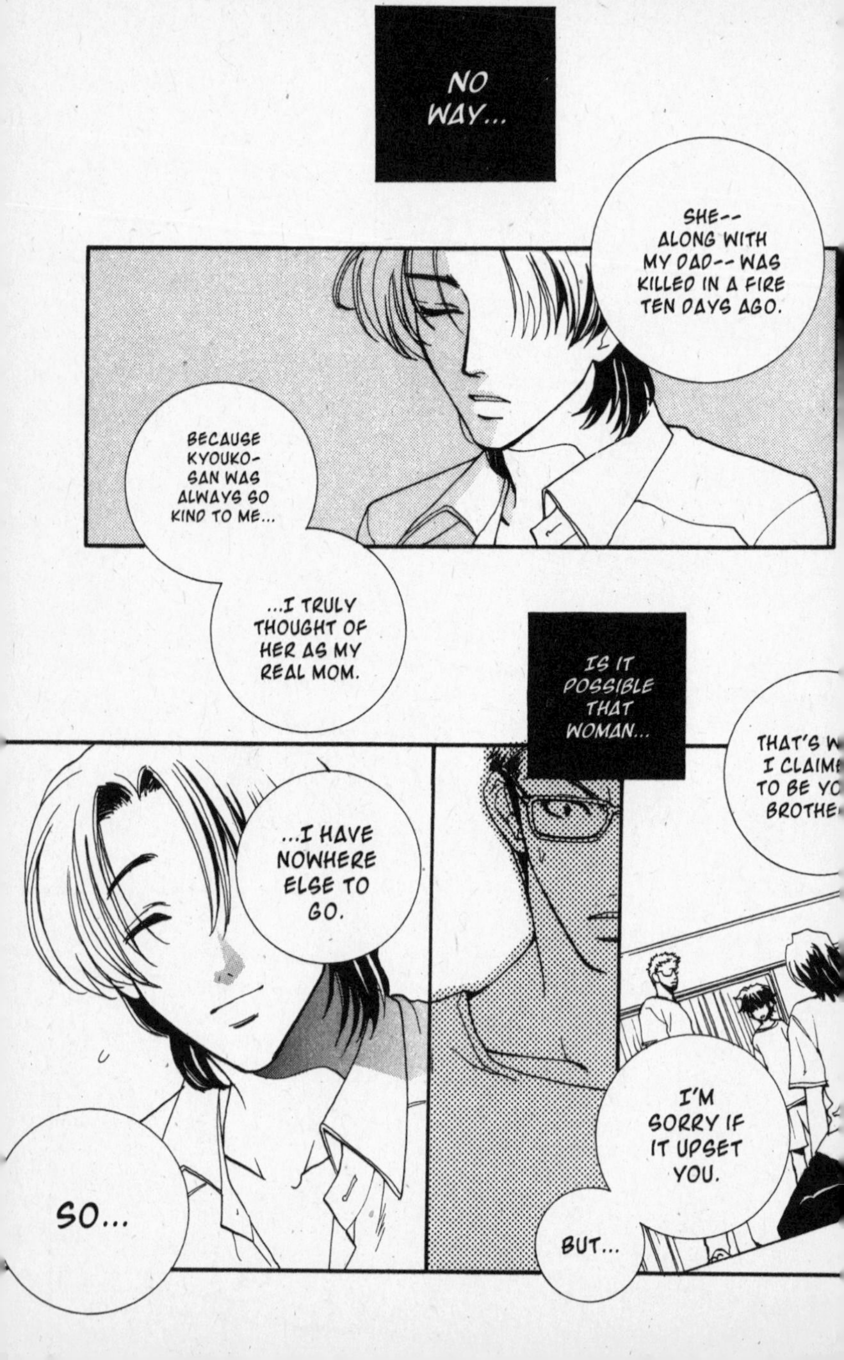
NO WAY...
SHE-- ALONG WITH MY DAD-- WAS KILLED IN A FIRE TEN DAYS AGO.
BECAUSE KYOUKO-SAN WAS ALWAYS SO KIND TO ME...
...I TRULY THOUGHT OF HER AS MY REAL MOM.
IS IT POSSIBLE THAT WOMAN...
THAT'S W I CLAIME TO BE YO BROTHE
I'M SORRY IF IT UPSET YOU.
BUT...
...I HAVE NOWHERE ELSE TO GO.
SO...

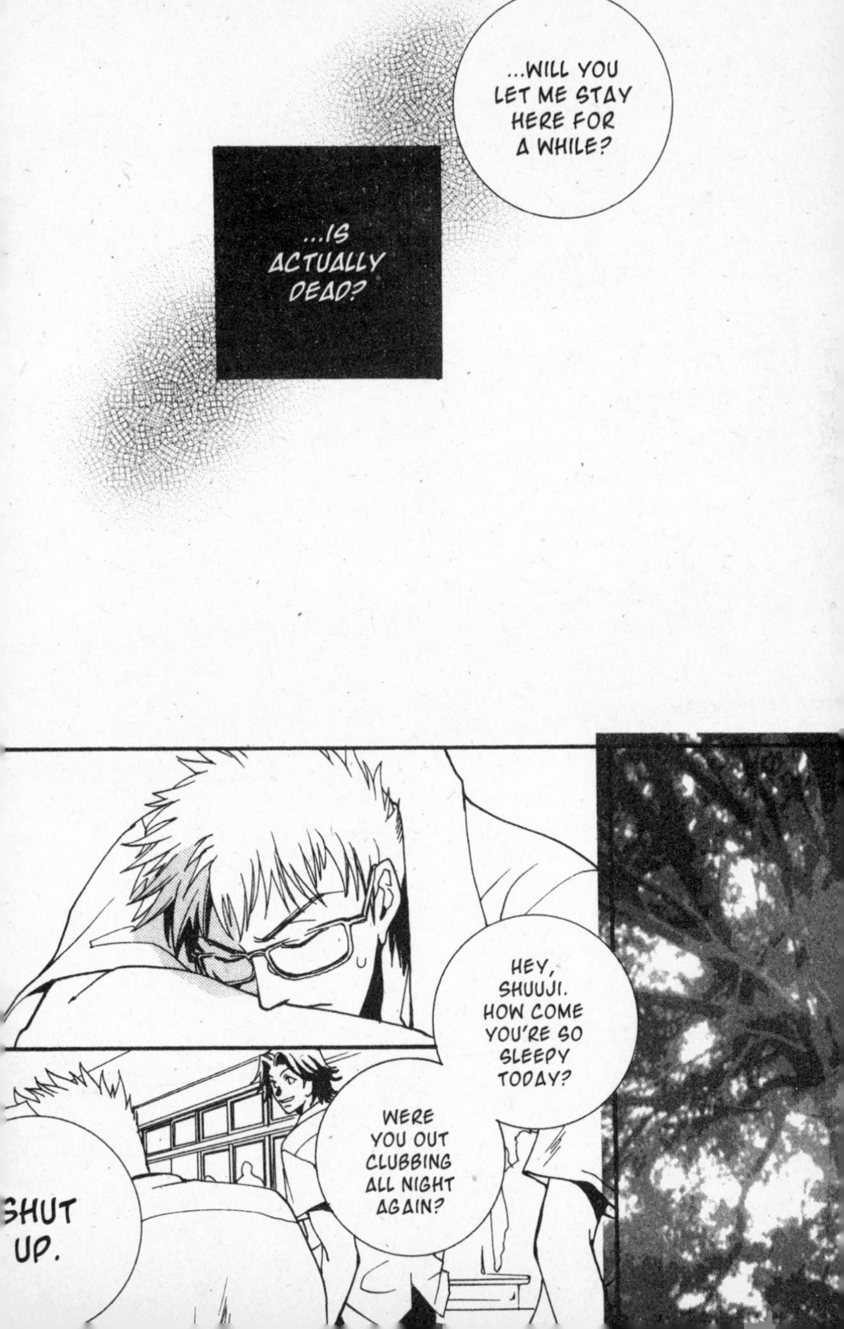
...WILL YOU LET ME STAY HERE FOR A WHILE?
...IS ACTUALLY DEAD?
HEY, SHUUJI. HOW COME YOU'RE SO SLEEPY TODAY?
WERE YOU OUT CLUBBING ALL NIGHT AGAIN?
SHUT UP.

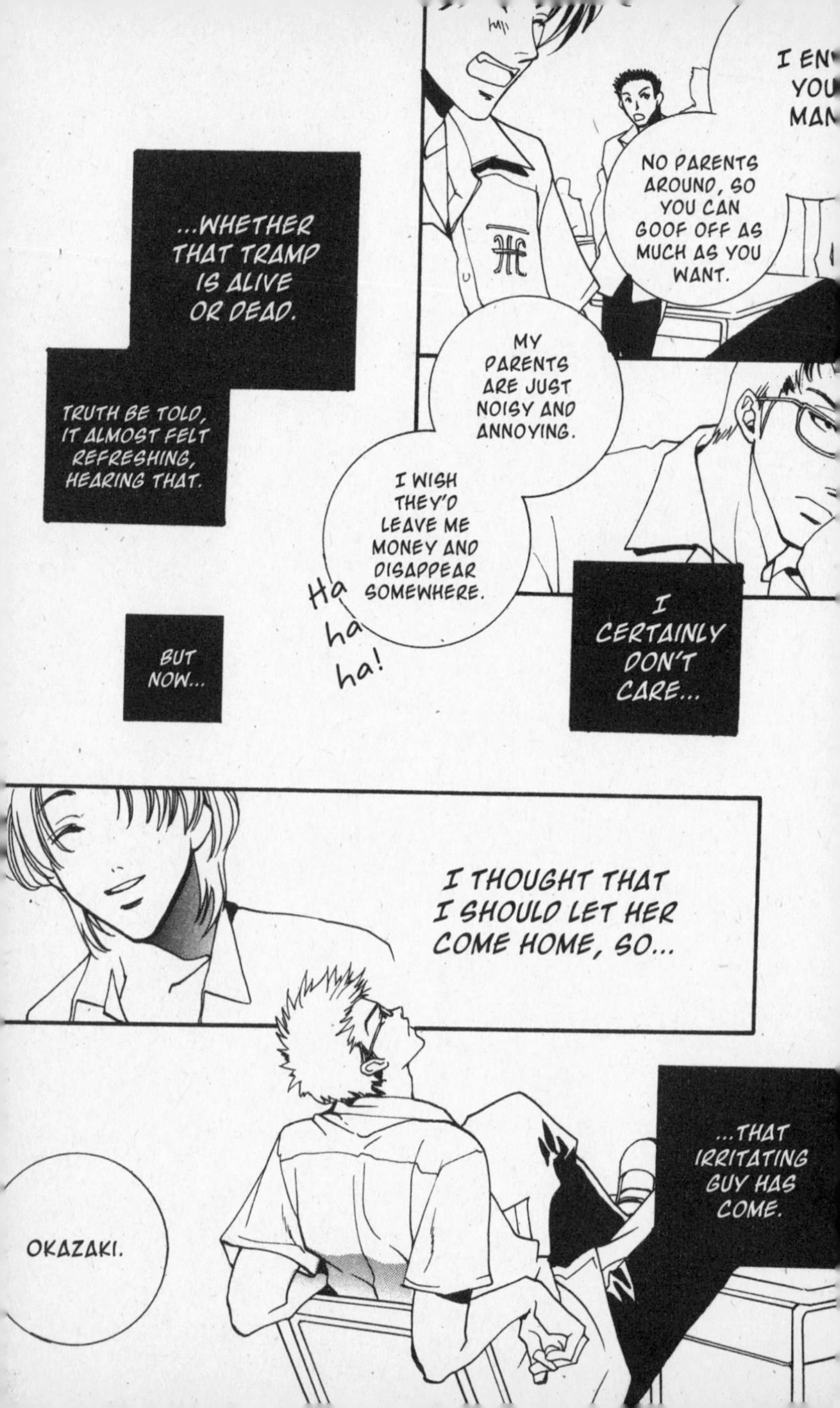

NO PARENTS AROUND, SO YOU CAN GOOF OFF AS MUCH AS YOU WANT.
MY PARENTS ARE JUST NOISY AND ANNOYING.
I WISH THEY'D LEAVE ME MONEY AND DISAPPEAR SOMEWHERE.
Ha ha ha!
I CERTAINLY DON'T CARE...
...WHETHER THAT TRAMP IS ALIVE OR DEAD.
TRUTH BE TOLD, IT ALMOST FELT REFRESHING, HEARING THAT.
BUT NOW...
I THOUGHT THAT I SHOULD LET HER COME HOME, SO...
...THAT IRRITATING GUY HAS COME.
OKAZAKI.

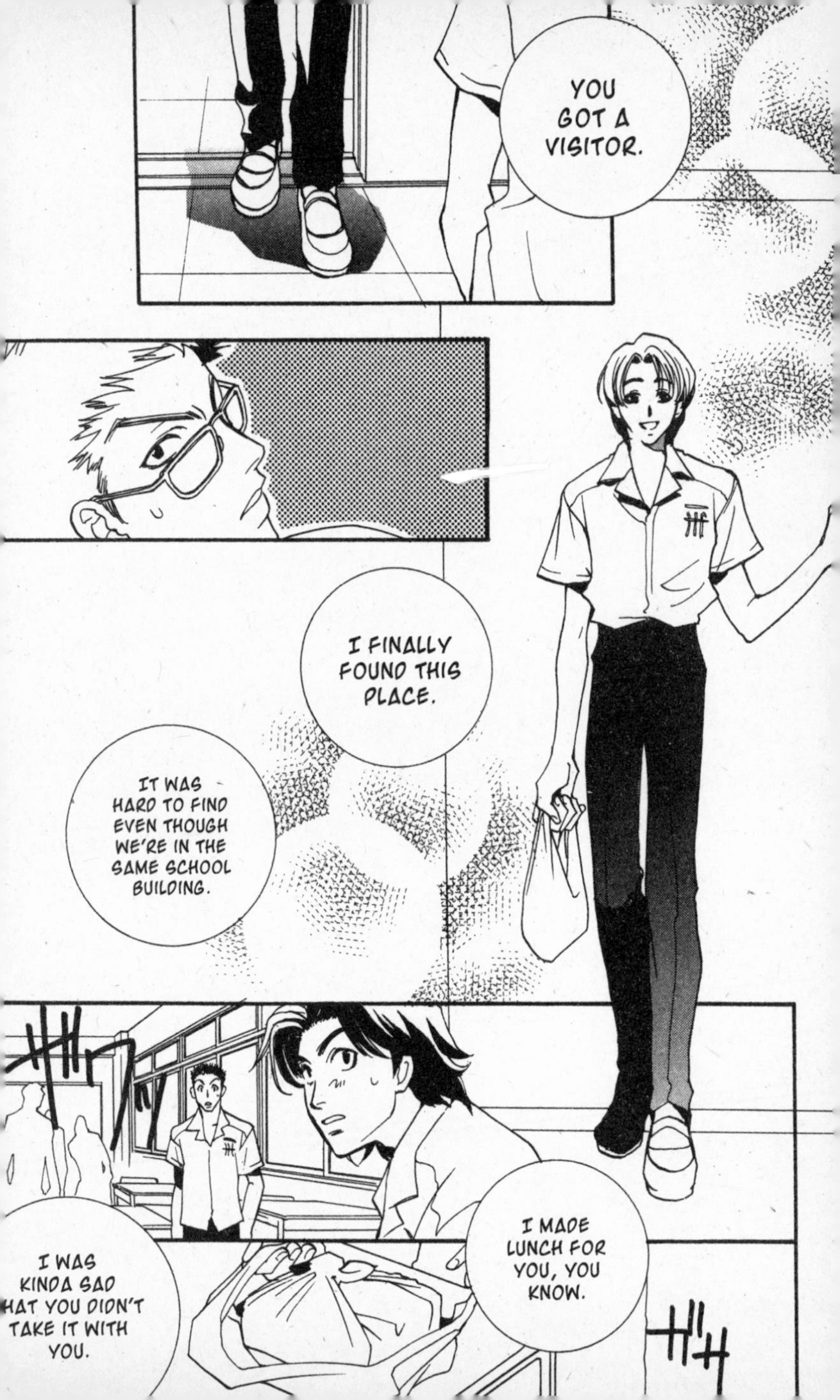
YOU GOT A VISITOR.
I FINALLY FOUND THIS PLACE.
IT WAS HARD TO FIND EVEN THOUGH WE'RE IN THE SAME SCHOOL BUILDING.
I MADE LUNCH FOR YOU, YOU KNOW.
I WAS KINDA SAD HAT YOU DIDN'T TAKE IT WITH YOU.

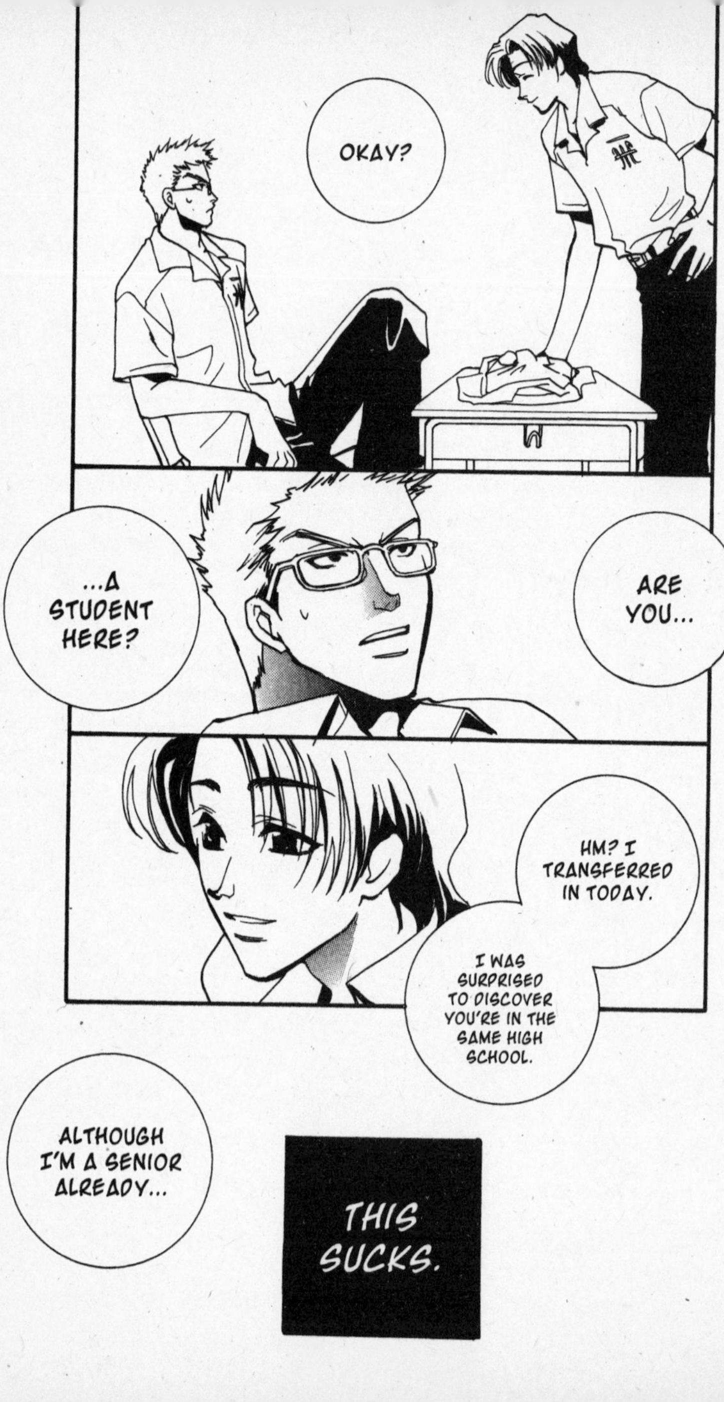

OKAY?
ARE YOU...
...A STUDENT HERE?
HM? I TRANSFERRED IN TODAY.
I WAS SURPRISED TO DISCOVER YOU'RE IN THE SAME HIGH SCHOOL.
ALTHOUGH I'M A SENIOR ALREADY...
THIS SUCKS.

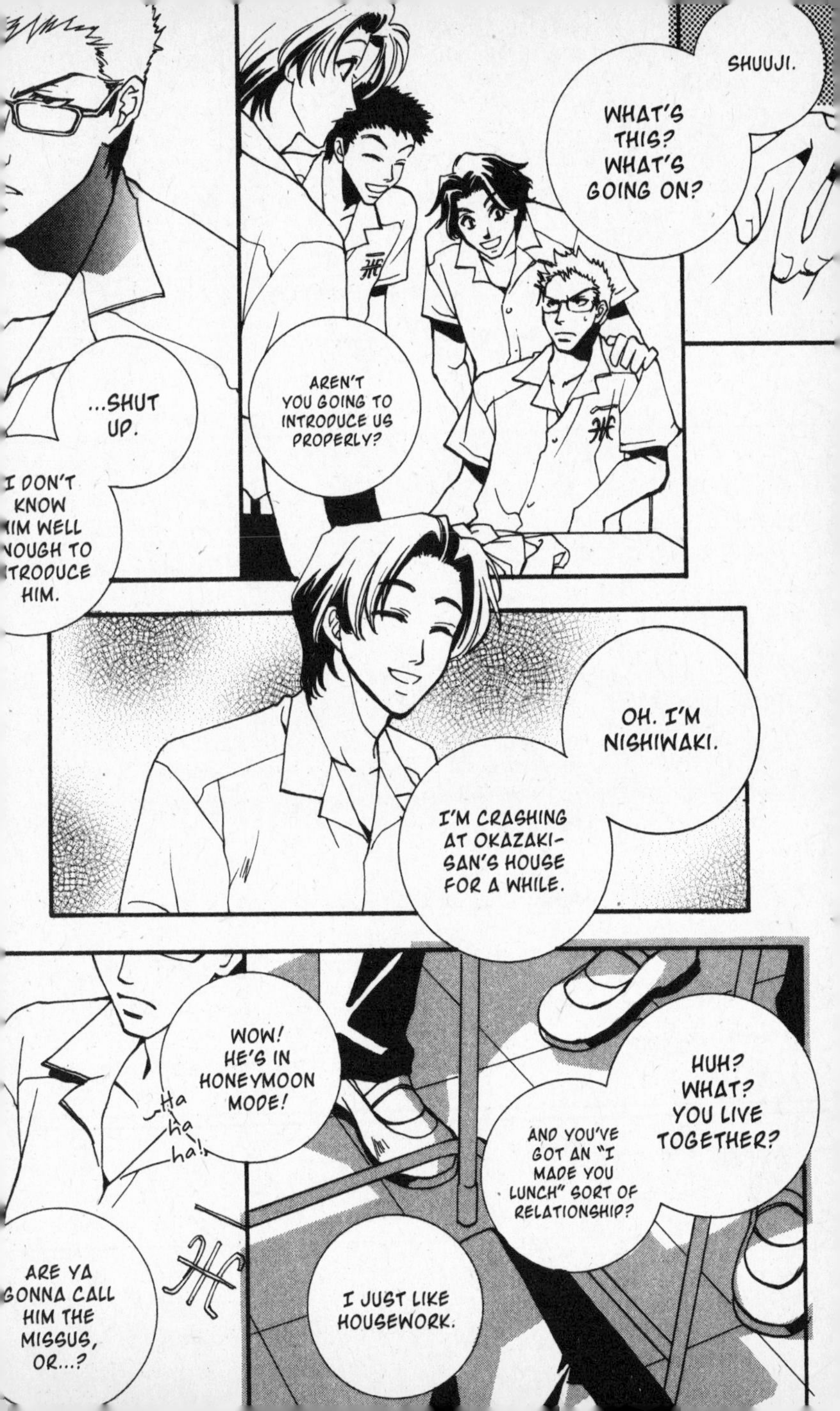
SHUUJI.
WHAT'S THIS? WHAT'S GOING ON?
AREN'T YOU GOING TO INTRODUCE US PROPERLY?
...SHUT UP.
I DON'T KNOW IM WELL NOUGH TO TRODUCE HIM.
OH. I'M NISHIWAKI.
I'M CRASHING AT OKAZAKI-SAN'S HOUSE FOR A WHILE.
HUH? WHAT? YOU LIVE TOGETHER?
AND YOU'VE GOT AN "I MADE YOU LUNCH" SORT OF RELATIONSHIP?
I JUST LIKE HOUSEWORK.
WOW! HE'S IN HONEYMOON MODE!
Ha ha ha!
ARE YA GONNA CALL HIM THE MISSUS, OR...?

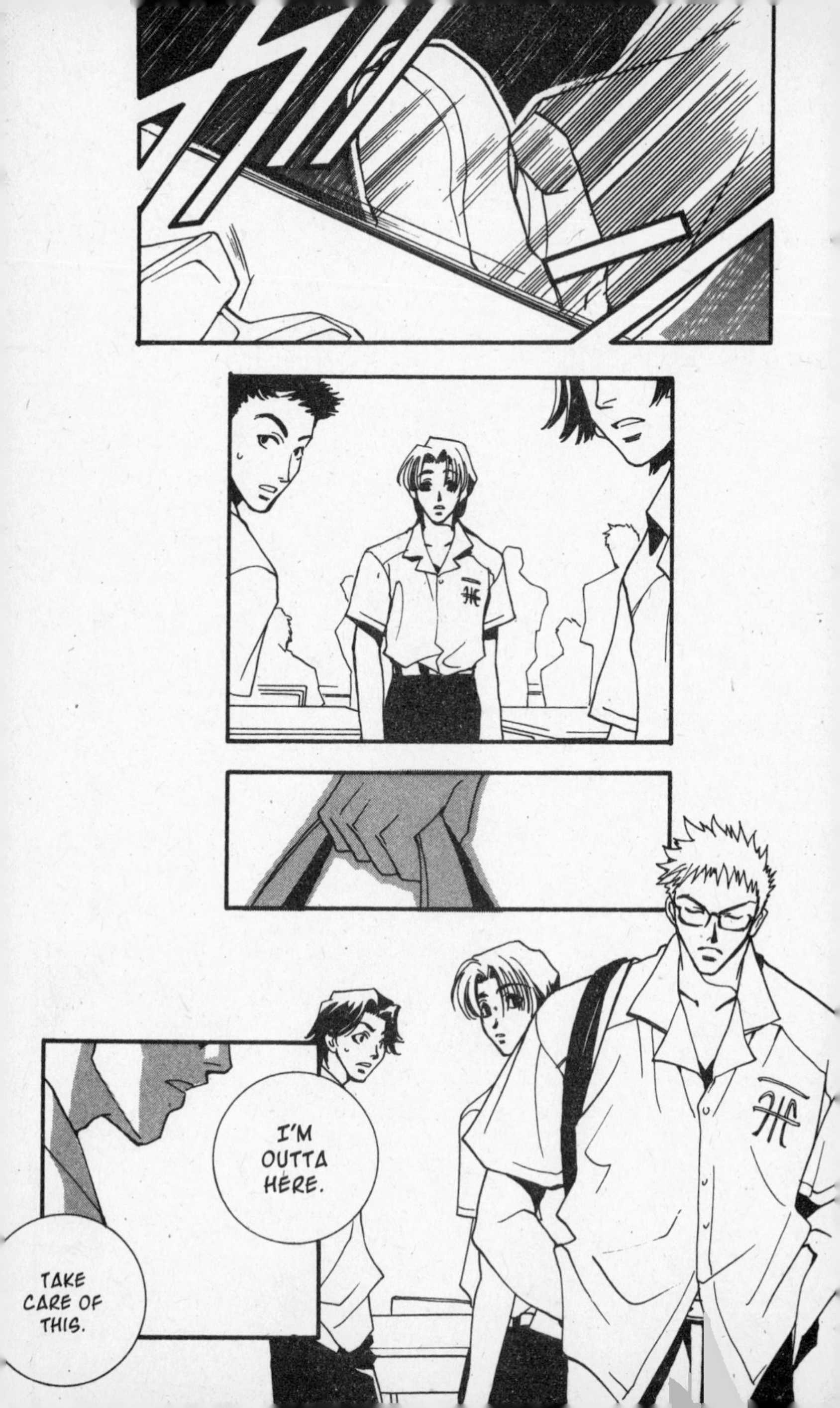
I'M OUTTA HERE.
TAKE CARE OF THIS.

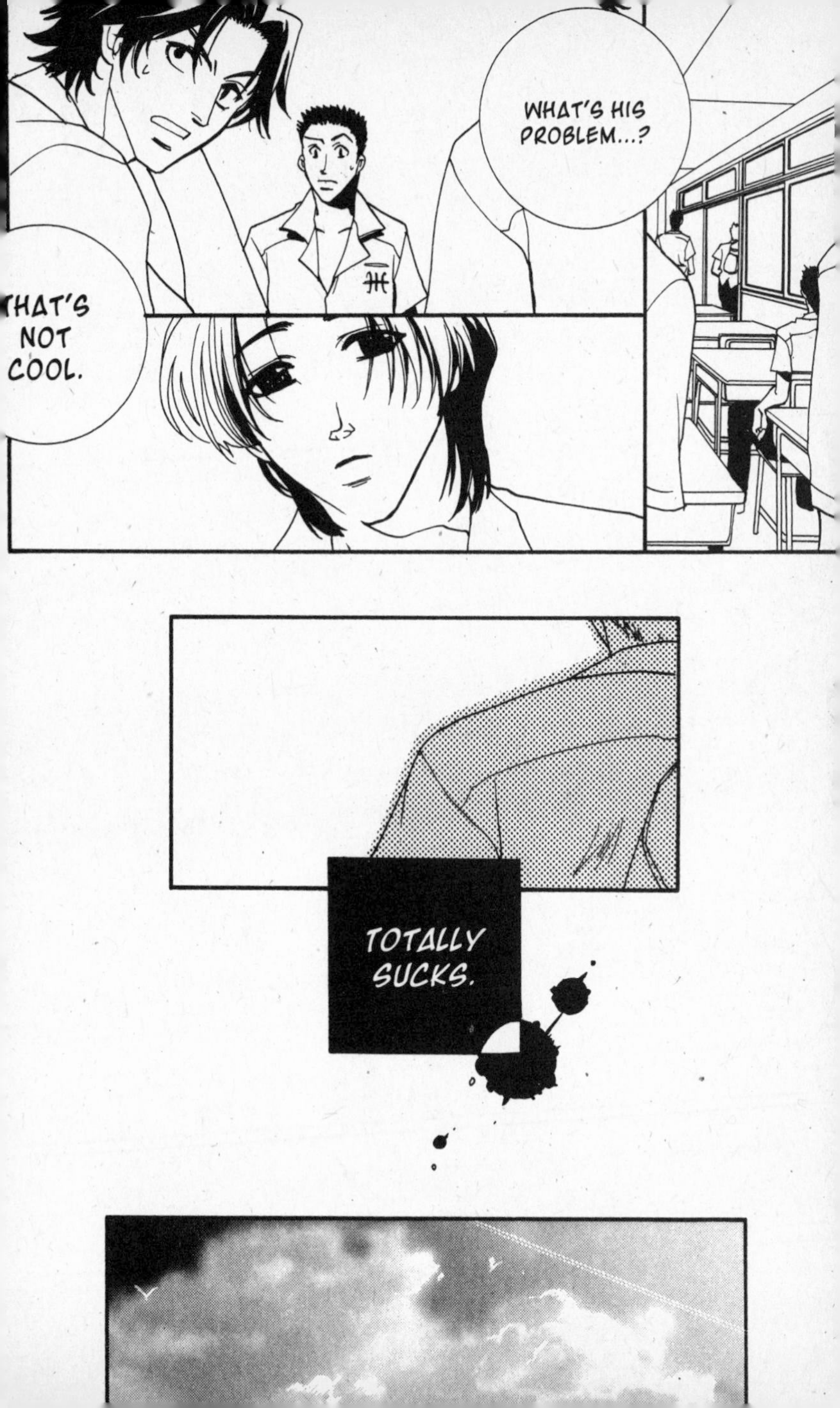
WHAT'S HIS PROBLEM...?
THAT'S NOT COOL.
TOTALLY SUCKS.

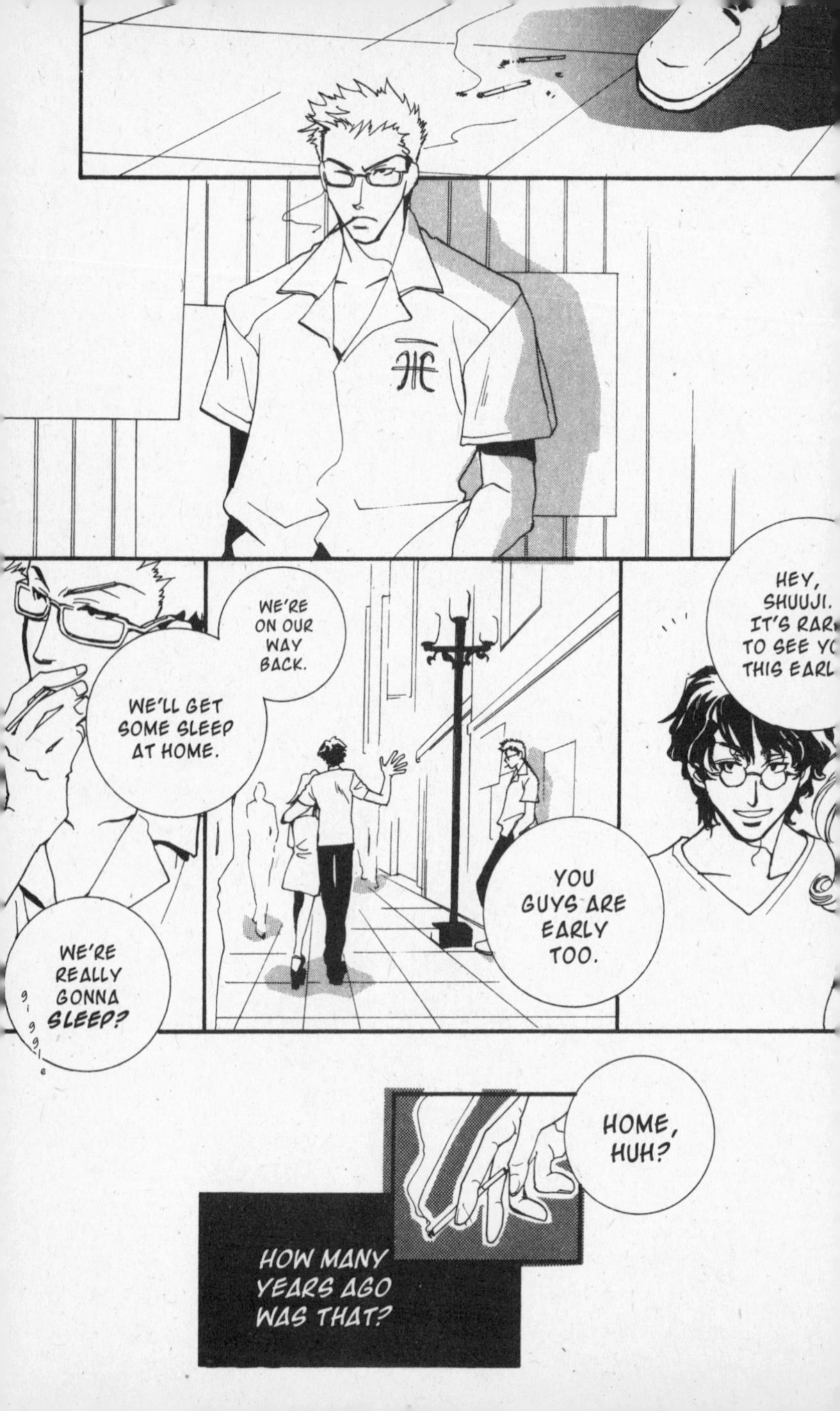
HEY, SHUUJI. IT'S RAR TO SEE YO THIS EARL
YOU GUYS ARE EARLY TOO.
WE'RE ON OUR WAY BACK.
WE'LL GET SOME SLEEP AT HOME.
WE'RE REALLY GONNA SLEEP?
giggle
HOME, HUH?
HOW MANY YEARS AGO WAS THAT?

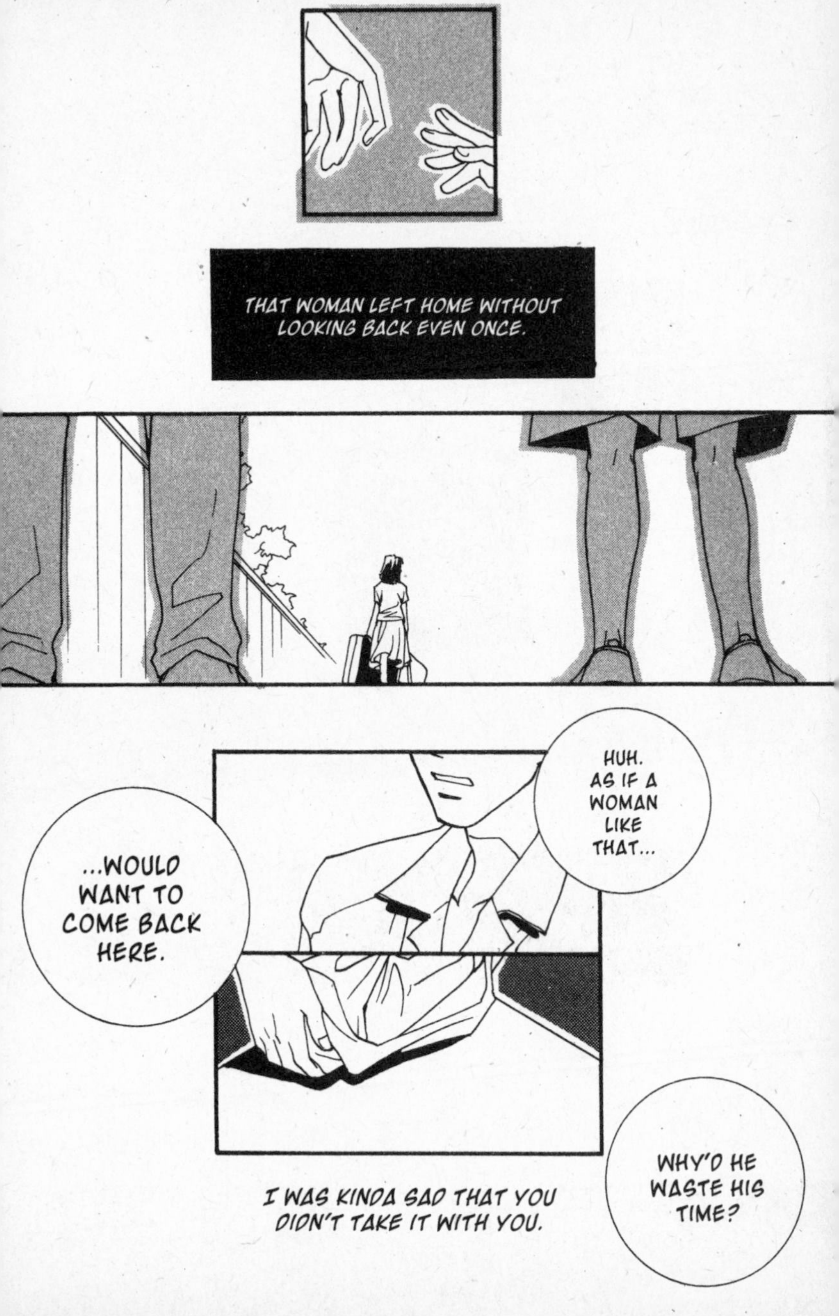
THAT WOMAN LEFT HOME WITHOUT LOOKING BACK EVEN ONCE.
HUH. AS IF A WOMAN LIKE THAT...
...WOULD WANT TO COME BACK HERE.
WHY'D HE WASTE HIS TIME?
I WAS KINDA SAD THAT YOU DIDN'T TAKE IT WITH YOU.

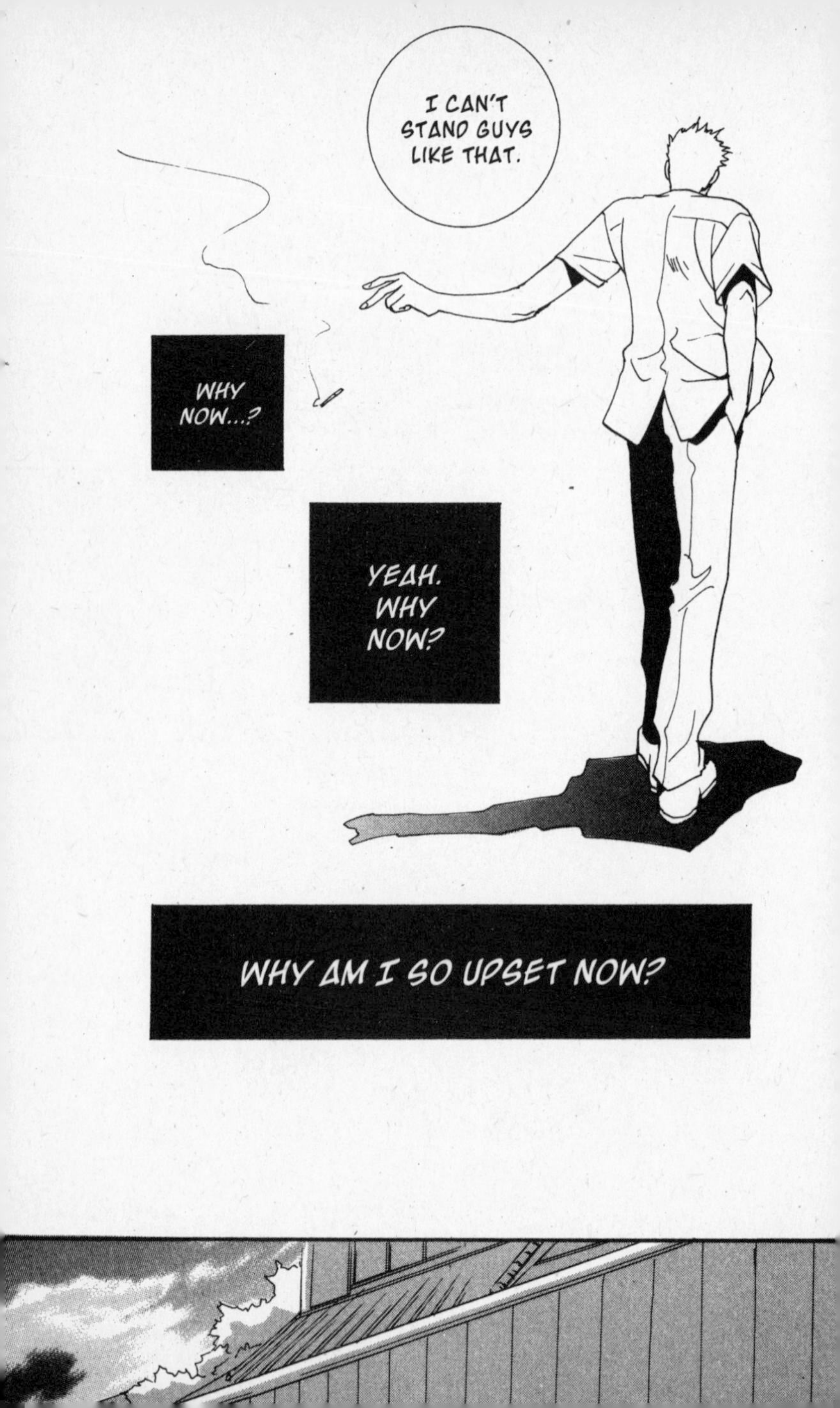
I CAN'T STAND GUYS LIKE THAT.
WHY NOW...?
YEAH. WHY NOW?
WHY AM I SO UPSET NOW?

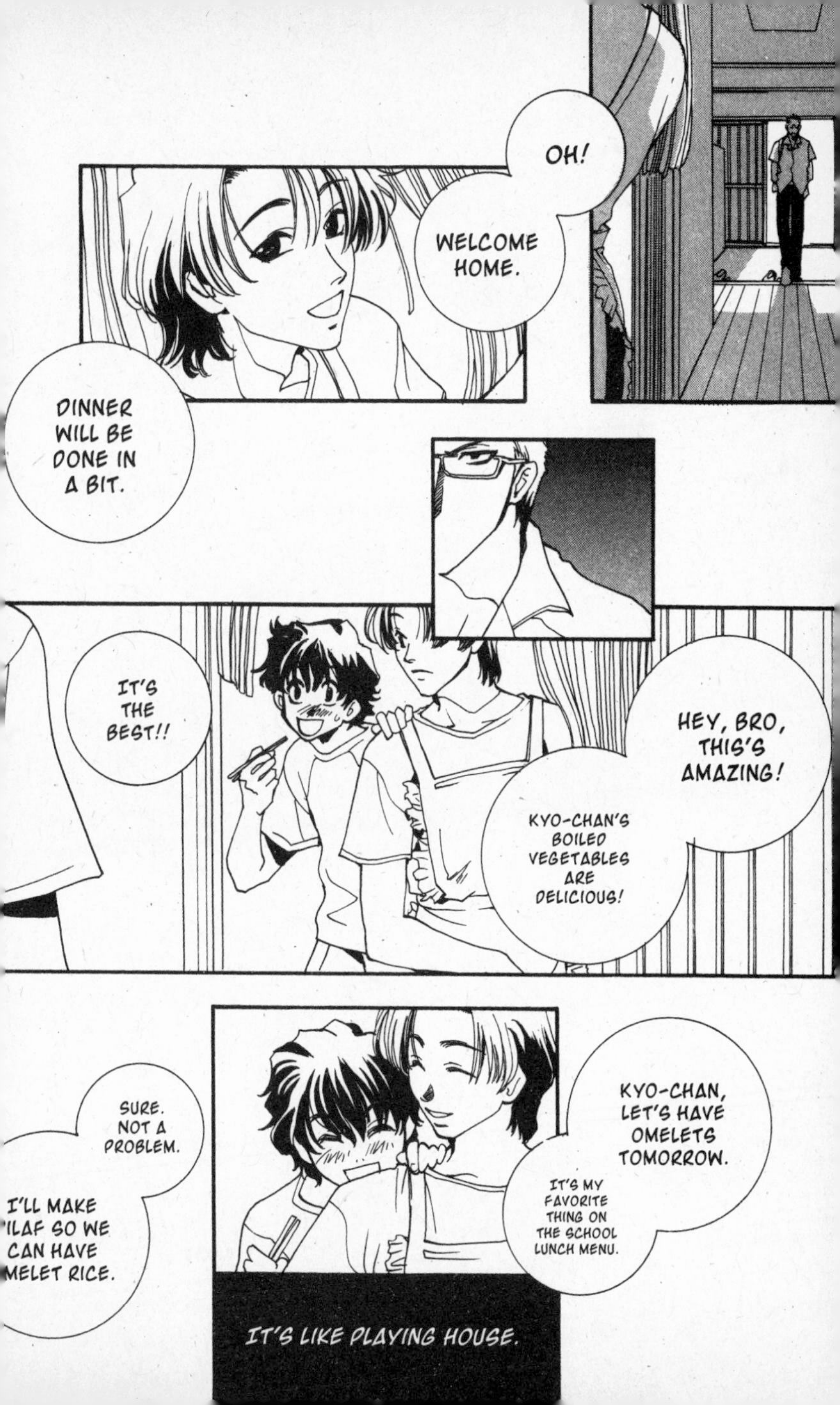
OH!
WELCOME HOME.
DINNER WILL BE DONE IN A BIT.
HEY, BRO, THIS'S AMAZING!
KYO-CHAN'S BOILED VEGETABLES ARE DELICIOUS!
IT'S THE BEST!!
KYO-CHAN, LET'S HAVE OMELETS TOMORROW.
IT'S MY FAVORITE THING ON THE SCHOOL LUNCH MENU.
SURE. NOT A PROBLEM.
I'LL MAKE ILAF SO WE CAN HAVE MELET RICE.
IT'S LIKE PLAYING HOUSE.

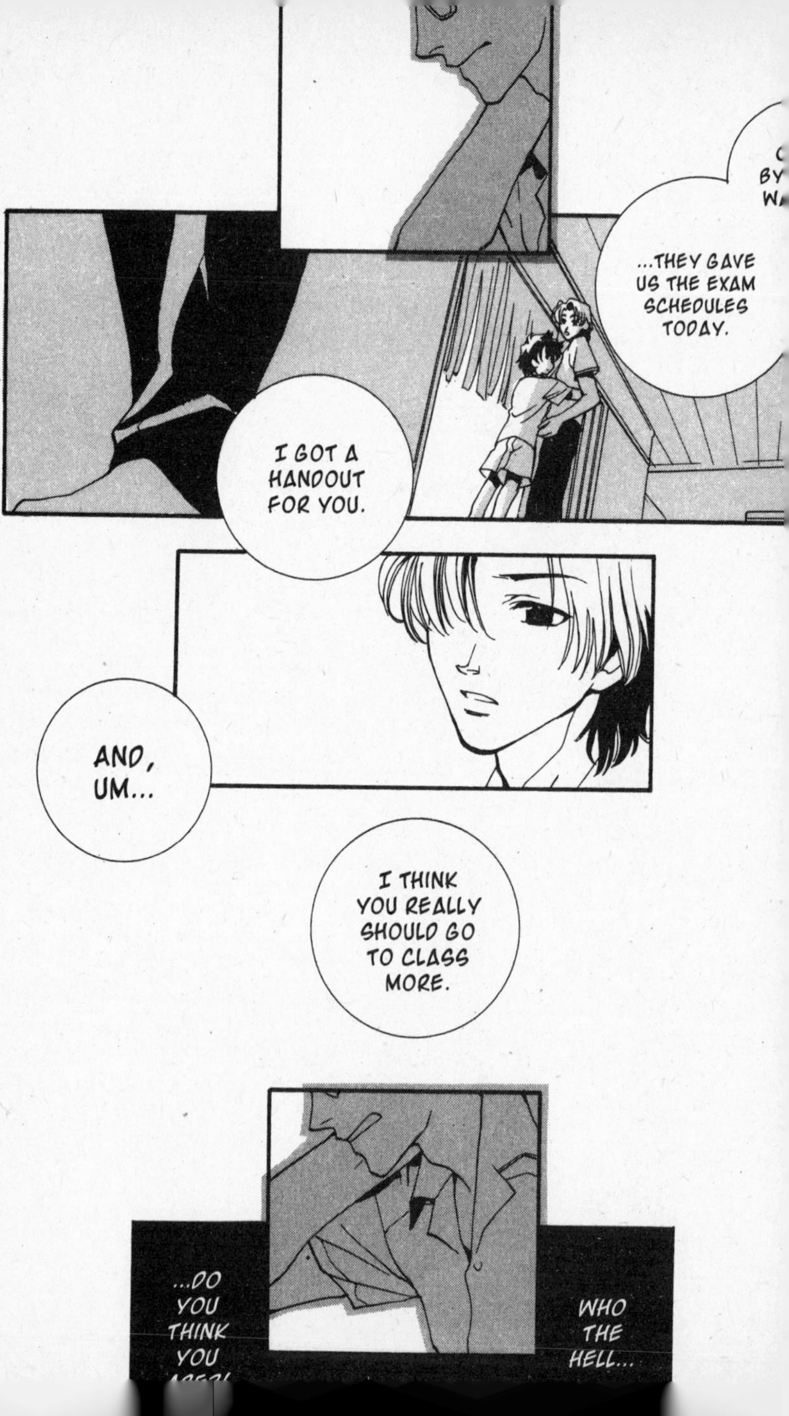
...THEY GAVE US THE EXAM SCHEDULES TODAY.
I GOT A HANDOUT FOR YOU.
AND, UM...
I THINK YOU REALLY SHOULD GO TO CLASS MORE.
WHO THE HELL...
...DO YOU THINK YOU

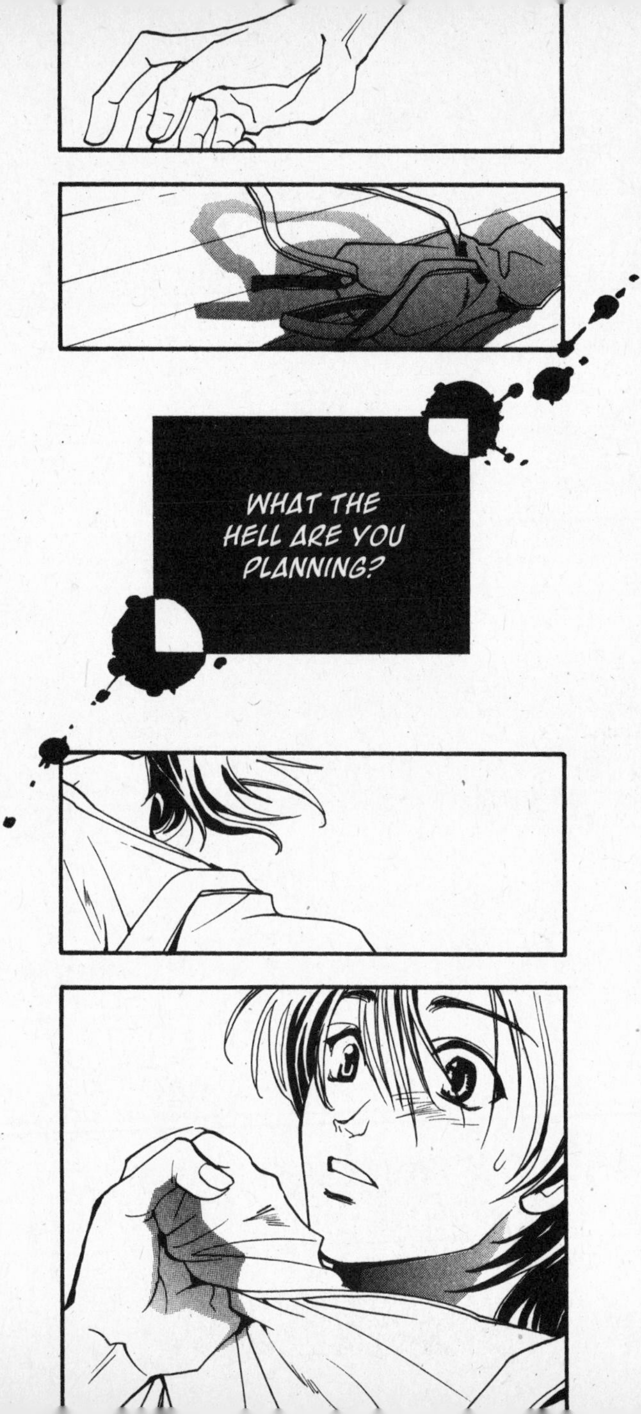
WHAT THE HELL ARE YOU PLANNING?

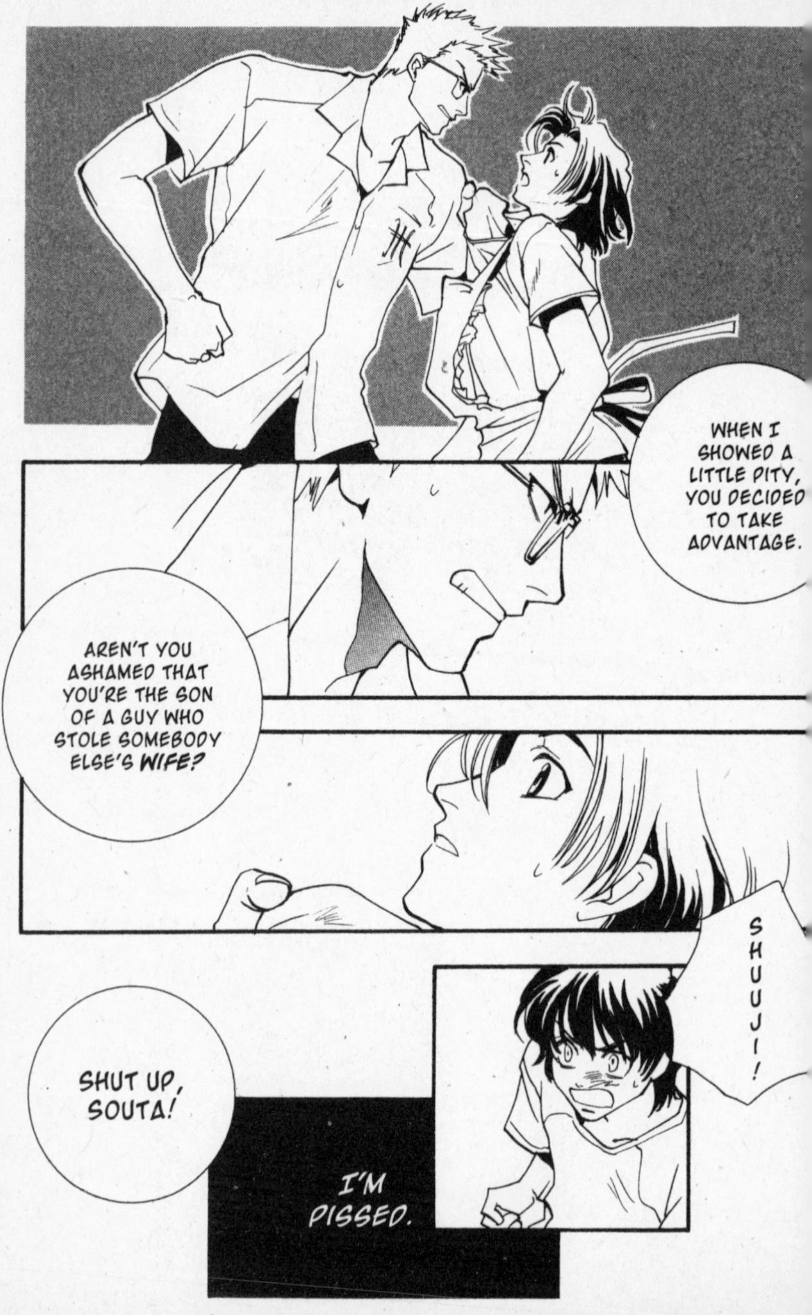
WHEN I SHOWED A LITTLE PITY, YOU DECIDED TO TAKE ADVANTAGE.
AREN'T YOU ASHAMED THAT YOU'RE THE SON OF A GUY WHO STOLE SOMEBODY ELSE'S **WIFE?**
SHUUJI!
SHUT UP, SOUTA!
I'M PISSED.

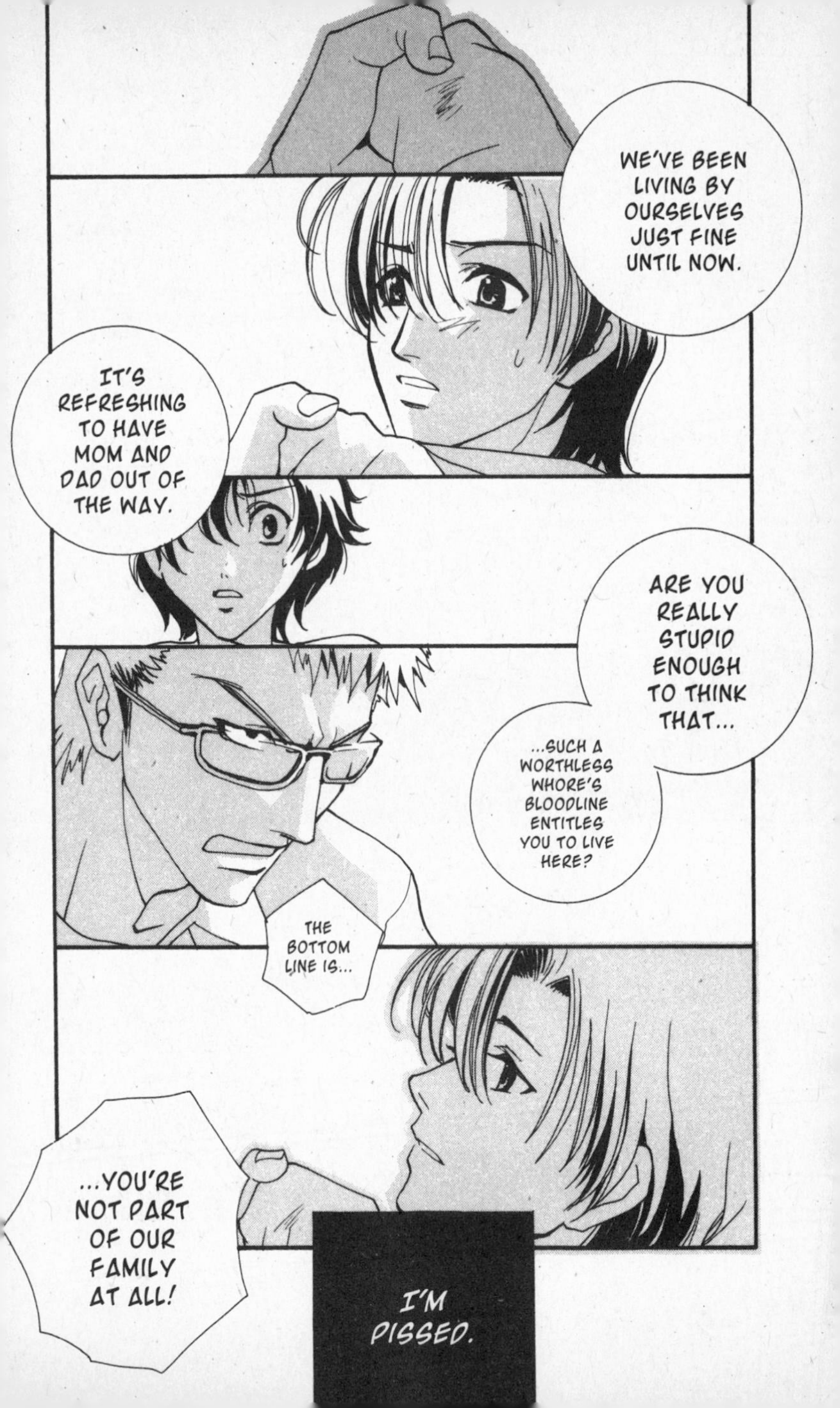
WE'VE BEEN LIVING BY OURSELVES JUST FINE UNTIL NOW.
IT'S REFRESHING TO HAVE MOM AND DAD OUT OF THE WAY.
ARE YOU REALLY STUPID ENOUGH TO THINK THAT...
...SUCH A WORTHLESS WHORE'S BLOODLINE ENTITLES YOU TO LIVE HERE?
THE BOTTOM LINE IS...
...YOU'RE NOT PART OF OUR FAMILY AT ALL!
I'M PISSED.

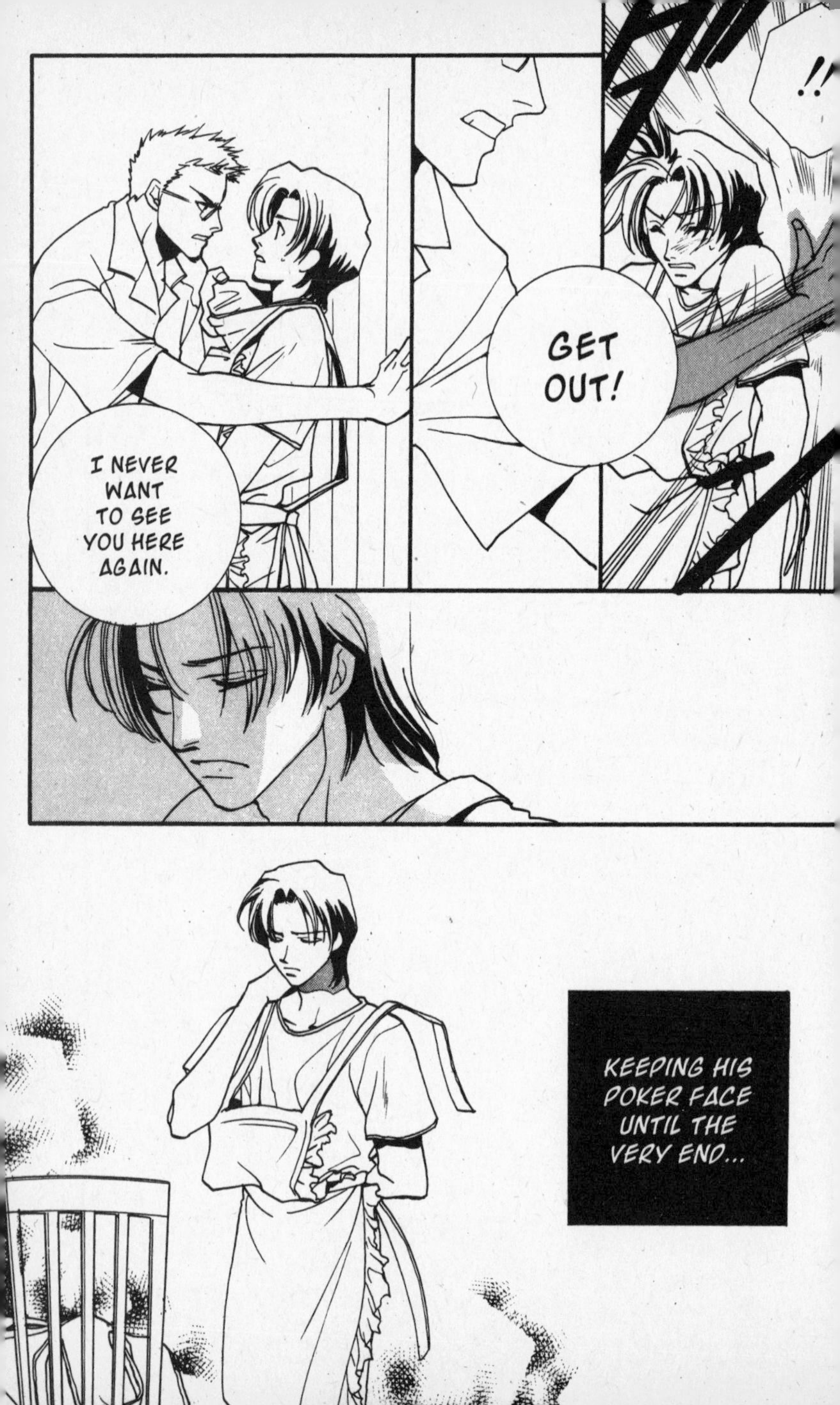
!!
GET OUT!
I NEVER WANT TO SEE YOU HERE AGAIN.
KEEPING HIS POKER FACE UNTIL THE VERY END...

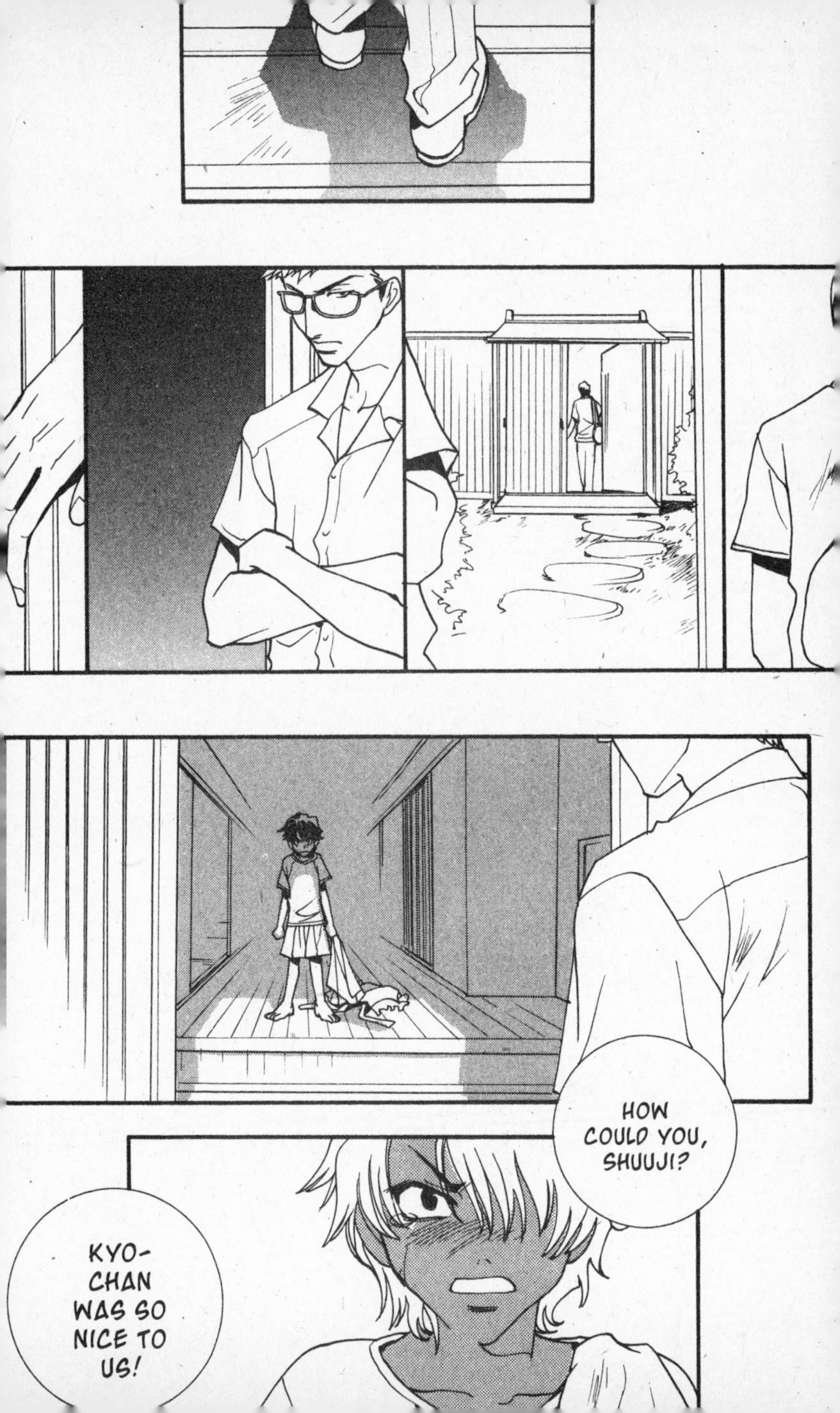
HOW COULD YOU, SHUUJI?
KYO-CHAN WAS SO NICE TO US!

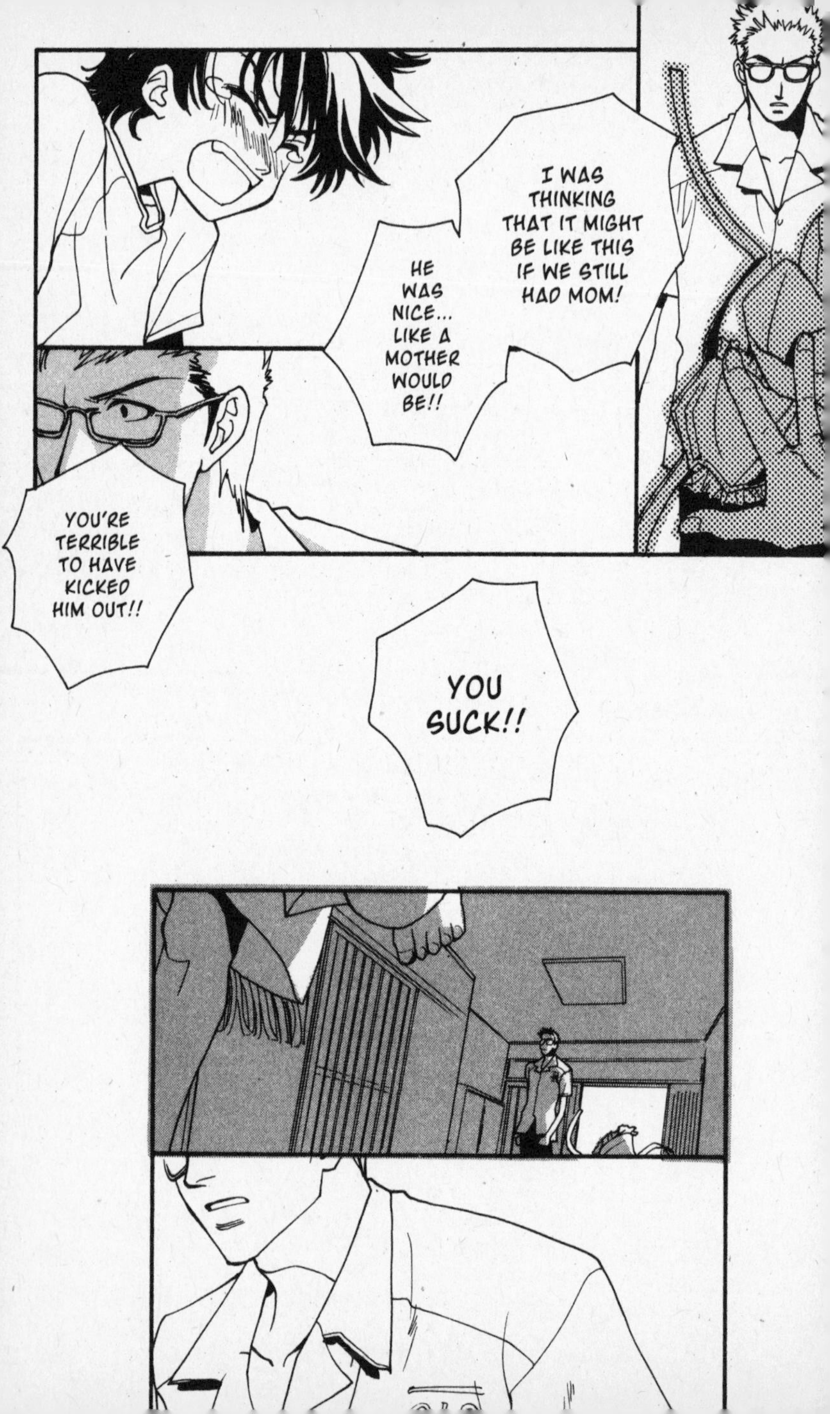
I WAS THINKING THAT IT MIGHT BE LIKE THIS IF WE STILL HAD MOM!
HE WAS NICE... LIKE A MOTHER WOULD BE!!
YOU'RE TERRIBLE TO HAVE KICKED HIM OUT!!
YOU SUCK!!

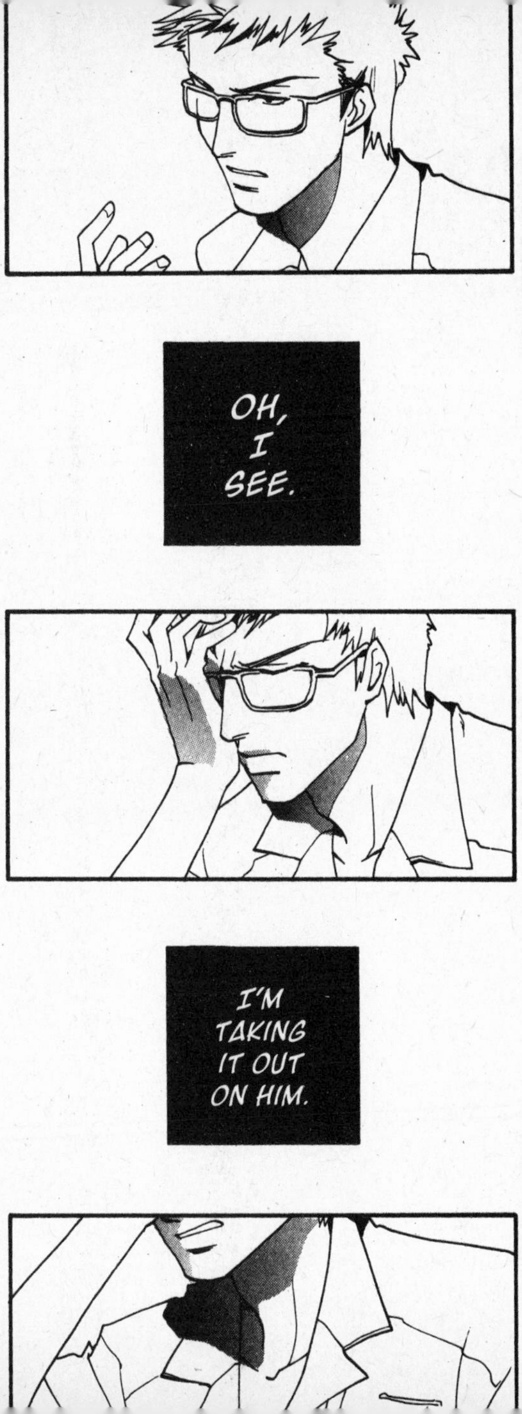
OH, I SEE.
I'M TAKING IT OUT ON HIM.

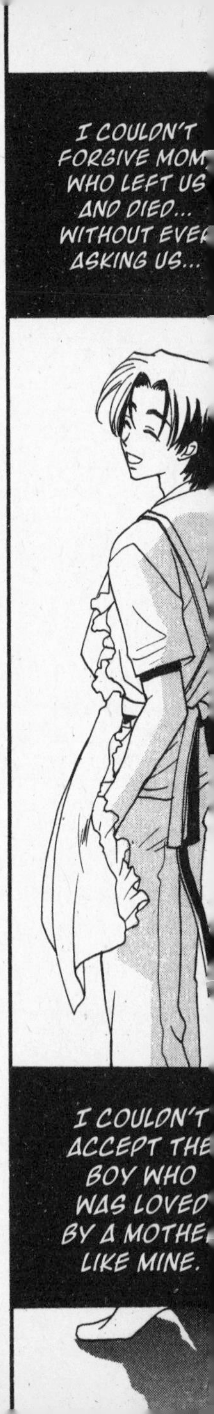
I COULDN'T FORGIVE MOM, WHO LEFT US AND DIED... WITHOUT EVER ASKING US...
I COULDN'T ACCEPT THE BOY WHO WAS LOVED BY A MOTHE LIKE MINE.

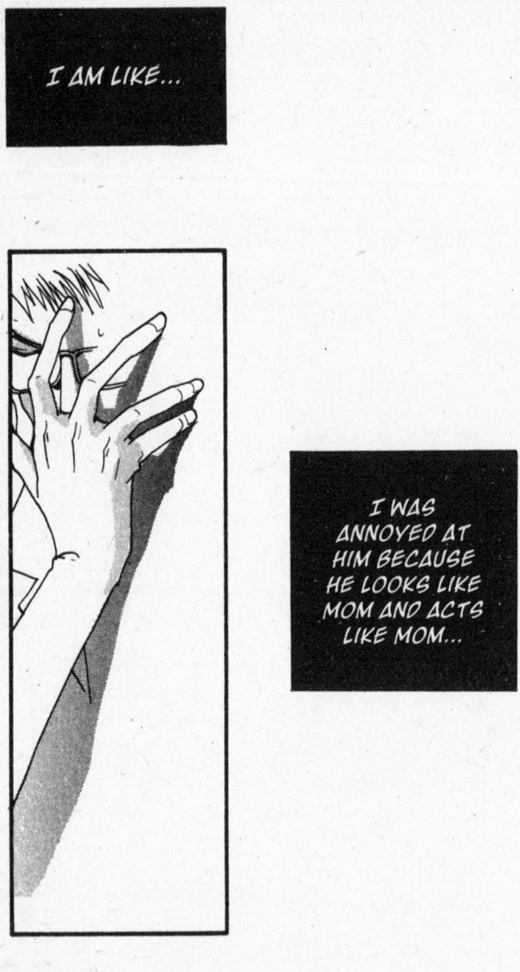
I AM LIKE...
...A KID WHO'S STARVING FOR LOVE.
I WAS ANNOYED AT HIM BECAUSE HE LOOKS LIKE MOM AND ACTS LIKE MOM...

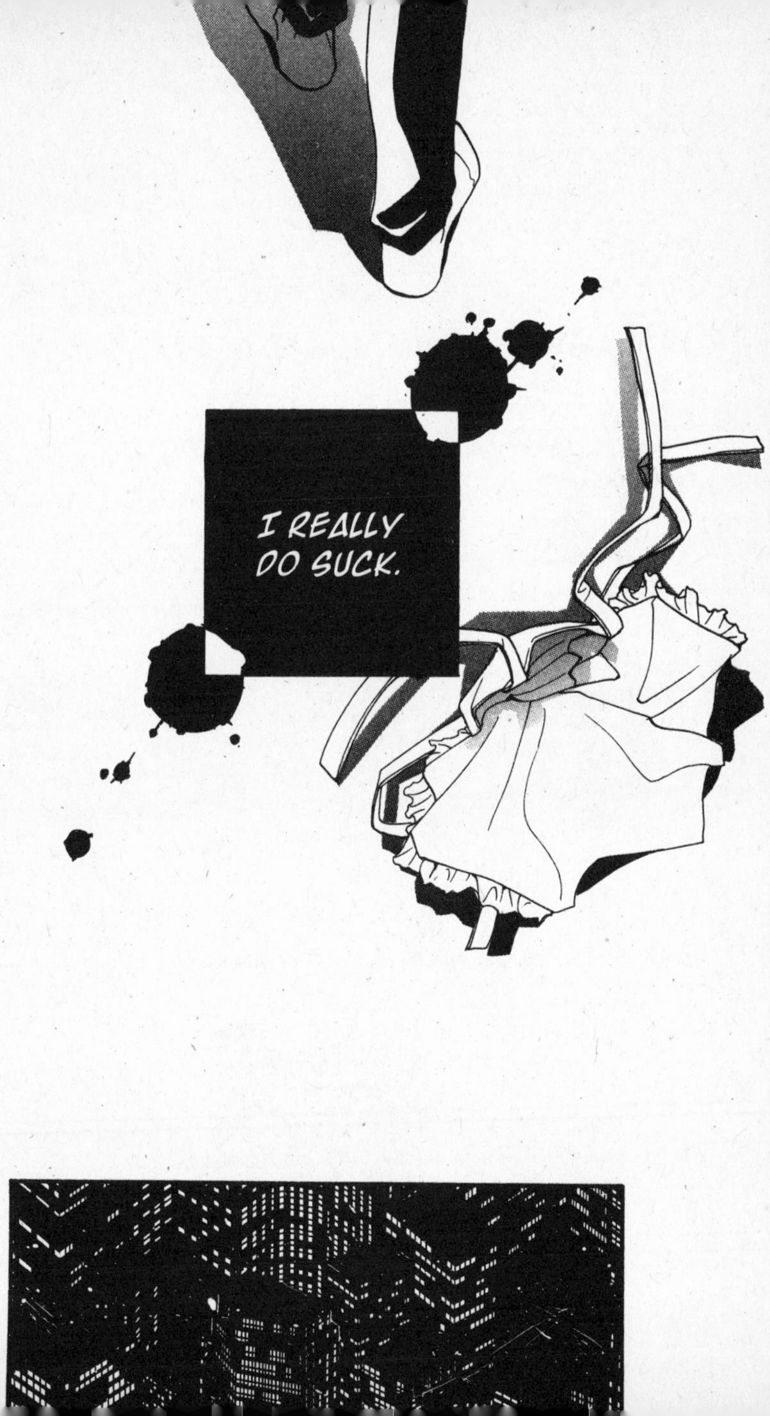
I REALLY DO SUCK.

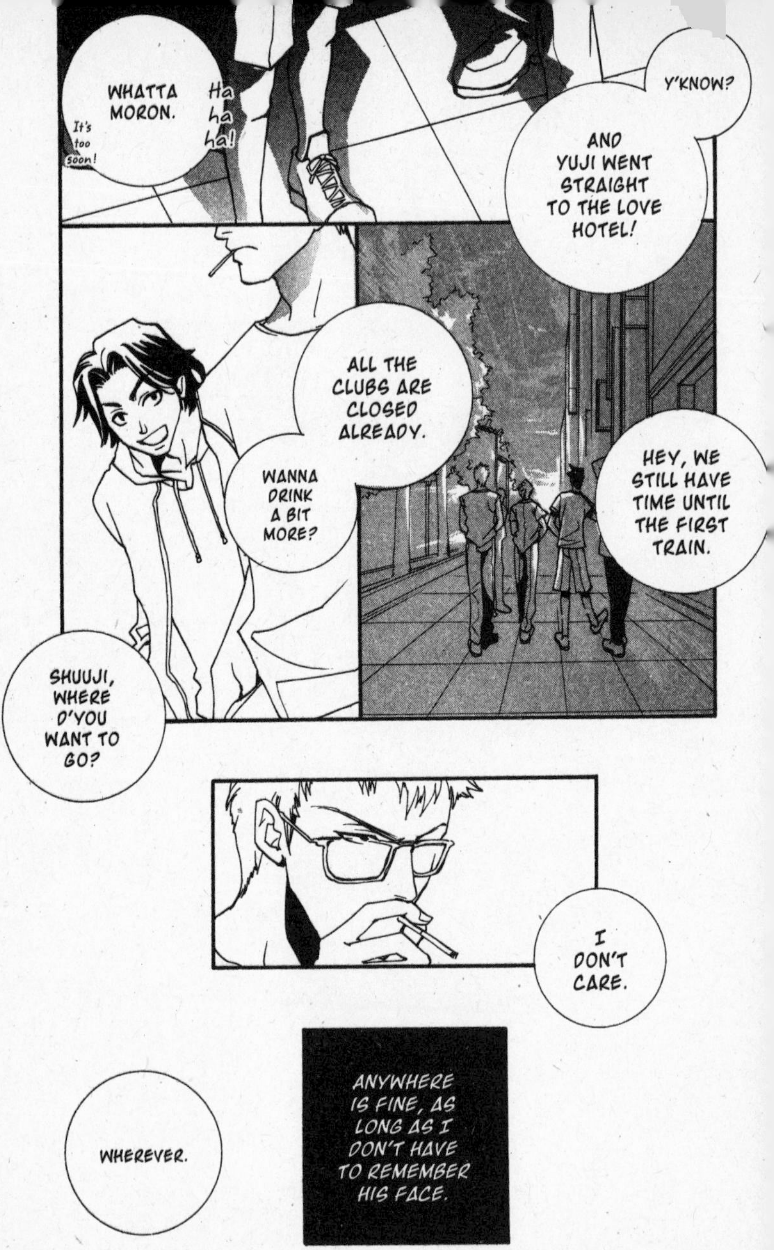
Y'KNOW?
AND YUJI WENT STRAIGHT TO THE LOVE HOTEL!
Ha ha ha!
WHATTA MORON.
It's too soon!
HEY, WE STILL HAVE TIME UNTIL THE FIRST TRAIN.
ALL THE CLUBS ARE CLOSED ALREADY.
WANNA DRINK A BIT MORE?
SHUUJI, WHERE D'YOU WANT TO GO?
I DON'T CARE.
ANYWHERE IS FINE, AS LONG AS I DON'T HAVE TO REMEMBER HIS FACE.
WHEREVER.

HIS QUIET
EYES KEEP
GUILTING ME.

I'M GOING
TO GO
CRAZY.

MAN, THERE'S GOTTA BE SOME CHICK GETTING OFF THE NIGHTSHIFT NOW, RIGHT?

WHAT, YOU WANT TO WALK HER HOME?

ASSHOLE, I'D GET HER TO STAY AND PARTY!

Ha ha ha!

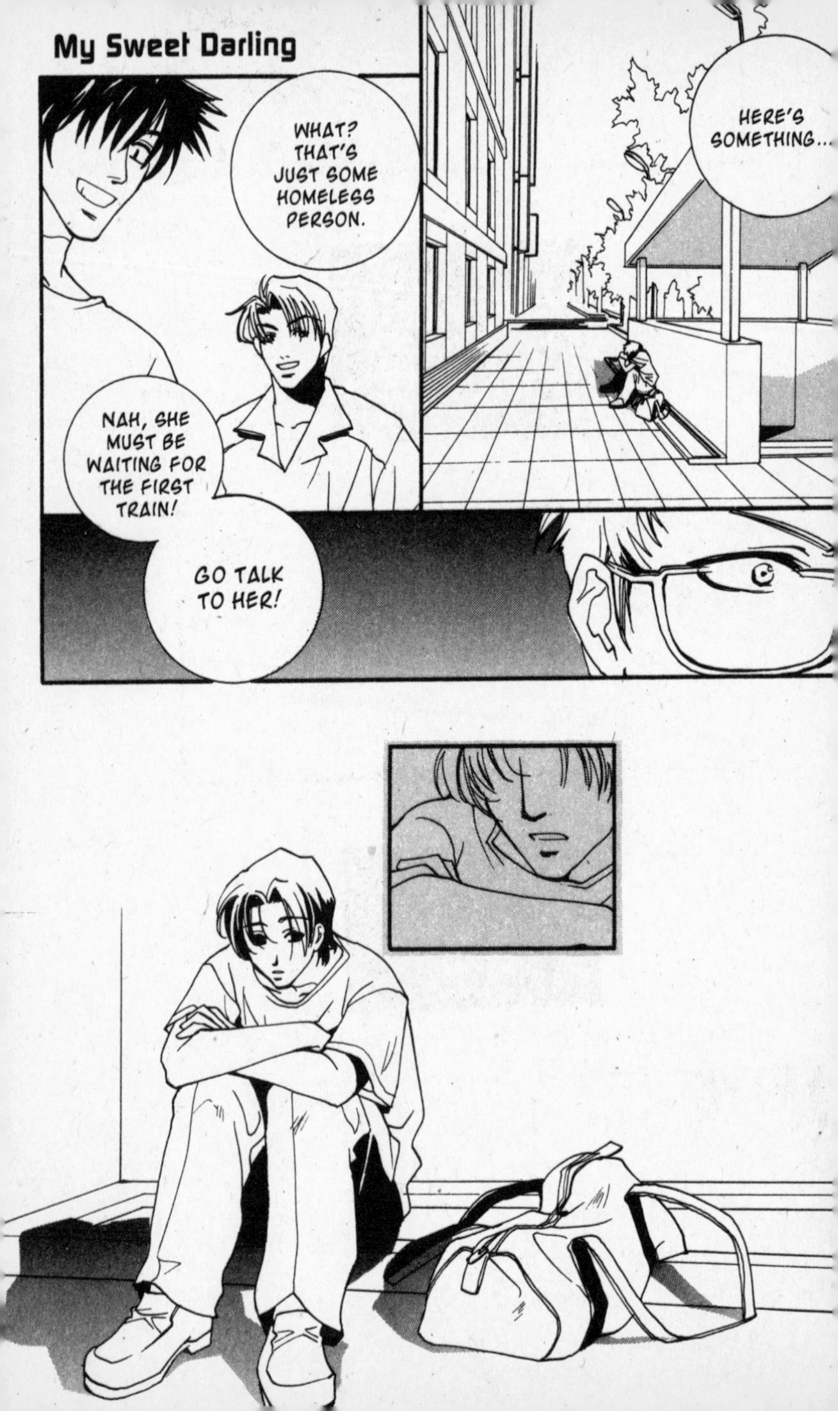
HERE'S SOMETHING...
WHAT? THAT'S JUST SOME HOMELESS PERSON.
NAH, SHE MUST BE WAITING FOR THE FIRST TRAIN!
GO TALK TO HER!

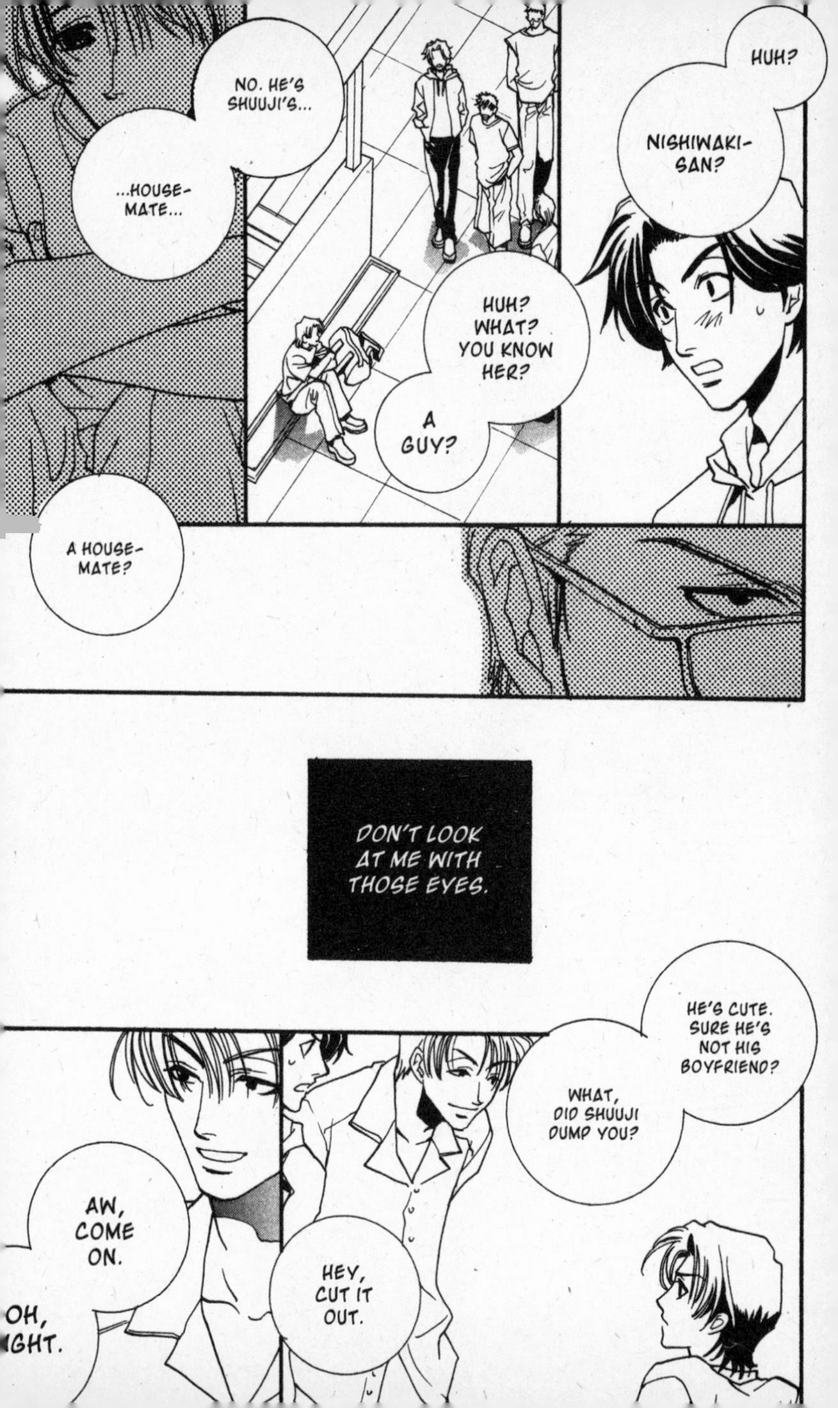
HUH?
NISHIWAKI-SAN?
HUH? WHAT? YOU KNOW HER?
A GUY?
NO. HE'S SHUUJI'S...
...HOUSE-MATE...
A HOUSE-MATE?
DON'T LOOK AT ME WITH THOSE EYES.
HE'S CUTE. SURE HE'S NOT HIS BOYFRIEND?
WHAT, DID SHUUJI DUMP YOU?
HEY, CUT IT OUT.
AW, COME ON.
OH,

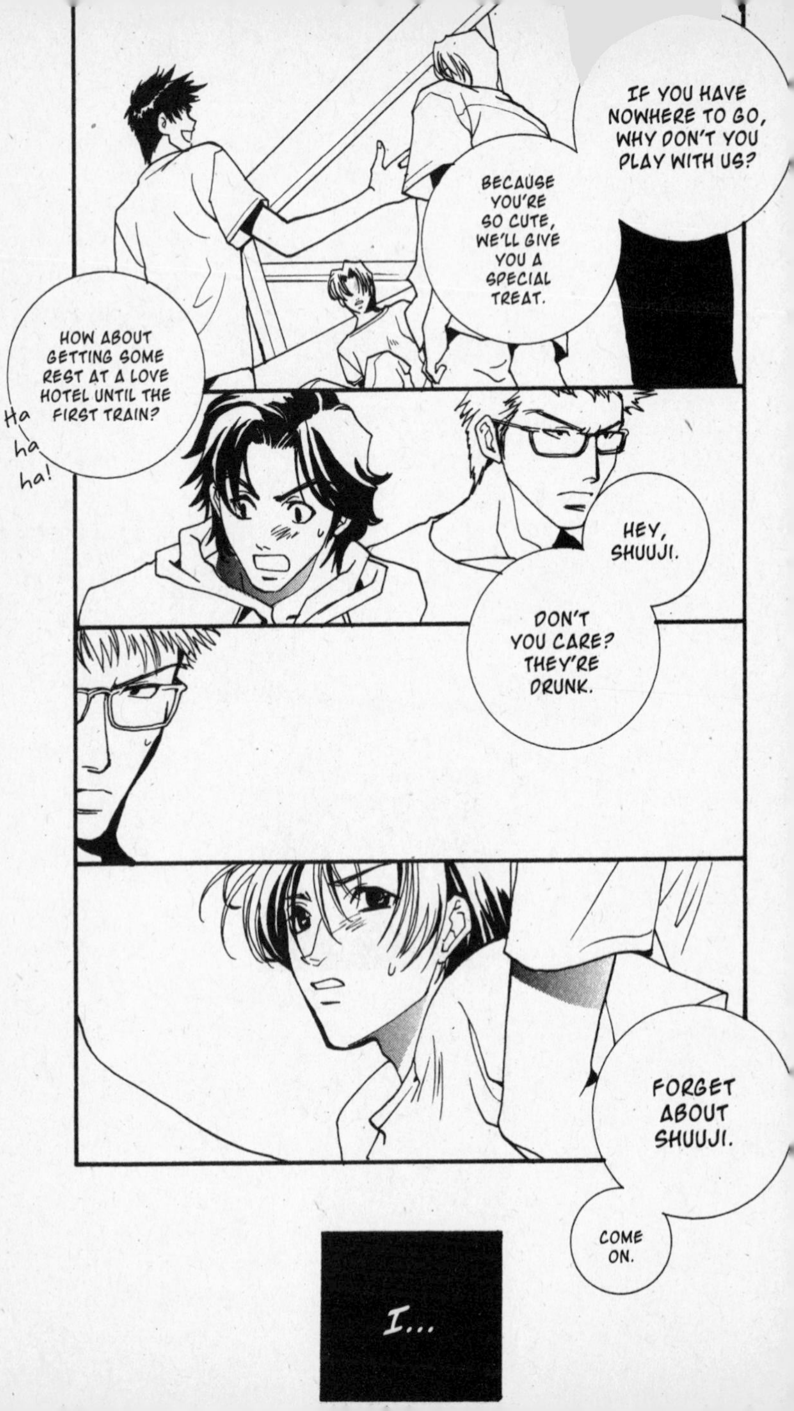
IF YOU HAVE NOWHERE TO GO, WHY DON'T YOU PLAY WITH US?
BECAUSE YOU'RE SO CUTE, WE'LL GIVE YOU A SPECIAL TREAT.
HOW ABOUT GETTING SOME REST AT A LOVE HOTEL UNTIL THE FIRST TRAIN?
Ha ha ha!
HEY, SHUUJI.
DON'T YOU CARE? THEY'RE DRUNK.
FORGET ABOUT SHUUJI.
COME ON.
I...

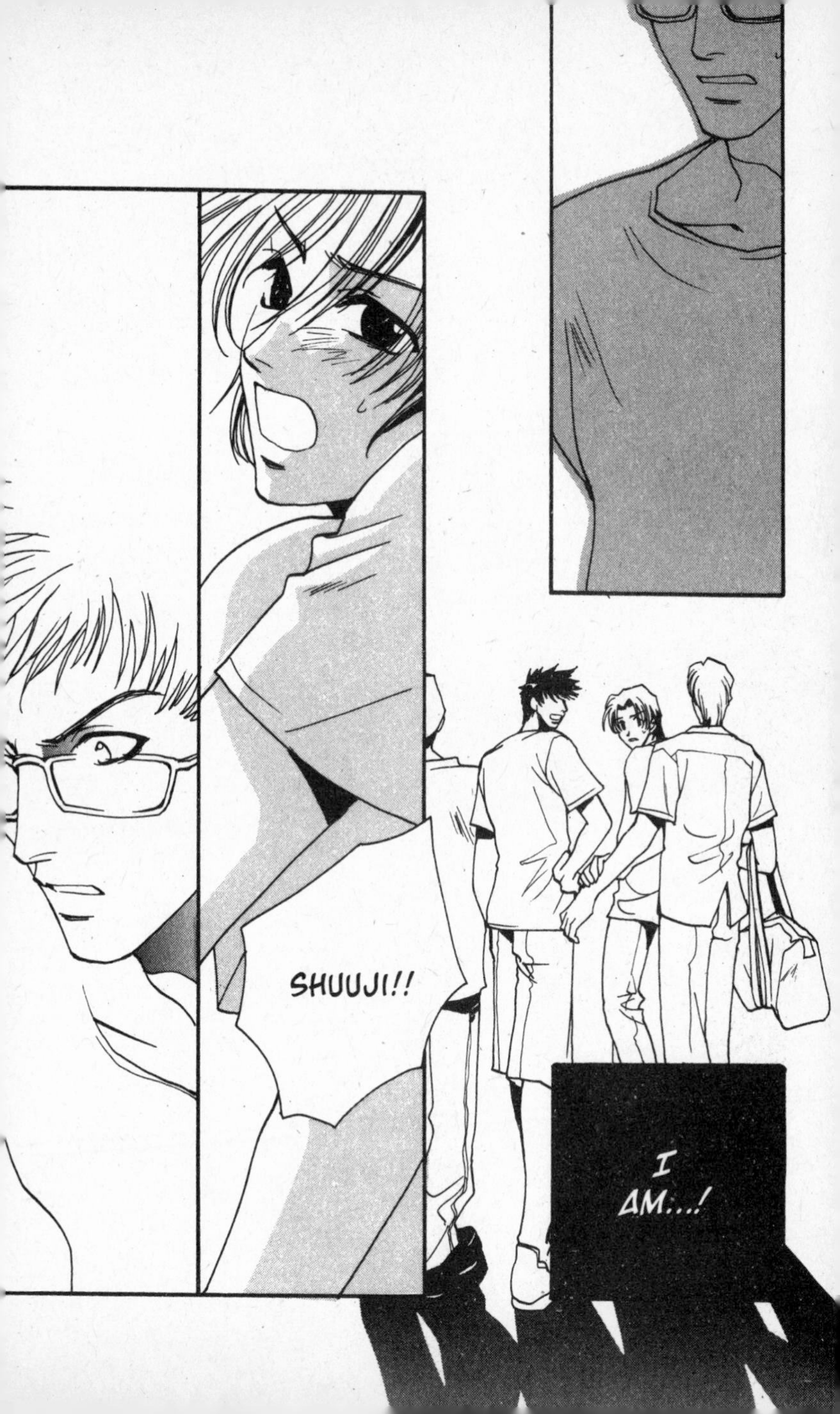
SHUUJI!!
I AM...!

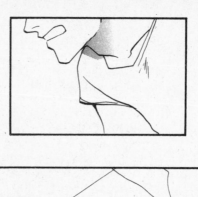

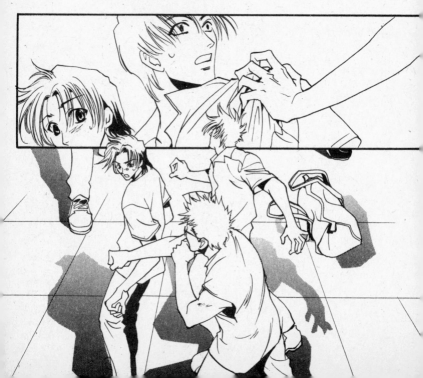

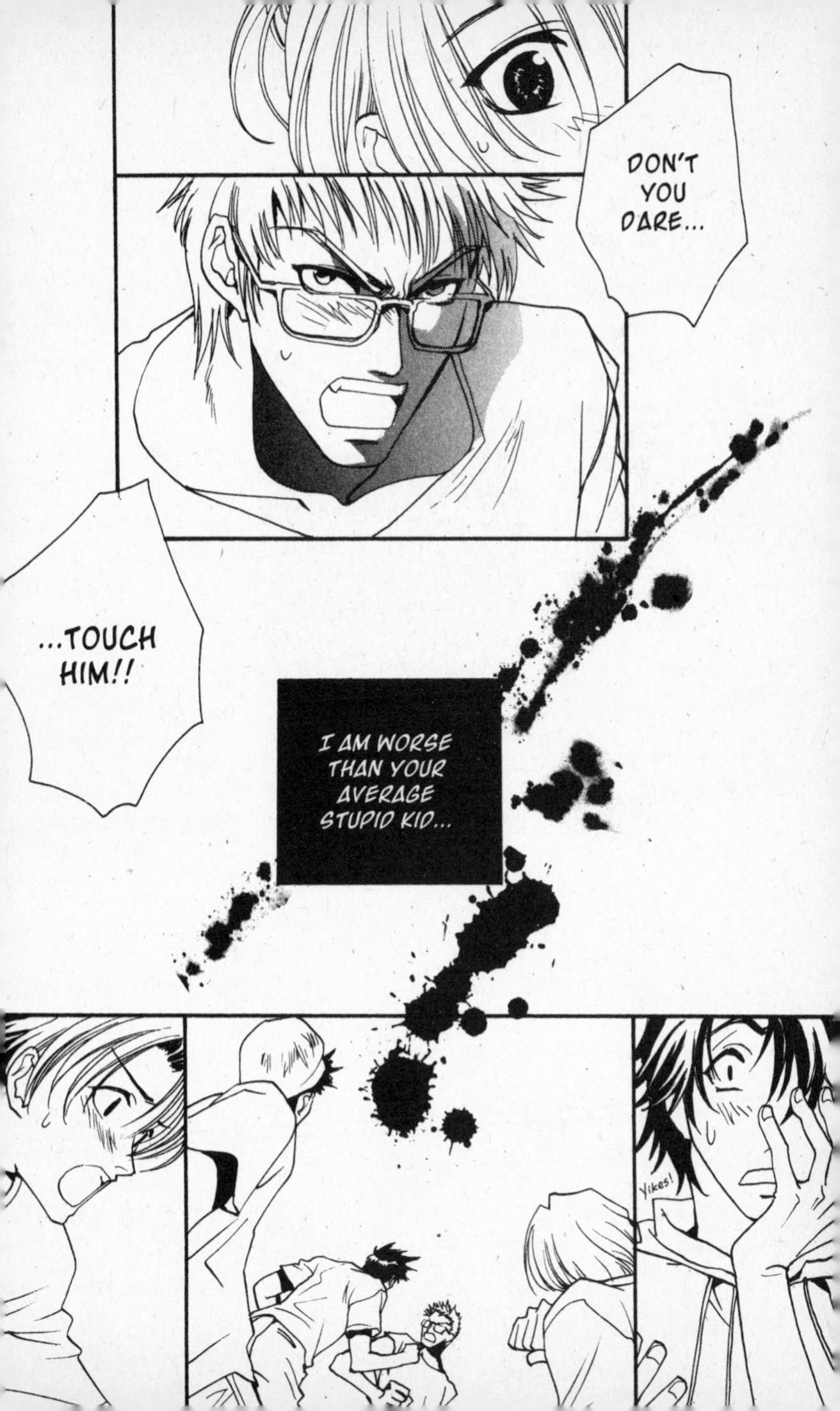
DON'T YOU DARE...
...TOUCH HIM!!
I AM WORSE THAN YOUR AVERAGE STUPID KID...
Yikes!

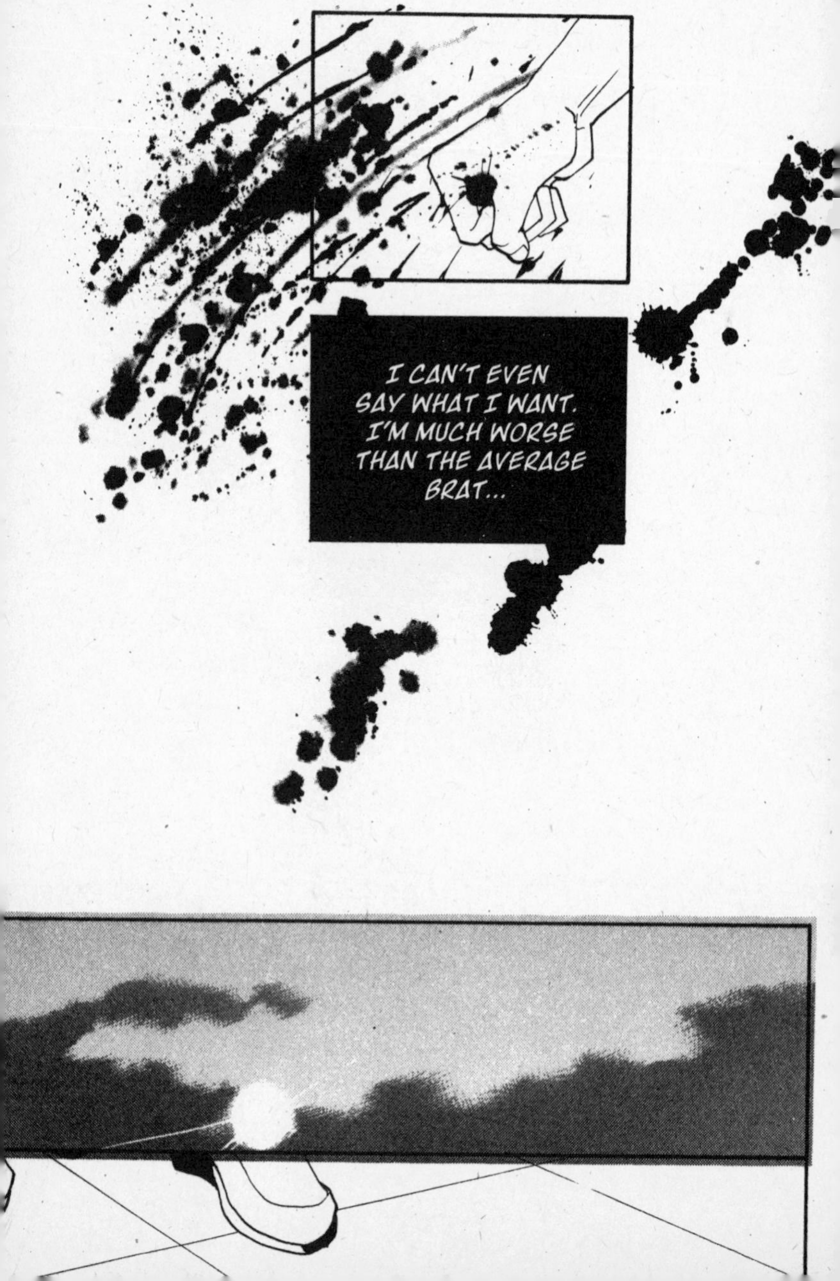
I CAN'T EVEN SAY WHAT I WANT. I'M MUCH WORSE THAN THE AVERAGE BRAT...

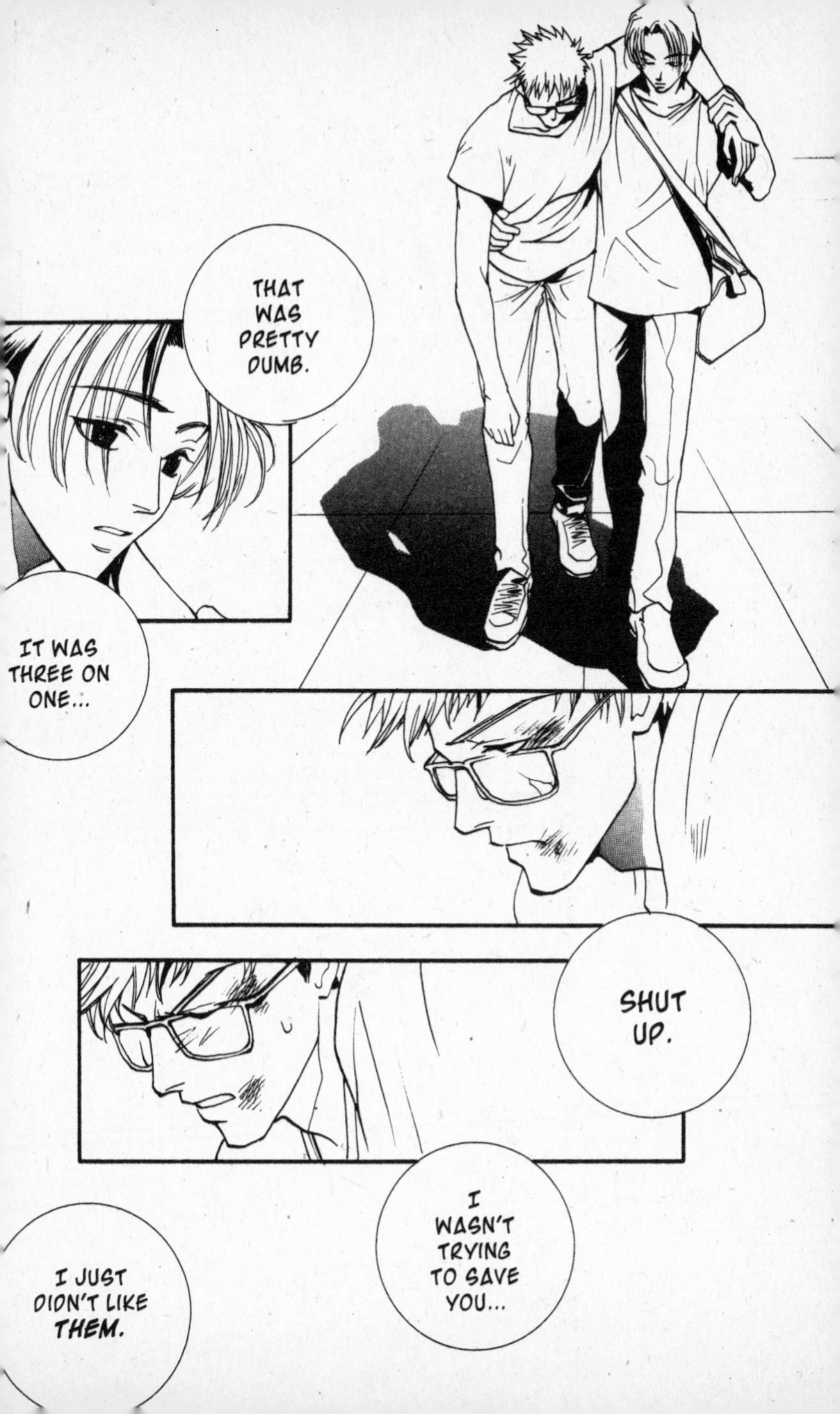
THAT WAS PRETTY DUMB.
IT WAS THREE ON ONE...
SHUT UP.
I WASN'T TRYING TO SAVE YOU...
I JUST DIDN'T LIKE **THEM.**

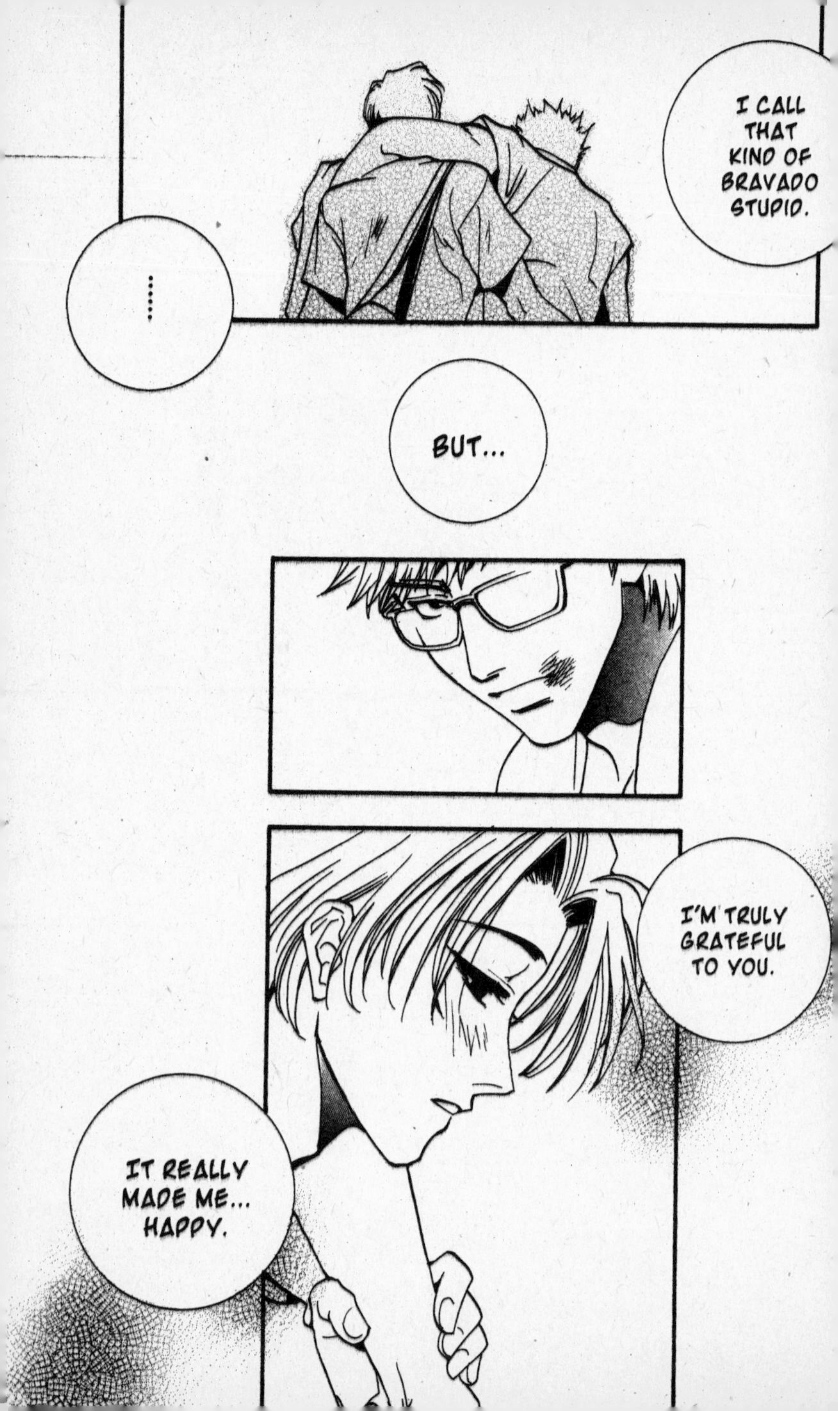
I CALL THAT KIND OF BRAVADO STUPID.
......
BUT...
I'M TRULY GRATEFUL TO YOU.
IT REALLY MADE ME... HAPPY.

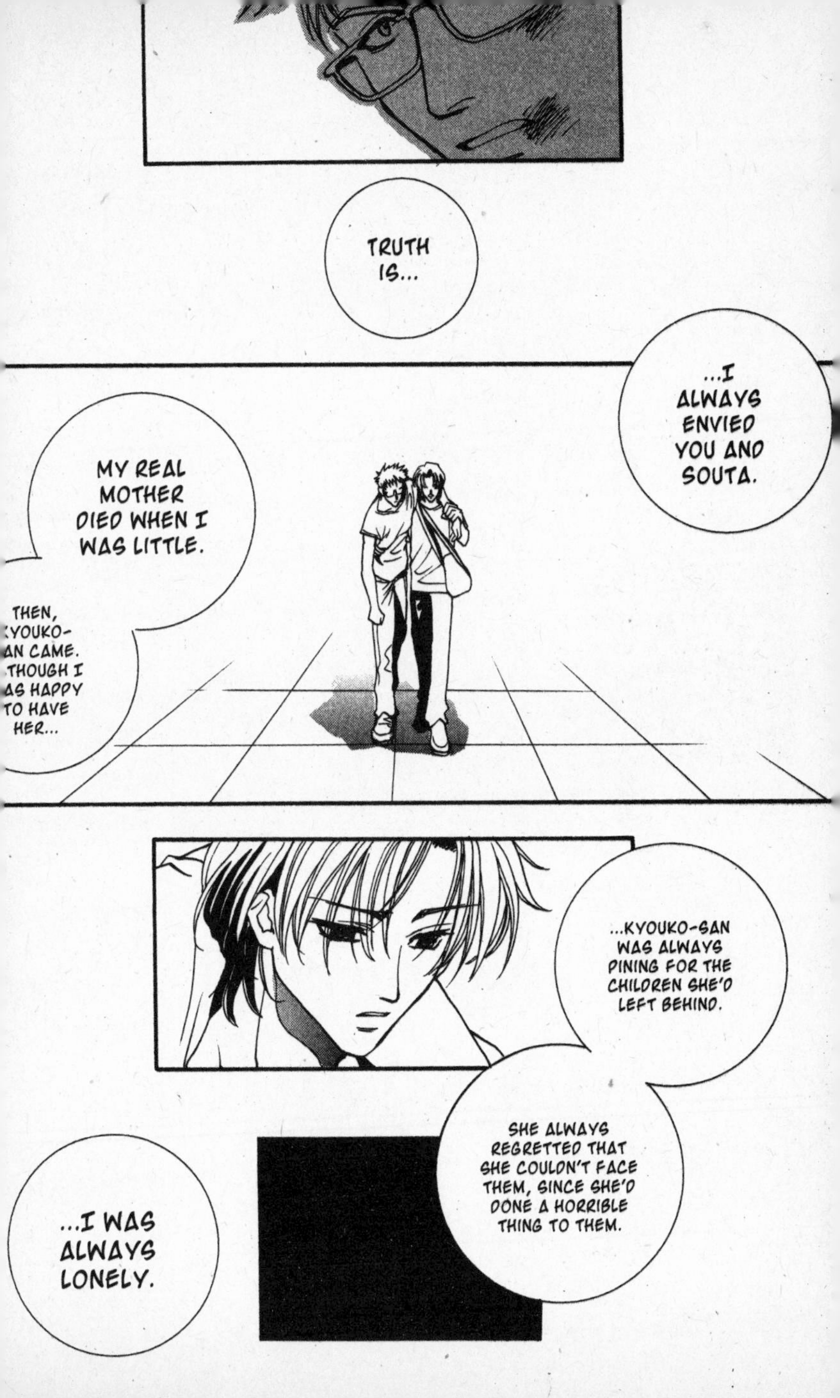
TRUTH IS...
...I ALWAYS ENVIED YOU AND SOUTA.
MY REAL MOTHER DIED WHEN I WAS LITTLE.
THEN, YOUKO- AN CAME. THOUGH I AS HAPPY TO HAVE HER...
...KYOUKO-SAN WAS ALWAYS PINING FOR THE CHILDREN SHE'D LEFT BEHIND.
SHE ALWAYS REGRETTED THAT SHE COULDN'T FACE THEM, SINCE SHE'D DONE A HORRIBLE THING TO THEM.
...I WAS ALWAYS LONELY.

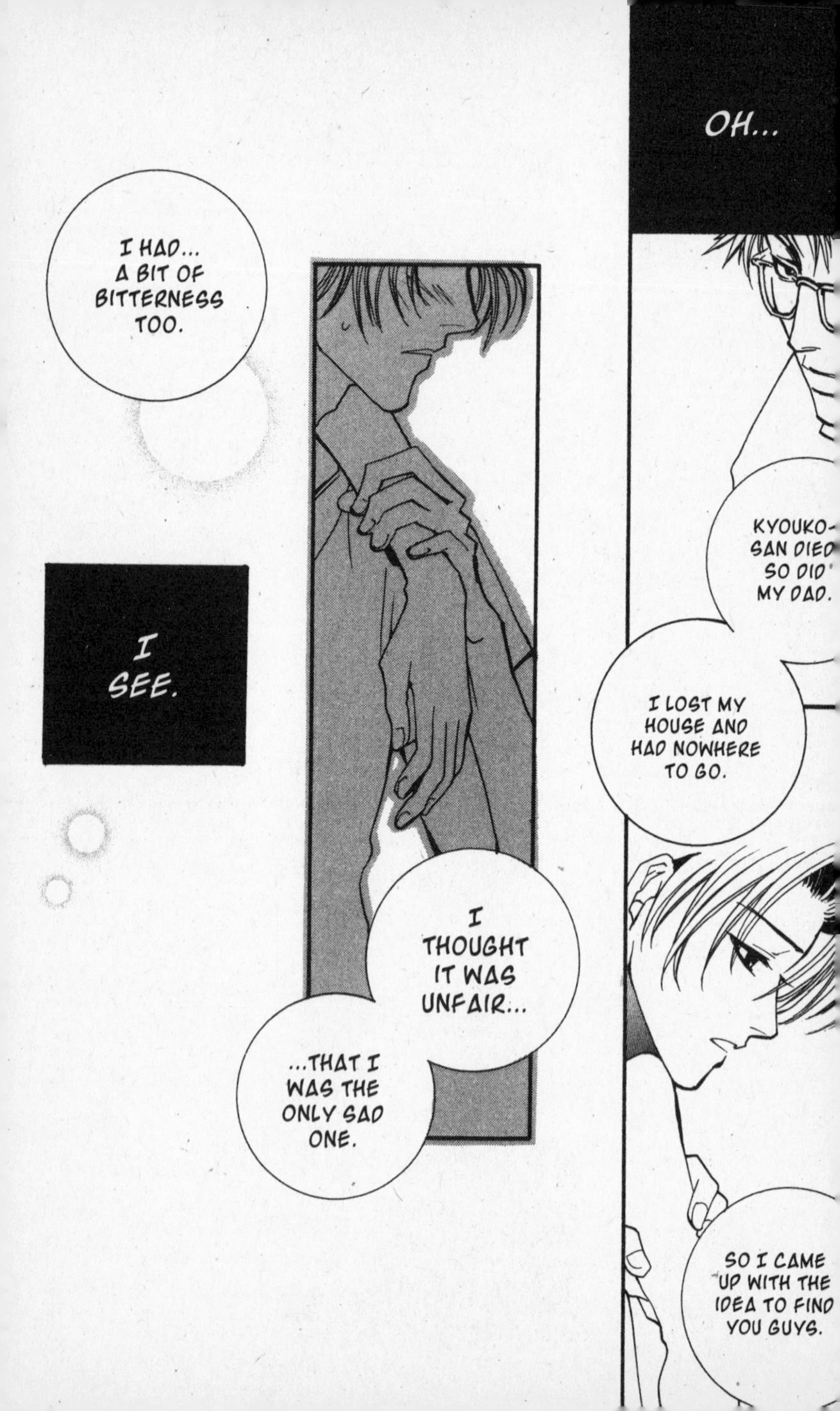
OH...
KYOUKO-SAN DIED SO DID MY DAD.
I LOST MY HOUSE AND HAD NOWHERE TO GO.
SO I CAME UP WITH THE IDEA TO FIND YOU GUYS.
I HAD... A BIT OF BITTERNESS TOO.
I SEE.
I THOUGHT IT WAS UNFAIR...
...THAT I WAS THE ONLY SAD ONE.

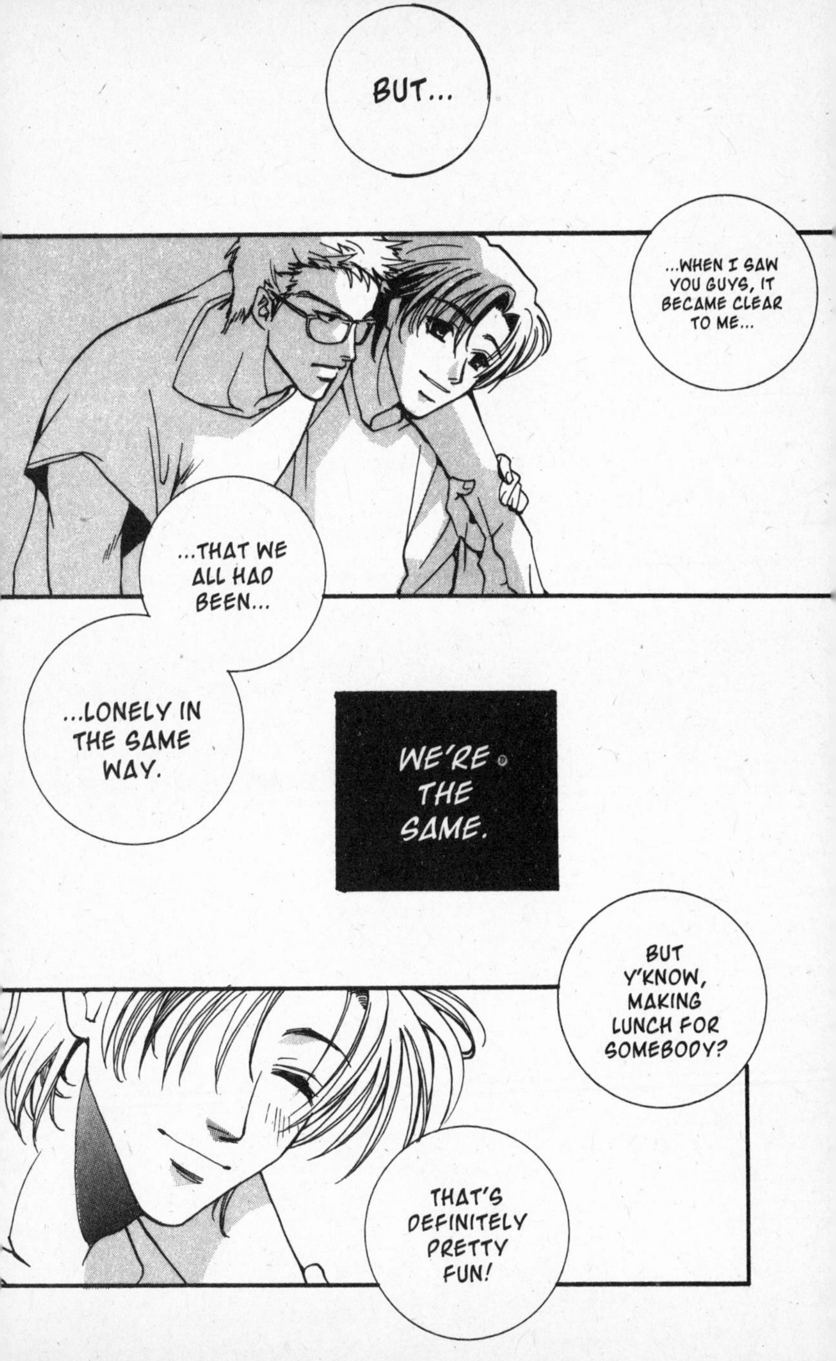
BUT...
...WHEN I SAW YOU GUYS, IT BECAME CLEAR TO ME...
...THAT WE ALL HAD BEEN...
...LONELY IN THE SAME WAY.
WE'RE THE SAME.
BUT Y'KNOW, MAKING LUNCH FOR SOMEBODY?
THAT'S DEFINITELY PRETTY FUN!

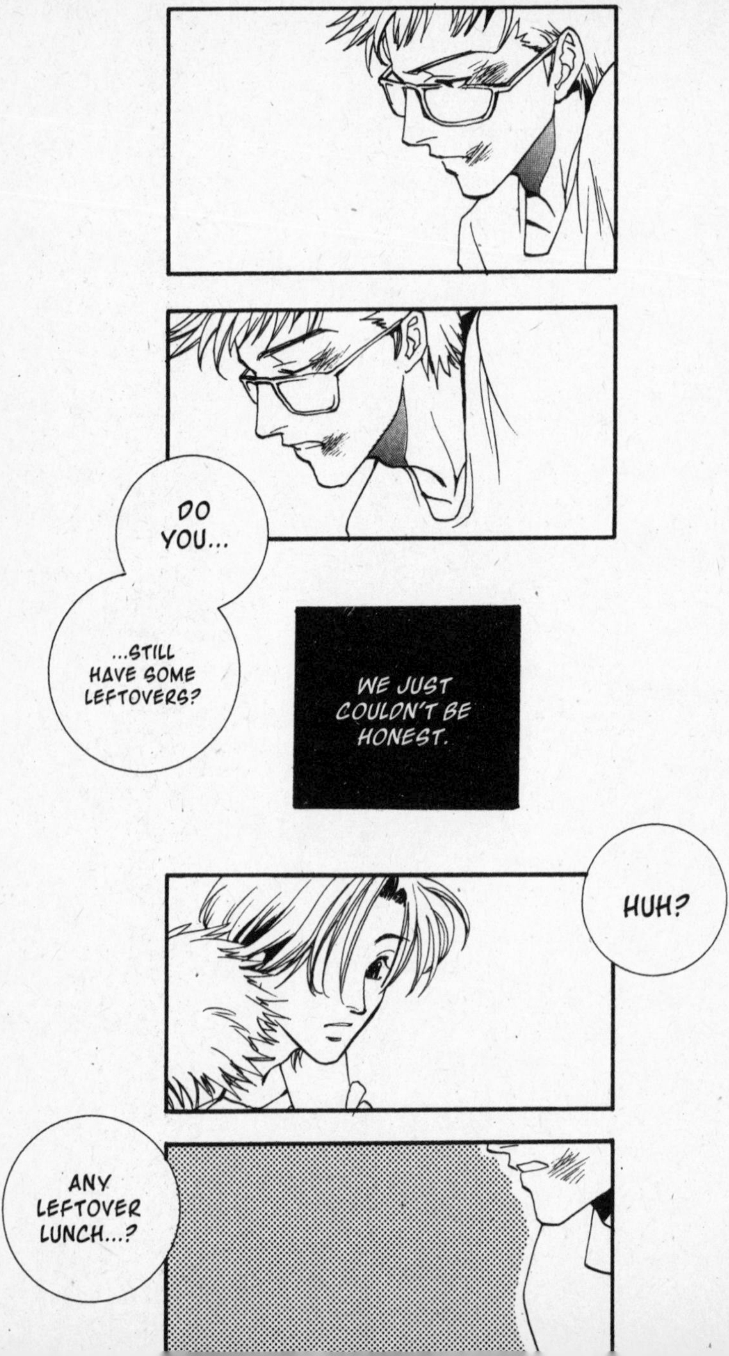
DO YOU...
...STILL HAVE SOME LEFTOVERS?
WE JUST COULDN'T BE HONEST.
HUH?
ANY LEFTOVER LUNCH...?

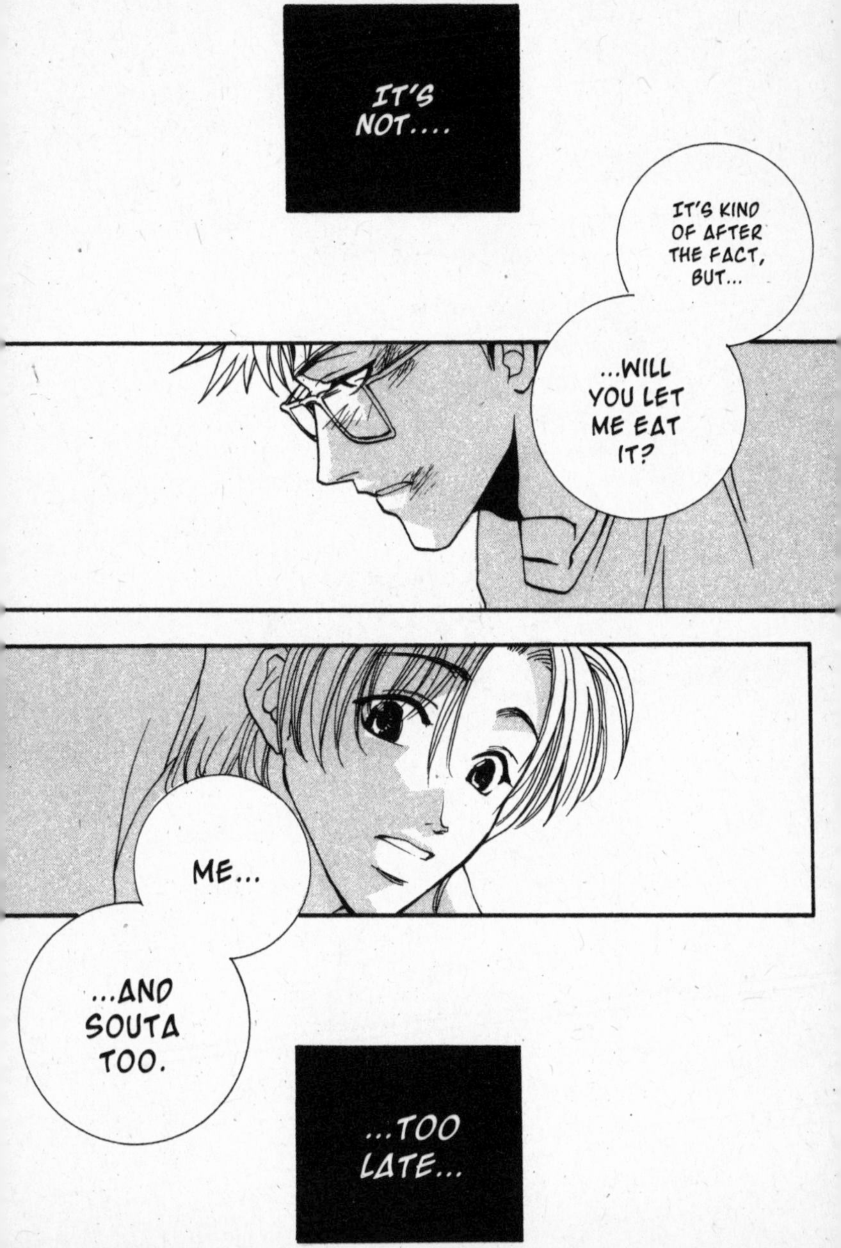
IT'S NOT....
IT'S KIND OF AFTER THE FACT, BUT...
...WILL YOU LET ME EAT IT?
ME...
...AND SOUTA TOO.
...TOO LATE...

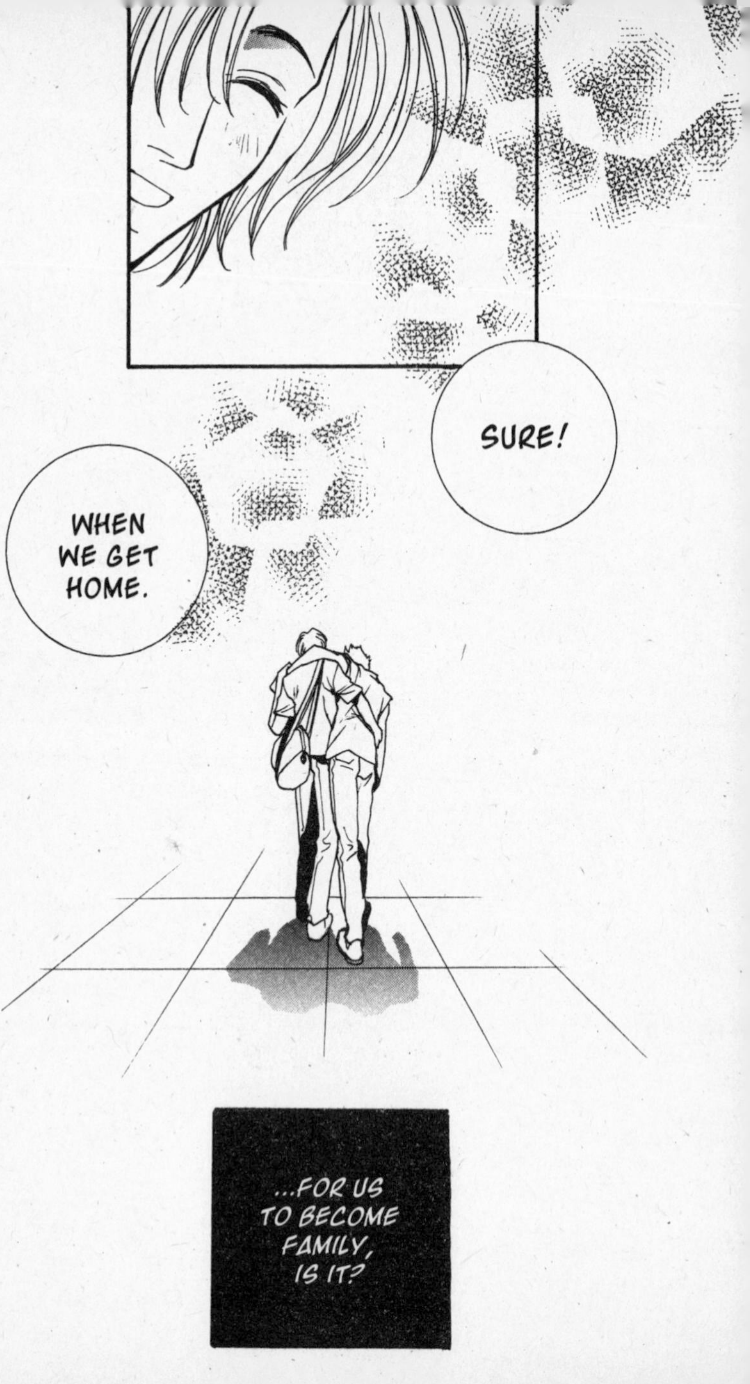
SURE!
WHEN WE GET HOME.
...FOR US TO BECOME FAMILY, IS IT?

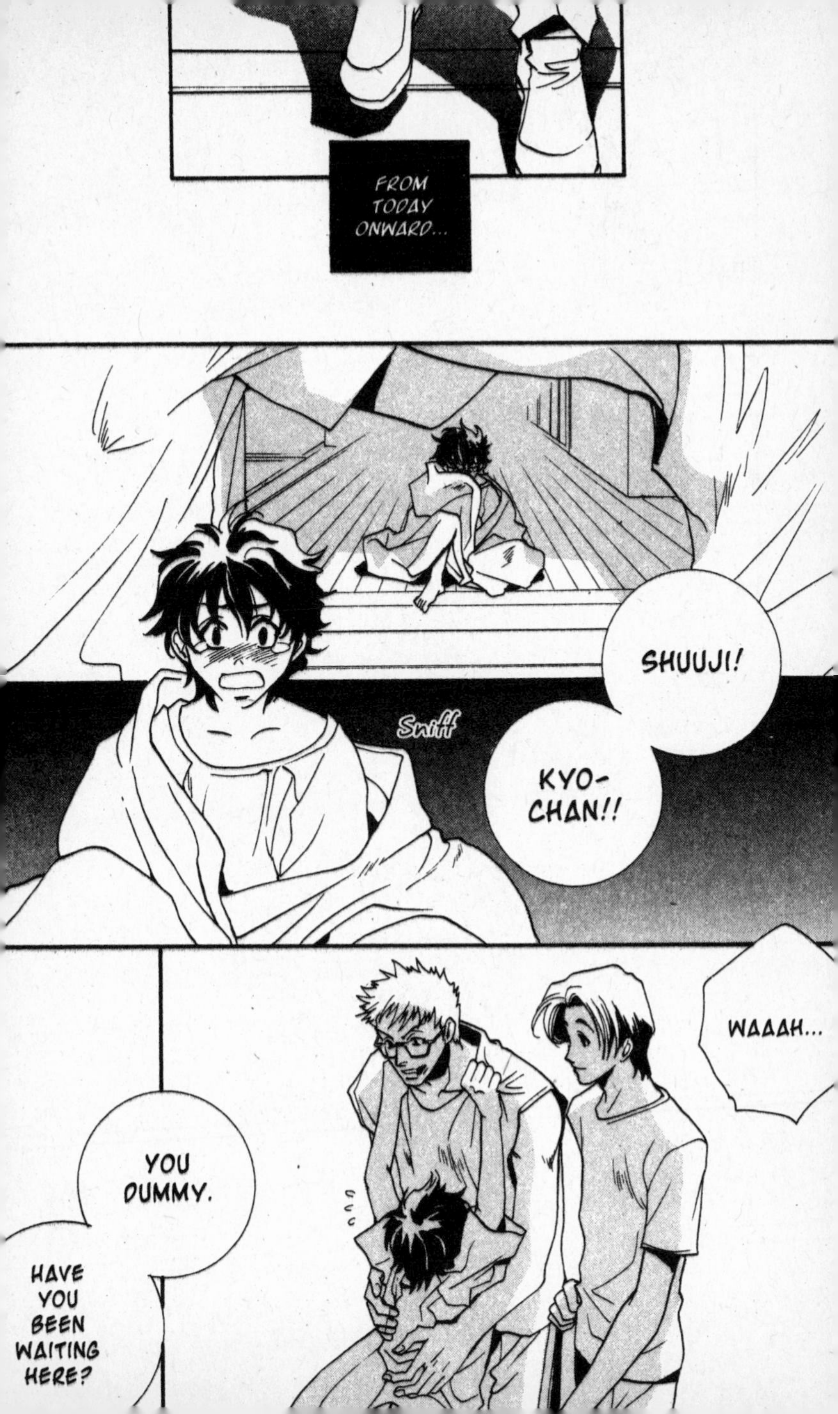
FROM TODAY ONWARD...
SHUUJI!
Sniff
KYO-CHAN!!
WAAAH...
YOU DUMMY.
HAVE YOU BEEN WAITING HERE?

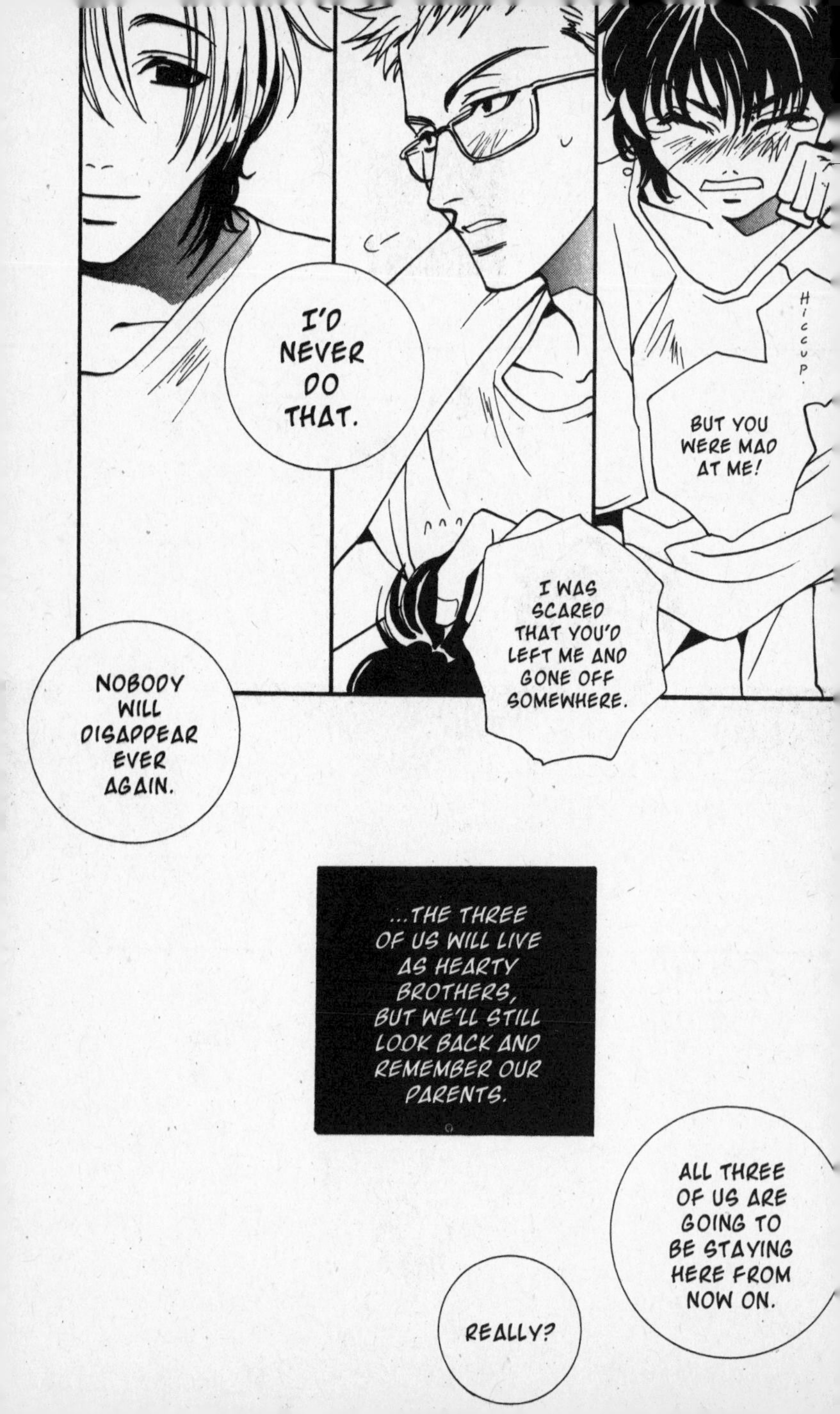
HICCUP.
BUT YOU WERE MAD AT ME!
I WAS SCARED THAT YOU'D LEFT ME AND GONE OFF SOMEWHERE.
I'D NEVER DO THAT.
NOBODY WILL DISAPPEAR EVER AGAIN.
...THE THREE OF US WILL LIVE AS HEARTY BROTHERS, BUT WE'LL STILL LOOK BACK AND REMEMBER OUR PARENTS.
ALL THREE OF US ARE GOING TO BE STAYING HERE FROM NOW ON.
REALLY?

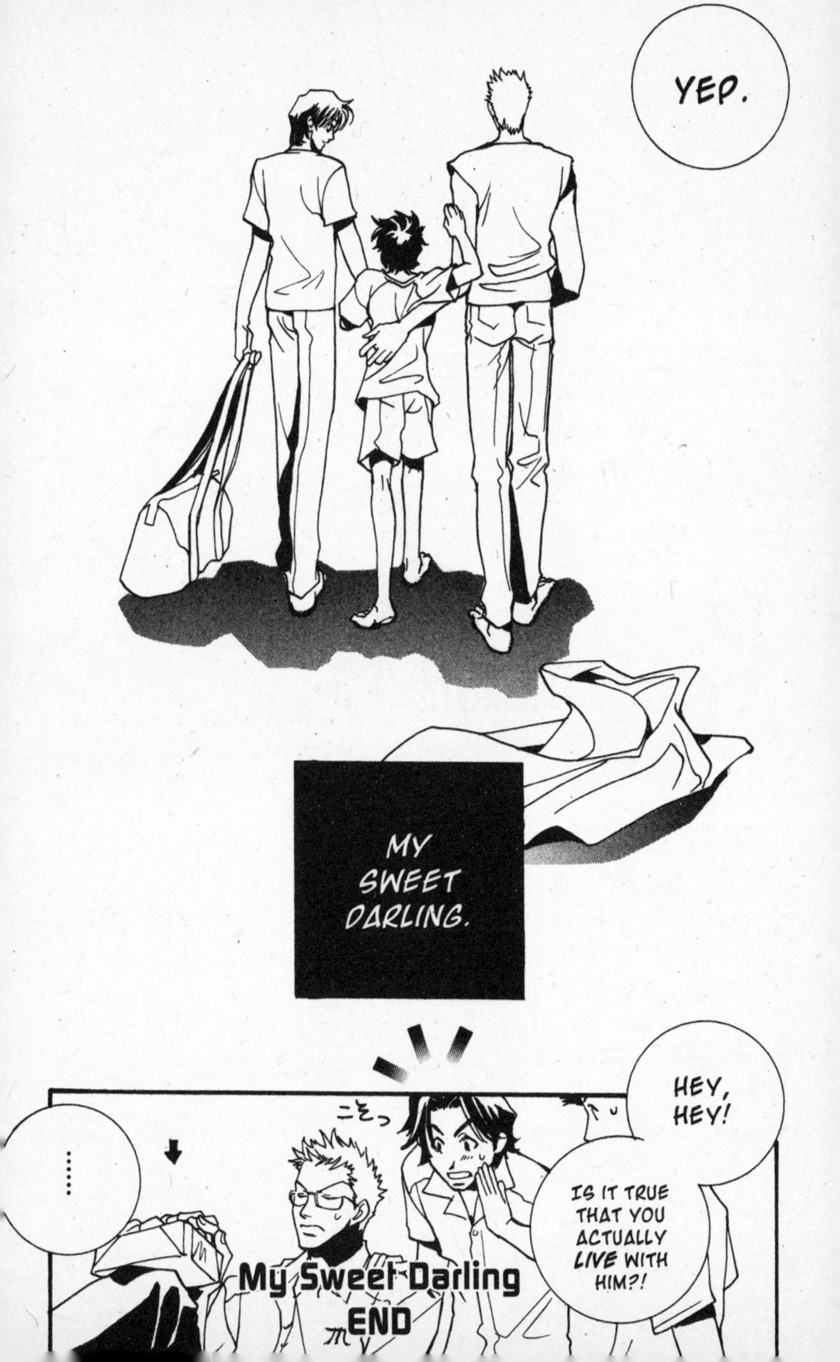
YEP.
MY SWEET DARLING.
HEY, HEY!
IS IT TRUE THAT YOU ACTUALLY LIVE WITH HIM?!
......
My Sweet Darling
END